MW00582056

OXFORD LEGAL PHILOSOPHY

Series Editors: TIMOTHY ENDICOTT, JOHN GARDNER, and LESLIE GREEN

Ignorance of Law

OXFORD LEGAL PHILOSOPHY

Series Editors Timothy Endicott, John Gardner, and Leslie Green

Oxford Legal Philosophy publishes the best new work in philosophically-oriented legal theory. It commissions and solicits monographs in all branches of the subject, including works on philosophical issues in all areas of public and private law, and in the national, transnational, and international realms; studies of the nature of law, legal institutions, and legal reasoning; treatments of problems in political morality as they bear on law; and exploration in the nature and development of legal philosophy itself. The series represents diverse traditions of thought but always with an emphasis on rigor and originality. It sets the standard in contemporary jurisprudence.

ALSO AVAILABLE IN THIS SERIES

Allowing for Exceptions
A Theory of Defences and Defeasibility in Law
Luis Duarte d'Almeida

Corrective Justice
Ernest J. Weinrib

Why Law Matters
Alon Harel

The Nature of Legislative Intent
Richard Ekins

The Ends of Harm
The Moral Foundations of Criminal Law
Victor Tadros

Conscience and Conviction
The Case for Civil Disobedience
Kimberley Brownlee

Ignorance of Law

A Philosophical Inquiry

Douglas Husak

OXFORD
UNIVERSITY PRESS

OXFORD
UNIVERSITY PRESS

Oxford University Press is a department of the University of Oxford. It furthers the University's objective of excellence in research, scholarship, and education by publishing worldwide. Oxford is a registered trademark of Oxford University Press in the UK and certain other countries.

Published in the United States of America by Oxford University Press
198 Madison Avenue, New York, NY 10016, United States of America.

© Oxford University Press 2016

Library of Congress Cataloging-in-Publication Data
Names: Husak, Douglas N., 1948- author.
Title: Ignorance of law : a philosophical inquiry / Douglas Husak.
Description: New York : Oxford University Press, 2016. | Series: Oxford legal philosophy |
    Includes bibliographical references and index.
Identifiers: LCCN 2016001845 | ISBN 9780190604684 (hardback : alk. paper)
Subjects: LCSH: Ignorance (Law)—Philosophy.
Classification: LCC K5083 .H87 2016 | DDC 340/.1—dc23 LC record available at
http://lccn.loc.gov/2016001845

9 8 7 6 5 4 3 2

Printed by Sheridan Books, Inc., United States of America.

Note to Readers

This publication is designed to provide accurate and authoritative information in regard to the subject matter covered. It is based upon sources believed to be accurate and reliable and is intended to be current as of the time it was written. It is sold with the understanding that the publisher is not engaged in rendering legal, accounting, or other professional services. If legal advice or other expert assistance is required, the services of a competent professional person should be sought. Also, to confirm that the information has not been affected or changed by recent developments, traditional legal research techniques should be used, including checking primary sources where appropriate.

(Based on the Declaration of Principles jointly adopted by a Committee of the American Bar Association and a Committee of Publishers and Associations.)

**You may order this or any other Oxford University Press publication
by visiting the Oxford University Press website at www.oup.com.**

*To the international community
of criminal law theorists*

Contents

Series Editors' Preface

"Ignorance of the law is no excuse" is a venerable legal maxim, one that is well known among laypeople as well as lawyers. It is mentioned by Aristotle and observed, with few qualifications, in Roman as well as common-law systems. But is it a good principle? As the number and technicality of statutory offenses continues to grow in most countries, the ability of people, even lawyers, to have a good command of what the law requires of them declines. Douglas Husak is inspired by this worrying aspect of contemporary life to offer a wide-ranging re-evaluation of the old maxim, exposing its troubling presuppositions and implications with characteristic wit and style as well as rigor and insight. In the process he introduces us to many interrelated and crosscutting themes that no other author has brought together. The book opens up numerous avenues of further exploration for the reader, and luminously explains the relations among them. The work is a major contribution to the study of legal and moral responsibility more widely, and not only a searing critique of received legal wisdom on the subject of how to deal with understandable ignorance.

February 2016

Timothy Endicott
John Gardner
Leslie Green

Acknowledgments

I have spent my entire professional life as a philosopher of law, and as a philosopher of criminal law in particular. Throughout what is now becoming a lengthy career, I have had the good fortune to associate closely with the finest criminal theorists in the Anglo-American world (and beyond). We attend conferences and roundtables together; we read and comment on each other's work; we jointly contribute to symposia in books and journals. My scholarly work has been built upon these exchanges. But these associations have been even more gratifying personally than professionally. I have cultivated a close friendship with many of the leading philosophers of criminal law, and these friendships have proved even more stimulating and important to me than our frequent professional interactions.

My interest in the topic of ignorance of law—like my interest in so many of the problems in criminal theory—was sparked by a provocative comment made by George Fletcher in his monumental *Rethinking Criminal Law*. Fletcher briefly questioned whether the "practice of disregarding mistakes of law" should be regarded as "a form of strict liability."[1] I was initially puzzled that anyone might construe strict liability to encompass the punishment of legally ignorant defendants. Something about this conceptualization seems intuitively correct, yet something about it is clearly erroneous. Liability is typically regarded as strict when it is imposed in the absence of culpability. Fletcher knows full well that persons who act in ignorance of

---

[1] George Fletcher: *Rethinking Criminal Law* (Boston: Little, Brown and Co., 1978), p.730.

law might have any of the culpable states required for penal liability. For example, a defendant might possess a substance he knows to be cocaine even though he does not know such possession to be illegal. As he knowingly possesses cocaine, he is regarded as culpable. How, then, could the imposition of liability on such a person possibly qualify as an instance of strict liability? Nonetheless, I continued to feel the pull of the contrary position. Initially, my puzzlement drove me to try to clarify the concept of strict liability—a concept I came to see as multiply ambiguous.[2] Only later did I approach this topic by reflecting on ignorance of law itself. Although Fletcher himself did not develop his provocative remark in much detail, the arguments I offer in this book might be interpreted as an extended effort to understand and vindicate his insight. Ultimately, I believe that our general practice of disregarding mistakes of law *is* aptly described as an instance of strict liability. Thus its justification rests on whether and to what extent strict liability is justifiable. As strict liability is almost always unjustified, our general practice of disregarding mistakes of law is almost always unjustified too.

My first foray into this topic consisted of a collaboration with my friend, co-teacher, and former Rutgers colleague Andrew von Hirsch titled "Culpability and Mistake of Law."[3] We argued that existing doctrine is far too restrictive, and that a broader defense should be recognized. At the very least, legally ignorant defendants should be exculpated when their mistake is *reasonable*. I continue to believe that this essay makes a tolerable start in addressing a number of normative difficulties. Still, further reflection persuaded me that the problem is far more complex than we believed at the time. Many more philosophical problems must be confronted in order to resolve it adequately. I explored some of these additional complexities in a later article titled "Mistake of Law and Culpability."[4] Even here, however, I failed to situate my position in a broader conception of criminal responsibility. This failure is crucial. I now appreciate that rival positions on whether and to what extent ignorance of law has exculpatory force depend almost entirely on the general theory of responsibility on which they rest. If the theory of responsibility I invoke in this book is roughly acceptable, ignorance

[2] See Douglas Husak: "Varieties of Strict Liability," VIII *Canadian Journal of Law and Jurisprudence* 189 (1995).
[3] In Stephen Shute, John Gardner and Jeremy Horder, eds: *Action and Value in Criminal Law* (Oxford: Clarendon Press, 1993), p.157.
[4] In 4 *Criminal Law and Philosophy* 135 (2010).

of law has some degree of exculpatory significance in circumstances far beyond those countenanced in either of my earlier essays. Thus my views have evolved considerably. Throughout the lengthy period in which I have written about this topic, I should add (insofar as I am able to introspect) that I did not begin with a conclusion and then twist the arguments to support it. Instead, I have allowed the arguments to take me where they will. Readers will quickly discover that these arguments take me to some surprising places—places where no criminal theorist has gone before. What I characterize as an *evolution* of my thought others would describe as a *regression*.

When I began my career in penal theory, philosophers of criminal law were obsessed with the problem of justifying punishment. Their obsession led them to neglect most other important issues. I long complained that criminal theorists paid too little attention to the topic of *criminalization*: the normative conditions that must be satisfied before the state is warranted in enacting and enforcing a penal statute. Although my complaint was trenchant at the time(s) I made it, no one can say that contemporary philosophers of criminal law continue to neglect this topic. Countless books, symposia, conferences, roundtables, and workshops have focused on the issue of criminalization. In my judgment, the problem of criminalization is important largely (but not exclusively) because of its conceptual connection to punishment. On my view, a statute is part of the *criminal* law when it subjects those who violate it to state punishment. If no one were ever punished for violating an alleged criminal law, we would care far less about whether the content of that law conformed to a normative theory of criminalization. Penal statutes must meet an exacting standard of justification mostly because state punishment must meet an exacting standard of justification. We cannot decide whether punishment is justified in the absence of presuppositions about what punishment should be imposed *for*. Thus the obsession with punishment that dominated the philosophy of criminal law several decades ago continues to this very day. The problem of justifying punishment provides the backbone that holds together most of the work in the philosophy of criminal law. My topic of ignorance of law is important because the doctrines the penal law implements on this matter directly affect who is punished and who is not.

In my opinion, Antony Duff and Michael Moore are the two best living philosophers of criminal law in the world. I am incredibly fortunate to count both as personal friends. Their influence on my thought has been enormous and can easily be seen throughout the pages that follow. Yet in one respect, it is notable that their influence does not extend even further. Although Duff and Moore have helped me to construct the general philosophical framework in which I operate, neither of these giants of criminal theory has been *especially* interested in ignorance of law—the issue on which I focus. They have graciously provided the space in which an original contribution can be made.

Nonetheless, I have had *lots* of help—the quantity and quality of which most academics can only dream. One event stands out. On September 10–11, 2015, more than a dozen of the world's most distinguished penal theorists were brought to Yale Law School for a workshop to discuss a draft of my manuscript. Every invitee agreed to attend (although Duff was forced to withdraw because of an injury). The participants included Larry Alexander, Mitch Berman, Kim Ferzan, Steve Garvey, Alexander Guerrero, Heidi Hurd, Michael Moore, Gideon Rosen, Re'em Segev, Ken Simons, Holly Smith, Victor Tadros, Peter Westen, Gideon Yaffe, and Michael Zimmerman.[5] I thank them all. How could anyone fail to learn after spending two days in a room surrounded by such brainpower? I hope to speak for each attendee in characterizing the workshop as remarkable.[6] Our discussions confirmed my belief that the topic of ignorance of law is unbelievably difficult and divisive. Although significant numbers of incredibly bright philosophers of criminal law disagreed with just about any given substantive claim I made, several others who are equally knowledgeable were on my side. Those who rejected my view on one issue flipped allegiance and concurred with me when the discussion turned elsewhere. This astounding meeting demonstrated the complete absence of a consensus about how any of these issues should be resolved. It would be foolish to react to such occasions with anything other than humility and a sense of one's own limitations. I will forever be grateful to Gideon Yaffe, who organized the event, and to each of those who took part—many of whom had to endure long travel delays caused by bad weather. Only a handful of authors have had the luxury of receiving so much help from so many experts before their book appears in print.

---

[5] Westen merits special thanks, as he continually bombarded my inbox with constructive criticisms, many of which I have been unable to answer.

[6] After initial reticence, I eventually warmed up to the description of this event as the "Husak-fest."

I have received additional assistance, even though it pales in comparison with what I gained at the Yale workshop. I delivered various parts of earlier versions of this manuscript at colloquia in philosophy departments and law schools throughout the world. I fear it would be tedious and even egotistic to list them all. I mention only two. First, Gabe Mendlow required students in his criminal theory seminar at the University of Michigan to read my entire unpublished manuscript and to prepare critical comments to keep me honest. Second, I must express my special thanks to graduate students in my seminars at Rutgers, many of whom recommended significant improvements despite their lacking an extensive background in legal philosophy. Ben Bronner, David Black, Brittany Shupe, Beth Henzel, James Goodrich, and Nevin Johnson helped me tremendously. Their input proved yet again that the caliber of my colleagues and our graduate program are the main reason Rutgers is such a wonderful place to do philosophy.

Introduction

How should the criminal law treat persons who breach penal laws of which they are ignorant? This is a crude approximation of the basic question I will address throughout this book. For three reasons, my conclusions resist a simple summary. First, I will find it necessary to repeatedly refine and clarify the basic question itself. Virtually every aspect of this deceptively straightforward issue demands analysis and explication. A satisfactory answer requires that we recognize more epistemic states than knowledge and ignorance. In addition, the object of ignorance may not actually be *the law* when ignorance is exculpatory. Second, the position I will defend is complex, nuanced, and highly qualified. Different kinds of cases must be distinguished, so no single response can be given for each of the many instances in which defendants are ignorant of law. Third, large parts of my answer will be tentative; I admit to uncertainty about how many central issues should be resolved. Judgments about responsibility, which form the cornerstone of any inquiry into ignorance of law, are among the most controversial in all of philosophy.

Still, an oversimplified summary of my provisional conclusions would be helpful. Roughly, I conclude that an ideal penal code should explicitly allow far more exculpatory significance to ignorance of law than is presently granted in existing systems of Anglo-American criminal justice. Persons who breach criminal laws of which they are unaware deserve *some* degree of exculpation in *nearly* every case. Defendants are fully responsible only when their wrongful actions are akratic, that is, when they are contrary to the balance of moral reasons they themselves believe to apply to their conduct. As a result, *full* responsibility for criminal wrongdoing turns out to be unusual.

But lesser degrees of responsibility should also be recognized. When defendants are aware of a substantial and unjustifiable risk their conduct might be wrongful, they should be punished, albeit to a lesser extent than defendants who know their acts are proscribed. To oversimplify my conclusions in a single sentence, I contend that the mens rea of a criminal offense should be construed to require not only knowledge of the relevant facts but also knowledge of the applicable law.

I contend that ignorant defendants are entitled to a less severe punishment than the maximum that is authorized even in extreme cases, which the majority of legal philosophers would immediately take to be a reductio of my position. These conclusions place me out on a limb. No criminal theorist allows an exculpatory consideration as broad or far-reaching as I defend in this book, although a few prominent moral philosophers have argued in favor of positions that are similar (but by no means identical) to those I reach here. I try hard to downplay the apparent implications of my claims that seem the most radical. I repeatedly emphasize that most of my investigation involves what I call *ideal* criminal theory. I appreciate that the exculpatory consideration I favor could only be implemented in a penal code that aspires to model the extent of criminal liability and the severity of punishment on the degree of moral blameworthiness and desert of particular defendants. For a number of largely pragmatic reasons, criminal codes in the real world must retreat from this ideal. We should not, however, settle for a non-optimal solution too quickly. Any deviation from this ideal is an unfortunate and regrettable compromise between justice and practical realities.

Why would a criminal theorist write an entire book about ignorance of law? And, just as important, why does he think legal philosophers and theoretically sophisticated legal scholars should invest the time and energy to read it? I offer eight distinct but related reasons, most of which will receive further elaboration in the pages that follow. First, few if any positions currently adopted by our system of penal justice are more normatively indefensible. I can think of no core area of the substantive criminal law more ripe for fundamental reform. Second, many interesting facets of the methodology I believe legal philosophers should pursue are revealed when we seek to identify the direction reform should take. We can appreciate the strengths (and perhaps the weaknesses) of a philosophical examination of the criminal law by focusing on this topic.

Third, laypersons and legal scholars alike betray massive confusion about this issue. *Ignorantia juris non excusat* is among the handful of adages about the substantive criminal law of which ordinary citizens profess confidence.[1] If my subsequent arguments are cogent, however, this adage is inadequate descriptively and unpersuasive morally. Thus I challenge conventional wisdom at its foundations. Still, my challenge is not heretical. As we will see, most of us are ambivalent about whether and to what extent the plea of ignorance of law should have exculpatory significance. Evidence of this ambivalence can be detected in positive law itself and exploited for my normative purposes. Fourth, this issue offers an excellent opportunity to demonstrate how careful thought about one topic has important implications for others. A sensible position on ignorance of law has repercussions that echo throughout the whole of legal and moral theory, so an examination of this question helps to shed light on a number of surrounding controversies. From this starting point, we can arrive almost anywhere. Although I advertise this book to be about ignorance of law, it is really about a good deal more—a substantial chunk of criminal theory and moral philosophy.

Fifth, this issue has considerable practical significance in the real world. If my general conclusions are correct, it is probable that a great many defendants are treated unjustly and stand to benefit from the exculpatory consideration I defend here. I argue that the conditions that would render an ignorant wrongdoer eligible for the maximum sentences authorized by law are rarely satisfied. Countless matters that have received far more attention from legal theorists—such as the parameters of self-defense against non-culpable aggressors—have much less impact on actual penal practice. Thus my claims have the potential to make a dent on the epidemic of over-punishment from which commentators on all points along the political spectrum agree we presently suffer. Whether this potential is realized, however, depends on a host of complex factors I will discuss.

Sixth, this issue is enormously deep and complex—surprisingly so. As we will see, many intractable philosophical disputes need to be resolved before a firm position on *ignorantia juris* can be defended. A comprehensive theory on this topic must address questions criminal

---

[1] These Latin adages are translated somewhat differently. My favorite is the "not very lofty English" translation of *"tough luck."* Sanford H. Kadish: "Excusing Crime," 78 *California Law Review* 257, 268 (1987).

theorists have rarely even asked. I would prefer to have succeeded in resolving some of these disputes, and thus to have reached a more definitive set of conclusions. At the very least, however, I am confident I can show why and at what points this topic is so difficult.

Seventh, my position does not depend on a political ideology or orientation. In this era of polarization, reforms get nowhere if they are backed by one political party but opposed by the other. Although liberals tend to be associated with pleas to reduce sentences, much of the recent impetus for an expansion of the defense of ignorance of law has come from conservatives.[2] Thus the stage is set for progress in the real world. Finally, no thorough treatment of this issue is available. Although theorists have written a fair amount about ignorance of law, much of it is repetitive, and little of it can withstand critical scrutiny. The problem of ignorance of law has yet to receive the sustained, careful, and systematic attention it merits from legal philosophers.

Thus I hope that both philosophers of criminal law as well as theoretically minded law professors and practitioners will find this book to be worthwhile. But what about a lay audience? The topic should be of broad interest. Who among us has not suffered from making a mistake of law—by misconstruing the cryptic instructions on a maze of No Parking signs, for example?[3] Alas, I am skeptical that many readers outside of the academy will find this book to be accessible. Painful experience has taught me that few persons beyond the walls of higher education are willing and able to slog through philosophy at a level that can be expected to attract specialists. I am convinced it is possible to write a respectable book about ignorance of law that is engaging to laypersons, but I am pretty sure I have not done so. Obviously, I would be delighted if my pessimism about this matter were unfounded.

Again, a rough approximation of my central question is how the law should judge defendants who violate penal laws of which they are unaware. Under what conditions should such persons be acquitted of their crimes, and when should they be punished? More specifically,

---

[2] For example, see Orin Hatch: Press Release, September 15, 2015, http://www.hatch.senate.gov/public/index.cfm?p=releases&id=090FFA70-5ABF-4160-8ED5-D512EBEBEB6F.

[3] This example provides some of the impetus for this book. When she was taking me to dinner after a talk at Harvard, Carol Steiker and I spent several minutes attempting to decipher the instructions on a battery of "No Parking" signs on a street in Cambridge. Somehow, the policeman who wrote the ticket was able to fathom what the signs prohibit. I sometimes wonder whether he had been issued a secret book unavailable to citizens that told him exactly where cars are permitted to park.

should they be excused? If they are not excused and eligible for penal sanctions, should the severity of their sentences be reduced below those inflicted on offenders who commit the same crime but realize their conduct is illegal? What additional information do we need—and what additional distinctions must we draw—before these questions can be answered? Must we ask *which* law has been violated? Must we contrast so-called *mala in se* from *mala prohibita* offenses, confining the scope of the defense to the latter while denying it to the former? Do we require further data about *why* the person is ignorant, and whether he is somehow blameworthy for his failure to know the law? Do we need to answer a counterfactual question: would the person who broke the law of which he is ignorant have complied with it if he had been aware of it? What else do we need to know before we can give a comprehensive answer to my central question? For what exact purpose is any of this further information needed? And if none of it *is* needed, why do so many legal theorists seem to believe otherwise?

Superficially, I ask what the law should be when a person B engages in conduct Φ that violates a criminal law L, when B did not know Φ amounts to a violation of L at the time he performed it. Assume that B was not aware Φ amounts to a violation of L not because he is mistaken about some *factual* property of his act or circumstance, but rather because he is mistaken about the existence, application, or meaning of L itself. In order to try to answer this question, it will prove helpful to ask whether and under what conditions the penal law should differentiate between A and B, if the former commits the same act Φ that violates the same law L but differs only in that he knows Φ violates L. Somewhat more formally, I will examine what the law should say about the following schema:

(1) A's conduct Φ violates law L, and A knows that Φ violates L.
(2) B's conduct Φ violates law L, but B does not know that Φ violates L.

I then seek to answer the following *basic question* (Q):

(Q) Ceteris paribus, how should the severity of A's punishment for Φ compare to that of B? More specifically, should B be sentenced less severely than A, or should A and B be sentenced to the same degree for Φ?

In the course of my endeavors to answer (Q), it will be necessary to refine the question itself. Some of these clarifications are easy to anticipate, but others are somewhat surprising. For example, as I explain in some detail in Chapter 2(D), if L is an instance of a type of law that is increasingly prevalent in penal codes, the above schema turns out to be literally incoherent. As formulated above, (Q) *cannot possibly* be answered.

I approach my inquiry as a legal philosopher. Unless the reader is a complete novice, she is bound to share a general understanding of how we philosophers of law think and argue. But great differences can be found within the camp of legal philosophers, and I would like to situate myself more narrowly within the group in which I claim membership. Some excellent legal philosophers are philosophers first and foremost. They write entire books that illuminate the law without mentioning a single case or statute. Other notable legal philosophers are mostly legal theorists. Although they draw from and are informed by philosophy, their knowledge is not especially deep, and is rarely up to date. I believe my own work falls squarely between these two extremes. I have spent most of my professional life careening back and forth between academic philosophy departments and law schools, and I hope this book demonstrates a reasonable proficiency with both the law and its philosophical underpinnings. Over time, however, I have come to recognize the pitfalls of my peculiar orientation: it is all too easy to fall between the cracks that divide the two disciplines I straddle. I constantly worry that I produce work that is too legalistic for philosophers but too philosophical for legal theorists. Sometimes I am guilty of belaboring points that are familiar to philosophers but less well known to legal academics (and vice versa). Despite my struggles to retain the best of both philosophy and legal theory, my biggest fear is that I capture the worst of each.

Readers of both legal periodicals and philosophy journals know the single most visible difference between the publications that appear in one venue or the other: the number and length of footnotes. Even though I believe philosophers have the better convention, I have tended to compromise on this matter, hoping the style of my manuscript will be foreign neither to academic philosophers nor to legal theorists. I have included more footnotes than appear in typical philosophy monographs, but fewer than appear in most law books. I trust that the many legal and moral philosophers who have contributed to the topics I discuss will not feel slighted when I do not credit their insights. Readers will have no difficulty finding a mountain of additional publications on most of the issues I examine here.

In my judgment, the most formidable challenge in writing a book is not merely to offer good arguments and decide what material is relevant or irrelevant. An equally difficult problem is to distinguish the relevant positions that are essential to defend from the relevant positions that can be presupposed. We risk losing a sharp focus on the specific topic of ignorance of law by pursuing broader moral and legal tangents that have been addressed at length elsewhere. Because these issues are canvassed in such detail by a number of other philosophers, this book would lose the originality I hope it to possess were I simply to rehash the work so many others have done before me. If everything that bears on my topic had been included, this book would become impossibly long. The main drawback in writing a lengthy book is that fewer people will have the patience to read it. Thus I have made some *very* hard editorial decisions, and readers are bound to disagree with several of them. Far too often, I apologize that a given topic is "beyond the scope of this project." Uncharitable reviewers will fault me for these frequent evasions. I plead guilty. My only response in mitigation is that a detailed examination of each of these issues would take us too far afield.

Thus I am forced to make several assumptions about the criminal law and the methodology I use to illuminate it. Although quite a few legal philosophers will regard these presuppositions as platitudinous, others will reject several of them outright. Candor about these background assumptions is crucial for a variety of reasons. Most obviously, those who do not share my presuppositions or the normative framework in which my reasoning is situated will almost certainly be unconvinced by many of my arguments. Less obviously, these assumptions have several interesting implications when conjoined. I suspect that some readers will share my sense that I sometimes paint myself into a corner. To escape from a given predicament, it may be necessary to re-examine one or more assumptions that seem fairly innocuous when considered in isolation. The problem of how to deal with defendants who are ignorant of law may seem insoluble unless one or more of these presuppositions is jettisoned. Which should we abandon? Surely the most vulnerable pillar is the theory of responsibility on which my account is constructed. If the foundation crumbles, the edifice loses its support. In any event, if I am ultimately mistaken, I hope at least to be mistaken for interesting reasons. A major payoff of focusing on the present topic is its potential to yield a fresh perspective on a broad range of issues in the philosophy of criminal law.

Let me cite several examples of positions that bear directly on my project but I will not endeavor to defend. Legions of political and legal philosophers have examined the age-old problem of how punishment is justified. If we seek to justify punishment *morally*—as surely we should—it would seem that persons must have engaged in moral wrongdoing rather than simply violating a law before the state has a sound basis to treat them punitively. I share a view held by many (and perhaps most) legal philosophers: the law per se does not automatically create moral reasons of compliance—even when that law is enacted in a democratic liberal state. I do not provide much by way of *argument* for this contested position; controversy about political authority and the alleged obligation to obey the law has been the subject of countless books and articles.[4] As far as I can determine, however, the implications of this view for the topic of ignorance of law have not been discussed. If the law per se does not create moral obligations of compliance, it is hard to see how *knowledge* of the law can add to our responsibility to conform to it. If I am correct so far, it is equally difficult to fathom how *ignorance* of the law could release offenders from a moral obligation they did not have in the first place. How, then, can either knowledge or ignorance of law have any significance from a moral point of view? Moreover, even if I am wrong and persons *do* have an obligation to obey the law per se, we need altogether separate arguments to show that the failure to discharge this obligation makes wrongdoers *responsible*. Presumably, these arguments will be *moral*. The entire focus on *law* begins to seem misplaced. I am unsure I can respond adequately to this set of worries, but at least I grapple with them rather than evade them.

In addition, I frequently invoke the concept of desert, but do not try too hard to rationalize it. Various *desert skeptics,* who reject most or all references to desert in moral and legal discourse, will be disappointed by my uncritical acceptance of this controversial moral concept. Even more important, I pay scant attention to controversies about free will and determinism, or indeed to other grounds for global skepticism about responsibility. I take the easy way out and presuppose that *some* persons are responsible for *some* of their conduct, and begin with the clearest examples in which nearly all readers should agree

---

[4] For example, see Stephen Perry: "Political Authority and Political Obligation," in Leslie Green and Brian Leiter, eds.: *Oxford Studies in Philosophy of Law* (New York: Oxford University Press, Vol. 2, 2013), p.1.

that attributions of responsibility are warranted. As Stephen Morse continually reminds us in responding to putative challenges from neuroscience, the criminal law adopts a folk psychological view of the person, and will continue to do so throughout the foreseeable future.[5] If no one is ever responsible for anything, an inquiry into the responsibility of defendants who are ignorant of law becomes moot. Of course, the metaphysics that underlie my assumption must ultimately be defended, although I make no effort to do so here.[6]

Unless one purports to rely solely on intuitions, I have come to appreciate that a position on exculpation and ignorance of law stands or falls mostly on the general theory of criminal responsibility it invokes. My own theory locates responsibility in our capacity to be *rational* or *reason-responsive*. Persons who possess this capacity but exercise it incorrectly, according to their own lights, are the best candidates for blame and punishment. My embellishment and support for this familiar theory, however, is admittedly thin and adds little to the voluminous philosophical literature that already exists. As a result, the application of this theory to the problem of ignorance of law is the most vulnerable part of my project. I do not tackle the difficult problems of explicating the idea of reason-responsiveness in great detail or of responding to well-known objections to it. I mention competitive theories and note some of their weaknesses, but I make no concerted effort to attack them directly. Although clearly crucial to the normative project I pursue here, some philosophical debates have taken on a life of their own and are best pursued as stand-alone inquiries. In short, I have resisted the temptation to write a book about responsibility; a more extended defense of a general theory of blameworthiness would require a separate volume. Still, I encourage those legal philosophers who are unpersuaded by my conclusions to identify the account of criminal responsibility on which their views rely. Too few of those who have contributed to the commentary on ignorance of law pay sufficient attention to the general theory of criminal responsibility their account presupposes. I hope at least to shine a bright light on this dependence.

[5] Stephen J. Morse: "Lost in Translation?: An Essay on Law and Neuroscience," *Law and Neuroscience*, 13 Current Legal Issues 529 (ed. Michael Freeman, 2010).

[6] See Michael Moore: "Stephen Morse on the Fundamental Psycho-Legal Error," 10 *Criminal Law and Philosophy* (forthcoming 2016).

I also pay little attention to a critique of what theorists have said about *ignorantia juris* throughout legal history. I neglect this matter to avoid a tendency I find frustrating in discussions of related topics by legal philosophers. For example, several books have recently been published in which the author discovers anew that each of the well-known theories of punishment is problematic. The weaknesses of these theories are recounted in painstaking detail, despite the fact that they are familiar even to nonspecialists. Almost as an afterthought, the author finally articulates his own original contribution: how the law *should* treat criminal offenders in order to avoid the problems he has uncovered with punishment. The shortcoming, however, is that the "new" theory is even more problematic than the old theories that are rejected, and far too little effort is expended to respond to these problems. When the going gets tough, the book comes to an end. I propose to devote more time developing my own account of ignorance of law and to examine only those positions that contain at least a grain of truth and have not been refuted time and time again. Thus I expend correspondingly less effort surveying legal history and showing where previous commentators have gone wrong.

Moreover, I have little to say—too little, I am sure—about how ignorance of law is handled in legal systems that are not Anglo-American. I have a simple explanation for this glaring omission. Like most legal theorists in the United States, I am relatively uninformed about comparative law. As a result, I would be forced simply to repeat what more knowledgeable commentators have said. This repetition would make my book more comprehensive, but less original. Fortunately, other legal scholars have done a commendable job discussing this topic in continental systems as well as in international law.[7] I do, however, briefly comment about the law in Germany, as the problem has generated enormous scholarly controversy over the years and has produced a doctrine that resembles (but is far from identical) to what I defend here.

In addition, I do not examine the conditions under which persons are *praiseworthy*. My neglect of praiseworthiness is hardly surprising in a discussion of the criminal law, inasmuch as systems of penal justice are not much interested in positive as opposed to negative desert. Because I base criminal responsibility on moral responsibility,

[7] For example, see A. van Verseveld: *Mistake of Law* (The Hague: T.M.C. Asser Press, 2012).

however, my lack of attention to praise may be problematic. Arguably, praiseworthiness and blameworthiness are symmetrical, and much can be learned about the latter by careful attention to the former. Despite my skepticism about this alleged symmetry, I adopt no explicit position on whether it holds. In any event, I do not pursue the opportunity to gain insights into the grounds of blameworthiness by inquiring into the foundations of praiseworthiness.

I often conclude that one wrongdoer is *fully* responsible whereas another is *less* than fully responsible. The practical import of these judgments is that only the former defendant is eligible for the maximum sentence authorized by law for her offense. The latter qualifies for a lesser punishment. This connection between degrees of responsibility and the amount of punishment for which persons become eligible is sensible only if the sentences the law actually imposes for given offenses approximate justice. They approximate justice, in turn, only if they conform to a principle of proportionality: the severity of the sentence is (ceteris paribus) a function of the seriousness of the crime, which in turn is a function of the culpability of the offender. But I make almost no effort to provide further content to the principle of proportionality or to respond to familiar difficulties about how it might be implemented in the real world. If sentences tend to be disproportionately harsh—as is certainly true in existing systems of criminal justice throughout the United States—a less-than-fully responsible wrongdoer might actually be given a longer sentence in the real world than is deserved by a fully responsible offender. When sentences are manifestly unjust in the first place, applications of judgments of *full* or *partial* responsibility will inherit this injustice. Thus my project makes the heroic assumption that sentencing schemes can be revised to roughly approximate principles of proportionality and retributive justice.

Just as authors must decide which issues must be confronted and which can be safely bypassed, they also must decide how much work should be done to place their topic in a broader framework. On this matter, I labor at some length. A sampling of the issues I touch along the way include the nature and importance of the contrast between justification and excuse, the determination of whether beliefs must be occurrent or latent to ground responsibility, the content of moral and legal wrongs and the rationale for supposing the former but not the latter to be strict, the contrast between offenses and defenses, the limits of subjectivism in moral and legal philosophy, the relevance of past wrongdoing to present blameworthiness, the importance of the principle of legality, the credibility of intuitions and the conditions under which they are likely to be contaminated, the connections between morality and law, the significance of whether a wrong is public or private, the foundations of responsibility, the consequentialist grounds to compromise with ideal theory, and a great many others. Because each of these topics is so difficult, I am certain I bite off more than I am able to chew. To some readers, I suspect that the connections I explore between *ignorantia juris* and broader questions in the philosophy of criminal law will be the most interesting parts of my project. To others, however, these discussions will be tedious distractions from the meat of my inquiry. I pursue many of these tangents at the beginning of my manuscript, and worry I take too long a windup before delivering my first pitch. Reasonable persons will disagree about how to strike the ratio between background and foreground.

One feature of my project is absolutely crucial to clarify at the outset, and is sufficiently important to merit frequent repetition. I do not delve too deeply into what might be called matters of first-order morality or law: a determination of what conduct Φ ought to be legal or illegal. Obviously, an answer to this question is extremely important and continues to divide legal theorists. I have spent much of my professional career addressing this topic and continue to believe that many of the problems in the substantive criminal law could be ameliorated by adopting a better theory of criminalization.[8] Subject to a few complications that can be put aside for the moment, however, my topic begins only *after* these first order judgments have been made. We want to know not *when* conduct Φ breaches a penal statute and thus is legal or illegal, but whether, under what conditions, and to what extent persons are *responsible for* and thus eligible to be *punished* for their illegal conduct. In fact, subject to some complexities I again put aside, it is reasonably clear that my basic question (Q) *presupposes* that persons A and B have acted unlawfully. *Unless* their conduct Φ amounts to a penal offense, questions of punishment should not arise; no legal system deliberately sentences persons for conduct it concedes to be permissible. The failure to grasp this very basic point—and the erroneous supposition that I am talking about wrongfulness or permissibility rather than about responsibility or its absence— threatens to make hash of my entire project. Admittedly, as we will

---

[8] Douglas Husak: *Overcriminalization* (Oxford: Oxford University Press, 2008).

see, first and second-order questions *can* be hard to distinguish.[9] But anyone who proposes to allow persons to evade punishment for violations of L when they are unaware of it is bound to be accused of not taking L seriously.[10] Moral and legal philosophers are less likely to confuse first-order questions (about wrongfulness) with second-order questions (about responsibility), but laypersons do so routinely.

At first blush, my conclusions about *ignorantia juris* seem extraordinarily radical. Affording some degree of exculpation to nearly all defendants who commit crimes in ignorance of law would represent a major departure from current legal doctrine. Should we really jump into this abyss? I offer two quick replies. First, as I will emphasize repeatedly, my position is not nearly as revolutionary as appearances may suggest.[11] One of the central themes of my approach is its "give and take": most aspects of my position are favorable to defendants relative to the status quo, but quite a few others are not. I *contract* the scope of liability in most respects, but actually *expand* it relative to what a number of prominent theorists recommend. In any event, I will argue that no major upheaval in the real world of criminal justice need occur if my view is implemented—especially when it is tempered by the practical concerns I introduce in my final chapter. Second, a conclusion that helps to reduce the severity of sentences should be welcomed rather than resisted. Legislators and citizens alike have begun to appreciate what legal theorists have understood for a long time: jurisdictions in the United States punish too many people with too much severity. We would label our ongoing experiment with mass incarceration as radical if only we were not so accustomed to it. My arguments should not be dismissed as heretical simply because they show a number of criminal defendants deserve lesser sentences and some deserve no punishment at all.

---

[9] See Re'em Segev: "Moral Rightness and the Significance of Law: Why, How, and When Mistake of Law Matters," 64 *University of Toronto Law Journal* 33 (2014).

[10] Much of the recent commentary on legislative proposals to enlarge the scope of the defense of ignorance of law exhibit this mistake. Those who propose to allow ignorance of law to exculpate wrongdoers who contaminate the environment, for instance, are accused of not caring about environmental protection.

[11] Some legal theorists concur. "To say that legal process must determine, in cases of uncertainty, that the actor actually knew what she was doing was wrong before punishment is justified may not impose a demanding new limitation in criminal law." Samuel W. Buell: "Culpability and Modern Crime," 103 *Georgetown Law Journal* 547, 602–603 (2015).

A quick summary of my organizational structure is as follows. Chapter 1 contains three parts in which I describe some preliminary matters that are crucial to my undertaking. In Part A, I formulate several nearly equivalent versions of what I take to be the basic question (Q) about ignorance of law I address throughout this book. The framework I construct invokes the closely related concepts of desert, blameworthiness, and responsibility. In Part B, I identify what I regard as the primary objective of the philosopher of criminal law: to specify what the criminal law should be. I argue that we should pursue this objective by recognizing a presumption that the law should adopt answers to normative questions that mirror those given in moral philosophy. This presumption is of moderate strength and can be overcome for myriad reasons, some of which may apply to the question at hand. Nonetheless, conformity between morality and law represents an ideal to which we should aspire. In Part C, I discuss the role that intuitions play in my inquiry. I am especially anxious to describe several grounds on which I believe intuitions on the topic of ignorance of law are unlikely to be reliable.

Chapter 2 purports to examine the law as it is. Even so, moral philosophers should not neglect this material. I do not survey existing law for its own sake, but rather because it contains a great deal of accumulated wisdom from which legal philosophers should draw. In Part A, I survey what courts and commentators have said about the topic. I describe a few cases that would seem to reveal the hardships of the conventional rule that ignorance of law is no defense. I speculate why existing cases do not produce outcomes even *more* unfavorable to these defendants. Legions of commentators have tried to identify what is correct or incorrect about existing doctrine, and their efforts reveal many insights we should try to preserve. In Part B, I describe the situations in which ignorance of law *is* a defense to a criminal charge. When *notice* to prospective offenders is somehow defective, all Anglo-American jurisdictions countenance a defense for defendants who are ignorant of law. But the scope of this defense is extremely narrow. In Part C, I examine the analytical project that has consumed many courts and commentators: distinguishing mistakes of law from mistakes of fact. Penal codes are far more lenient toward defendants who make mistakes of fact than toward those who make mistakes of law. A number of theorists, however, are skeptical that the contrast between the two kinds of mistakes can be drawn at all. I conclude that these skeptics are incorrect, and that the two kinds of mistake can be clearly demarcated—even if the distinction is ultimately unimportant for normative purposes. Our best theory of responsibility and blameworthiness should aspire to symmetry and afford much the same degree of exculpation to defendants who are guilty of either kind of mistake. In Part D, I situate the exculpatory consideration I ultimately favor in a broader framework of criminal law defenses. I explain why quite a few defendants who successfully plead ignorance of law *need* no defense because their ignorance entails that they have not breached the law in the first place. I suggest that many leading cases in which the mens rea terms of statutes are construed to exculpate "innocent" defendants suggest that it is the lack of moral wrongdoing, rather than ignorance of the law itself, that provides the rationale for acquittal. Eventually I will inquire whether the basis of exculpation in such cases—which I call a *denial of mens rea*—should be made available to ignorant defendants more extensively.

Chapter 3 engages the parallel treatment of my basic question undertaken by moral philosophers. Not coincidentally, this chapter is the most speculative and tentative in my book. Although they speak with many different voices on the topic, moral philosophers have done more work than their legal counterparts to try to identify whether and under what circumstances persons are blameworthy when they are ignorant their acts are wrongful. As I accept a presumption that the outcomes of the criminal law should conform to those reached in moral philosophy, the contributions of these moral philosophers are directly relevant to my project. I invoke a subjectivist theory of reason-responsiveness to support exculpation for persons who are ignorant of law. The theory sometimes presented as its main competitor—a quality of will theory—is best construed to support a defense as well. As we will see, however, many moral philosophers who otherwise would agree that B deserves some degree of exculpation relative to A for his wrongful act Φ withhold such exculpation when B is somehow at fault for his ignorance. If most persons who do not realize their act is wrongful are culpable for being ignorant, few will turn out to deserve any amount of exculpation. Subject to a few exceptions I discuss later, I express doubts that persons who are ignorant of law should be denied exculpation for their crimes because they are culpably rather than non-culpably ignorant.

In Chapter 4, I make a number of important refinements and qualifications of the central thesis about responsibility defended above. I begin by clarifying *what* the knowledgeable offender A must believe *about* his wrongful conduct in order to be fully responsible for it. In particular, his beliefs about the wrongfulness of his conduct need only be latent rather than occurrent. I also describe actual and possible exceptions—cases in which defendants might be fully responsible despite their ignorance of law. Offenders who are willfully ignorant, for example, deserve no exculpation. The basis for recognizing additional exceptions, however, is far more speculative. Cases of *mala prohibita* are probably the most difficult category—those in which conduct is not wrongful prior to or independent of law. What could it mean to say that defendants are ignorant of the morality that underlies such laws?[12] I try to answer this question, although no single solution can be given for each *malum prohibitum* offense. I also inquire briefly whether negligent mistakes of law—those a reasonable person in the actor's situation would not have made—should ever give rise to liability.

In Chapter 5, I discuss how the theory of ignorance of law I develop and defend would play in the real world. With the refinements and exceptions from Chapter 4 in mind, I describe in Part A how my theory of ignorance of law could be implemented in existing systems of penal justice. I invoke the structure of exculpatory claims described in Chapter 2(D) to question whether ignorance of law might best be conceptualized as what I called a denial of the mens rea of criminality. I decide that ignorance of law should probably function as an excuse even though it contests mens rea, and suggest that this conceptualization actually maintains the symmetry I generally favor between law and fact. I conclude in Part B with speculation about how the adoption of my views would bring about empirical consequences both good and bad. Many of the effects of my theory would be favorable. Nonetheless, I end with a note of pessimism and even cynicism. Misunderstanding and deliberate distortion might actually make it unwise to adopt my views. All aspects of political justice have become extraordinarily politicized. Significant compromises with ideal justice may well be necessary if a theory of ignorance of law is to preserve respect for law and not produce consequences more harmful than beneficial in the real world.

---

[12] I frequently refer to the morality that *underlies* a law, but the relationship between a given law and the moral reasons to conform to it is more complex than this term suggests. See my discussion of triggering reasons in Chapter 4(C).

1

Methodological Assumptions

How to Approach a Philosophical Inquiry Into the Topic of Ignorance of Law

Much of this chapter is not *directly* about ignorance of law. Those who are keenly interested in the topic but become impatient with lengthy preliminaries may be tempted to skip this chapter and move immediately to subsequent discussions of the central issue of how ignorance of law bears on responsibility. I urge readers not to succumb to this temptation. Admittedly, I expend a great deal of time setting up the problem, and fully understand the desire to get to the heart of my substantive position. I admit to misgivings about taking such a long windup before delivering my first pitch. But much of the debate about philosophical issues—including those in legal philosophy—involves controversy about how we should expect progress to be made. In my judgment, this controversy is especially prevalent in the context of ignorance of law, as so much of the existing commentary proceeds within a consequentialist normative framework that differs from my own. In what follows, I describe many of my presuppositions and commitments as well as the methodology I pursue.

I believe each of the many assumptions I make in this chapter represents orthodoxy—at least within the circle of criminal theorists in which I travel. But it is hard to be sure, because some of these assumptions are given a novel twist that may be decidedly *un*orthodox. In any case, I need to be explicit about my methodology because nearly all of it is contentious, and philosophers who do not share my foundation may reject the arguments I build upon its edifice. I have little choice but to take a great many crucial assumptions for granted; their defense would take us too far afield and require a separate treatise. A few of my assumptions are relatively innocuous and are disputed by only a small handful of legal philosophers. Others, however, place my inquiry within a framework several prominent philosophers reject. Even without attempting to defend these assumptions, it is important to identify the exact points at which substantive disagreement is most likely to occur.

In addition, detailed work on a specific topic in the philosophy of criminal law—such as whether and to what extent persons should be punished when they are ignorant they have committed an offense— is interesting not only for its own sake, but also because of what it tells us about related issues in criminal law theory. How does a focus on ignorance of law bear on the contrast between wrongdoing and culpability, the nature of criminal responsibility, the similarities and differences between morality and law, and the significance of the debate about the obligation to obey the law? These and many other questions are raised by the problem on which I focus. The framework I construct around this topic may engage philosophers as much as my arguments about ignorance of law itself.

A. The Basic Question

Legal philosophy includes many diverse parts that share little in common. Some theorists construe the objective of jurisprudence, for example, to consist in the identification of necessary truths about law. Whether or not this description is accurate elsewhere in analytical legal philosophy, it is light years away from the task I undertake here. My project lies in the domain of criminal theory or (in terms I use interchangeably) the philosophy of criminal law. The primary objective of this domain is normative, even though a considerable amount of conceptual spadework is needed to achieve this normative goal. I understand inquiries in the philosophy of criminal law to consist (directly or indirectly) in attempts to articulate and defend a conclusion about *what the criminal law ought to be* on given topics. These topics might be substantive or procedural, although my concern in what follows is almost solely with the former. My specific aspiration is to identify what the criminal law ought to be when defendants breach a criminal law but are unaware they have done so.

Almost certainly we need to retreat from the ideal I defend, but it is instructive to identify the ideal from which retreat must occur.

The task of identifying what the law ought to be is not an *interpretation* that seeks to achieve a *fit* with precedent or existing penal codes. My account would be doomed at the outset if we accept this desideratum. I need not be reminded that my conclusions about ignorance of law are at odds with Anglo-American law as it is. Admittedly, the discrepancy between my view and existing law is a reason to tread carefully; one should suspect the law has *some* reason to favor the status quo. As we will see, however, the fit between my theory and existing law is not quite as bad as initial appearances may suggest; our penal justice system manifests quite a bit of ambivalence about defendants who are unaware their conduct is criminal. Reform is in the air. Strains in current law are not hard to detect—or to exploit. In any case, my position should not be dismissed because it fails to satisfy an alleged desideratum of fit.

As I explain repeatedly in the pages that follow, my initial description of my project will require considerable refinement and qualification. These refinements and qualifications are absolutely crucial. A preliminary objective of any philosopher is to clarify the question that need to be addressed. The failure to pose the right questions has contributed greatly to confusion among scholars and practitioners about whether and under what circumstances ignorance of law should exculpate. As a result, virtually all of Part A—and, indeed, the bulk of Chapter 1—strives to clarify the basic question I propose to address. The ultimate payoff of these efforts, I hope, is to facilitate my normative endeavors in subsequent chapters.

I begin with a rough approximation of my question before I introduce the complexities we ultimately need. Superficially, I ask how the criminal law should treat defendants who have broken the law but are unaware they have done so. Should these persons be exculpated? If not, why not; if so, why and under what conditions? If they should be exculpated at least sometimes, what form should their exculpation take? Should they be granted a complete defense and be acquitted? Or should they be entitled to mitigation, that is, should they be punished less severely than those defendants who are convicted of the same offense but understand their conduct is illegal? Or should their ignorance be wholly irrelevant to the severity of their punishments? Even a superficial formulation of these questions should lead readers to suspect that categorical answers will not be forthcoming. Thus we need to inquire into the additional issues that need to be confronted before progress can be made. Should we try to decide, for example, whether the defendant is culpable for being ignorant in the first place? Does it matter whether the statute these persons breach is a *malum in se* or a *malum prohibitum?* What other mental states of defendants or facts about their situation are material to the sanction the law should impose? I wrestle with these complexities later. At this time, I focus simply on how we should understand the topic itself. What exactly are we trying to construct a theory *about?*

To begin to provide a more precise account of the basic question to be addressed, I propose we try to determine what the law should say about the following schema. Suppose:

(1) A knows his conduct Φ violates law L.
(2) B does not know his conduct Φ violates law L.

Assume that B does not know that Φ amounts to a violation of L not because he is mistaken about some *factual* property of his act or circumstance, but rather because he is mistaken about the content or application of L itself. I then seek to answer the following question, which I repeatedly describe as the *basic question* (Q):

(Q) *Ceteris paribus*, how should the severity of A's punishment for Φ compare to that of B's? More specifically, should B be punished less severely than A, or should A and B be punished to the same degree?

Throughout this book I will refer to this schema repeatedly, adding modifications and qualifications as needed.

Several points of clarification about this basic question are in order, and they will consume us throughout this part of the chapter. As formulated above, (Q) asks about the *severity of punishment* that should be imposed on defendants depending on whether they are aware they have committed a crime. Throughout this book, however, I will provide several different versions of (Q), intending these different formulations to unearth much the same basic question— variations that express issues I believe must be resolved in the course of answering (Q). Subject to a few complications I put aside for the moment, I make two assumptions. First, I assume that any respectable argument to establish that B (the ignorant defendant) should be punished less severely than A (the defendant who is aware his act is illegal) for Φ would show that B *deserves* to be punished less severely than A for Φ. Second, I assume that any sound argument to establish that B deserves less punishment than A for Φ because of her ignorance of L would reveal her ignorance of law to be *exculpatory*. I intend this second assumption to be far less controversial than the first. I simply use the generic term *exculpation* to include all of the diverse factors that show one offender to deserve a less severe punishment than another for committing the same crime L. Exculpation, then, refers to whatever entitles an offender to a reduced sentence. B's sentence is reduced relative to that of A, who (*ceteris paribus*) is eligible for the maximum sentence authorized for a violation of L.

The first assumption, however, carries enormous philosophical baggage and will be greeted with skepticism by some philosophers of law. My decision to construe the basic question (Q) in terms of desert locates my project squarely within the *retributive* tradition in penal philosophy. The nature and defining features of this tradition are often misunderstood, so I am well advised to use the label with caution. Retributivism is a very broad umbrella, and little of substance unites all of the many theories that fall within its shadow. In my judgment, retributivism should be understood to include any theory that affords a central place to desert in efforts to justify impositions of the penal sanction.[1] The details of how desert is alleged to enter into the correct theory of punishment can and do differ widely from one retributivist to another.[2] I encourage legal philosophers not to saddle my project with a particularly implausible account of the nature of retributivism in order to discredit it—a tendency all too common among foes of the retributive tradition. I will have a bit more to say about desert below, although I make no concerted effort to address the many worries that have led several prominent philosophers to deny its existence. My present point, however, is that I construe (Q) to ask whether B deserves some degree of exculpation relative to A. I comment briefly in subsequent chapters about possible

---

[1] "Retributivism without *desert* ... is like *Hamlet* without the Prince of Denmark." Hugo Bedau: "Retribution and the Theory of Punishment," 75 *Journal of Philosophy* 601, 608 (1978) (emphasis in original).

[2] I ask how much punishment is deserved rather than how much punishment should be imposed, all things considered. This distinction is important, because the determination of whether and to what extent punishment should actually be imposed is governed mostly by instrumentalist considerations and is not simply a function of the desert of the offender. See Douglas Husak: "Why Punish the Deserving?" in Douglas Husak, ed.: *The Philosophy of Criminal Law* (Oxford: Oxford University Press, 2010), p.393.

non-desert bases for differentiating between their punishments, but these considerations are not the focal point of my inquiry.

Thus I ask:

(Q)   *Ceteris paribus,* how does the severity of the punishment A deserves for Φ compare to the severity of the punishment B deserves for Φ? More specifically, does B deserve less punishment than A, or do A and B deserve the same severity of punishment for Φ?

I now make a further explicit assumption: *ceteris paribus,* the relative amount of punishment A and B deserve should be determined by their relative degree of *blameworthiness.* That is, if B deserves to be punished less severely than A for Φ, then B is less blameworthy than A for Φ. I suggest, then, the following interpretation of (Q):

(Q)   *Ceteris paribus,* how does the blameworthiness of A for Φ compare to that of B? More specifically, is B less blameworthy than A, or are A and B equally blameworthy for Φ?

I offer a final suggestion about how to interpret (Q). We should be interested in the relative degree of blameworthiness of A and B because of its connection to *responsibility.* To be sure, responsibility is a prerequisite for more than blame. At the very least, it is also a prerequisite for praise as well as for a host of other reactive attitudes. I take state punishment imposed through institutions of criminal justice, however, to allocate blame and responsibility. Thus I propose to decide whether A should be punished more severely than B by assessing their relative amount of responsibility. In other words, I propose to construe (Q) to ask:

(Q)   *Ceteris paribus,* how does the responsibility of A for Φ compare to that of B? More specifically, is B less responsible than A, or are A and B equally responsible for Φ?

Hence I move seamlessly back and forth from punishment to desert, from desert to blameworthiness, and from blameworthiness to responsibility.[3] None of these transitions is unproblematic. Not much

---

[3] Some philosophers incorporate each of these concepts in a single sentence. Derk Pereboom, for example, writes: "For an agent to be morally *responsible* for an action in the sense at issue is for it to belong to him in such a way that he would *deserve blame* if he understood that it was morally wrong." John Martin Fischer, et al.: *Four Views on Free Will* (Malden, MA: Blackwell, 2007), p.197 (emphasis added). Pereboom himself defends a forward-looking conception of responsibility without commitment to retributive desert.

in philosophy *is*. Terms such as *desert, blameworthiness*, and *responsibility* have a multiplicity of distinct meanings I will seldom bother to contrast. Addressing each of the several ways my assumptions might be challenged could easily comprise a separate volume.[4]

Still, I am aware that many legal theorists will reject my invitation to move so smoothly between judgments about the severity of the punishment that should be inflicted on A relative to B and judgments about the relative desert of A and B. Some of this resistance is bound to derive from misunderstandings. I do not contend that blameworthiness, responsibility, and desert *suffice* to justify punishment; the connection among them is much more indirect and partly dependent on instrumentalist rationales.[5] But on any sensible interpretation of their relationship, increases in blameworthiness, responsibility, and desert provide a ground to increase punishment. Other bases of resistance understand me all too well. As I have said, a number of philosophers of criminal law are desert skeptics, at least when desert is negative and involves the suffering or disutility punishment inevitably inflicts.[6] Some (but not all) of the criminal theorists who resist my interpretation of (Q) in terms of desert contend that the extent of punishment that should be imposed on A and B is *solely* a function of forward-looking considerations rather than backward-looking judgments. The most important of these consequentialist considerations is deterrence, both general and special. Indeed, as we will see in Chapter 2, conjectures about deterrence have loomed large (far *too* large) among theorists who have sought to defend an approximation of the position the law currently adopts about *ignorantia juris*. As I will emphasize in the next part, however, the normative framework that animates my project is deontological. I accept constraints on the authority of the state to pursue the good—in this case, the good of crime reduction. Desert, I submit, creates one such deontological constraint. Maximizing

---

[4] In particular, judgments of blameworthiness seemingly lend themselves to matters of degree more readily than judgments of responsibility. For some additional challenges, see David Shoemaker: "On Criminal and Moral Responsibility," in Mark Timmons, ed.: *Oxford Studies in Normative Ethics* (Oxford: Oxford University Press, Vol. 3, 2013), p.154.

[5] See Douglas Husak: "What Do Criminals Deserve?" in Kimberly K. Ferzan and Stephen Morse, eds.: *Legal, Moral, and Metaphysical Truths: The Philosophy of Michael S. Moore* (Oxford: Oxford University Press, forthcoming, 2016).

[6] The most vehement critics of desert include Derek Parfit: *On What Matters* (Oxford: Oxford University Press, 2011), chapter 39; and Victor Tadros: *The Ends of Harm* (Oxford: Oxford University Press, 2011), chapter 4.

deterrence is a worthy objective, but should not be achieved at the price of treating offenders in ways they do not deserve.

A few additional presuppositions are as follows. First, I stipulate that A and B are sane adults. Philosophers of law disagree about why and to what extent juvenile and mentally abnormal offenders should be punished less severely than sane adults when they commit the same crimes. These disagreements should not be allowed to infect our efforts to answer the basic question (Q). Determining whether and to what extent ignorance of law exculpates is already difficult; we should not compound this difficulty by adding the uncertainty that applies to the blameworthiness of juveniles and the mentally abnormal. Note also that (Q) asks about whether A and B are subject to comparable amounts of punishment for their conduct Φ that violates law L. I intend *conduct* to include both acts and omissions, however this elusive contrast is drawn.[7] Even more important for present purposes, I emphasize the crucial *for* relation in (Q), which I hope not to be inexplicable or mysterious.[8] I am uninterested in so-called *whole life* conceptions of desert, and confine the scope of my inquiry to what A and B deserve solely *for* Φ.[9] As we will see in Chapter 3, some arguments for punishing A and B equally for Φ cite some *other* act Ω that B has performed that allegedly makes her eligible for the same quantum of punishment as A. Among the difficulties in assessing these arguments is to understand how the commission of this other act Ω can render B eligible to be punished *for* Φ. In other words, even if B has committed this other act Ω, how does this concession advance our inquiry? After all, (Q) asks whether the degree of punishment to be inflicted on B should be similar to or different from the degree of punishment that should be inflicted on A *for* conduct Φ that breaches L. Any attempt to answer (Q) must preserve this stipulation.

Moreover, my basic question (Q) includes a *ceteris paribus* clause. What are these words designed to preclude? Obviously, any variables other than ignorance that might affect the severity of deserved punishment must be held constant between A and B. Still, I make no concerted effort

---

[7] For a taste of many of the complexities, see Randolph Clarke: *Omissions: Agency, Metaphysics, and Responsibility* (Oxford: Oxford University Press, 2014).

[8] See Douglas Husak: "Reply: The Importance of Asking the Right Question: What Is Punishment Imposed For?" in Russell L. Christopher, ed.: *Fletcher's Essays on Criminal Law* (Oxford: Oxford University Press, 2013), p.53.

[9] For a dizzying array of distinctions about desert, see Shelly Kagan: *The Geometry of Desert* (New York: Oxford University Press, 2012).

to identify what each of these variables might be. Most obviously, A and B must have committed the same offense Φ. Moreover, if a defendant is a recidivist who has violated L on a previous occasion, nearly all theorists agree his punishment for Φ should be increased—despite disagreement about why this sentencing enhancement is deserved. In the present context, of course, it is hard to see how a defendant *could* be ignorant that his act Φ violates L on more than a single occasion in which he is arrested. To be sure, B could have committed multiple infractions before she is apprehended and her ignorance is rectified. In any event, I intend all variables other than ignorance that might affect the severity of the punishment deserved by A relative to B—whatever they may be—to be precluded by the *ceteris paribus* clause.

One clarification is perhaps more crucial than any other. My topic is *not* about whether conduct Φ is criminal or non-criminal. Subject to a few complexities I leave aside for the moment, my basic question (Q) arises only *after* this first order judgment has been made. We want to know not *when* conduct Φ breaches a penal statute and thus is legal or illegal, but whether, under what conditions, and to what extent persons should be punished *for* their illegal conduct Φ. In fact, I hope it is clear that (Q) *presupposes* that A and B have acted unlawfully. *Unless* their conduct Φ is illegal, questions of deserved punishment do not arise; no legal system deliberately punishes persons for conduct it concedes to be lawful. I do not allow for a category of *blameworthy but legal* conduct: a category Michael Zimmerman helpfully describes as *accuses* in the moral domain.[10] Whether it is ever sensible for morality to blame persons for doing what is permissible, I do not recognize a counterpart of this category in the criminal arena. It would be hard to frame an indictment to represent how a person could be legally blameworthy in the absence of wrongdoing. Presumably, such a person would be responsible *for* his mental states—a position nearly every criminal theorist would be quick to resist. The principle of legality, prohibiting punishment in the absence of a violation of law, has a special salience in the legal sphere. As we will see, some features of my theory (and quite a few other theories) make it hard to understand exactly *why* legality should have this importance. I will have more to say about the significance of legality in Chapters 4 and 5.

---

[10] Michael Zimmerman: *Living with Uncertainty: The Moral Significance of Ignorance* (Cambridge: Cambridge University Press, 2008), p.194ff. Zimmerman expresses reservations about whether we should countenance accuses in the legal domain.

I should also clarify what I mean by affirming (or denying) that A and B should be punished equally (or unequally). In raising this issue, I have in mind *state* punishment. That is, I ask how the state should sanction offenders through its formal institutions of criminal justice. Although I typically omit reference to the state in my subsequent discussions, I realize that not all punishments are imposed by the state.[11] Even so, we cannot answer (Q) unless we are able to recognize given treatments as instances of state punishment. This topic is extraordinarily important in its own right; persons are entitled to many procedural safeguards when the state threatens to punish them, but these protections are unavailable when the state proposes to treat them in ways that do not amount to punishment. For present purposes, however, a definition is needed simply to appreciate what would count as an answer to (Q). On my view, a state response constitutes a punishment when it deliberately expresses condemnation or stigma and imposes a deprivation or hardship on the offender. Each of these components is important. Some commentators neglect the condemnatory aspect of punishment and focus only on the degree to which it deprives persons of goods and liberties. This focus is too narrow. Especially in white-collar contexts, many defendants are more willing to pay hefty fines than to accept the stigma that attaches to their wrongdoing. But punishments involve both. Moreover, a treatment is not punitive because it *happens* to deprive and condemn. Taxes and license revocations are rarely punitive. The very *purpose* of a response must be to deprive and to stigmatize if that response is to qualify as punitive. That is, punishments *intentionally* impose condemnation and deprivation. Armed with this definition, we can further clarify the basic inquiry. The question whether A and B should be punished with equal or unequal severity asks whether the state should deliberately impose a comparable degree of stigma and inflict a comparable quantum of deprivation on A and B. If B should be punished less severely than A, she should be condemned to a lesser degree and/or suffer a smaller amount of deprivation than A for having performed the same conduct Φ that breaches the same law L.[12] This definition, like virtually everything else in this part, is certainly subject to challenge. Is it really true that the criminal

---

[11] See Leo Zaibert: *Punishment and Retribution* (Burlington, VT: Ashgate, 2006).

[12] I avoid commitment about whether an increase in condemnation can offset a decrease in deprivation to make the severity of two punishments equal, all things considered.

law should be fixated on condemnation and blameworthiness? What would the criminal law look like—and how would it be improved—if this stipulation were relaxed? These foundational questions cannot be discussed.

Next, it is imperative to recognize that my basic question (Q) raises a *comparative* issue. I ask how the severity of the sentence or punishment of B, who is ignorant of the law L she breaks, should differ in severity from that of A, an otherwise similarly situated defendant who knows his conduct violates L. I express (Q) in comparative terms to avoid an uncertainty that derives from my conceptualization of questions about the punishment that should be imposed on defendants in terms of their desert. As skeptics of retributive desert frequently point out, it is exceedingly hard to anchor sentencing schemes, make non-comparative judgments of desert, or attach cardinal numbers to a quantum of deserved punishment.[13] What exact amount of punishment does a defendant deserve for committing arson or kidnapping, for example? These questions are nearly impossible to answer, not only because types of crimes include tokens that vary enormously in their degree of seriousness. This latter problem might be overcome by including every relevant detail in given examples. But even when a very specific scenario is before us, we tend to offer wildly different answers, and it is unclear how our disagreement should be adjudicated. Fortunately, there is far more consensus about comparative and ordinal judgments of desert. Respondents and sentencing authorities are much more likely to concur about whether one defendant deserves *more* or *less* punishment than another. The benchmark of my inquiry, then, is A, who knows his conduct Φ violates law L. Although I join the large chorus of reformers who believe punishments tend to be far too severe across the board throughout the United States, I do not specify the quantum of punishment A deserves. *Whatever* amount of punishment he deserves for Φ, I ask whether B should be punished less severely. Thus my project can be pursued whether we think the punishment A deserves for breaching L is probation or death. That is, we can make headway in answering (Q) even though we may be unclear about the cardinal, non-comparative extent of punishment deserved by either A or B.

---

[13] See Andrew von Hirsch: *Censure and Sanction* (New Brunswick: Rutgers University Press, 1987).

At the risk of alienating readers who regard the philosophical proclivity for Greek symbols as tedious, it will sometimes prove convenient to refer to the *difference* in the quantum of punishment A and B deserve for violating law L. As I am noncommittal about the exact amount of punishment deserved by either, it is impossible to represent this difference by a cardinal number. Thus I occasionally refer to this difference by yet another symbol: μ. Of course, if ignorance of law has no exculpatory significance whatever, μ will be equal to 0. But μ may turn out to be quite large. In any event, because my basic question (Q) asks about the quantum of punishment deserved by A relative to that of B, it can be construed to ask whether, under what conditions, and to what extent the value of μ is greater than zero.

Perhaps I should have formulated the basic question (Q) somewhat more neutrally in order to beg fewer questions. We cannot rule out the possibility that B might actually deserve *more* punishment than A because she acts in ignorance of law. A handful of commentators seem attracted to this possibility in a limited range of cases. That is, they are tempted to suppose that B, who is unaware Φ is illegal, might sometimes be more culpable and deserve a more severe sentence than A, who knows Φ to be unlawful. A few mistakes about the content of law seem so elementary that they could only be made by monsters (supposing the defendant to be a sane adult). Eventually I will dismiss the possibility that B ever deserves more punishment than A. I hold that ignorance of law exculpates B relative to A if it creates any difference in the punishments they deserve.

My formulation of (Q) sidesteps a related issue that merits some attention. I typically refer to ignorance of law as potentially *exculpatory* rather than to knowledge of law as potentially *inculpatory*. Logical space allows for the possibility that A is subject to a greater quantum of punishment than B not because *ignorance* of the law *exculpates* B but rather because *knowledge* of the law *inculpates* A. Especially when ignorance of L is the norm and knowledge of L is unusual by comparison, it might be sensible to begin from a baseline of ignorance and conceptualize knowledge of illegality as an inculpatory or aggravating factor rather than to begin from a baseline of awareness and conceptualize ignorance of illegality as an exculpatory or mitigating factor. I take this alternative fairly seriously, even though I am unsure whether it is functionally distinct from the position I spend most of my time exploring. In Part B of this chapter I will briefly speculate how the possibility that (Q) might be understood in

METHODOLOGICAL ASSUMPTIONS 29

terms of inculpation of A rather than exculpation of B could bear on the credibility of our intuitive judgments about their relative desert. I discuss a variant of this possibility yet again in Chapter 2.

I should explain why my formulation of (Q) is not couched in more familiar terms. Theorists typically ask whether and under what circumstances ignorance of law should *excuse* a defendant from criminal liability. Often I will pose my inquiry in these very terms. As we will see in Chapter 2(D), however, not all of those exculpatory considerations that warrant an acquittal should be conceptualized as excuses. We cannot rule out the possibility that some other kind of defense might apply to persons who are ignorant of law. For that matter, an offender who is ignorant of law might deserve to be acquitted even though he has nothing we would call a defense at all. Peculiar as it may seem, some defendants who are ignorant of law *cannot* breach the law for which they are prosecuted. Moreover, ignorance of law might well play an important exculpatory role in our criminal justice system even though a defendant who is unaware of her offense is not entitled to an acquittal. Perhaps this defendant deserves to have her sentence mitigated or reduced. Because these very real possibilities must be kept open, I generally ask whether and under what circumstances ignorance of law is an exculpatory consideration rather than an excuse. One of my primary objectives is to decide what *kind* of exculpatory consideration ignorance of law should be, and we should not simply assume that an excuse is the best alternative.

Additional elaboration will eventually be needed of some of the terms in (Q) that initially seem straightforward. The central issue may not exactly involve *ignorance,* and the object of ignorance may not really be the *law.* Although further clarification of these cryptic remarks will be provided in the chapters that follow, I comment very briefly on them here. In the first place, I regard ignorance or mistake as consisting in a false belief. Perhaps these terms function somewhat differently in ordinary language than the way I employ them here. We would have no difficulty comprehending someone who used the term *mistake* to include an accident, as when I jostle you on a subway. Moreover, some philosophers find it useful to distinguish ignorance from mistake. According to a conventional way to mark this contrast, a person is *mistaken* about a given proposition p when his belief about it is false, whereas a person is *ignorant* about p when he holds no belief about it one way or the other. I will not contrast mistake from ignorance in these exact terms, but I construct a taxonomy of culpable mental states that recognizes much the same difference implicitly. A richer array of contrasts is needed because the epistemic states I believe to be normatively relevant to judgments of responsibility extend beyond those we would describe as ignorance or knowledge. A defendant may be neither totally ignorant nor wholly knowledgeable of the law; more possibilities within these extremes must be countenanced. I borrow a more refined inventory of culpable states from the way modern penal codes govern mistakes of *fact*. Briefly, a defendant may have a purpose or intention that a fact obtains, or she may know that a fact obtains, or she may be reckless about whether a fact obtains, or she may be negligent about whether a fact obtains. The same is true of persons with respect to the law, and each of these distinct culpable states plays a role in my subsequent analysis. A defendant may have a purpose or intention to break the law, or he may know that he is breaking the law, or he may be reckless about whether he is breaking the law, or he may be negligent about whether he is breaking the law. I will describe the relevance of these contrasts when I finally present my own normative theory of ignorance of law in Chapters 3 and 4. For the moment, I stress only that my approach draws more distinctions among the possible culpable states of defendants toward the law than is suggested by the oversimplified description of my project in (Q). We create an incomplete and misleading dichotomy when we suppose that a given offender either knows or does not know he violates L.

Moreover, it can be misleading to contend that a defendant is or is not ignorant of the law simpliciter. One reason to offer a more nuanced account of the object of her ignorance—of what she is ignorant *of*—is fairly easy to grasp. In some cases, defendant A might be able to recite the law perfectly, whereas defendant B might have no inkling that his conduct is covered by a criminal proscription. But cases on neither pole of this dichotomy lie within the purview of my inquiry. A and B may be ignorant of different aspects of the law they breach, and it is hardly obvious they should be treated comparably. Should we equate the defendant who is wholly unaware the law proscribes sex with very young women with another who is unaware of the exact age at which young women are able to convey effective consent? Should we equate the defendant who is wholly unaware that income is subject to taxation with another who is unaware of exactly which gains qualify as income? Ultimately, I will deny that these distinctions are very important for purposes of identifying the blameworthiness of defendants who are ignorant of law. Still, we should not preclude the possibility that we have to decide *how much* of law L, or which *elements* of law L a given person needs to know before we can assess whether and to what extent she deserves exculpation.

Less obviously but even more importantly, ignorance of *the law* that is breached may not be what ultimately matters to judgments of how much punishment is deserved. Instead, knowledge or ignorance of L may be a rough surrogate for what *really* matters: knowledge or ignorance that Φ is *morally wrong*. It is not easy to understand how the truth or falsity of a defendant's belief about the content of the law *could* make a difference to the punishment she deserves. More plausibly, the case for or against exculpation derives from considerations that bear more directly on matters of morality. Unless the very existence of L automatically has moral significance, knowledge or ignorance of L would seem to be a proxy for something else that is relevant to desert. In Chapter 5(A) I will concede that we have little option other than to use this proxy in the real world, but we should not confuse a surrogate for the real thing. Again, I will offer further clarification in subsequent chapters of these admittedly sketchy remarks.

How should we go about answering (Q)? It would be instructive to pose my basic question to academic philosophers. Non-academic respondents, however, are more able to think about concrete cases than about abstractions. If we really care about the views of ordinary citizens, the normative objectives of criminal theory might better be served by reflecting on specific examples. As I will explain below, however, no single case forms a sound basis for a broad generalization. In this context, it is almost certain that distinctions must be drawn between one kind of example and another, and I will describe many different types of case in the pages that follow. But two particular examples will receive repeated attention. I introduce these illustrations here, although I deliberately omit crucial details until later. Depending on how these details are filled in, respondents may well differ in their intuitive judgments about whether the person I describe should receive any degree of exculpation relative to a defendant who is not mistaken that Φ is wrong.

First, consider the case of **Jacob**. Like nearly all persons (especially undergraduates), Jacob recognizes environmental protection as a moral imperative. He is often unaware, however, of the details of the laws that are designed to achieve this end. In particular, he is unfamiliar with the contents of the penal regulations that govern the disposal of batteries. When the batteries on his flashlight burn out on his camping trip, he throws them into the garbage along with his leftover food. Although he is aware that his failure to recycle these batteries might be unlawful, he is not sure one way or the other. Unfortunately, Jacob happens to be in a jurisdiction that requires this kind of battery to be recycled. I ask how the severity of the sentence or punishment of Jacob, who is ignorant of the battery-recycling law he breaks, should compare (*ceteris paribus*) to the severity of the sentence or punishment of A, an otherwise similarly situated defendant who knows her disposal of batteries violates the law. Even though additional details are almost certainly needed to answer this question, I will frequently return to the example of Jacob.[14]

Second, consider the case of **Hernan**. Like nearly all sane adults, Hernan recognizes that each person should be treated with a modicum of concern and respect. He is sincerely convinced, however, that it is lawful for individuals conquered in war to be used as slaves. Therefore he buys and enslaves persons who have been defeated in battles waged by the soldiers of his nation. He is unaware, however, that enslaving the persons he purports to own has recently been outlawed by a treaty negotiated by his state. I ask how the severity of the sentence or punishment of Hernan, who is ignorant it is a crime to enslave his victims, should compare (*ceteris paribus*) to the severity of the sentence or punishment of A, an otherwise similarly situated defendant who knows that enslaving conquered people is a crime. Again, further

---

[14] I became interested in the example of battery disposal at the same time I began thinking seriously about the normative problems involving ignorance of law. Coincidentally, I soon attended a conference (on an unrelated topic) of criminal law professors at Columbia University who (during a coffee break) happened to disagree among themselves about the content of these very laws. Neither law professors nor ordinary citizens have very accurate information about what recycling laws allow or prohibit. Of course, my ambition is not to conduct research and present the truth about these matters. Regrettably, however, it turns out that even a fair amount of research is not especially helpful in clarifying the issue. Each state has a very different framework of laws and regulations that pertain to recycling, the details of which can vary from one municipality to another. The first hit on my first Internet search took me to a website that states that ordinary AA flashlight batteries should be recycled if they are "reusable alkaline manganese (rechargeable)," but not if they are "alkaline (manganese)." This information confirmed my belief that this example helps to demonstrate that uncertainty is pervasive and ignorance of law is not rectified so easily. But the point of my example is to illustrate the problems in trying to assess the culpability of ordinary persons who risk acting wrongfully on the basis of the beliefs they actually have.

details about Hernan's case may (and almost certainly do) influence our answer.

Philosophers of criminal law stand a reasonable chance of making progress toward their normative objective in light of the several foregoing clarifications of (Q). But the process of refinement and modification has only begun, and more is on the way. Still, I hope to have made a tolerable start in identifying the basic question this book will address. My attempts to answer it will advance what I take to be the primary goal of criminal theory: defending a position about what the content of the law ought to be.

B. Critical Morality and the Criminal Law

Ignorantia juris non excusat is among the handful of adages about the criminal law laypersons profess to know for certain. But this adage, as I will demonstrate at length throughout this book, is inadequate descriptively and oversimplified normatively. In this part, I focus on a second adage that is crucial for my project and enjoys a comparable amount of currency among laypersons (even though it is less often dignified by a Latin slogan): *the law should not enforce morality*. Or, expressed a bit differently: law is one thing, morality is another. But this adage, to an even greater extent than its predecessor, is hopelessly confused. It contains a grain of truth that should be preserved, but conceals an even larger kernel of falsity. If the normative objective I propose to pursue in this book is cogent, we cannot evaluate the former adage unless we understand what is mistaken about the latter.

I describe my project as an attempt to defend a conclusion about what the law ought to be when persons are ignorant their conduct violates a penal statute. How should we assess given positions on this topic? In particular, how should we decide whether one alternative is *better* than another, or *improves* on the status quo as embodied in legislation and the common law? The best answer to this question is that *critical morality* provides the standard by which competitive positions should be assessed as superior or inferior to one other. In other words, when we pursue the objective I have assigned to criminal theory and investigate *what the law ought to be* on a given topic, the sense of *ought* in this inquiry is *moral*. Moreover, the morality in question is *critical*; its content is ascertained through philosophical argument rather than a sociological poll. Inasmuch as critical morality informs my project, it turns out to be profoundly misleading (to say the least) that the law should not enforce morality. What else but morality would anyone think the law *should* enforce? No alternatives are viable. It is respectable to claim that the rules and doctrines of the *civil* law should aspire to maximize efficiency. Economic analysis has reshaped our normative theories of tort and contract, often for the better. The comparable claim about the *criminal* law, however, is indefensible. For good reason, economic analysts have had almost no impact in reforming the substantive criminal law. As long as the focus of our inquiry is limited to the content of the penal law, no other position about what the law ought to enforce is remotely plausible. I conclude that the criminal law should derive from, be based on, conform to, or mirror critical morality. More precisely, I will argue that we should recognize a *presumption* that the criminal law should derive from, be based on, conform to, or mirror critical morality.

Antony Duff appears to dissent, but the differences are less than meet the eye. Duff contends that we should begin with political philosophy rather than moral philosophy when assessing the rules and doctrines of the criminal law, especially as they pertain to criminalization. Thus political philosophy specifies the criteria by which one theory improves over another.[15] After all, criminal justice is a state institution, and its structure and limits are part of a political theory of the liberal democratic state. As a result, Duff argues that we should proscribe and punish only *public* wrongs, that is, those wrongs that concern both the political community as well as the particular individual who is victimized. I concur that only public wrongs should be criminalized, and that too many philosophers of criminal law neglect the role of the state and the political dimensions of penal justice. But I see less reason to think that political philosophy rather than moral philosophy must be the *starting* point of the inquiry. Where we begin is less important than the arguments we accept and the place we end. On this matter, Duff and I almost entirely agree. Public wrongs are a subclass of wrongs, and we must look to moral philosophy to identify those wrongs the community may legitimately proscribe. Even more importantly, moral philosophy is crucial in determining whether and to what extent persons deserve to be

---

[15] See R.A. Duff: "Towards a Modest Legal Moralism," 8 *Criminal Law and Philosophy* 217 (2014); and "Legal Moralism and Public Wrongs," in Ferzan and Morse, eds.: *op.cit.* Note 5.

punished when they commit these wrongs. A normative position on ignorance of law, I hope Duff would agree, should be drawn both from moral philosophy and from a political theory of the liberal democratic state.

Positive arguments support recognizing a presumption that the criminal law should conform to critical morality. The best such argument, I submit, begins by identifying the nature of the criminal law itself. By definition, the *criminal* law is that domain of law that subjects offenders to *state punishment*. In other words, if a given law really is part of the criminal law of a state, those who violate it become eligible for a punitive sanction. For any number of reasons, of course, punishment may not actually be inflicted on those who meet its eligibility conditions: offenders may not be detected; those who are caught might be spared through exercises of police, prosecutorial, or judicial discretion; some who are tried might be justified or excused; or defendants who are guilty and lack a defense may be acquitted by mistake, especially when the standard for conviction is proof beyond a reasonable doubt. Thus only a small minority of offenders actually suffer the state punishment for which their conduct renders them eligible. But if a violation of a law L does not at least make persons subject to state punishment, we have ample reason to deny that L is part of the state's criminal law.

The next step in the argument is that state punishment must be *justified*. What is it about punishments that require justification? This question has already been answered. Punishment, as I have indicated, necessarily involves an intentional imposition of both hard treatment and stigma. No one denies that deliberate impositions of hard treatment and stigma—in other words, punishments—treat persons in ways that would amount to a gross violation of their rights in the absence of a special justification. We would be horrified by a state practice that intentionally condemned persons and deprived them of goods and liberties to which they were otherwise entitled unless we were confident that this practice is defensible. What *kind* of defense would be needed to assuage our reservations? The sense of justification we seek can only be *moral*. Philosophers since at least the time of Plato have struggled to produce a moral rationale for punitive practices, and the controversy remains very much alive to this day. We are not simply interested in a *legal* defense of state punishment. A legal defense is relatively easy to produce; in most cases we have little difficulty deciding whether punishments are imposed in conformity with whatever principles and procedures are mandated by law. But a legal defense leaves our central question untouched. We must justify the very principles and procedures used to impose punishment legally, and the type of justification we require is moral. In short, a moral question—what justifies state punishment?—must be given a moral answer. Any attempt to provide a legal answer to a moral question misfires by changing the subject. The adage that the law is one thing and morality is another should not be invoked to show that the moral assessment I undertake here is somehow misguided or confused.

I want to explicitly indicate how to understand my basic question (Q) in light of the presumption I invoke. As we have seen, I move seamlessly back and forth between punishment and desert, desert and blameworthiness, and blameworthiness and responsibility. Each of these terms is multiply ambiguous in ordinary language. It should now be clear, however, that the senses of *responsibility, blameworthiness,* and *desert* in question are *moral*. As we have a presumptive reason to conform our criminal law to critical morality, liability and punishment for conduct will presumptively depend on whether we are *morally* responsible and blameworthy for engaging in it. After all, we are interested in the question of what the law ought to be when persons breach criminal laws of which they are ignorant, and the sense of *ought* in this question is moral. And we are concerned with whether and under what circumstances persons deserve to be punished when they break laws of which they are unaware, and the sense of desert in this question is moral as well. If there is such a thing as *legal* desert as opposed to *moral* desert,[16] we should be uninterested in it qua philosophers unless we can learn something about moral desert from the inquiry.

I suggest, then, the following interpretation of (Q):

(Q)   *Ceteris paribus,* how does the moral responsibility/blameworthiness/desert of A for Φ who breaches law L compare to that of B? More specifically, is B less morally responsible/blameworthy/deserving than A, or are A and B equally morally responsible/blameworthy/deserving?

---

[16] I share skepticism about this matter with Mark Greenberg. See his "How Mistakes Excuse: Genuine Desert, Moral Desert, and Legal Desert," 11 *APA Newsletter on Philosophy and Law* 8 (2011).

In some guise or another, I trust that questions of this kind are familiar to moral philosophers.[17]

My interpretation of (Q) in terms of moral blameworthiness is sensible only insofar as violations of the substantive criminal law are moral wrongs that make offenders eligible for moral blame. How can A or B deserve *any* amount of moral blame for performing Φ in violation of L unless Φ is morally wrong? *Do* the rules of the substantive criminal law proscribe moral wrongs? The answer—which seems patently obvious to me—is that some do and some do not. When L does *not* proscribe a moral wrong, persons do not deserve to be punished for breaching it. Most important, persons do not deserve to be punished for breaching it even when they know it exists. If knowledge of such laws does not add anything to a justification of when persons deserve punishment, ignorance of such laws does not subtract anything from a justification of when persons deserve punishment. My contention that both knowledge and ignorance of these laws is immaterial to a moral justification of punishment presents a fascinating set of issues for a philosophical analysis of ignorance of law—issues with which criminal theorists have yet to grapple.

Admittedly, not all legal philosophers accept my invitation to examine the topic of ignorance of law by considering whether such offenders are morally responsible, and their reluctance might give us pause. Gideon Yaffe, for example, has defended a sophisticated position on ignorance of law, and I agree with (and will make ample use of) a great deal of his reasoning.[18] In a crucial respect, however, his project is very unlike my own. He explicitly purports to inquire whether and under what conditions the punishment of persons who breach laws of which they are unaware is compatible with *legal* desert as something distinct from *moral* desert. Consider, for example, Yaffe's discussion of *Surry Country Council v. Battersby*.[19] The defendant had made an agreement with a couple to take care of their children for five days each week; the children returned to their parents each weekend. But

---

[17] Although I will not use the term, (Q) raises issues often debated under the rubric of *moral worth*. "Why the same actions prompt us to morally praise (or condemn) some agents more or less than others is what I call the question of moral worth." Nomy Arpaly: *Unprincipled Virtue: An Inquiry into Moral Agency* (Oxford: Oxford University Press, 2003), pp.68–69.

[18] Gideon Yaffe: "Excusing Mistakes of Law," 9:2 *Philosophers' Imprint* 1 (2009).

[19] 2 W.L.R. 378 (Q.B. 1965).

Battersby did not have a license to provide foster care, as mandated by law. She was prosecuted for violating a statute requiring persons to obtain a license if they accept money to care for children for more than thirty consecutive days. Battersby defended on the ground that she did not know she needed a license because she thought Friday and Monday were not consecutive. The court found her to be liable because it held Friday and Monday *are* consecutive days for purposes of the statute. Thus she was found guilty despite her mistake of law. Yaffe is quick to agree there is "something wrong" with the court's judgment in *Battersby*. But he holds that "what's wrong is not that she does not deserve the punishment she receives. She deserves it legally and does not deserve it morally," and "it is only legal desert that concerns us when deciding whom to punish under the law."[20]

Of course, Yaffe is entitled to pursue any project he likes. Nonetheless, I address a different question (Q). If legal desert means anything at all, I propose to put it aside; my topic is whether such persons as Battersby *morally* deserve criminal liability and punishment when they breach penal laws of which they are unaware. Yaffe, of course, is a professor of philosophy as well as a professor of law. Why then, would he frame his inquiry to exclude moral desert? His motivation, I suspect, is to provide a unified account of when persons deserve criminal liability and punishment in cases of both *mala in se* and *mala prohibita*. The concern underlying this motivation is perfectly sensible. Suppose we contrast *mala in se* from *mala prohibita* as follows: offenses are *mala in se* when they proscribe conduct that is morally wrongful prior to and independent of law, whereas offenses are *mala prohibita* when they proscribe conduct that is not morally wrongful prior to and independent of law. If these characterizations are roughly acceptable, the pressing issue is how it is possible for persons to be morally blameworthy for perpetrating a *malum prohibitum* offense—as one might regard the statute in *Battersby*. Indeed, this problem is enormously difficult, and one can sympathize with Yaffe's desire to circumvent it by confining his project to the preconditions of *legal* blame and desert. What could morality possibly have to say about whether weekends are included in the period of time persons need a license to provide foster care? As morality would seem to be silent about Battersby's conduct, it is tempting to frame the inquiry to involve something other than moral desert. When construed to

---

[20] *Op.Cit.* Note 18, p.20.

put morality aside, the investigation can range over all penal statutes, including those that are *mala prohibia*. Nonetheless, the moral difficulty persists, as Yaffe is well aware. If we *are* interested in determining whether and under what conditions persons deserve moral blame for committing offenses of which they are unaware—many of which are *mala prohibita*—the problem must be confronted head-on rather than evaded. It is easy to see how persons breach moral obligations when they perpetrate rape and murder and other *mala in se*. But how do they breach moral obligations if L is a *malum prohibitum* offense? I will devote Chapter 4(C) to this difficult topic.

As my latest version of (Q) is phrased in terms of moral blameworthiness, it may be useful to say a bit about blameworthiness and how it differs from blame. To help clarify this matter, let me contrast four analytically distinct stages through which responses to wrongdoing might (and often do) pass. Suppose Harry knowingly and inexcusably rapes Sally. I assume without argument that a set of Strawsonian reactive attitudes are apt or appropriate for Sally. As Strawson famously indicates, normal individuals feel indignation and resentment toward those who wrong them.[21] I think we should say—although Strawson himself did not put the matter in quite this way—that it is fitting and appropriate for Sally to judge Harry to be *blameworthy* for what he has done. Still, Sally might decline to share her feelings and attitudes with anyone, regardless of how fitting and appropriate they may be. Thus a second stage through which her response to wrongdoing might pass takes place when she expresses her feelings and attitudes through verbal or nonverbal behavior. She might confide in her friends or therapist, for example. If and when Sally moves to this second stage, we might say that she no longer merely judges Harry to be *blameworthy;* she *blames* him. Next, these feelings and attitudes might be conveyed or somehow made known to the wrongdoer himself. The expression of Sally's feelings and attitudes *to Harry* represents yet a third contingent stage in her response to Harry's act. Blame expressed to the wrongdoer himself might be called *directed blame*.[22] Finally, these feelings and attitudes might be conveyed more widely in some

---

[21] Peter F. Strawson: "Freedom and Resentment," 48 *Proceedings of the British Academy* 1 (1962).

[22] Distinctions between overt and directed blame are usefully drawn by Michael McKenna: "Directed Blame and Conversation," in D. Justin Coates and Neal A. Tognazzini, eds.: *Blame: Its Nature and Norms* (Oxford: Oxford University Press, 2013), p.119.

sort of public, formal setting. The expression of these judgments in a public, formal setting might be said to involve *censure*.

It *might* be thought that the *desert* of wrongdoers is exhausted at the first of these four stages. If what Harry deserves is that Sally has a set of reactive attitudes about him that are fitting and appropriate, how can his desert extend to any of the subsequent stages—to the outward expression of these attitudes to others, let alone to Harry himself? Is the expression of a reactive attitude defended by the same rationale that applies to the attitude itself; does the aptness or appropriateness of feelings or attitudes transmit to their expression?[23] What is the rationale for making wrongdoers such as Harry aware of the attitudes victims such as Sally hold about them? The answer, I think, is fairly clear: it is equally appropriate that persons other than Sally have feelings and attitudes about Harry too. If so, these persons must be made aware of what Harry has done. But Harry deserves not only that other persons have apt attitudes and feelings about him in virtue of his deed. He also deserves to *know* that others have these feelings and attitudes. After all, we are interested in identifying what *wrongdoers* deserve, not merely how victims are entitled to feel when they are wronged. It is hard to see that what Harry deserves is simply that other persons have whatever feelings or attitudes are appropriate under the circumstances. The most obvious way to ensure that Harry is made aware of these feelings and attitudes is for Sally (or someone on her behalf) to direct them to him. According to this account, to blame someone is to target him with the appropriate reactive emotions; blame is typically what is *deserved* by the blameworthy.[24]

So much for my cursory treatment of blame and blameworthiness. If one accepts my interpretation of the basic question (Q) in terms of moral blameworthiness and desert, it should be clear that any attempt to answer it that does not depend solely on intuitions must be rooted in a theory of moral responsibility. That is, we cannot aspire to identify the conditions under which ignorance of

---

[23] For some doubts, see Coleen Macnamara: "Blame, Communication, and Morally Responsible Agency," in Randolph Clarke, Michael McKenna, and Angela M. Smith, eds.: *The Nature of Moral Responsibility: New Essays* (New York: Oxford University Press, 2015), p.211.

[24] For a list of several philosophers who subscribe to this account and a discussion of how it is often taken for granted by others, see D. Justin Coates and Neal A. Tognazzini: "The Contours of Blame," in Coates and Tognazzini: *Op.Cit.* Note 22, pp.3, 13.

law does or does not reduce the moral responsibility of wrongdoers without drawing from the more general criteria that make anyone morally responsible for anything. A huge problem, however, will plague us throughout this entire project. As I follow what I take to be philosophical orthodoxy in reserving the scope of the penal law to persons who are morally blameworthy, it becomes crucial to contrast moral blameworthiness with closely related properties the possession of which renders persons eligible for a host of negative reactive attitudes *other* than moral blame. This task is extraordinarily hard; the difficulty of delineating the scope of moral from nonmoral evaluation is among the trickiest in all of ethical theory.[25] Individuals can be stupid, obstinate, humorless, or stubborn, or suffer from similar defects that few are likely to confuse with moral blameworthiness. But what about callousness, thoughtlessness, narcissism, or carelessness? Or viciousness, brutality, lust or avarice? If actions that manifest these defects render wrongdoers eligible for *moral* blame, the penal sanction could be employed far more broadly than if they did not. Even those commentators who concur that penal justice purports to impose moral blame are certain to disagree with some of my judgments about when non-moral rather than moral blame is present.

Without pretending to have drawn this crucial distinction, I return to some loose threads about the connection between critical morality and criminal law. It is important not to proceed too quickly and destroy the grain of truth in the adage that the law should not enforce morality. When construed charitably, this adage has two implications that should be preserved. First, for several reasons I will discuss mostly in Chapter 5, perfect conformity between law and morality is not a realistic goal. Thus I hold that the rules and principles of the criminal law should conform to morality *presumptively*. That is, the rules and principles of the criminal law should mirror morality in the absence of good reason to the contrary. Unless such good reasons exist, the penal law should correspond to morality. The default position— the position to which we should gravitate if insufficient reasons are marshaled in favor of the opposing point of view—is that the criminal law should conform to critical morality.

---

[25] For thoughtful progress, see Gary Watson: "Two Faces of Responsibility," 24 *Philosophical Topics* 227 (1996); and Neil Levy: "The Good, the Bad and the Blameworthy," 1 *Journal of Ethics and Social Philosophy* 1 (2005).

I intend this claim about the connection between criminal law and morality to be fairly modest and uncontroversial. As it stands, it is relatively uninformative. No one should be quick to challenge it without understanding the *strength* of this presumption. Theorists lack an accepted metric to depict such strength. Generally, a presumption is strong when few reasons suffice to rebut it, and weak when it is overcome relatively easily. If this crude device is applied, the presumption I invoke here should be characterized as moderate. Its strength falls somewhere between these two extremes—it is neither as strong nor as weak as a good many other presumptions with which we are familiar. Although it is far from trivial, I believe that quite a few good reasons can be found for the rules and doctrines of the criminal law to diverge from those of critical morality. Chapter 5 explores some of the bases for a departure in the context of the rules pertaining to ignorance of law. Do difficulties of proof allow a divergence? To what extent should our rules be altered to ensure that deterrence is not weakened? Do expectations that my conclusions will be deliberately distorted by my ideological opponents warrant nonconformity? At the present time, however, I do not address these questions. I simply point out that the thesis that the law should conform to morality presumptively does not tell us a great deal—and is more innocuous than it might appear—because the presumption in question is only moderately strong and can be overcome on any number of grounds.

I digress briefly to note an irony in commentary about my topic. As we will see in Chapter 2, perhaps the most common basis for *denying* exculpation to wrongdoers who act in ignorance of law is also couched in terms of a presumption. Courts and commentators repeat over and over again that everyone is presumed to know the law. It is hard to know how to understand this peculiar statement. Like the presumption I invoke in favor of conforming criminal law to morality, the supposed presumption that everyone knows the law is remarkably uninformative. That is, its alleged existence does not tell us much unless we are able to assess its strength and identify the weight of the reasons needed to rebut it. Remarkably, however, the majority of commentators neglect this point when they invoke the presumption that everyone knows the law. In other words, they rarely discuss the weight of this supposed presumption. Indeed, unless notice is somehow defective, they typically appear to treat it as an irrebuttable rule of law. As far as I can see, virtually *no* consideration adduced by the ignorant defendant is deemed sufficient to outweigh it. Needless to say, an irrebuttable rule of law is a far cry from a true presumption. The statement that everyone is presumed to know the law can no more support a conclusive rule about knowledge than the statement that everyone is presumed to be innocent can support a conclusive rule about innocence. If we really propose to treat everyone as though they know the law, we should not disguise this proposal by expressing it as a presumption—unless, of course, we proceed to explain how this presumption can be rebutted.

What is equally perplexing, however, is that most commentators miss this same point when they *reject* the supposed presumption that everyone knows the law. Depending on the weight assigned to it, however, the existence of this presumption is not nearly as preposterous as many critics have alleged. James Fitzjames Stephen, for example, said this presumption was like "a forged release to a forged bond."[26] John Austin claimed it to be "notoriously and ridiculously false."[27] Edwin Keedy called it "absurd."[28] It seems apparent, however, that these critics are so incredulous because they too conceptualize this presumption as an irrebuttable rule. In fact, however, there is nothing outlandish about regarding knowledge of the law as the default position—the position the law should reach in the absence of good reason to believe otherwise. As so construed, the practical import of this presumption would be to allow the burden of proof to be allocated to the defendant. That is, the state could require the defendant to show (by some unspecified standard) that she did *not* know her conduct breached the law. In the absence of such evidence, the presumption would stand as *not* rebutted (although not as *irrebuttable*). As we will see, positive law tends to embrace this view about where the burden of proof should be allocated. In those unusual instances in which ignorance of the law functions as a defense, most jurisdictions require the defendant to prove his ignorance by a preponderance of the evidence.[29] This allocation has led to no outcry from commentators who ridicule (in the exceptionally strong language I have quoted) the supposed existence of a presumption that everyone knows the law. But this allocation makes perfect sense if such a presumption exists—as long as we are

[26] James Fitzjames Stephen: *A History of the Criminal Law of England* (London: Macmillan, Vol. 2, 1883), p.95.
[27] John Austin: *Lectures on Jurisprudence* (New York: Henry Holt and Co., 5th ed., 1885), pp.481–482.
[28] Edwin R. Keedy: "Ignorance and Mistake in the Criminal Law," 22 *Harvard Law Review* 75, 77 (1908).
[29] *Model Penal Code* §2.04(4).

careful not to conflate true presumptions with irrebuttable rules of law. In any event, we cannot *really* understand much about what is involved in accepting a presumption unless we have some idea of what amounts to a good reason to deviate from it.

Why is it important to conceptualize the criminal law as presumptively conforming to morality, even while recognizing a number of rationales to allow a deviation? To insist that law should mirror morality presumptively helps to remind us that conformity between the two domains is an aspiration or goal. An argument for a given departure should be viewed with suspicion, scrutinized carefully, and never accepted too readily. The deviations we permit should be regarded as occasions for regret, as invitations to try to do better. Even if punishments must sometimes be imposed on those who do not deserve them, such treatments *wrong* persons who have a legitimate basis for complaint. Fortunately, many (but not all) of the reasons typically provided for allowing the rules that pertain to ignorance of law to depart from those of morality are far less weighty than commentators seem to suppose. If they should be rejected as insufficient to rebut the moderately strong presumption in favor of conformity, we should retreat to the default position that the doctrines governing ignorance of law should mirror those of morality.

I turn now to a second grain of truth in the adage that the criminal law should not enforce morality. In at least one class of cases, I recognize an exception to the presumption that the criminal law should conform to morality. By describing a class of cases as an *exception*, I mean that the presumption, if it exists at all, is *always* overcome or defeated when applied to members of this class.[30] When is this so? Earlier I mentioned that Duff believes the philosopher of criminal law should begin with political theory rather than with moral philosophy. Although I demur about starting points, I concur that private immorality represents a class of cases in which the presumption has no significance. In other words, when wrongdoing is private, the polity is not permitted to intervene and punish wrongdoers. In a liberal democratic state, the criminal law is not equivalent to an institutionalized form of moral philosophy. Such a state is constituted partly by its ongoing commitment to respect the

---

[30] For a defense of the claim that this presumption exerts *some* weight even when wrongdoing is private, see James Edwards: "Reasons to Criminalise," *Legal Theory* (forthcoming).

privacy of its members, and this commitment is reflected (inter alia) in the content of the criminal law it aims to enforce.

Quite a few legal philosophers have challenged my contention that private wrongdoing lies beyond the purview of the criminal law as a matter of principle.[31] In order to decide whether I am correct to hold that any presumption to enforce morality is nonexistent or always overcome when wrongdoing is private, we need criteria to categorize given instances of wrongful conduct as public or private. Of course, I can offer examples with which I trust all readers will agree. I act wrongly when I behave rudely or am ungrateful to my friends and family, yet the criminal law would not be permitted to intervene in these situations.[32] These wrongs are private. On the other hand, my supposition that rape is a public wrong is part of what motivated my claim that persons other than the victim should be made aware of what Harry has done to Sally. Admittedly, efforts to move beyond easy examples and produce criteria to distinguish the public from the private are problematic.[33] Ultimately, a theory of public wrongs requires nothing less than a theory of the state. But the difficulty of producing such a theory, however formidable it may be, should not lead us to conclude that the contrast between the two kinds of wrongs is illusory. I take comfort in the fact that efforts to contrast the public from the private are bitterly contested in *any* sphere, so we should not expect this distinction to be any less controversial when the penal law is involved.[34] However the contrast is drawn, we should not neglect the significance of privacy when we turn to the role of the criminal law in enforcing morality.

---

[31] See Michael S. Moore: "A Tale of Two Theories," 28 *Criminal Justice Ethics* 27 (2009); and Heidi M. Hurd: "Paternalism on Pain of Punishment," 28 *Criminal Justice Ethics* 49 (2009).

[32] See Leo Katz: "Villainy and Felony," 6 *Buffalo Criminal Law Review* 100 (2002).

[33] See S.E.Marshall and R.A.Duff: "Criminalization and Sharing Wrongs," 11 *Canadian Journal of Law and Jurisprudence* 7 (1998); and Ambrose Lee: "Public Wrongs and the Criminal Law," 9 *Criminal Law and Philosophy* 155 (2015).

[34] I mention only three of many current disputes. In the domain of criminal procedure, courts continually struggle to decide whether privacy is invaded by novel methods of domestic law enforcement. In the area of social media, Internet users question whether the information they post can be harvested for commercial purposes. In the context of national security, citizens disagree about the lengths to which states should go in protecting them from harm. These questions will *always* be debated in a liberal state. At least *part* of the motivation for safeguarding privacy in these diverse domains is to insulate private wrongdoing from state scrutiny and legal proscription.

I hope, however, to sidestep the debate about whether and how the presumption in favor of conforming law to morality applies to both public and private wrongdoing. My project is to decide what the criminal law ought to be when persons are unaware they breach its proscriptions. As I emphasize repeatedly, it is an altogether different question whether the law they violate is a legitimate proscription in the first place. This latter question, although crucially important, is (mostly) beyond the scope of my project. I mention private immorality for two reasons. First, it provides a kind of case in which the law should *not* conform to morality. Legal philosophers should be more willing to concede the existence of the presumption I presuppose if they recognize its immunity from potential counterexamples drawn from the private sphere. Second, this exception to the conformity I otherwise favor will play a role when we return in Chapters 4(B) and 5(A) to the question of why the state should respect a principle of legality when persons commit wrongs that have not been proscribed.

Because I believe the rules and doctrines of the criminal law should presumptively conform to those of critical morality, many of my ensuing arguments refer indiscriminately to both morality and law. I often refer to ignorance of generic *wrongdoing* with no further specification of whether the wrongdoing in question is moral or legal. Criminal theorists who disagree with me about the presumptive connection between these two domains are bound to find these references to be maddening. I hope their irritation will not lead them to dismiss my project as misguided. Many of the claims in which I refer indiscriminately to law or morality could be rewritten to be restricted to one domain or the other. In any event, a great many of my subsequent arguments *do* treat morality and law separately. Chapter 2, for example, is almost solely about existing law. Most of Chapter 3, by contrast, barely mentions law, attempting to identify the relevance of ignorance of moral wrongdoing to moral blameworthiness. Thus I frequently examine law and morality separately, even though I believe they are intimately related.

A proposal to model the criminal law on critical morality requires some discussion of the nature of morality. To *what* conception of critical morality should the criminal law presumptively conform? I hope to be excused for making no systematic effort to answer this question by providing a moral theory. I simply repeat the assumption mentioned above: the morality to which the criminal law should presumptively conform is not wholly consequentialist in nature. It contains a number of deontological constraints that limit what may be done to persons to maximize the good. Many of these limitations can be derived from something akin to a Kantian prohibition against using persons as a mere means for the greater good. I do not enter the debate about exactly how this *means principle* should be formulated or defended.[35] The details, I hope again, are mostly unimportant for my larger purposes. I insist only that a deontological rather than a consequentialist framework should be applied to assess the merits of various answers to the basic question of how our criminal justice system should treat persons who are unaware their conduct violates the law. This insistence will be immediately dismissed by some but accepted with a shrug by others. The majority of criminal theorists embrace a deontological perspective. But scholars from related disciplines—criminologists, economists, and law professors not trained in philosophy—tend to be attracted to some version of consequentialism. In partial defense of my assumption, I point out that the historical turn from utilitarianism to deontology that took place within philosophical circles in the middle part of the twentieth century originated largely with counterexamples to consequentialism drawn from the sphere of criminal justice. In particular, objections to attempts to increase deterrence by punishing persons known by the authorities to be innocent led many philosophers to appreciate that efforts to maximize good consequences needed to be constrained by deontological principles. Criminal justice is perhaps the most obvious domain in which we should be unwilling to use persons as a mere means to achieve utilitarian objectives.

I believe that few of the claims I have made in this part will strike philosophers of criminal law as novel or radical. I think the majority of Anglo-America penal theorists concur that the criminal law should conform to critical morality presumptively. This presumption reflects an aspiration that informs my thoughts about ignorance of law. If my approach is followed, it should be clear that our rules about exceptions from penal liability should conform presumptively to morality just as much as the rules of liability themselves. Theorists implicitly invoke such a presumption in their writings about defenses: self-defense, duress, insanity, and the like—topics that generally are examined

---

[35] See the papers in the special issue on the *means principle* in 11 *Criminal Law and Philosophy* (forthcoming, 2016). See also Alec Walen: "Transcending the Means Principle," 33 *Law and Philosophy* 427 (2014).

within a deontological framework. Curiously, however, most scholarly treatment of the present topic stands as a stark exception to this generalization. A great many theorists assess what the law ought to be when wrongdoers are uninformed of its proscriptions by trying to identify the answer that would produce the best consequences overall. Obviously, I do not pursue this line of thought. As I have said, a number of prominent moral philosophers have been willing to withhold moral responsibility from persons who are unaware their conduct is wrongful. Philosophers of criminal law, by contrast, tend to resist the parallel position in the domain of penal liability. Why has the criminal law been so slow to adopt a deontological framework and incorporate the insights of moral philosophers about this particular topic? This question demands an answer, although I can only briefly speculate about what that answer might be.

I entertain three hypotheses about why criminal theorists have been reluctant to afford a greater degree of exculpatory force to ignorance of wrongdoing, even though several moral philosophers have been inclined to do so. First, the adage "ignorance of law is no excuse" exerts a powerful pull on us all. As propagandists appreciate, an adage repeated frequently comes to gain a halo of respectability it may not warrant. Students, professors, and laypersons alike seem confident that this adage is correct, and thus are less likely to demand arguments for something they regard as unassailable. Obviously, the parallel adage in the moral sphere—"ignorance of morality is no excuse"—does not enjoy a comparable stature.

My second hypothesis is that criminal theorists are and ought to be more cautious than moral philosophers. The claims I will defend in this book may well have radical implications for the penal law; their implementation would require a drastic rethinking of the circumstances under which wrongdoers should be punished. Exactly *how* far-reaching these implications might be depends on a number of factors, including empirical conjectures about the extent of ignorance.[36] In any event, moral philosophers have more latitude than their counterparts in the legal academy to defend novel positions with revolutionary implications. Suppose it is true that fewer persons are

[36] For empirical evidence that even many violent offenders believe they are acting permissibly, see Alan Page Fiske and Tage Shakti Rai: *Virtuous Violence: Hurting and Killing to Create, End, and Honor Social Relationships* (Cambridge: Cambridge University Press, 2014). See also Chapter 4(A).

morally blameworthy than non-philosophers are inclined to think. Does this conclusion simply require that we edit whatever entries we make in the moral ledger we use to keep track of the blame individuals deserve? Obviously, no such ledger really exists. Systems of criminal justice and punishment, by contrast, are ubiquitous. Changes in these latter institutions would have sweeping ramifications for the lives of countless persons in the real world.

My third and final hypothesis is important for understanding my project, and requires a bit more familiarity with the structure of the criminal law itself. Like moral philosophers, penal theorists should be willing to contrast wrongdoing—which takes place when defendants engage in an act proscribed by a penal statute—from culpability, which must be present in order to subject wrongdoers to liability and punishment. In the absence of this contrast, my inquiry is barely intelligible. But what do these philosophers of criminal law mean by *culpability*? To some penal theorists, defendants are culpable whenever their conduct satisfies each of the elements of a statute with whatever mental (or quasi-mental) state the legislature specifies. The Model Penal Code made a major contribution to clarity and uniformity by recognizing only four mental states that are relevant to the culpability of defendants: purpose, knowledge, recklessness, and negligence. I will have quite a bit more to say about these mental (or quasi-mental) states later. For now, the important point is that many criminal theorists unreflectively assume that a defendant has all of the culpability that is needed for liability and punishment when her conduct satisfies each element of a penal statute with whichever of these states the legislature designates. But this way of conceptualizing culpability is utterly alien to moral philosophers. They would be astounded to learn that inquiries into blameworthiness could be resolved by an assurance that a person had engaged in wrongful conduct with one of the foregoing mental states—that is, with purpose, knowledge, recklessness, or negligence. The story related by criminal theorists may be partially correct, but many parts remain untold. Why simply assume that a person is blameworthy when she commits a criminal act purposely, for example? Surely a great many additional conditions must obtain before offenders become eligible for moral blame.

To be sure, thoughtful criminal theorists would concede on reflection that culpability *cannot* be exhausted solely by the account I have sketched above. Persons who act in self-defense, for example, are not blameworthy for their conduct, even when they kill an aggressor purposely—the highest degree of culpability known to the criminal law. Nor are juvenile offenders blameworthy for their con-duct, even when they kill knowingly. Thus these theorists implicitly recognize that more remains to be said about criminal responsibility than is contained in the simple story I have told so far. I mark their recognition of this insight by contrasting *broad* from *narrow* culpa-bility.[37] The latter is generally contained in the content of offenses and obtains when a defendant breaches a statute with whatever mental state the law requires. All remaining inquiries into whether responsibility is deserved are consigned to the former category. Broad culpability includes such matters as voluntariness, sanity, the absence of a substantive defense, and any other matter needed for criminal responsibility. Once this contrast is drawn, questions about the crim-inal responsibility of wrongdoers who are ignorant of law should be conceptualized as an inquiry into their broad culpability. Although George Fletcher did not draw this distinction in so many words, he must have had something like broad culpability in mind when he speculated that a system of criminal justice that does not recognize ignorance of law as exculpatory imposes a kind of *strict liability*—that is, an instance of liability without culpability.[38] In any event, it is broad as well as narrow culpability that should concern us when we aspire to model the criminal law on morality. To illustrate my point, consider the two specific examples to which I promised to return. I stipulated that Jacob knows he is throwing away batteries, and Hernan is aware he is enslaving human beings. If *this* is all we need to know to deem them to be culpable, the question of whether wrongdoers deserve blame when they act in ignorance of law becomes simple. *Too* simple. Trivially, these persons have all of the narrow culpability the law requires to pronounce them liable and subject to punishment. But the truth about their broad culpability—the culpability that matters to my inquiry—is far more complex.

Perhaps I am mistaken in my conjectures about why moral philosophers tend to be more willing to exculpate ignorant wrongdoers than penal theorists. However this discrepancy is explained, I encourage the criminal law to move in the direction favored by the moral philosophers whose views I will soon discuss.

---

[37] See Douglas Husak: "'Broad Culpability' and the Retributivist Dream," 9 *Ohio State Journal of Criminal Law* 449 (2012).

[38] George Fletcher: *Rethinking Criminal Law* (Boston: Little, Brown and Co., 1978).

We should applaud such a movement if we believe the criminal law should conform to critical morality presumptively. And this conformity is important to achieve, notwithstanding the grain of truth in the adage that the law should not enforce morality. The morality this presumption should implement recognizes a zone of privacy and includes deontological constraints that limit what states may do to persons to maximize good consequences. If deontological moral philosophy offers cogent support for a greater amount of exculpation for offenders who are ignorant of their wrongdoing—as I will argue in Chapter 3(B)—the criminal law has a presumptive reason to do so as well.

C. Intuitions and Their Limitations

An enormous problem remains even if we agree that the rules and doctrines of the criminal law should presumptively conform to critical morality. As we all know, reasonable people disagree about the content of morality. Disagreement is probably even more vehement among those who reject consequentialism and concur that the criminal law should include deontological constraints. Thus we need a methodology to help us to decide whether a given rule or principle conforms to or deviates from critical morality. Nearly all philosophers respond to this predicament by relying to some extent on their *intuitions*: judgments they make when reflecting on particular examples or general principles.[39] I will do so as well. After all, normative inquiry must begin *somewhere*. Nonetheless, my main objective in this part is to urge skepticism and caution about this methodology as applied to the basic question of whether and under what circumstances ignorance of law is exculpatory.

I do not concede for a moment that my own judgments are *un*intuitive. Law professors who have struggled unsuccessfully to rationalize *ignorantia juris* in their classes may think the answer to (Q) is obvious: *of course* defendants who are ignorant of law deserve some degree of exculpation. Still, I am painfully aware that many respondents report initial intuitions that are very much at odds with

---

[39] Generally, see Michael Huemer: *Ethical Intuitionism* (New York: Palgrave MacMillan, 2005).

those I defend throughout this book. The moral philosophers with whom I am inclined to agree are equally aware that readers will tend to regard their views as absurd. Michael Zimmerman admits that his judgment that persons are rarely blameworthy for their actions will strike readers not only as mistaken but as "positively obscene."[40] Gideon Rosen is equally candid in describing his similar views as "preposterous."[41] Like Zimmerman and Rosen, I cannot pretend my conclusions about responsibility correspond to the intuitions initially reported either by academic philosophers or by laypersons. And many of these intuitions are strongly held and said to warrant a high level of credence.[42]

Legal philosophers who resist my proposal are even quicker to point out its inherent implausibility. Yaffe rhetorically asks:

Does every single person who is deserving of criminal punishment believe himself to be acting illegally? It does not seem likely. A person committing murder, again, is doing something worth prohibiting in part because he disregards the value of another person's life, placing his good above the life of another. To say that he also needs to believe himself to be acting illegally if he's to be doing something deserving of criminal punishment is to elevate a reverence for the law beyond morally tolerable bounds ... It is important to see that what was just offered is not an *argument* for the claim that desert of criminal punishment does not require a belief that one is acting illegally; it was, rather, a set of considerations that make that claim seem plausible.[43]

I hazard three replies to Yaffe's passage. First, whatever its demerits might be, no one can accuse my position of "elevat[ing] a reverence for the law beyond morally tolerable bounds." As I will emphasize repeatedly, what justifies punishment is awareness that one is acting immorally, not awareness that one is acting illegally. Thus I elevate only a respect for morality, but not beyond what I take to be its

---

[40] Michael Zimmerman: "Ignorance as a Moral Excuse" (forthcoming).

[41] Gideon Rosen: "Culpability and Ignorance," 103 *Proceedings of the Aristotelian Society* 61, 83 (2003).

[42] In this context, one commentator seems confident that "moral practice is often wiser than theory." See Randolph Clarke: "Negligent Action and Unwitting Omission," in Alfred Mele, ed.: *Surrounding Free Will* (Oxford: Oxford University Press, 2015), pp.298, 299.

[43] Yaffe: *op.cit.* Note 18, p.8.

tolerable bounds. Second, I agree that part of what makes murder worth prohibiting is that it "disregards the value of another person's life." But the question, as Yaffe understands, is not the first-order question of which acts are wrongful and why, but whether and under what circumstances persons are responsible for performing wrongful acts. Finally, if designed as an answer to the latter question, a controversial theory is presupposed by the claim that persons become responsible when they disregard the value of another person's life. I believe my own account of responsibility improves on the particular theory Yaffe apparently holds. In any event, my theory does not become implausible simply because it produces outcomes that differ from those of its competitors.

In this part I question whether we should have much confidence in the reliability of our intuitions about these matters. I will not challenge the trustworthiness of *all* of our moral intuitions, even though such global skepticism is remarkably hard to combat: Why suppose any of our judgments track cross-cultural, transhistorical, and cross-linguistic moral truths? I will evade this bigger debate. Instead, I will describe some of the reasons our intuitions are *especially* likely to go awry on the topic on which I focus: the blameworthiness of persons who are ignorant their conduct is wrongful. I begin with the intuitions themselves. Philosophers have only recently begun to conduct systematic polls to find out what members of criminal justice communities happen to believe about given questions. This trend is welcome; all too frequently, lone philosophers are content simply to report their *own* intuitive judgments. George Sher, for example, is hardly unusual in beginning his book about the responsibility of persons who act in ignorance by describing a number of examples in which he is confident "we would normally judge that the agent is responsible and blameworthy for what he does."[44] The cases Sher presents involve inadvertence, forgetfulness, and other kinds of negligence. I am ambivalent about whether I share his intuitions; they seem more like borderline cases than clear examples around which theories should be constructed. In any event, they are a perilous place to begin a philosophical investigation.

At the very least, little credence should be afforded to our intuitions unless they are widely shared. Surely we need a larger sample if we

---

[44] George Sher: *Who Knew?: Responsibility without Awareness* (Oxford: Oxford University Press, 2009).

purport to incorporate intuitions into the legal domain that purports to speak for the community. We are not interested in idiosyncratic responses, but in the moral judgments *most of us* would make about specific cases after careful reflection. Thus we have reason to investigate more broadly. The task of collecting a small army of respondents would seem to be the easy part. Once these persons are assembled, the bigger challenge is how to present the issue to them. I doubt we should pose the basic question (Q) in quite the way I have formulated it so far. To be sure, we could simply ask how the severity of A's sentence for Φ should compare to that of B when (*ceteris paribus*) A knows his conduct violates law L but B does not. But even though this question may be intelligible to philosophers, I fear it is too abstract for typical respondents. It fails to present a sufficiently concrete example about which most persons have a clear opinion. Thus we need a specific case. With what example should we begin? My own experience soliciting intuitions from undergraduates as well as from law students confirms that no single example provides an ideal place to start. Depending on the content of law L and the conduct that instantiates Φ, respondents tend to report different judgments with varying degrees of confidence. The two specific examples I invoke most frequently—**Jacob** and **Hernan**—elicit distinct intuitions, especially when they are embellished with different details. And, to get a bit ahead of myself, some of the cases I later discuss—involving wrongdoers who act akratically—elicit distinct intuitions as well.

A few methodologically-sophisticated experiments that seemingly support this conclusion have actually been conducted by legal philosophers. Paul Robinson has spent the latter part of his professional life arguing that the moral authority of the penal law depends largely on whether it conforms to intuitions of justice shared by members of the criminal justice community.[45] Thus he believes we should solicit lay intuitions about controversial rules and principles of the substantive criminal law in order to determine whether existing doctrine conforms to or deviates from them. Some of these surveys involve ignorance of law. Some of his frequent collaborators have presented a series of hypothetical cases (typically but not always to Princeton undergraduates) in which defendants vary in the extent to which they evoke sympathy from respondents. In the first example in

---

[45] Paul H. Robinson: *Distributive Principles of Criminal Law: Who Should Be Punished How Much?* (Oxford: Oxford University Press, 2008).

such a series, the defendant is a coral reef researcher. In her efforts to preserve endangered species, she collects specimens of dead coral in a manner she knows does not damage the reef. She is unaware of a new law prohibiting the removal of dead or living coral from the place she works. In the second example in the series, the defendant is the CEO of a cigarette manufacturing company. He advertises cigarettes on Internet sites that cater to teenagers, most of whom are too young to smoke legally. He is unaware of a new law extending the ban on cigarette advertising to the Internet. In each case, respondents were asked whether they would favor conviction if they served on a jury. Ninety-four percent were willing to convict the cigarette manufacturer, but only 24 percent opted to punish the coral reef researcher.[46] The authors conclude that "participants resisted allowing a person who acted with wrongful intent to escape punishment even if he or she was genuinely ignorant of the laws proscribing that action. If, on the other hand, a person committed an illegal act during the course of either moral or neutral behavior, then ignorance of the laws against these specific illegal acts was taken to provide a valid defense or at least a reason to mitigate the sentence given for the offense."[47]

It is easy to challenge what these experimental results *really* show. Unlike the CEO of the cigarette company, the coral reef researcher is not engaged in the conduct that causes the very harm the statute is designed to prevent. Indeed, her acts are designed to have the opposite effect. Nonetheless, these experiments strongly suggest (in case there was any doubt) that we should not try to answer our basic question (Q) in the absence of additional information about the nature of the law L and the reasons A and B violate it. Judgments are likely to be sensitive to whether one defendant but not the other behaves in ways we approve. I suspect the intuitions of many readers of this book vary along these same dimensions. Many professional philosophers of law concur with lay respondents and categorically reject any degree of exculpation when non-virtuous defendants commit wrongful acts they are unaware are proscribed by law.[48] I cannot name a single criminal theorist who is on record for believing otherwise, although a number of moral philosophers dissent from this consensus. In short,

---

[46] Adam L. Alter, Julia Kernochan and John M. Darley: "Morality Influences How People Apply the Ignorance of Law Defense," 41 *Law & Society Review* 819 (2007).

[47] *Id.*, p.843.

[48] See Dan M. Kahan: "Ignorance of Law Is a Defense: But Only for the Virtuous," 96 *Michigan Law Review* 127 (1997).

commentators express few reservations about punishing ignorant perpetrators who breach laws that are *mala in se*. If respondents are prepared to convict a person who markets cigarettes on the Internet without realizing his conduct is illegal, one can only imagine their response to a slave-owner like Hernan who believes his victims are unprotected by the criminal law. Other examples are even more horrendous. The specter that serial rapists would escape their just deserts because they manage to convince themselves that non-consensual sex is morally permissible has colored countless discussions of the topic of *ignorantia juris*.

Despite this apparent consensus among philosophers of criminal law, I will argue that we should not take the foregoing data *too* seriously. I do not construe these intuitions as providing strong support for the proposition that the penal law should afford exculpation to sympathetic, morally motivated defendants while withholding it from unsympathetic, nonmorally motivated defendants. In Chapter 3(B) I will defend the conclusion that *some* degree of exculpation should be extended to nearly *all* persons who are ignorant their conduct is wrongful, regardless of the specific crime they commit. If I am correct, I must explain why so many commentators appear to believe otherwise. To begin, notice that the foregoing experiments did not require respondents to make judgments about the relative desert of two persons who perform the *same* act Φ, which one but not the other knows to violate the same law L. Recall that my basic question (Q) is *comparative*; it asks about the *relative* blameworthiness of two persons who engage in the same wrongful conduct when one is ignorant of law but the other is not. Moreover, (Q) asks about exculpation generally, not simply about the black-or-white determination of acquittal or conviction. It bears repetition that denying any degree of exculpation to the wrongdoer who is unaware his act is illegal entails that the two individuals deserve to be treated exactly the same under the law. Any reduction of sentencing would be wholly discretionary. In my opinion, this result is manifestly *unintuitive*. The claim that a defendant who is ignorant of law deserves to be treated exactly like the defendant who commits the same crime but understands his act is illegal is much less intuitively secure than criminal theorists seem to have supposed.

But I cannot win the battle simply by reporting that my own intuitions differ from those described above. I need independent reasons to doubt my position is undermined by the conflicting responses of others. My reservations on this score draw from research conducted by experimental philosophers that purport to specify the conditions under which our intuitions are likely to be credible or to lead us astray. Several factors play a role in confounding our judgments about the impact of ignorance of law on the culpability of defendants who commit illegal acts, even when these acts are clearly wrongful. In the remainder of this part I will discuss five separate grounds on which I believe we have special reason to be skeptical that our intuitions on this matter are reliable.

The first of these five factors involves the difficulty of imagining a particular example that is presented to us for our intuitive response. We should have more confidence in the reliability of our intuitions about cases with which we are reasonably familiar and do not tax our imaginations too greatly.[49] Crucial facts are often omitted when unrealistic situations are described to us, and respondents tend to fill in these gaps in unspecified ways that shape the judgments they report. I believe this phenomenon applies to many of the cases in which respondents are reluctant to exculpate: those in which a person commits a serious moral wrong of which he is ignorant. Dan Kahan, for example, invites us to imagine a person "who engaged in sexual relations with a ten-year-old, and who professed to be unaware that such conduct was immoral (much less illegal)." He concludes: "Rather than being a ground for sympathy, that person's moral ignorance would itself provide grounds for condemning her, for it would reveal that she doesn't care about things ... the psychological and physical well-being of children—that she ought to care about."[50] Kahan infers from such examples (and from his survey of recent precedents) that ignorance of law is and ought to be a defense "only for the virtuous." Ultimately, I will accept *some* parts of his analysis. To implement his conclusion, however, we must be careful to apply the correct theory of virtue (or of responsibility). Kahan's own remarks indicate that he regards the statutory rapist in his example as blameworthy because his act reveals a defect in what he cares about. Thus Kahan presupposes what I later will call a *quality of will* theory—a theory I will critically examine in Chapter 3(B) that grounds our responsibility in the

---

[49] See Jakob Elster: "How Outlandish Can Imaginary Cases Be?" 28 *Journal of Applied Philosophy* 241 (2011).
[50] Kahan: *Op.Cit.* Note 48, p.144.

nature of our *wills*. At present, however, my point is that the story he asks us to imagine is incomplete.

It is hard to imagine how any sane adult (in this time and place) could believe non-consensual sex to be permissible. How would this perpetrator explain the fact that *other* persons with whom he is acquainted bother to obtain consent, and do not achieve sexual gratification through force? Respondents are bound to suspect these rapists are lying about their beliefs, harboring this suspicion even if the philosopher who designs the experiment stipulates otherwise. Stipulations are not always accepted as true, especially when they are fantastic. Notice that Kahan himself specifies his statutory rapist "professes" ignorance of law. Why not stipulate he *is* ignorant of law? Apparently, even the author of the hypothetical has trouble believing his own stipulation. Respondents will be even less willing to accept his narrative without skepticism.

Let us pause to contemplate how a sane adult *could* suppose a given act of rape is legally permitted. Perhaps a recent visitor from a very different culture might think his spouse is not permitted to withhold sex from him. Once this additional information is furnished to respondents, the defendant in question immediately gains some degree of sympathy. Many theorists contend that the law should recognize a *cultural defense* that would at least reduce the sentence of persons who commit criminal acts that are permissible in the place from which they come.[51] To the extent that this defense has normative appeal, it might be conceptualized in at least two different ways. Different forms of socialization and acculturation could provide agents with varying capacities to recognize and respond to moral considerations in different contexts.[52] But suppose cultural deprivations do not actually reduce capacities to conform. In such cases, I suspect that support for something akin to a cultural defense is simply a proxy for the belief that ignorance of law is exculpatory when we construct a realistic scenario of how sane adults could possibly be unaware of the wrongfulness of their conduct. At least, I can think of no *other* reason we would be tempted to exculpate defendants from other cultures whose capacities are intact unless their background causes them to be

---

[51] See Allison Dundes Renteln: *The Cultural Defense* (Oxford: Oxford University Press, 2004).

[52] See Manuel Vargas: *Building Better Beings: A Theory of Moral Responsibility* (Oxford: Oxford University Press, 2013).

ignorant their acts are wrong. My point is just this: as further details of these extreme cases render them easier to imagine, we become more likely to grant some degree of exculpation to the wrongdoers in question. As long as the cases remain difficult to contemplate, our intuitions withholding exculpation are less likely to be credible.

It should be simple to anticipate how the foregoing considerations might apply to **Hernan**. Recall that Hernan believes he is legally and morally permitted to treat conquered peoples as slaves. Clearly, this example is under-described. If Hernan lives in a time and place where sane adults hold this moral view, the case for some degree of exculpation would become more compelling. Suppose he is a conquistador who hails from an Old World country in which nearly everyone believes that Native Americans may be enslaved when they are defeated in battle. To add detail, suppose the very peoples he enslaves own slaves themselves who were won in earlier wars. The question to be asked is comparative: Does Hernan really deserve as much punishment as a person who commits the same acts but understands perfectly well that slavery is wrong? When embellished in this way, intuitions on this question budge in the direction I favor. And if intuitions do *not* move in this direction, we should ask how *else* respondents are able to fathom how a sane adult could have the bizarre beliefs I have attributed to Hernan. However the details are filled in, Hernan is bound to gain sympathy.

A second reason to be skeptical of the reliability of intuitions in the context of *ignorantia juris* derives from the presuppositions and biases both professional and nonprofessional respondents bring to the table. The methodology of soliciting intuitions about particular examples works best when subjects have no prior views about the truth or falsity of the principles at stake. For example, college freshmen probably have no strong preconceptions about whether persons are more responsible for causing harm they intend than for harm they foresee. As a result, hypothetical examples are helpful in allowing us to sharpen our views about this principle. But it would be hard to find respondents who have not internalized the rule of *ignorantia juris*. Subjects are in much the same position as jurors who are instructed to decide a case solely on the basis of the evidence admissible in court, even though they have antecedent opinions about the very issue to be resolved. Consider how intuitive reactions are likely to differ about examples in which persons use provocative words in the United States, relative to places without established traditions of freedom of speech. The fact that persons think they know the correct response—that speech is privileged or that ignorance of law is no defense—is bound to skew the judgment they favor. When I ask my own students to grapple with hypothetical cases, many automatically apply the rule they have learned at an early age. When I press them about why they have reached the judgment they deliver, they confidently read from a mental script and recite the very doctrine I designed the experiment to test.

My third reason to be skeptical of supposed intuitions in this domain comes from experience I am confident we all share in the real world. Intuitions about *ignorantia juris* should be taken with a grain of salt when they diverge from how respondents think and behave in situations in which pleas of exculpation are requested. I see no reason to privilege responses in artificial experiments over what we know people actually say and do in their everyday lives. Whatever students may report when asked to complete a questionnaire in a classroom, most of us are quick to plead ignorance as an excuse when our own unwitting wrongdoing is brought to our attention. At some time or another in our lives, each of us has violated a rule of which we were unaware. How did we respond when detected? I recently observed a stranger talking on a mobile phone in an area where such conversations are prohibited by Homeland Security. It is easy to predict how the offender reacted when an authority confronted him. He did not reply, "I have nothing to say on my own behalf—ignorance of law is no defense." Instead, he responded, "I am sorry—I did not know I was not allowed to use my phone here." If I am correct to assume that this latter reply is nearly universal and the former is unusual or nonexistent, I make two observations. First, the offender must have believed he was entitled to leniency—some degree of exculpation—if his plea were accepted as true. He would not have responded, for example, "my father has a lot of money," or "rules are made to be broken." These latter retorts, I am sure he would realize, would get him nowhere. Second and just as important, the plea of ignorance is often *accepted* as wholly or partially exculpatory by the authority who confronts the offender. One would be astonished to learn that this person did not actually *receive* some degree of leniency relative to an offender who knew mobile phones were prohibited but made a call anyway. If the intuition that ignorance of law is no excuse were as entrenched as many commentators allege, we would be puzzled by the fact that ordinary persons plead it so frequently and authorities accept it so readily. But these familiar facts are *not* puzzling. A comprehensive perspective on the culpability of ignorant defendants must explain rather than neglect these truisms.

My next two reasons are somewhat more speculative. The fourth of these factors has the potential to contaminate intuitions across a broad range of issues in moral philosophy, but is probably more worrisome in the context of ignorance of law than in most other contexts. Social psychologists have long understood that intuitive responses to questions are subject to framing effects.[53] Different judgments become more or less prevalent as changes are made to the sequence in which the questions are asked. Even more worrisome is the finding that incompatible answers are given to two questions that are logically equivalent but phrased differently. On many substantive topics, respondents are more likely to agree that A is more blameworthy and deserves more punishment than B than to agree that B is less blameworthy and deserves less punishment than A. For example, respondents are more inclined to say that males who rape strangers are worse than males who rape their dates than to say that males who rape their dates are not as bad as males who rape strangers. Even though the desert of A>B, it is not the case that the desert of B<A. Obviously, this pair of judgments is incoherent. Perhaps this framing effect reflects an overall punitive attitude on the part of respondents; they are more inclined to agree that a quantum of punishment should be *increased* than that it should be *decreased*.

In my experience conducting polls of undergraduates and first-year law students, this tendency plays a role when respondents are asked about the relative blameworthiness of wrongdoers who are aware or unaware that their act is illegal. The person who is ignorant may not deserve less punishment than the person who is knowledgeable, but the person who is knowledgeable deserves more punishment than the person who is ignorant. If so, the tests actually used to solicit intuitions may unwittingly prompt respondents to answer that ignorance of law is not exculpatory. Experiments invariably ask whether ignorance should mitigate rather than whether knowledge should aggravate—even though these questions are functionally equivalent. Simply on the basis of the intuitions they report to the question that is posed,

---

[53] See Walter Sinnott-Armstrong: "Framing Moral Intuitions," in Walter Sinnott-Armstrong, ed.: *Moral Psychology: The Cognitive Science of Morality: Intuition and Diversity* (Vol. 2, Cambridge, MA: MIT Press, 2008), p.47.

respondents are less likely to afford exculpatory significance to ignorance of law than if the issue were phrased differently—that is, if it asked whether a factor increases blameworthiness rather than whether a factor decreases it.

Experiments could control for this phenomena by framing (Q) differently. Instead of asking whether B deserves less punishment than A, we could ask whether A deserves more punishment than B. When I formulate (Q) in this way, however, respondents become confused. Can we grasp what it would mean to hold knowledge of law as aggravating? We are accustomed to thinking of ignorance of law as exculpatory if it has any significance at all. It is peculiar to inquire whether the absence of a defense can serve as a ground to enhance a sentence. Does the lack of duress, for example, increase desert? It is far more natural to suppose that the presence of duress decreases it. As we will see, however, ignorance need not be conceptualized as a defense of any kind. If we can bring ourselves to regard ignorance as the baseline—which it may well be in many situations—it would be instructive to inquire what to say in the relatively unusual case in which the wrongdoer possesses knowledge her act is wrong.

Fifth, recall what our intuitions on this topic are *about*. At face value, they are about the extent to which persons A and B should be *punished* for engaging in the same conduct Φ that breaches law L. My inquiry does not involve what might be called matters of first-order morality or law: determinations of whether conduct Φ is wrongful or illegal in the first place. Obviously, positions on this latter question are extremely important. As I repeatedly emphasize, however, my topic arises only *after* these first-order judgments have been made. We want to know not *when* conduct Φ breaches a penal statute and thus is illegal, but whether, under what conditions, and to what extent persons should be punished *for* conduct we stipulate to be illegal. Again, I hope it is clear that my basic question (Q) *presupposes* that A and B have acted unlawfully. *Unless* their conduct Φ is illegal, questions of punishment do not arise. My own experience with law students, however, confirms that they have difficulty separating first-order from second-order questions. Even judges and law professors sometimes have trouble separating wrongdoing from culpability. Especially when wrongs are egregious, many of us allow our judgments about wrongfulness to infect our judgments about responsibility—a phenomenon that also plagues intuitions about other excuses. But separation can also be difficult in more everyday situations. Recall the foregoing experiment in which respondents were prepared to grant an ignorance-of-law defense to a coral reef researcher whose behavior is designed to protect the environment. Respondents are more likely to offer some degree of exculpation to a defendant who performs Φ to the extent they are uncertain it is wrongful. That is, doubts about whether and to what extent Φ is wrongful are reflected in judgments about whether and to what extent persons should be responsible for it. To a great extent, this tendency is laudable. Respondents *should* be unwilling to punish conduct that is morally permissible. Nonetheless, this tendency contaminates the use of intuitions in the present context. When respondents succumb to this tendency, their intuitions are not responsive to the basic question I propose here. Their ambivalence about the wrongfulness of Φ infects their judgments about the degree to which A or B are blameworthy. As long as respondents conflate questions of wrongdoing with those of responsibility, their reports of intuitions about the latter topic become suspect.

I make a final point about the general significance of intuitions. Intuitions are not taken by moral philosophers to represent the *end* of moral inquiry. Instead, they play a role in a particular argument structure that is widely employed. These thought experiments contain four stages. First, a particular example is presented in more or less detail: you awaken to find that your kidneys have been attached to those of a fatally ill violinist, or a trolley speeding down a track is about to run over five innocent victims, and you can divert it to a spur with only one innocent person. Next, a moral judgment is requested from the respondents to whom the example has been presented: it is permissible for you to disconnect yourself from the violinist, or you are permitted to throw the switch so that the trolley will kill one rather than five. Third, the moral judgment made about the particular example is generalized to support a moral principle: no one may be required to allow his body to be used to keep another alive, or anyone may cause the death of one if five others would die otherwise. Finally, this principle is applied to a new example that is similar to but different from its predecessor: suppose a fetus needs your womb to survive, or a doctor proposes to harvest the organs of a single healthy victim to save the lives of five innocent patients who need transplants. If the principle originally identified in the third stage of this argument produces counterintuitive outcomes when applied to the new example introduced in the final stage, refinements and qualifications are added to achieve a better fit—*reflective equilibrium*—between the two. Philosophers employ some version of this methodology every day. Although the details can vary widely, I hope the version of the model I have sketched is roughly familiar.

If the intuition that ignorance of law were deeply entrenched, it would be fairly difficult to find examples in stage four that produce results most respondents would recognize as counterintuitive. In other words, the principle of *ignorantia juris,* formulated at stage three, could be applied broadly to resolve a great many cases to which it pertains. In fact, however, it turns out to be easy to present cases in which respondents are quick to revise and qualify the principle that ignorance of law is no defense. Several such examples are discussed in later chapters. When these cases are assembled and their underlying rationale is brought to light, little is left of the original principle. Respondents can be persuaded to accept so many refinements and qualifications to the original rule that *ignorantia juris* becomes distorted almost beyond recognition. Or so I will contend.

At the end of the day, I deny that my position is especially counterintuitive. But it is hard to be sure; it is notoriously difficult to defend intuitions to those who do not feel their pull. Despite the several foregoing factors that militate in favor of caution, little progress can be expected in this inquiry unless readers share *some* pre-theoretical judgments about the relative desert of A and B. But more than intuitions are needed. If I am correct that intuitions tend to be unreliable in this context, we have an even greater incentive to try to bring them into reflective equilibrium with more general rules and principles. I try to achieve this feat in what follows. Moreover, if the case for allowing a more expansive defense of ignorance of law is as compelling as I will suggest, one would expect that some amount of support for my conclusion could be detected within positive law itself. As I will explain in Chapter 2, existing law reveals strains that can be relieved by enlarging the scope of *ignorantia juris.*

I conclude that we should apply more than the usual dose of skepticism toward intuitions in favor of punishing B, who is ignorant of law, to the same extent as A, who knows his conduct is illegal. Although we have little recourse but to rely on our intuitions at some point in the inquiry, we should be reluctant to generalize from them in our attempts to reach deep insights into the broader question before us. I have described several reasons to question the credibility of our intuitions when we reflect on whether and to what extent ignorance of law should be exculpatory, even when law L is a *malum in se.* Inasmuch as little weight should be assigned to allegations that my position is counterintuitive, I hope we become more receptive to my claim that ignorance of law has exculpatory significance.

Conclusion

In this chapter I have constructed much of the conceptual framework needed to make progress on the topic of ignorance of law. I have introduced a schema that gives rise to what I call my basic question (Q). If the conduct Φ of both A and B violates law L, and neither is mistaken about the relevant facts, but only A knows Φ violates L, I ask:

> (Q)   *Ceteris paribus*, how should the severity of A's punishment for Φ compare to that of B? More specifically, should B be sentenced *less* severely than A, or should A and B be punished to the same degree?

I have tried to clarify this question by recasting it in terms of desert, blameworthiness, and responsibility—central concepts in the retributive tradition I invoke. As I have indicated, many legal philosophers are likely to disagree with my subsequent positions about ignorance of law, because they reject some of the presuppositions I have made in this chapter. Perhaps they reject my account of the objectives I have assigned to the philosopher of criminal law. Or they may believe it is misguided to suppose that law should mirror morality, even presumptively. Maybe they have more confidence than I in their intuition that nearly everyone who violates a law of which she is ignorant deserves punishment and no amount of exculpation. Or they may hold more radical views, such as that no one is ever responsible or blameworthy for anything.

I suspect the most likely source of disagreement, however, is that criminal theorists will reject my particular account of responsibility or blameworthiness, preferring a competing analysis that has different implications for the basic question (Q). I turn to questions of responsibility for Φ in Chapter 3(B). For now, I simply reveal my assumptions and indicate my awareness that any number of distinguished moral and legal theorists hold contrary positions against which I do not pretend to have argued. Philosophers must resist the urge to try to comment definitively on every topic that bears on their project—even those they admit to be central. I hope that the presuppositions I have made here are shared to a sufficient extent to induce most legal philosophers to read further and to evaluate the position about ignorance of law I build upon the edifice I have constructed.

2

Existing Law, Scholarly Commentary, and What to Learn from It

My basic question is what the law ought to be when A and B engage in the same conduct Φ that violates the same law L but differ only in that A but not B knows Φ violates L because of B's mistake of law. How does Anglo–American law answer this question at the present time? Laypersons and first-year law students express supreme confidence in their answer. The claim that *ignorance of the law is no excuse* (or *no defense*) is among the handful of adages about the law about which ordinary citizens profess to be certain. As I have indicated, their antecedent confidence about this claim skews their intuitions about examples designed to test it. My ambition in this book is to mount a normative challenge to this adage and to defend an alternative approach I hope will conform more closely to our sense of justice as embellished by moral philosophers. In this chapter, however, I spend much of my time examining this claim *descriptively*—in our current system of penal justice. As we will see, the adage *ignorantia juris* contains more than a grain of truth, but is wildly oversimplified. Existing law qualifies and amends this generalization in several ways I will recount at length. These amendments and qualifications are important to anyone who aspires to understand the law as it is.

It would be remarkable if a book-length examination of ignorance of law did not at least superficially acquaint readers with existing doctrine. But why should *legal philosophers* care very much about what the law actually *is*? I offer three replies. First, the objective of the philosopher of criminal law is to determine what the law ought to be in order to improve it. The law as it is represents the baseline against which alleged improvements should be measured. Second, even though I will argue that existing doctrine on this topic is woefully deficient, it is almost certain to contain valuable insights that should be preserved. Here, as elsewhere, the common law embodies a great deal of accumulated wisdom. Finally, if the existing rule of *ignorantia juris* requires the fundamental rethinking I will recommend, it would be surprising if the law did not contain tensions that exhibit deficiencies and point to the direction where reform is most needed. Indeed, many such tensions can be found and exploited for my purposes. In this chapter I will suggest how some of the postures positive law has taken toward ignorance of law are useful in formulating my own normative theory—a theory introduced in Chapter 3 and refined and qualified in the chapters that follow.

Part A begins by offering two hypotheses about the relative dearth of cases in which applications of the adage seem manifestly unjust. I then survey how a few of the most distinguished commentators in the history of Anglo-American jurisprudence have attempted to rationalize this body of law. This narrative is far from comprehensive; I discuss only those theorists whose positions on the topic are original or insightful. Many legal scholars have explored the basis of current doctrine and have tried to understand its several qualifications, and contemporary philosophers of criminal law have much to learn from both their successes and their failures. Their observations are useful in identifying the flaws in positive law that need to be rectified. The improvements I ultimately suggest are partly built upon the foundations these commentators helped to construct.

In Part B I describe the grounds on which a consensus has emerged that ignorance of law *should be* recognized as an excuse. When *notice* to prospective offenders is somehow defective, all Anglo-American jurisdictions countenance a defense for defendants who are ignorant of law. As commentators have repeatedly pointed out, however, the law is incredibly stingy in the criteria by which notice is deemed to be inadequate. As a result, exculpation is typically withheld from defendants who are ignorant of law. A more robust requirement of notice would undoubtedly succeed in exculpating greater numbers of defendants than the law currently allows. Still, it would not begin to compensate for what I regard as the more fundamental normative defect with the rule of *ignorantia juris*.

In Part C, I examine the analytical project that has consumed many courts and commentators: distinguishing mistakes of law from mistakes of fact. Penal codes are far more lenient toward defendants who make mistakes of fact than toward those who make mistakes of law. A number of theorists, however, are skeptical that the contrast between the two kinds of mistakes can be drawn at all. If they are correct, how should our criminal justice system respond? Should our doctrines about ignorance of law more closely resemble those pertaining to mistakes of fact, or should the converse be true? I ultimately conclude that these skeptics are incorrect, and that the two kinds of mistake *can* be clearly demarcated. It is an altogether different question, however, whether the attempt to contrast mistakes of fact from mistakes of law is worth the effort. In the final analysis, I will contend that our best theory of responsibility should aspire to *symmetry* by affording the same degree of exculpation to defendants who are guilty of either kind of mistake.

Finally, in Part D I analyze the complex structure of exculpatory claims. I recount how our penal code sometimes manages to exculpate defendants who are ignorant of law *without* purporting to regard ignorance as an excuse or indeed as a defense of any kind. A rapidly growing number of penal statutes contain elements that entail that defendants who are ignorant of law do not breach the law at all. The use of this device to exculpate "innocent" defendants is perhaps the best evidence of the strain the rule of *ignorantia juris* places upon existing law. Why should such elements be included in some statutes but not others? Efforts to answer this question offer clues that might well allow us to extend the exculpatory significance of ignorance of law well beyond its present boundaries.

A. Selected Cases and Commentary

As a crude approximation, the adage *ignorantia juris non excusat* is an established part of all Anglo-American systems of criminal law. The rule itself is ancient and can be traced at least to Roman times. English common law adopted it long ago, eventually exporting it to the United States.[1] It appears in countless state and federal cases, and first was cited

---

[1] See Edwin Meese III & Paul J. Larkin, Jr.: "Reconsidering the Mistake of Law Defense," 102 *Journal of Criminal Law & Criminology* 725 (2012).

in one of the earliest opinions of the Supreme Court: "It is a common maxim, familiar to all minds, that ignorance of the law will not excuse any person, either civilly or criminally."[2] It is only a slight exaggeration to say that the foregoing statement remains true to this day, as the adage is alleged to be "as firmly settled a legal doctrine as any rule could hope to be,"[3] holding an "almost mystical power ... over the judicial imagination."[4] These statements are emphatic. Nonetheless, in this part I will argue that a closer look at the decisions of courts and the writings of commentators reveals quite a bit of ambivalence about *ignorantia juris*. This ambivalence is reflected in some pending legislative reforms that would have a major impact on current law.

One might reasonably anticipate that thousands of actual cases could be cited to illustrate the rule and the hardship it brings. Recall the example of **Jacob,** who throws his dead batteries into his garbage and is unaware that the laws of his jurisdiction mandate recycling. If the adage were applied to him, courts would not differentiate his fate from that of another defendant who commits the same offense while knowing her conduct is illegal. Surprisingly, however, relatively few actual cases can be found that shock our sense of justice.[5] After introducing three of my favorite examples, I will offer two very different hypotheses about why cases that exhibit the injustice of the doctrine are not more prevalent.

My first example is *State v. Striggles,*[6] in which the Supreme Court of Iowa affirmed a conviction for the offense of "keeping a gambling house." Striggles had installed an unusual vending machine in his restaurant; buyers were not always informed of exactly what they would receive when they placed a nickel in the slot. Striggles had been apprehensive about whether the machine qualified as a "gambling device" within the meaning of the penal statute. In 1923, a decree of the municipal court of Des Moines specified that this type of machine was *not* a gambling device. The distributors of the machine then secured a certified copy of the decree, and brought to Striggles a letter

---

[2] *The Joseph,* 12 U.S. (8 Cranch) 451 (1814).

[3] Paul J. Larkin, Jr.: "Taking Mistakes Seriously," 28 *B.Y.U. Journal of Public Law* 104–105 (2015).

[4] A.T.H. Smith: "Error and Mistake of Law in Anglo-American Criminal Law," 14 *Anglo-American Law Review* 3 (1985).

[5] Textbooks often include the (overly complex) case of *People v. Marrero,* 507 N.E.2d 1068 (1987).

[6] 202 Iowa 1318 (1927).

from the county attorney as well as from the mayor of the city assuring him that the device in question was perfectly legal. He then installed the machine in his place of business. Nonetheless, the county grand jury indicted him. At trial, Striggles offered in evidence a certified copy of the judicial decree of the court, as well as the letters from the county attorney and the mayor. Objections to his proffer of evidence were sustained. A unanimous Supreme Court held that a defendant could not rely upon decisions of inferior courts when committing acts alleged to be criminal. The Court indicated that citizens were entitled to rely on judgments of the highest court of the state, but decisions of lower courts could not serve as a defense. Striggles's conviction was affirmed even though it seemed he had done all that was humanly possible at the time to assure himself he had complied with the law.

My second example is drawn from federal law, and involves a very different pattern of facts, but also illustrates the effects of the doctrine of *ignorantia juris*. In *United States v. McNab*,[7] the defendant appealed his conviction and sentence of ninety-seven months imprisonment for importing undersize lobsters from Honduras in violation of the Lacey Act, a federal law prohibiting the importation of "fish or wildlife taken, possessed, transported, or sold in violation of . . . any foreign law." If the lobsters had not been illegal to transport under Honduran law, no violation of the Lacey Act could have occurred. McNab challenged the validity of the Honduran law in question, requiring the U.S. court to undertake its own determination of foreign law. In making this determination, the court relied on affidavits from Honduran officials that the lobsters had indeed been harvested illegally pursuant to "Resolution 030–95." After the defendants were convicted, however, the Honduran government recanted its original affidavits, admitting that the resolution was invalid at the time the lobsters had been shipped. The Honduran Constitution itself required the invalidation of Resolution 030–95 to be applied retroactively, so McNab's conviction would have been reversed had his case been tried in Honduras. Nonetheless, the U.S. court held that the lobsters had been harvested illegally at the time of the defendants' conduct. The concession that Honduras would not hold the defendants liable for past shipments of the lobsters did not change the fact that the shipments violated then-valid Honduran laws and the Lacey Act. So far, the outcome of the case seems to depend solely on what Honduran law *is*. But McNab proceeded to argue that

[7] 324 F.3d 1266 (2003).

he did not know and could not have been expected to keep abreast of interpretations and changes of foreign resolutions, and that the district court abused its discretion by excluding evidence at trial about his lack of knowledge of Honduran law. The court curtly responded that this argument was "without merit."

My third and final example involves illicit drug law, a domain in which I believe injustice is ubiquitous. In *State v. Fox*,[8] the defendant was convicted of the illegal possession of ephedrine, a controlled substance requiring a medical prescription under state law. Fox was charged in January 1991, although compounds containing ephedrine had been available as an over-the-counter treatment for asthma until November 1990. The defendant had placed his order by calling a toll-free number of a national outlet located in a state in which the substance was uncontrolled. Fox sought at trial to introduce evidence of several magazines that carried advertisements for the mail-order service he had utilized. His proffered evidence was held not to be relevant because knowledge that ephedrine was illegal was not material to his guilt. The court followed numerous other precedents in holding that the drug possession statute only requires the defendant to know he possesses a drug, not that the drug he possesses is illegal. It continued: "Ignorance of the law is no defense." Possession statutes, however, are nearly always construed to allow defendants a reasonable opportunity to dispose of the illegal substance. If this opportunity were unavailable, liability and punishment for possession would be unfair. But defendants have no reason to avail themselves of this opportunity unless they believe the substance they possess is illegal. Thus the line of cases that follow *Fox,* and punish persons for possessing something they did not realize to be illegal, raise serious questions.

Again, one would think that applications of the doctrine of *ignorantia juris* would create the potential for massive injustice. Surprisingly, however, the foregoing cases are somewhat unusual. Why are more cases that illustrate the injustice of *ignorantia juris* not reported? Two very different explanations might be given. On the one hand, the fact that such cases do not number into the tens of thousands is probably a testament to the grip the adage exerts on legal practice. In all likelihood, efforts to challenge such an established rule in court would be futile. Would a seasoned lawyer advise Jacob to plead innocent to the charge of violating the recycling laws of his jurisdiction? Almost

---

[8]   866 P.2d 181 (1993).

certainly, he would be told that his plea of ignorance of law would be summarily rejected. On the other hand, the paucity of precedents may indicate that the potential injustice caused by *ignorantia juris* is often rectified. Andrew Ashworth speculates that the dearth of appellate cases on *ignorantia juris* may be due to the fact that exculpation "is often accommodated in other ways."[9] It is tempting to believe that exercises of police and prosecutorial discretion spare many defendants who are ignorant of law from arrest and punishment. Recall my example in Chapter 1(C) of the person who talks on his mobile phone in a place where he does not know his use is prohibited. It would be remarkable if this person were arrested, prosecuted, and convicted. Of course, the same is true of Jacob.

Thus Ashworth is probably correct. Still, it is nearly impossible to collect reliable data about how discretion is exercised generally, much less in cases in which persons are suspected by police and prosecutors of being ignorant of the law they violate. In the real world of criminal justice, when persons are arrested and prosecuted in bulk, exercises of discretion are less likely to be effective in sorting those who deserve liability and punishment from those who do not. Among the many problems with assembly-line justice is that overworked police and prosecutors are unable to learn very much about the specific circumstances of the individuals they process. Thus they cannot hope to distinguish those who deserve a full quantum of punishment from those who deserve some degree of exculpation.[10] If this diagnosis is accurate, defendants who are ignorant of the law they violate are often lumped together with those who are not, and the recognition of a wider exculpatory consideration would bring about little improvement. Hence the punishment of persons who are ignorant of law may be a very real problem in our system of criminal justice that would not be fully rectified by reforms in the substantive criminal law.

The worrisome cases that *are* reported, however, lend some support to Ashworth's conjecture, revealing efforts to alleviate the harsh rule of *ignorantia juris* even while purporting to affirm the adage. In *Striggles,* for example, the court indicated "in passing" that a county attorney who exercised his discretion to dismiss the case "would not

---

[9] Andrew Ashworth: *Principles of Criminal Law* (Oxford: Oxford University Press, 5th ed., 2006), p.236.

[10] See Josh Bowers: "Legal Guilt, Normative Innocence, and the Equitable Decision Not to Prosecute," 110 *Columbia Law Review* 1655 (2010).

be subject to criticism."[11] Any injustice of conviction that occurred through prosecution was allegedly rectified when Striggles was made to pay only the minimum fine authorized by law. Presumably, then, *Striggles* answers our basic question (Q) by extending some degree of exculpation. But is *this* the appropriate legal response? Prosecution *did* occur. Striggles was not entitled to exculpation as a matter of substantive law, but rather as a matter of sentencing discretion. Arguably, he should have been *acquitted,* not merely punished less severely. Reliance on the sensible exercise of discretion by sentencing judges is always a poor substitute for getting our substantive rules right in the first place. It is hard to believe that Striggles deserves any of the stigma of conviction or the collateral consequences that follow from it.

But is the injustice in these cases really so grave? Even though the failure to acquit in each of these situations may *seem* unjust, this appearance can be challenged. None of these three defendants is an especially sympathetic character; they do not possess an abundance of what Dan Kahan calls *virtue.* Those who profit by installing a gambling device in a restaurant or by depleting the stock of lobsters in the ocean are not exemplary members of the community. Even Fox bought a quantity of ephedrine that could not possibly have been for his personal use in combatting asthma. Thus I doubt that the police, prosecutor, or judge really *believed* him to be wholly innocent or unaware of his wrongdoing. Nonetheless, I find these precedents to be worrisome. The rule of law applied in these cases indicates that the plea of ignorance would not have been accepted even if it *had* been believed.

Thus the verdict about existing case law is decidedly mixed. Even so, it is far more difficult to find cases in which courts have *granted* an ignorance of law defense. Unquestionably, the most famous such example from the Supreme Court is *Lambert v. California,*[12] reprinted in nearly every leading casebook assigned to law students. In *Lambert,* a peculiar set of circumstances combined to make the plea of ignorance of law compelling. As a convicted felon, Mrs. Lambert had violated a local ordinance against failing to report to the sheriff after being present in Los Angeles for five or more days. She responded that she had no way of knowing that her mere presence in the city amounted to a crime. Although the Court was careful to recite the familiar adage that

---

[11] *Op.cit.* Note 6, p.1321.
[12] 355 U.S. 225 (1957).

"ignorance of the law will not excuse," it nonetheless reversed her conviction. Commentators continue to divide about which of the unusual factors in *Lambert* was crucial in persuading the Court to decide in her favor.[13] Of special significance, however, is the conceptualization of Lambert's offense as an omission rather than an act. The Court claimed the conduct proscribed by the statute "is unlike the commission of acts, or the failure to act under circumstances that should alert the doer to the consequences of his deed." Thus it held "that actual knowledge of the duty to register or proof of the probability of such knowledge and subsequent failure to comply are necessary before a conviction under the ordinance can stand." One might have anticipated that *Lambert* would become the first in a long line of precedents in which convictions would be reversed because of ignorance of law. In fact, however, few cases have followed the reasoning in *Lambert*.[14] In his dissent, Justice Frankfurter accurately predicted that "the present decision will turn out to be an isolated deviation from the strong current of precedents—a derelict on the waters of the law."[15]

Lambert aside, the outcomes of these cases and the rule invoked to support them seem dubious. If I am correct that existing doctrine about the exculpatory significance of ignorance of law is so troublesome, it would be astonishing if other legal philosophers had failed to take notice. And they *have.* These shortcomings have come to the attention of legions of commentators who join me in pursuing the objective of the philosophy of criminal law: determining what the law ought to be. Despite its impressive pedigree, any number of legal philosophers have expressed misgivings about *ignorantia juris* and disagreed about whether it can be rationalized. Many favor a modest expansion in the scope of the defense—an expansion that, however sensible, falls far short of the sweeping reforms I eventually propose here.

Even those theorists who *accept* the doctrine have struggled mightily in their efforts to salvage it. The fact that many of the most distinguished scholars in Anglo-American legal history bothered to devise arguments in its support indicates that something about the adage disturbed them and led them to appreciate a defense is needed. After all, they did not feel a comparable urgency to explain, for example, why greed or lust is not

---

[13] See, for example, Peter W. Low and Benjamin Charles Wood: "*Lambert* Revisited," 100 *Virginia Law Review* 1603 (2014).

[14] But see *Conley v. United States,* No. 11-CF-589 (D.C. 2013).

[15] *Op.cit.* Note 12, p.232.

a defense to criminal conduct. Why treat ignorance of law differently?
The obvious answer is that the sentiment in favor of recognizing some
degree of exculpation is powerful. Indeed, attempts to undermine the
appeal of this rationale or to explain why the penal law should not be
swayed by it have produced some of the least impressive commentary
in the long history of criminal law theory. Many of the arguments
that have been offered are transparently unsound and suggest an air
of desperation. But my project is not historical. I see no reason to
recite what commentators such as Hale or Blackstone thought about
ignorance of law—unless they produced plausible arguments in favor
of retaining, qualifying, or abandoning the doctrine. Numerous writers
have done a thorough job exposing the fallacies in their arguments,
and nothing is gained by duplicating what several other scholars have
accomplished. I seek instead to identify insights that have not been
appreciated in the work of earlier theorists. Thus I will discuss only
those positions from which I believe something important remains to
be learned.

I begin my brief survey with the views of Oliver Wendell Holmes
Jr., even though his thoughts on the matter may seem cursory. In my
judgment, however, Holmes is the first theorist to comprehend what
the Anglo-American approach to ignorance of law reveals about the
normative framework that underlies our penal law. He candidly admits
that no deontological or retributive defense of the rule of *ignorantia
juris* is credible, and that the rejection of this exculpatory consideration
reflects an underlying commitment to utilitarianism. Holmes simply
takes for granted that the Anglo-American approach to this topic
demonstrates that "the law does undoubtedly treat the individual as a
means to an end, and uses him as a tool to increase the general welfare
at his own expense." The rule of *ignorantia juris* is "evidence that our law
exceeds the limits of retribution, and subordinates consideration of the
individual to that of the public well-being . . . [This doctrine] cannot
be satisfactorily explained on any other ground."[16] Admittedly, Holmes
does not explicitly *argue* for these sweeping claims. Still, I believe he is
absolutely correct to suggest that no respectable deontological support
for the doctrine can be found. Where Holmes went wrong, of course,
is to uncritically accept a utilitarian moral framework in which persons
may be used as a mere means for utilitarian ends.

---

[16] Oliver Wendell Holmes, Jr., in Mark DeWolfe Howe, ed.: *The Common Law*
(Boston: Little, Brown and Co., 1963), p.40.

Still, we must presuppose the very utilitarian framework espoused by Holmes in order to understand many of the efforts commentators have made to defend the adage. Two concerns loom large among those who concur with existing doctrine. First, legal philosophers frequently caution that courts would be overburdened if the defense were allowed. John Austin, for example, went so far as to predict that "ignorance of the law would be alleged . . . in almost every case" if the excuse were granted.[17] A closely related worry is that the plea would be nearly impossible to disprove, thereby producing a rash of false acquittals. These fears, of course, avoid rather than address the issue of whether persons *deserve* punishment when they are ignorant of the law they violate. In addition, these worries seem grossly exaggerated even in utilitarian terms. Neither of these concerns has led our criminal justice system to reject the exculpatory significance of mistake of *fact*, even though such mistakes seem little different from mistakes of law in their potential to acquit the guilty or to unduly burden judges or juries. Finally, to the extent these fears are warranted, their impact could be minimized by allocating the burden of proof about ignorance of law to the defendant. This decision about where to place the burden of proof may be objectionable on other grounds, but it would diffuse the difficulty I examine here.

In a similar vein, other theorists have insisted that the criminal law should not create incentives for ignorance. If the defense were recognized, they caution, persons would have no reason to inform themselves of their legal duties, and misinformation about the law would be even more pervasive than it is today. These allegations involve empirical speculation, and no evidence is typically marshaled to support them.[18] To the extent they are correct, it is arguable that states have reason to expand the exculpatory force of this plea in order to reward persons who have made good-faith efforts to ascertain their legal duties. Individuals (such as Striggles) who go to extraordinary lengths to understand the law—say, by studying judicial opinions prior to engaging in whatever conduct turns out to be illegal—almost certainly should be acquitted by a criminal justice system that purports to incentivize diligence. More to the point, it is hard to believe that large

---

[17] John Austin: *Lectures on Jurisprudence* (Robert Campbell, ed., 5th ed.,Vol. 1, 1885), p.483.
[18] Some of the difficulties in analyzing the empirical effect of *ignorantia juris* on encouraging knowledge of the law are examined by Richard Posner: *Economic Analysis of Law* (Aspen: Kluwer, 7th ed., 2007), pp.233–234.

numbers of potential defendants would actually cultivate ignorance, secure in their knowledge that they could not be convicted in the event they faced prosecution. Moreover, as I will explain in Chapter 4(A), in extreme situations in which ignorance *is* cultivated—involving *willful ignorance*—exculpation should be denied.

Finally, utilitarian concerns are paramount among those many commentators who argue that the rule of *ignorantia juris* should be retained because it promotes general deterrence. Again, the proposition that the excuse must be rejected in order to reduce crime is asserted more often than it is defended. I reply only that this rationale could be marshaled against *any* excuse, each of which can be thought to erode the deterrent efficacy of the penal law.[19] But the real problem with the foregoing allegations is not that they prove too much or rest upon unsupported empirical conjectures. Instead, the most obvious difficulty is the moral framework they invoke. A criminal conviction is a heavy price to pay to encourage diligence or increase deterrence. Although a given rule that sacrifices individuals for the greater good might well be useful in minimizing crime, no legal philosopher who takes rights and justice seriously would be persuaded to adopt it on this ground. As "threshold deontologists" point out, only a near-catastrophe or serious public harm could justify the trade-off Holmes encourages the state to make routinely. In short, utilitarianism generates wrong answers about the desert and culpability needed for criminal liability and punishment generally, and these shortcomings become glaring when we focus on the defense of ignorance of law. No contemporary theorist, I hope, would be as eager as Holmes to openly flout the Kantian "means principle" and embrace the punishment of blameless defendants without apology or embarrassment.

I offer a final note about consequentialist perspectives on this topic. Although I have alleged that utilitarians produce little or no evidence about the supposed instrumentalist disadvantages of excusing defendants who are ignorant of law, an additional problem with their rationale is equally troublesome: these commentators rarely weigh the likely *advantages* of recognizing the defense. Those defendants who would otherwise suffer the imposition of penal sanctions are the most obvious beneficiaries of the changes I later recommend. Although it is at least arguable that the suffering inflicted on offenders should be

---

[19] See H.L.A. Hart: *Punishment and Responsibility* (Oxford: Oxford University Press, 2d ed., 2008), especially p.77.

discounted when it is deserved, my subsequent arguments are designed to show that the suffering inherent in the punishment of ignorant defendants is *un*deserved. Finally, as I will explain in Chapter 5(B), allowing this defense would be likely to bring about positive effects throughout the criminal justice system as a whole. The utilitarian verdict on the defense might look decidedly different if both its positive and its negative effects were included in the balance.

Even though I believe Holmes was correct to identify the moral framework we must assume to be operative if we have any hope of supporting the adage of *ignorantia juris*, subsequent commentators persisted in their efforts to construct a non-consequentialist rationale. I turn next to Jerome Hall, the first writer to devote a large chunk of his treatise to the topic of ignorance of law.[20] Hall takes seriously the difficulties of defending the rule; his refutations of the many attempts of previous commentators are perhaps the most impressive part of his uneven book. His positive argument on behalf of the adage, however, has not withstood critical scrutiny. Hall contends that accepting the plea of ignorance would undermine the objectivity of law by contravening the principle of legality. "If that plea were valid, the consequence would be: whenever a defendant in a criminal case thought the law was thus and so, he is to be treated as though the law were thus and so, *i.e., the law actually is thus and so.* But such a doctrine would contradict the essential requisites of a legal system, the implications of the principle of legality."[21] As George Fletcher pointed out a generation later, Hall's argument is unsound in failing to distinguish justification from excuse.[22] The former, but not the latter, is plausibly included in a complete description of the conduct the law proscribes. We might say, for example, that the law prohibits intentional killings *except* when committed in self-defense. But a state that allows an *excuse* of ignorance of law would not alter the objective content of penal proscriptions one whit—no more than a state that allows an excuse of duress or insanity. In posing my basic question (Q), recall that both A and B engage in the same conduct Φ that *violates* law L. Just as no one should believe the insane do not violate a law for which they are excused, no one should believe the ignorant do not violate a law of which they are unaware.

---

[20] Jerome Hall: *General Principles of Criminal Law* (Indianapolis: Bobbs-Merrill, 1947), chapter XI.

[21] *Id.*, pp.382–383 (italics in original).

[22] George Fletcher: *Rethinking Criminal Law* (Boston: Little, Brown and Co., 1978), pp.733–735.

The fallacy of Hall's reasoning is easy to appreciate when justification and excuse are contrasted. Of course, Hall's argument is fallacious only if Fletcher is correct that the exculpatory significance of ignorance of law is best conceptualized as an excuse—a somewhat controversial point to which I will return in Chapter 5(A).

It is fascinating to speculate what Hall *would* have concluded had he recognized his novel argument in favor of *ignorantia juris* to be unsound. As I have indicated, his critiques of alternative rationales for the doctrine are devastating. When the single consideration advanced by a philosopher in support of a debatable position is shown to be fallacious, he can either rethink its truth or continue to believe it while casting around for yet another argument on its behalf. The second of these tacks—sometimes called *dumbfounding*—is common. After all, few legal philosophers have abandoned their efforts to justify state punishment, even after they become persuaded of the inadequacies of their own attempts to do so. The rule of *ignorantia juris* may be comparable. The adage is so ingrained that I strongly doubt that Hall would have emerged as the first leading penal theorist to openly repudiate it. Like punishment itself, the rule has proved more resilient than any particular argument advanced in its support.

I turn next to Fletcher, who I credit for reviving an interest in criminal theory throughout the United States in the final quarter of the twentieth century. Fletcher merits special attention not only for exposing the fallacy in Hall's defense of *ignorantia juris,* but also for becoming the first Anglo-American commentator to suggest that the "practice of disregarding mistakes of law" might well be regarded as "a form of strict liability."[23] As I have indicated, strict liability is typically conceptualized as liability in the absence of culpability. But many defendants who act in ignorance of law are highly culpable in the narrow sense; they may commit the actus reus of their crimes with some degree of mens rea that pertains to matters of fact. If ignorance of law precludes narrow culpability or mens rea, Fletcher could not have regarded it as an *excuse,* as excuses are compatible with mens rea. Thus it becomes plausible to construe *ignorantia juris* as an instance of strict liability only if we construe culpability broadly, to encompass all of the many variables that bear on whether a defendant is blameworthy and responsible. It is precisely this broad conception of culpability Fletcher must have had in mind when making his insightful remark. If we agree

[23] *Id.,* p.730.

that defendants who act in ignorance of law lack broad culpability, and agree that broad culpability should be a necessary condition of liability and punishment, we are well on our way toward accepting ignorance of law as exculpatory. The resistance criminal theorists have long felt about strict liability should transfer to how they should feel about the rule of *ignorantia juris.*

It is noteworthy, however, that Fletcher himself did *not* explicitly draw this radical conclusion. Although he is skeptical of strict liability generally, and apparently construes existing doctrine about ignorance of law to be an instance of it, he could not quite bring himself to openly repudiate the adage of *ignorantia juris.* Instead, he launches into a lengthy digression into German doctrine on the topic, which he clearly (and correctly) regards as superior to its counterpart in the United States. Most legal systems afford more exculpatory significance to mistake of law than those in Anglo-America,[24] but none is quite as liberal as that in Germany. It allows a defense of ignorance of law when the actor "could not have avoided this mistake," and even mitigates punishment when the mistake is avoidable.[25] Needless to say, applications of this provision have given rise to twists and turns about whether given mistakes of law are avoidable.[26] At the risk of oversimplification, mistakes of law provide a basis for acquittal when they are reasonable, that is, when they are non-negligent—a position long endorsed by many legal philosophers, including myself, in my earliest contribution to this debate.[27] It is hard to believe that persons should *ever* be punished when they behave reasonably. If criminal negligence should be rare, strict liability should be rarer still. My present point, however, is that Fletcher himself missed a golden opportunity to openly embrace the implications of his own thought. Curiously, he does not return from his discussion of German law to unequivocally state his own thesis about how Anglo-American law should answer my basic question (Q).

Not all legal philosophers have been so reticent. Among contemporary criminal theorists, Andrew Ashworth has gone to the greatest

---

[24] See A.A. van Verseveld: *Mistake of Law* (The Hague: T.M.C. Asser Press, 2012).

[25] §17 StGB.

[26] C. Roxin: *Strafrecht Allgemeiner teil, Band I, Grundlagen, der Aufbau der Verbrechenslehre* (4th ed., C.H. Beck, Munich, 2006).

[27] Douglas Husak and Andrew von Hirsch: "Mistake of Law and Culpability," in Stephen Shute, John Gardner and Jeremy Horder, eds: *Action and Value in Criminal Law* (Oxford: Clarendon Press, 1993), p.157.

lengths throughout his distinguished career to repeatedly challenge the doctrine of *ignorantia juris*. Although he seldom uses such strong language, Ashworth does not mince words in describing the existing rule as "preposterous." The adage rests on "insecure foundations within the criminal law and on questionable propositions about the political obligations of individuals and of the state."[28] Even Ashworth, however, explicitly denies that defendants who are ignorant of law deserve some degree of exculpation in nearly every case. He thinks "it is only fair and right to expect citizens to acquaint themselves with the criminal law and wrong to give them an incentive to remain ignorant."[29] Thus his solution to the injustice caused by *ignorantia juris* is to beef up the requirement of notice—a topic I address in Part B and again in Chapter 5(B). Briefly, Ashworth contends that a state that is prepared to punish defendants who are ignorant of law must do more to inform its citizens of their legal obligations. I sympathize with these remarks. At the very least, however, we need to know what the law ought to be with respect to ignorant defendants until Ashworth's proposals are implemented. For the foreseeable future, defendants will continue to violate laws of which they are ignorant. How should we assess their blameworthiness relative to that of persons who know their conduct is criminal? Why should we equate the responsibility of offenders who breach their alleged duty to know law L with those who breach L knowingly? I will endeavor to answer these questions in Chapter 3(B) and the chapters that follow. For now, suffice it to say that my position on these matters is even more far-reaching than that of Ashworth.

As I have indicated, a great many reformers have sought to limit the harshness of the prevailing rule of *ignorantia juris* by contending that ignorance of law should be a defense when it is *reasonable*. Reasonable behavior is non-negligent, that is, behavior that a reasonable person in the actor's situation (sometimes called RPAS) would not have performed. Thus a defendant should be granted a defense of mistake of law when a reasonable person in her situation would have made the same mistake. As a *substantive* matter, the position I will ultimately defend is very different. Before liability should be imposed, I require a defendant to have actual awareness that her conduct is or might be wrongful. At no point in this analysis do I resort to what a hypothetical

---

[28] Andrew Ashworth: "Ignorance of the Criminal Law, and Duties to Avoid It," in Andrew Ashworth, ed.: *Positive Obligations in Criminal Law* (Oxford: Hart Publishing, 2013), p.81.
[29] *Id.*, p.86.

reasonable person would have known in the defendant's situation. As a *practical* matter, however, my position may not differ much from that proposed by the above reformers. These two substantively distinct positions will tend to converge in practice because of the means by which third parties are likely to gain evidence of what a particular person believes. Criminal defendants have ample incentives to lie about the content of their beliefs. In many circumstances, the best evidence that a defendant *actually* believes p is that a reasonable person in her situation *would* have believed p. Unless she can tell a plausible story about why she does not believe what judges and jurors are convinced a reasonable person in her situation would have believed, third parties will be inclined to conclude she is lying. For this reason, applications of the two standards tend not to differ appreciably in the real world. Still, as a matter of substance, the two positions diverge considerably. If the defendant herself does not at least suspect that her conduct is wrongful, liability would be imposed in the absence of the culpability I will argue the law should require.

The rule that reasonable mistake of law should exculpate is so compelling that many contemporary lawmakers have proposed its adoption in codes. Separate bills currently pending before the Senate and the House to improve federal criminal law are aptly described as "the most significant liberalization of America's criminal justice laws since the beginning of the drug war."[30] The House Bill, known as the Criminal Code Improvement Act of 2015, provides: "If no state of mind is required by law for a Federal criminal offense—(1) the state of mind the government the Government must prove is knowing; and (2) if the offense consists of conduct that a reasonable person in the same or similar circumstances would not know, or would not have reason to believe, was unlawful, the Government must prove that the defendant knew, or had reason to believe, the conduct was unlawful."[31] The Senate Bill, knows as the Mens Rea Reform Act of 2015, provides for a default mens rea of willfulness for most federal crimes, defined so

---

[30] Matt Apuzzo and Eric Lipton: "Rare White House Accord with Koch Brothers on Sentencing Frays," *New York Times* (Nov. 24, 2015), p.A1, http://www.nytimes.com/2015/11/25/us/politics/rare-alliance-of-libertarians-and-white-house-on-sentencing-begins-to-fray.html?r=0.

[31] "Criminal Code Improvement Act of 2015" Subchapter C, §11. For critical commentary, see Orin Kerr: "A Confusing Proposal to Reform the 'Mens Rea' of Federal Criminal Law," *The Volokh Conspiracy* (November 25, 2015), https://www.washingtonpost.com/news/volokh-conspiracy/wp/2015/11/25/a-confusing-proposal-to-reform-the-mens-rea-of-federal-criminal-law/.

that "the person acted with knowledge that the person's conduct was unlawful."[32] Orin Hatch, the former Chairman of the Senate Judiciary Committee who introduced the Senate bill, explains that "without adequate *mens rea* protections—that is, without the requirement that a person know his conduct was wrong, or unlawful—everyday citizens can be held criminally liable for conduct that no reasonable person would know was wrong. This is not only unfair; it is immoral. No government that purports to safeguard the liberty and the rights of its people should have power to lock individuals up for conduct they didn't know was wrong. Only when a person has acted with a guilty mind is it just, is it ethical, to brand that person a criminal and deprive him of liberty."[33] The fate of these bills is uncertain. They indicate, however, that the ideas they express are no longer outside the mainstream.

Whether these ideas will carry the day remains to be seen. Opposition comes largely from liberals, who fear that exculpation will mostly benefit white-collar, corporate criminals—individuals who are difficult to convict even without a new defense of reasonable ignorance of law. Consider the reception this bill has received in the media. A recent editorial in *The New York Times* admits that "many federal laws are sloppily drafted, and some may need to be re-examined and re-written." But it cautions that "a broad, sloppy fix is not a solution." Exactly why is this "fix" inadvisable? The answer is that "ignorance of the law is generally not an excuse for breaking it, and it certainly should not be turned into an excuse when the action inflicts serious harm to large numbers of people or to the environment."[34] It is hard to understand, however, why the *magnitude* or *type* of harm caused (e.g., to the environment) provides a principled reason to punish a defendant who would otherwise be blameless. Recall that Jacob, our confused camper, risks harming the environment, but this fact does not seem to provide a special reason to hold him responsible. The implicit assumption is that granting an ignorance of law defense for wrongdoers who breach a given law L somehow proves that L is not taken seriously. To my mind, the tenor of the recent discussion of this

---

[32] "Mens Rea Reform Act of 2015, §(A)(4)" (https://www.govtrack.us/congress/bills/114/s2298/text).

[33] Press Release, September 15, 2015, http://www.hatch.senate.gov/public/index.cfm?p=releases&id=090FFA70-5ABF-4160-8ED5-D512EBEBEB6F.

[34] "Don't Change the Legal Rule on Intent," *The New York Times* (December 6, 2015), p.8.

issue in the media demonstrates the need for the kind of scrutiny a legal philosopher is able to provide.

Even a truncated survey of existing positions on the topic of ignorance of law should mention puzzling aspects of what some commentators have *not* said about it. The adage is so engrained that legal philosophers seem unwilling to contest it, even when their overall theory militates against it. Consider, for example, the recent reconceptualization of the substantive criminal law undertaken by Larry Alexander and Kim Ferzan.[35] No commentators are more eager to preserve individual subjective culpability throughout the whole of the penal law. According to Alexander and Ferzan's "unified" conception, "criminal culpability is always a function of what the actor believes regarding the nature and consequences of his conduct and what the actor's reasons are for acting as he does in light of those beliefs."[36] Maybe so. But *what* must the actor believe about the nature of his conduct to be culpable for it? Objective considerations play no apparent role in this unified conception. For example, Alexander and Ferzan are prepared to hold a defendant culpable and subject to criminal liability if she believes, however unreasonably, that she is imposing an unjustified risk on another by casting an evil spell upon him. Wrongdoing itself is too "objective" for these theorists; a homeowner who believes it is impermissible to water his lawn is culpable for activating his sprinkling system even if he is mistaken about the existence of the proscription. If these authors are willing to take subjectivism so far, one might have expected them to be prepared to spare a defendant from blame if he believes, reasonably or not, that his conduct is neither wrongful nor criminal. But even Alexander and Ferzan balk at this implication of their unified theory of culpability when they turn to the topic of ignorance of law. In this context, they explain their retreat from subjectivism by asserting that "at least with respect to crimes that are *mala in se,* ignorance that the conduct they proscribe is legally prohibited does not undermine culpability."[37] Alexander and Ferzan maintain that "self-centeredness, avarice, and other vices that are revealed in unjustified risk impositions explain culpability rather than negate it."[38] But why accept *this* theory of culpability—a theory I will describe as a quality of will theory in

[35] Larry Alexander and Kimberly Kessler Ferzan with Stephen Morse: *Crime and Culpability* (Cambridge: Cambridge University Press, 2009).
[36] *Id.,* p.41.
[37] *Id.*
[38] *Id.,* p.153. The authors express misgivings about their own analysis in p.153n76.

Chapter 3(B)? Why the sudden shift from the subjective perspective of the defendant to objective criteria of blameworthiness? Apparently the pull of the principle that ignorance of law is no defense is so powerful that even commentators who embrace a radical subjectivism about culpability and punishment are unwilling to resist it in situations in which persons sincerely believe their conduct is morally and legally permissible.

So much for my quick tour of scholarly commentary. What else about existing law merits brief attention? As I explained in my Introduction, I have almost nothing to say about comparative law—about how ignorance of law is handled outside of Anglo-American jurisdictions. But inasmuch as I have briefly described the more favorable treatment German law affords to defendants who are ignorant of law, I would be remiss not to at least mention Jewish law, which goes further than any system of which I am aware in exculpating wrongdoers who do not know they have committed an offense.[39] Transgressors who violate Jewish law intentionally (with due warning) are subject to the death penalty. Unintentional violators, however, are not. Most important for present purposes, unintentional transgressors include those who are unaware they have breached a prohibition. Are unintentional wrongdoers exculpated altogether? It is hard to be sure. Violators who are ignorant of law are required to bring a sin offering to the Temple. According to one interpretation, the latter requirement is not a mode of punishment at all, but rather a method of expiation demanded in the absence of culpability. On a second interpretation, however, the sacrifice indicates that ignorant wrongdoers *are* culpable, albeit less so than intentional wrongdoers.[40] In the latter event, the alleged difference in the degree of culpability between the knowing and unwitting offender represents a chasm. The death penalty and the need for a Temple sacrifice are as far apart in severity as two punishments can be.

Before we conclude this brief survey of what courts, commentators, and different systems have or have not said about ignorance of law, it is worthwhile to mention two different but equally curious exceptions to the general doctrine that are widely recognized. First, existing law does an about-face and is remarkably generous when mistakes of law

---

[39] See Arnold Enker: "Error Juris in Jewish Criminal Law," 11 *The Journal of Law and Religion* 23 (1994–1995).

[40] See Jed Lewinsohn: "Philosophy in Halakhah: The Case of Intentional Action," 7 *Torah-U-Madda Journal* 97 (2006–2007).

are made by legal officials such as enforcement officers, prosecutors, or judges. Although the context obviously differs from one in which an individual is charged with a crime, the reasonable-mistake exception to the exclusionary rule, the qualified-immunity rule, and the harmless-error rule all protect officials who make reasonable mistakes about the content of law in the administration of criminal justice.[41] Even though these doctrines may be controversial, no one would think to oppose them on such fictitious grounds as "everyone is presumed to know the law." One can only wonder why mistakes of law are so readily forgiven when made by government officials rather than by private individuals.[42]

Second, ignorance of law can excuse defendants who are insane. Versions of the *M'naghten* test remain the most common formulation of the insanity defense used throughout the United States today. This criterion mandates acquittal when a defect of reason from a disease of the mind causes a defendant either not to know the nature and quality of his act or, if he did, not to know his act is wrong. Courts and commentators have long debated whether the last prong of this test refers to *legal* or *moral* wrongs. In either event, this prong of the test raises a puzzle: Why should ignorance of law constitute an excuse when it is caused by a mental disease or defect, but not when it is produced by some other source? Perhaps in 1843, when *M'Naghten* was decided, the content of the criminal law was so clear that only mental illness could plausibly explain how an adult could be unaware of its demands. But why does this part of the M'Naghten rule survive today? I have no speculation to offer. Fortunately, no rationale will be needed. If my subsequent arguments are sound, an exculpatory consideration for ignorant defendants should typically be available to the sane and insane alike. Thus we will have no need to explain why the plea should be reserved only for the latter categories of wrongdoers. The strain in existing law represented by an ignorance-of-law defense in the test of insanity will be resolved by granting some degree of exculpation to nearly all defendants.

In this part I have demonstrated what many theorists of the criminal law have known all along: the doctrine of *ignorantia juris* has the potential to produce injustice in particular cases, and almost certainly is impossible to defend without presupposing a utilitarian framework

---

[41] For a recent example, see *Heien v. North Carolina,* 135 S. Ct. 530 (2014). For critical commentary, see Kit Kinports: "Heien's Mistake of Law," Alabama Law Review (forthcoming, 2016).

[42] See Larkin, Jr.: *Op.cit.* Note 3.

that is not embraced elsewhere and ought to be rejected. The fact that such injustice does not occur more often probably reflects ambivalence about the adage among legal practitioners. But the rule itself survives largely intact, as even commentators who purport to reform the law stop short of embracing the implications of their own arguments. Nonetheless, as I hope to show, we have much to learn from a further examination of existing doctrine.

B. Notice

As I have indicated, a number of courts and commentators reject exculpatory claims of ignorance of law on the ground that everyone is presumed to know the law. No single rationale is cited more frequently as a basis for withholding complete or partial exculpation from a defendant who is unaware his act Φ violates law L. Earlier I asked how this *presumption* should be understood. I now ask how it can possibly be thought that everyone is presumed to have this arcane knowledge. The answer is that a liberal democratic state has a duty to provide *notice* to citizens of their legal obligations. In the absence of notice, the supposition that everyone is presumed to know the law is more than a fiction. It is, in Ashworth's words, preposterous. Thus the content of the requirement to provide notice is widely regarded as central to my topic. But even though virtually all criminal law textbooks devote quite a bit of attention to the cases and commentary that construe the notice requirement in their chapters on *ignorantia juris,* I will conclude there is less of interest here than meets the eye. The judicial opinions and scholarly articles about notice are not especially helpful in answering my basic question (Q). Nonetheless, a brief discussion of notice and its relation to responsibility and ignorance of law is in order.

Many commentators attach broad jurisprudential significance to the requirement of notice. Lon Fuller, for example, famously contends that a sovereign (imaginatively named King Rex) who fails to promulgate his commands not only fails to make good law, but fails to make law at all.[43] Thus Fuller construes the requirement of notice to be a corollary of legality itself, an implication of the principle that we are governed by the rule of law rather than by the rule of men. Whether or not

---

[43] Lon L. Fuller: *The Morality of Law* (New Haven, CT: Yale University Press, 1964).

we accept this jurisprudential thesis, Fuller is correct to suggest that spectacular failures of promulgation can undermine allegations about duties of compliance. "Certainly there can be no rational ground for asserting that a 'man can have a moral obligation to obey a legal rule that ... is kept secret from him ... or was unintelligible."[44] Fuller immediately recognized the difficulty of determining what counts as notice for purposes of satisfying this requirement. At this juncture, his analysis becomes opaque. He ends his discussion by remarking that "the requirement that laws be published does not rest on any such absurdity as an expectation that the dutiful citizen will sit down and read them all."[45] Unfortunately, he offers no detail about the expectation on which this requirement *does* rest. A number of courts and commentators have struggled to provide content to the obscure but crucial demand that the penal law must somehow be made available and intelligible to citizens who are expected to comply with it.[46] As we will see, Anglo-American law has failed abysmally to infuse this demand with substantive meaning. At least in Anglo-American law, in only the most extreme cases—not so unlike those involving Fuller's incompetent King Rex—is notice said to be sufficiently defective to persuade courts to afford exculpatory significance to the plea of ignorance of law.

Unlike Fuller, I make no explicit jurisprudential commitment about the nature of law or legal systems. Instead, I move directly to the position about notice taken by the celebrated *Model Penal Code*. By its own admission in its commentary, the Code's treatment of legal ignorance is conventional in following the common law. Thus the requirement of notice is *not* construed so that defendants must actually *know* (or even be *negligent* about whether) their conduct is criminal. Notice is *constructive* rather than actual. That is, notice is not deemed defective because the defendant herself has not actually noticed it. Consider those defendants who pay no attention to whatever allegedly notifies them their conduct is illegal. Some judicial responses to such persons are glib at best. According to Judge Posner, "when a defendant is morally culpable for failing to know or guess that he is violating *some* law (as would be the case of someone who committed

---

[44] *Id.*, p.39.

[45] *Id.*, p.51.

[46] For a defense of very demanding publicity criteria, see Bruno Celano: "Publicity and the Rule of Law," in Leslie Green and Brian Leiter, eds.: *Oxford Studies in Philosophy of Law* (New York: Oxford University Press, Vol.2, 2013), p.122.

a burglary without thinking—so warped was his moral sense—that burglary might be a crime), we rely on conscience to provide all the notice that is required."[47] It is hard to make sense of Posner's position; he seemingly presupposes this defendant is *already* culpable for what he *fails* to know. But why? It is extraordinary to suppose we can rely on conscience for whatever notice the law must supply—whether or not the moral sense of a defendant is "warped."

In any event, in Section 2.04(3) the Code recognizes an exception to its general rule of *ignorantia juris* by creating a genuine defense when notice is defective. Actually, the relevant provisions of this statute create *two* grounds for a defense of ignorance of law that should be distinguished. According to the first, "a belief that conduct does not legally constitute an offense is a defense to a prosecution for that offense based upon such conduct when (a) the statute defining the offense is not known to the actor and has not been published or otherwise reasonably made available prior to the conduct alleged."[48] No one is likely to contest this provision when the relevant statute "has not been published" at all. As Fuller pointed out, conviction for a "secret law" is universally regarded as an abomination. But in what other circumstances is a defendant to be acquitted because the relevant statute "has not been . . . reasonably made available prior to the conduct alleged?" This clause could be construed broadly or narrowly, and the fate of many a defendant depends on how courts elect to interpret it.

The official Comments provide little guidance, leaving most of the interpretive work to courts. The draftsmen indicate that "not every official announcement, however obscure, would necessarily constitute publication. That term should be construed in light of the principle that the basic issue is whether the law is reasonably available."[49] If this Comment is to be taken seriously, it would seem that the draftsmen intend to grant a defense of ignorance of law when the failure to know that conduct is illegal derives from a determination that the statute is reasonably unavailable. But when is the lack of availability reasonable? The draftsmen explicitly mention but fail to adopt further language that would have been helpful in clarifying the scope of this exception. They might have added that a law is not reasonably available when

---

[47] *United States v. Wilson,* 159 F.3d 280, 295 (1998) (Posner, J., dissenting).
[48] *Model Penal Code* §2.04(3)(a).
[49] Comments to *Model Penal Code* §2.04(3), p.276.

it can "not be discoverable through the exercise of due diligence," or when the defendant has "exercised all the care that a law-abiding and prudent person would exercise to ascertain the law."[50] Although a decision to embellish Section 2.04(3) with these remarks might have been momentous, the draftsmen ultimately chose not to include them. As a result, courts have almost always construed the foregoing clause narrowly. In only a small handful of situations have defendants prevailed because the statute in question was not reasonably made available to them at the time of their illegal action. It is remarkable what courts have held to constitute fair notice when defendants are ignorant of the law they breach. It seems to suffice that the statute is accessible to the handful of citizens who are skillful in navigating legal search engines such as Westlaw or Lexis/Nexis. Given the incredibly low bar of what passes for fair notice, it is hard to see how this requirement could support a presumption of universal knowledge of law. In any other context, support for an analogous presumption would be ludicrous. Each day, for example, *The New York Times* publishes a table indicating the total amount of precipitation in the current year. No one would infer from the availability of this data that everyone is presumed to know how much rain has fallen.

As I have indicated, Section 2.04(3) creates a second ground for a genuine defense of ignorance of law: "A belief that conduct does not legally constitute an offense is a defense to a prosecution for that offense based upon such conduct when ... (b) [the defendant] acts in reasonable reliance upon an official statement of the law, afterward determined to be invalid or erroneous, contained in (i) a statute or other enactment; (ii) a judicial decision, opinion or judgment; (iii) an administrative order or grant of permission; or (iv) an official interpretation of the public officer or body charged by law with responsibility for the interpretation, administration or enforcement of the law defining the offense."[51] The Comments indicate that this provision "deals with the situation in which the defendant is aware of the possible relevance of criminal legislation, but he is misled by reasonable reliance upon an official statement of the law that is afterward determined to be erroneous."[52]

---

[50] *Id.,* p.277.
[51] *Model Penal Code* §2.04(3)(b).
[52] Comments to *Model Penal Code* §2.04(3), pp.277–278.

Although its exact scope may be unclear, *some* version of this second basis for recognizing a defense of ignorance of law almost certainly is required by the due process clause of the Constitution.[53] Presumably, its rationale is roughly analogous to estoppel: a legal system that induces reliance should not be allowed to arrest and prosecute persons who act on the very reliance induced. Indeed, this defense is sometimes called "estoppel by entrapment," even though commentators have pointed out that it technically involves neither estoppel nor entrapment.[54] Some evidence of the confusion about the underlying rationale of this defense is provided by the fact that jurisdictions throughout the United States vary enormously in whether or in what form they have adopted it. Only nine states contain equivalent statutes, whereas a number do not include a provision even roughly comparable.[55] Notwithstanding these variations, the Code is clearly correct that the defense is required to afford justice to particular offenders: "There can be no point in punishing someone who neither knows his behavior is criminal nor has that information reasonably available to him."[56]

Suppose, then, that the above provision from the *Model Penal Code* became the law of the land. Recall *Striggles*, the case involving the businessman who was sentenced for installing a gambling device in his restaurant, despite having been given ample assurance the machine was legal. Presumably, he would have been exculpated had Section 2.04(3)(b) been applied to his case. Reliance on a judicial decision is expressly allowed by the statute, with no indication that that decision must be rendered by the highest court of a state. Thus Section 2.04(3) (b) amounts to important progress toward what I hope is agreed to be a just outcome. Nonetheless, its scope remains narrow. Generations of law students have struggled to answer exam questions in which they must decide whether a given "statement of law" on which a particular defendant "reasonably relies" has been issued by "the public officer or body charged by law with responsibility for the interpretation, administration or enforcement of the law defining the offense." Of course, not just *anyone* can provide a "statement of law" on which a defendant

---

[53] See *Raley v. Ohio,* 360 U.S. 423 (1959); *Cox v. Louisiana,* 379 U.S. 559 (1965); and *United States v. Pennsylvania Industrial Chemical Corp.,* 411 U.S. 655 (1973).

[54] See Gabriel J. Chin, Reid Griffith Fontaine, Nicholas Klingerman, and Melody Gilkey: "The Mistake of Law Defense and an Unconstitutional Provision of the Model Penal Code," 93 *North Carolina Law Review* 139 (2014).

[55] *Id.*

[56] Jeremy Horder: *Excusing Crime* (Oxford: Oxford University Press, 2004), p.276.

is entitled to rely. But the professionals who diligent laypersons are most likely to consult when uncertain of their legal obligations—licensed attorneys—are clearly outside the ambit of this provision. In nearly all jurisdictions, a defendant who follows the advice of his attorney but is nonetheless mistaken about his interpretation of the statute in question is not entitled to a defense of ignorance of law.[57] Of course, this provision need not have been construed so narrowly.[58] Still, the draftsmen go on to indicate that their refusal to allow a defendant to be exculpated when she relies on bad advice from her attorney is based on "serious problems of collusion and fabrication."[59]

Although some commentators concur that these problems are sufficiently grave to warrant a denial of the defense,[60] legions of scholars have argued that this second ground should be enlarged. Few parts of the Code have been subjected to more criticism than Section 2.04(3) (b). As Jeremy Horder has contended, fine lines between persons who are or are not authorized to provide official advice should not be decisive when a mistaken defendant seeks exculpation. Instead, the availability of the defense should depend on whether the particular defendant exhibits sufficient respect for law.[61] Following the pioneering work of Ashworth,[62] Horder holds that defendants show such respect when they behave like good citizens and make the very sort of inquiries the law should encourage. What more should we demand of persons who are threatened with the stigmatizing deprivation of the penal sanction?

Thus far I have critically discussed the requirement that potential defendants receive fair notice of the penal statute they violate. Perhaps surprisingly, the great bulk of actual cases dealing with possible defects of notice do not quite conform to this description. That is, few of these cases involve situations in which defendants allege that they

---

[57] New Jersey goes further than other states in allowing a defense when "[t]he actor otherwise diligently pursues all means available to ascertain the meaning and application of the offense to his conduct and honestly and in good faith concludes his conduct is not an offense in circumstances in which a law-abiding and prudent person would also so conclude." *N.J. Stat. Ann.* §2C:2-4(c)(3) (West 2005).

[58] The draftsmen explicitly state that they "did not address [this provision's] possible application to situations where subordinate government officers or private individuals employed by government officers exceed legal authority but claim they relied on a superior officer's statement of their duties." Comments to *Model Penal Code* §2.04(3), p.278.

[59] *Id.,* p.280.

[60] Miriam Gur-Arye: "Reliance on a Lawyer's Mistaken Advice—Should It Be an Excuse from Criminal Liability?" 29 *American Journal of Criminal Law* 455 (2002).

[61] Horder: *Op.cit.* Note 56, p.273.

[62] Andrew Ashworth: "Excusable Mistake of Law," *Criminal Law Review* 652 (1974).

lacked a reasonable opportunity to learn of the existence of the statute breached. Instead, they mostly involve situations in which the conduct proscribed is difficult to fathom, even when a defendant may be able to recite the terms of the statute verbatim. Defendants claim they could not have been expected to conform to the law because they could not make sense of its demands. Penal law scholars are fond of these cases because they are among the few in the domain of substantive criminal law that implicate the Constitution. The due process clause has been construed to require statutes to be written in a way that is intelligible to the persons expected to comply with them. Laws that do not satisfy this test can be held "void for vagueness." In famous language, the Court has said that "a statute which either forbids or requires the doing of an act in terms so vague that men of common intelligence must necessarily guess at its meaning and differ as to its application violates the first essential of due process of law."[63]

The vagueness doctrine has been especially important in the history of efforts to proscribe vagrancy and obscenity. A vague statute in the latter domain gave rise to one of the most well-known statements ever made by a Supreme Court justice. In the course of expressing despair about his inability to offer a verbal definition of pornography, Justice Stewart infamously said: "I know it when I see it."[64] Although I believe Stewart has been unfairly ridiculed for this remark, the problem with his statement is evident. Persons who are uncertain about how legislation is to be applied to their situation receive no guidance when they are assured that a particular justice will know how to categorize a given material when he subsequently examines it. Scholarly anxieties about definitions of pornography appear to have waned, but parallel worries about how to characterize the prohibited conduct in vagrancy statutes remain very much alive. Laws that punish persons who "remain in any one place with no apparent purpose," for example, require potential defendants who are standing on a street corner to guess whether they have or lack an "apparent purpose."[65] Defendants cannot but be ignorant of their legal duties when statutes are drafted so poorly.

Again, the foregoing defendants need not be unaware of the *existence* of the statute. As Samuel Buell and Lisa Griffin have recognized, if notice

---

[63] *Connally v. General Construction Co.*, 269 U.S. 385, 391 (1926).
[64] *Jacobellis v. Ohio*, 378 U.S. 184, 197 (1964).
[65] *City of Chicago v. Morales*, 527 U.S. 41 (1999).

is to serve as a condition for deserved punishment, offenders must be entitled not only to *category notice* but also to *within-category* notice. Even statutes that are not vague under constitutional standards can fail to provide the sort of notice Buell and Griffin have in mind. Although vagrancy statutes provide a good illustration, other vehicles for thinking about the problem of within-category notice include fraud, extortion, rape, and bribery. These behaviors frequently involve pressing issues of social, political, and economic policy. Moreover, these offenses inevitably present challenges of what Buell and Griffin call *embeddedness*. They take place in the midst of activities that are not only unobjectionable but socially welcome: sales, negotiations, sex, and politics. At the boundaries of these offenses, the argument continues, category notice (for example, "fraud is a crime") does not suffice. Arguably, a person should not be punished for the crime of fraud, extortion, rape, or bribery unless she knows what she did is an *instance* of fraud, extortion, rape, or bribery.[66] Suppose it is true that all citizens have adequate notice, for example, that a federal statute prohibits the destruction of "any record, document or tangible object" in order to obstruct law enforcement. Even so, how is anyone to divine whether this statute proscribes the act of tossing underweight fish back into the sea to stymie an investigation by the Fish and Wildlife Conservation Commission?[67]

Despite the enormous amount of commentary it has spawned, I do not believe the body of law involving notice is very helpful in answering my basic question (Q). I offer six related but distinct observations about notice to explain my subsequent neglect. First, judicial opinions about vagueness are often infused with normative concerns other than those involving ignorance. In particular, vague statutes allow or even encourage arbitrary and discriminatory enforcement and thus jeopardize the rule of law. For good reason, courts are perhaps even more worried about guiding officials than about providing fair notice to defendants.

Second, not all vagueness is pernicious; *some* is inevitable, and perhaps even beneficial.[68] Thus judges must be selective in voiding legislation on this ground. Understandably, judges are and ought to be more

---

[66] Samuel Buell and Lisa Kern Griffin: "On the Mental State of Consciousness of Wrongdoing," 75 *Law and Contemporary Problems* 213 (2012).

[67] See *Yates v. United States*, 574 U. S. ___ (2015).

[68] See Timothy Endicott: "The Value of Vagueness," in Andrei Marmor and Scott Soames, eds.: *Philosophical Foundations of Language in the Law* (Oxford: Oxford University Press, 2011), p.14.

prepared to find a statute void for vagueness when they disapprove of it on some unrelated ground.[69] Many of the precedents involve sympathetic defendants who breach statutes of dubious merit. In such cases, courts strain to find a rationale to acquit, and no one can be too sure that the absence of notice is the factor that explains their decision.

Third, courts have ample resources to mitigate problems that might otherwise result from inadequate notice. A recent trend is to preserve the constitutionality of vague legislation by confining its application to kinds of behavior that are especially egregious and no one would think are allowed. In *Skilling v. United States*,[70] for example, the Court responded to a vagueness challenge to the federal "honest service fraud" statute, which proscribes "a scheme or artifice to deprive another of the intangible right of honest services." This statute appears to be vague. On its face, it might be construed to punish such relatively innocuous conduct as the making of a personal call by a salaried employee during working hours. The Court, however, managed to save the statute by construing it to prohibit only bribes and kickbacks—even though nothing in the statute itself singled out these particular behaviors. If subsequent courts follow the strategy in *Skilling* and preserve the constitutionality of open-ended legislation by interpreting it to proscribe only conduct that is egregious, void-for-vagueness challenges will be even less successful than in the past.

Fourth, little of further interest is likely to be unearthed if the point of examining the existing law of notice is to discover whether and under what circumstances a plea of ignorance of law *should* exculpate. To my mind, problems of vagueness mostly involve the craft of legislative draftsmanship. In only a handful of cases is there evidence that the particular defendant *had* examined the statutory text in question and yet remained baffled about its demands. Important though it may be, my basic question (Q) does not ask whether a defendant would have been able to ascertain what a statute proscribed if only he had bothered to study it. Instead, the question is how to assess the culpability of a defendant who is aware of his legal duties, relative to a defendant who, for whatever reason, is not. Sloppy legislation simply adds an additional layer of complexity on top of this basic question.

---

[69] "Often, vagueness decisions, no matter what the theory, are not only about vagueness." Peter W. Low and Joel S. Johnson: "Changing the Vocabulary of the Vagueness Doctrine," (forthcoming).

[70] 561 U.S. 40, 130 S. Ct. 2896 (2010).

Fifth, some important issues regarding this topic do not literally involve ignorance of either category notice or within-category notice. Instead, they involve a closely related problem of uncertainty about the *enforcement* of a law the content of which is crystal clear. One can imagine the howls of protest that would greet decisions to strictly enforce speed limits as written. The driver who is ticketed for going 36 mph in a 35 mph zone would have a complaint that is barely distinguishable from ignorance of law. As is often the case, drug offenses provide an equally good illustration of the difficulty I have in mind. At the time of this writing, four states—Washington, Colorado, Oregon, and Alaska—are in the process of implementing a regime of marijuana decriminalization. Others are all but certain to follow soon. But marijuana continues to be proscribed for any and all purposes as a Schedule I substance under federal law. Because of the ongoing federal prohibition, many respectable financial institutions in these states are understandably reluctant to do business with the growing marijuana industry. Some transactions are explicitly illegal and trigger derivative liability for the very federal offenses perpetrated by the marijuana dispensaries themselves. Facilities licensed under state law frequently are forced to conduct business in cash, subjecting themselves to enormous risks of robbery. To help rectify this situation, the Obama administration has issued guidelines designed to assure banks they would not be prosecuted if they provide financial services to legitimate marijuana businesses. Not surprisingly, some banks remained unmoved. Assurance that prosecution would be inappropriate is not an obvious defense in the event that charges are filed. Reluctant banking officials are not ignorant of law in a literal sense; they remain painfully aware of the federal statutes they would be violating by making loans available. The only foolproof solution is to change federal law so that banks are permitted to do business with the marijuana industry.[71]

Finally, the requirement of notice of the law turns out to be somewhat beside the point on the theory of ignorance I will ultimately defend. What the responsible defendant really must know, I believe, is that his behavior is *wrongful*, not that it is *illegal*. If notice is somehow defective, but the conduct of the defendant is morally wrongful and he knows as much, why does he deserve any degree of exculpation? Conversely, if notice is adequate but the conduct of the defendant is morally

---

[71] See William Baude: "State Regulation and the Necessary and Proper Clause," 65 *Case Western Reserve Law Review* 513 (2015). See also Alex Kreit: "What Will Federal Marijuana Reform Look Like?" 65 Case Western University Law Review 689 (2015).

permissible and he knows as much, why does he deserve any amount of punishment? If the mere existence of a law cannot create a moral obligation, knowledge of the law does not do so either, and a failure to inform citizens of their legal obligations is not what ultimately matters to responsibility. I return to this topic in Chapter 5(A).

My final reason for claiming that notice of the law is largely immaterial in answering my basic question (Q) is easily misconstrued. I do not allege that notice is irrelevant for all normative purposes— that is, those that do not bear on the blameworthiness and desert of the defendant. The imposition of sanctions on those who have not had ample opportunity to avoid them produces a kind of *unfairness* that is important despite its lack of impact on responsibility. Consider, for example, two gunmen with no legitimate authority. The first bursts into a classroom and immediately kills an innocent student. The second differs in that he threatens to kill unless the student leaves the room immediately. The student disobeys and is shot. The first gunman perpetrates an injustice greater than the second. If I am correct, notice has an independent normative significance, whether or not the content of the norm is illegitimate. Even if I am correct that a penal law per se creates no moral reason to comply, those who are aware of it can at least avoid the evils of punishment by electing to obey it. I suspect that theorists who believe I pay too short shrift to the importance of notice are likely to misconstrue its normative significance. The absence of notice may create unfairness, but need not affect anyone's blame-worthiness and desert.

For these six reasons, I conclude that the enormous body of law and scholarly commentary involving notice is only marginally significant in a project that seeks to answer my basic question (Q). No one can object to a requirement that statutes avoid vagueness and be made available to citizens. But commentators who are obsessed with the details of notice run the risk of missing many of the deeper and more subtle normative issues surrounding *ignorantia juris*.

C. Fact and Law

To thoroughly understand existing doctrine—that is, to understand and assess how our legal system presently treats defendants who are ignorant of *law*—we must understand how our legal system presently treats defendants who are ignorant of *fact*. The juxtaposition of these two bodies of law presents a stark contrast. The hostility shown by our penal justice system to the plea of ignorance of law is almost entirely reversed when defendants plead ignorance of fact. To a great extent, the latter have exculpatory significance, whereas the former do not. Despite its familiar counterpart, the adage "ignorance of fact is no excuse" would never be voiced by laypersons or legal practitioners. In short, the disparate treatment existing Anglo-American criminal law affords to these two kinds of mistake is nothing less than extraordinary. Eventually we will have to inquire why this is so and whether it is defensible. I will argue that this disparity is almost entirely *in*defensible and that the state should respond to defendants who make mistakes of law in much the same way as it responds to those who make mistakes of fact. If the *presumptive symmetry* between fact and law for which I argue is preferable to the current rule of *ignorantia juris,* it would not be surprising if much of the scholarly commentary on the significance of the distinction between fact and law turns out to be confused. I hope to reveal some of these confusions in this part. First, however, I briefly recount existing legal doctrine on mistake of fact—the framework we should aspire to replicate for mistake of law. I do so by describing how such mistakes are conceptualized in the *Model Penal Code.* As I have emphasized, this Code is the most sophisticated such document ever drafted in the United States or indeed in any Anglo-American jurisdiction, and its novel treatment of mistake of fact is probably its crowning contribution to criminal theory. Although the outlines of this framework are certain to be familiar to nearly all readers—they are a staple of first-year classes in criminal law—I cannot afford to be too brief.

To begin, the Code implements what might be described as *elements* analysis.[72] That is, penal statutes are subdivided into component parts called elements. Murder, for example, involves the killing of another human being. Each of these elements is typically qualified by a culpable state, although the culpable state that attaches to one need not be identical to that which attaches to another. The culpable states that can attach to these elements are exactly four in number, each of which is carefully defined by the Code. Although the definitions of these four states slightly differ depending on whether they modify a conduct, circumstance, or result element of a statute, the following generalizations are roughly accurate: a defendant acts *purposely* when

---

[72] See Paul H. Robinson and Jane A. Grall: "Element Analysis in Defining Criminal Liability: The *Model Penal Code* and Beyond," 35 *Stanford Law Review* 681 (1983).

her conscious object is to engage in the conduct she performs, she acts *knowingly* when she is aware of the nature of her conduct, she acts *recklessly* when she consciously disregards a substantial and unjustifiable risk created by her conduct, and she acts *negligently* when she disregards a substantial and unjustifiable risk created by her conduct of which a reasonable person in her situation would have been aware.[73] Wrongful conduct performed with any of these culpable states is regarded as less serious than wrongful conduct involving any of its predecessors. That is, each state renders a defendant less blameworthy than she would have been if she had committed the same act with a higher degree of culpability. *Ceteris paribus*, a defendant is more culpable when she commits an act purposely rather than knowingly, is more culpable when she commits an act knowingly rather than recklessly, and is more culpable when she commits an act recklessly rather than negligently.[74]

The doctrines governing mistake of fact are a corollary of the above definitions of culpable states. Ignorance of fact precludes liability when it "negatives" the level of culpability attached to an element of the offense. This result follows from Section 2.04(1)(b) of the *Model Penal Code* and the analogous provisions in many state and federal codes. In terminology I will claim to be misleading, this statute provides: "(1) Ignorance or mistake as to a matter of fact or law is a defense if . . . (b) the law provides that the state of mind established by such ignorance or mistake constitutes a defense." As many commentators have pointed out, this provision is redundant and expresses a tautology; nothing of substance would change even if it were deleted. "The law" to which Section 2.04(1)(b) refers is the particular offense the defendant is accused of having breached. In essence, then, the statute says that something is a defense when the law specifies that it is a defense. Presumably, the draftsmen included an unnecessary provision in the Code to avoid the possible misunderstanding that could have occurred in its absence. In any event, as we will see, quite a bit of theoretical confusion results even when this exculpatory provision *is* included in a code.

Consider the example of theft to illustrate how a mistake of fact becomes exculpatory even though it is not a true defense. Suppose a statute attaches the mens rea of knowledge to each element of

---

[73] *Model Penal Code* §2.02(2).
[74] See Douglas Husak: "The Sequential Principle of Relative Culpability" in Douglas Husak, ed.: *The Philosophy of Criminal Law* (Oxford: Oxford University Press, 2010), p.177.

this offense. As a result, a defendant does not commit the crime of theft unless she knows the property she takes is not her own. If she is mistaken about this matter—if she knows she is taking something but falsely supposes that what she is taking is unowned or belongs to her—she simply does not commit the crime of theft. It is technically inaccurate, however, to say our confused defendant has an *excuse* for theft. Indeed, she does not even have a *defense* for theft. Although she is exculpated, she actually *needs* no defense, excuse or otherwise. Instead, she lacks liability because she fails to satisfy one of the elements of the statute. She does not fail to satisfy any of the actus reus elements of theft, but rather one of its mens rea elements. Thus I call this basis for exculpation a *denial of mens rea* (or a *denial of the mens rea of criminality*). A denial of mens rea is not only the *typical* mechanism by which the code secures the acquittal of defendants who make such mistakes of fact—it is the *only* mechanism.

This type of exculpatory claim—a denial of mens rea—should strike moral philosophers as perplexing. This perplexity becomes evident when we invoke either of the two presumptions I employ throughout this book: first, the criminal law should conform to morality; and, second, the law should treat mistakes of fact and law symmetrically. Although I hope these presumptions are plausible, each is jeopardized by the very existence of the category of exculpatory consideration I call a denial of mens rea. Other kinds of exculpatory claims have clear analogs in morality or, indeed, in any rule-governed enterprise. But exculpatory pleas that deny mens rea have no obvious moral counterparts. In moral philosophy, few wrongs contain mens rea. No one would think to formulate the moral wrong of rape, for example, to include a mens rea component in addition to its actus reus. This wrong is perpetrated not only by persons who are culpable about whether their victim has failed to consent. Instead, this wrong is perpetrated by anyone who engages in non-consensual sex—period. In moral philosophy, the absence of (the counterpart of) mens rea is nearly always an *excuse*, and the presence of culpability serves largely to affect the quantum of blame, if any, that perpetrators deserve. In short, the absence of culpability in a rapist would not lead a moral philosopher to conclude that the person could not possibly be a rapist at all. Criminal wrongs, on the other hand, tend to be formulated very differently; mens rea requirements almost always are included in penal statutes. Depending on the details of the particular statute, a defendant does not commit the crime of rape and become a rapist in law unless he acts with some degree of mens rea—typically recklessness.[75] Expressed somewhat differently, criminal offenses are rarely strict. Some degree of mens rea is required of all material elements—at least for long-standing crimes within the core of the penal law. Moral wrongs, by contrast, are usually strict; mens rea is not a part of the moral wrong to which criminal wrongs otherwise correspond. *If* I am correct, the very *content* of moral wrongs is unlike that of criminal wrongs.[76] *Why* criminal and moral wrongs should have a different content represents something of a mystery to which I will return in Chapter 5(A). But *that* they have this different content is harder to contest.

To be sure, my claims about the dissimilar content of criminal and moral wrongs can be challenged on several grounds. I mention three. First and most obviously, my generalization about the content of moral and criminal wrongs is riddled with exceptions on both sides: some moral wrongs contain a mens rea component, whereas some criminal wrongs do not. Next, I admit that my generalization is hard to defend against skeptics who contest it. Since the time when common law crimes were abolished, canonical formulations of penal wrongs are easily found. One need only consult the applicable statute. By contrast, canonical formulations of moral wrongs are controversial; disputes about their content are hard to resolve. Finally and most important, the fact that penal *statutes* contain a culpability requirement may not settle the question of whether the content of penal *wrongs* does so as well. Perhaps the wrong in a penal statute is only a subset of its material elements.

If we really propose to model the criminal law on morality, the realization that moral and criminal wrongs have a different content is deeply problematic. To preserve their presumptive symmetry, the absence of mens rea should be an excuse for the commission of a penal wrong, not a denial of a mens rea element of an offense. I am unaware, however, of a single contemporary philosopher of criminal law who explicitly endorses this idea;[77] the conceptualization of penal offenses to include culpability has a long and impressive history, and is widely recognized as one of the crowning achievements of the *Model*

---

[75] Thus the otherwise baffling title of Douglas Husak and George C. Thomas III: "Rapes without Rapists: Consent and Reasonable Mistake," 11 *Philosophical Issues* 86 (2001).

[76] For the most complete and sophisticated discussion of this structural dissimilarity, see R.A. Duff: *Answering for Crime* (Oxford: Hart, 2007), chapters 9 and 10.

[77] In recent history, a proposal to make penal wrongs strict was famously defended by Barbara Wootton: *Crime and the Criminal Law* (London: Stevens & Sons, 1963). Wootton's motivations, however, were completely unlike those discussed here. She aspired mostly to achieve greater flexibility in treating criminals to prevent them from repeating their offenses.

Penal Code. If we retain this feature of our statutes and continue to allow mistakes of fact to have exculpatory significance as a denial of mens rea, the outstanding question is whether we should do so as well when providing for the exculpatory significance of ignorance of law. Chapter 5(A) explores this complex issue in more depth.

However the foregoing puzzle is resolved, the exculpatory mechanism I call a denial of mens rea is *ordinarily* unavailable when defendants make a mistake of law. Although I will return to some important exceptions to this generalization in Part D below, these exceptions do not swallow the rule. A defendant who knows she is killing a human being but mistakenly supposes her deed to be lawful satisfies each of the elements of the offense with the requisite degree of culpability and thus is liable for the crime of murder. In case there is doubt, the Code specifically indicates: "Neither knowledge nor recklessness or negligence as to whether conduct constitutes an offense or as to the existence, meaning or application of the law determining the elements of an offense is an element of such offense, unless the definition of the offense or the Code so provides."[78] What I have called narrow but not broad culpability is an element of penal offenses.

Because existing legal doctrine is so much more lenient when defendants make mistakes of fact than when they make mistakes of law, it is imperative to devise some means to contrast propositions of fact from propositions of law. I have implicitly presupposed some such device can be found. In formulating my basic question (Q), I invoked a distinction between the two kinds of mistake. I stipulated that B, unlike A, is unaware Φ amounts to a violation of L not because she is mistaken about some *factual* property of her act or circumstance, but rather because she is mistaken about the existence or application of L. Indeed, unless at least a rough contrast between the two kinds of mistake can be drawn, it is hard to see how anyone could make sense of a narrow project purporting to ask whether and to what extent mistakes of law should have exculpatory significance. If the distinction could not be drawn, commentators should simply discuss the relevance of mistake simpliciter. Frankly, I believe the latter question—whether and under what conditions mistakes of *any* kind should have exculpatory force—*should* be the focus of an inquiry. This question should be addressed even though I will argue that the contrast between mistake of fact and mistake of law is not really so hard to draw.

---

[78] *Model Penal Code* §2.02(9).

Many and perhaps most commentators contend that the contrast between fact and law *is* very difficult to draw. A few even go so far as to describe it as "arbitrary."[79] Before I hazard a reply to these commentators, it is worthwhile to ponder the implications for my fundamental project if their challenge cannot be met. If the two kinds of mistake are really impossible to distinguish, it would seem that the law either should be *less* willing to exculpate defendants who make mistakes of fact or *more* willing to exculpate defendants who make mistakes of law. Surprisingly, however, some of those very commentators who believe the distinction is arbitrary continue to support the status quo and think the state should be much more lenient toward defendants who make mistakes of fact than toward those who make mistakes of law. I doubt, however, that this combination of positions is coherent. Presumably, an arbitrary contrast can support no normative weight, and a contrast that is *close* to arbitrary can support *little* normative weight. My own preference, as I have said, is for codes to grant some degree of exculpation to nearly all defendants who are mistaken about the law—as is already the case when defendants are mistaken about the facts. But I do not support this presumptive symmetry because of the supposed difficulties of drawing the contrast. I believe the problems of distinguishing mistakes of law from mistakes of fact are grossly exaggerated and rest on confusions that can be rectified fairly easily. Even so, I will conclude that criminal theorists need not struggle too much to draw a sharp line between mistakes of fact and mistakes of law because a defensible normative position on the latter is nearly identical to a defensible normative position on the former. At the present time, however, I simply focus on the supposed problems of drawing the contrast itself.

A number of theorists have made the task of distinguishing propositions of fact from propositions of law to be far more difficult than it is.[80] I doubt their confusion has a single source. On some occasions, they distort the issue by changing the subject. They sometimes speak as though the contrast between mistakes of fact and mistakes of law is a way to categorize *cases*. They ask, for example, whether a given case (such as those I have mentioned) is a "mistake of fact case" or a "mistake of law case." But the distinction, I hope it is clear, is not about

---

[79] Larry Alexander: "Inculpatory and Exculpatory Mistakes and the Fact/Law Distinction: An Essay in Memory of Mike Bayles," 12 *Law and Philosophy* 33 (1993).

[80] For a useful attempt to draw the contrast, see Peter Westen: "Impossible Attempts: A Speculative Thesis," 5 *Ohio State Journal of Criminal Law* 523, 535 (2008).

cases, but rather about *propositions*. On other occasions, their confusion is more subtle. Difficulty frequently ensues from their failure to precisely identify the proposition(s) that is allegedly hard to classify. In almost any real example, persons have beliefs about several distinct propositions that are material to their blameworthiness and liability. As both beliefs and propositions are individuated by their content, we can enumerate the number of material mistakes a defendant has made by counting the number of propositions about which he is mistaken. Following this strategy enables us to attend to the *source* of a defendant's confusion about the law and to realize that many are uncertain about the law *because* they are uncertain about the facts. A defendant who erroneously believes the substance in his hand is sugar rather than cocaine is mistaken that the law prohibits what he possesses. But no one should conclude from this truism that it is impossible to decide whether he has made a mistake of fact or a mistake of law. In all or virtually all cases, accurate categorization can be achieved by carefully individuating the proposition(s) about which the mistake is made.

Let me illustrate my strategy by reference to one of the many examples that supposedly stump commentators. Larry Alexander describes a law that prohibits hunting when a red flag flies over the Fish and Game Department but allows hunting when a green flag flies.[81] If a colorblind hunter mistakes red for green and green for red, Alexander asks whether he has made a mistake of fact or a mistake of law. His question is rhetorical; he thinks the categorization is "arbitrary" so that either answer is as good as the other. The key to resolving his hypothetical, I propose, is to appreciate that the hunter has made *both* kinds of mistake. Any perplexity this answer might be thought to engender is easily explained by contrasting the following distinct propositions.

p1: the flag flying over the Fish and Game Department is green

is a matter of fact; her error about p1 involves nothing remotely legal. On the basis of her factual mistake about p1, however, our hunter subsequently misapplies the law, the contents of which she understands perfectly. She can correctly recite the statute

p2: hunting is illegal when a red flag is flying but legal when a green flag flies over the Fish and Game Department.

[81] Alexander: *Op.cit.* Note 79.

No mistake of either sort is made about p2. She falsely believes, however, that the law allows her to hunt at the time she makes her factual mistake and is arrested.

p3: hunting is allowed today

is a false proposition of law. She is mistaken about p3 because she is mistaken about p1. But we have no difficulty in distinguishing propositions of fact from propositions of law as long as we are careful to unambiguously identify the object of her belief. This example—and a great many others with a similar structure—seems unproblematic to me.

In the event of doubt about how to sort a particular case, I propose the following heuristic. In any given example, simply insert the phrase "As a matter of fact, . . ." or "As a matter of law, . . ." before any proposition to be classified one way or the other. This device, I believe, will help to resolve nearly any allegedly troublesome case by individuating the proposition(s) about which the defendant is or is not mistaken. As a matter of fact, our colorblind hunter mistakenly believes a red flag to be green. As a matter of law, she correctly believes that hunting is allowed when green flags are flying. As a matter of law (again), she mistakenly believes that hunting is allowed on the day in which she misidentifies the color of the flag. Any perplexity we may have about whether the defendant has made a mistake of fact or a mistake of law results from a failure to identify the unique content of the propositions believed.

It would not be surprising, however, to encounter troublesome borderline cases. After all, philosophers are accustomed to vagueness and have long been familiar with the difficulty of deciding what a given proposition is *about*. But even this admission might concede too much. Consider, for example, the notorious case of *Nix v. Hedden,* which purported to decide whether tomatoes are a fruit or a vegetable for purposes of applying the Tariff Act of 1883.[82] The Supreme Court unanimously held that tomatoes are a vegetable, notwithstanding the contrary opinion of botanical experts who testified that tomatoes are better classified as a "fruit of the vine." Suppose Smith believes the proposition:

p4: tomatoes are vegetables.

---

[82] 149 U.S. 304 (1893).

Would he be making a statement of fact or law? In the absence of additional information, Smith might be doing either one, and my test helps to provide a determinative answer. We might invite Smith to insert the words, "As a matter of law, . . ." before his utterance. If he accepted this invitation, it is clear that his proposition would be true. But if he began "as a matter of fact, . . . " I doubt his utterance would be a mistake of either kind. Instead, pursuant to the authority of the botanical experts, his utterance would be *true*. One and the same utterance (such as "It is raining") can express different propositions, some of which are false while others are true. As formulated above, p4 does not express a unique proposition. Once we disambiguate the propositions expressed by the single utterance, I predict all allegedly hard or borderline cases for contrasting fact from law will become easy.

This device can be employed to show that no so-called *mixed* mistakes of law and fact occur. Although it is not exactly clear what is supposed to make a given case mixed, many commentators continue to find such examples challenging.[83] Consider the case reprinted in many criminal law textbooks: *R v. Smith (David Raymond)*,[84] in which the Court of Appeal accepted mistake as a defense to a violation of the Criminal Damage Act. When leaving his rental apartment, the defendant ripped out the wall panels and floorboards he had previously installed. He believed his act only damaged his own property. He misunderstood, however, the content of the relevant property law. Because the panels and boards he had installed were fixtures, they became the property of the landlord. As a result, his act damaged the property of another. Even so, the court held that the defendant lacked the required mens rea as to the actus reus of "destroying or damaging any property belonging to another." Most commentators regard this outcome as correct. In this case, however, I see no difficulty categorizing the defendant's mistake as one of law or fact. Utterances of the form "this object is mine" might express distinct propositions, either of fact or of law. Whether or not Smith made both kinds of mistake, he certainly made a mistake about how to apply the law of property. The real problem in this case is not to classify the proposition, but rather to explain why courts and commentators are willing to make an exception to the doctrine of *ignorantia juris* by granting a defense. But this latter question is

---

[83] See Kenneth W. Simons: "Ignorance and Mistake of Criminal Law, Noncriminal Law, and Fact," 9 *Ohio State Journal of Criminal Law* 487 (2012).

[84] *R v. Smith (David Raymond)* [1974] 1 All E.R. 632.

normative, not conceptual. One suspects that the supposed difficulty of contrasting fact from law in so-called mixed cases is really a subterfuge to gerrymander the distinction to achieve results intuitively recognized as just.

As I have said, most commentators probably regard the decision in *Smith* as correct. But *why* does the defendant qualify for a defense? Textbooks answer that courts are much more inclined to exculpate defendants who make mistakes of law when their mistakes are about *non-criminal* law, such as the law of property. A line of precedents supports this position, and many existing statutes do so as well. Penal codes often ensure that defendants are not liable for property violations when they are mistaken about their rights. State laws against property violations often include clauses such as " . . . knowing that [the defendant] is not licensed." For example, the New Jersey burglary offense requires knowledge that the defendant is unlicensed or unprivileged to remain in the structure,[85] the Pennsylvania criminal trespass statute similarly requires knowledge that entry is unlicensed or unprivileged,[86] and the New Jersey law proscribing invasions of privacy requires knowledge that an observation is unlicensed or unprivileged.[87] I will say a good deal more about statutes that contain this sort of clause in Part D. At present, I simply ask: Why is this statutory language used? The underlying rationale for including such provisions in these statutes is hard to reconcile with the general unwillingness to allow any degree of exculpation when defendants make mistakes about the criminal law itself. To my mind, this exception (or qualification) to the rule of *ignorantia juris* only serves as further evidence of the injustice of the generalization—that is, the generalization to which this line of precedents stands as an exception. The strain in existing law is evident. Instead of carving out an exception with a dubious rationale when defendants make a given *kind* of mistake described as mixed, it would be preferable to rethink the general rule itself.

Eventually we will have to explicitly confront the normative question: Regardless of whether or not I am correct to say the contrast is drawn easily, *should* the two kinds of mistake be treated dissimilarly? Despite some misgivings, my answer is no. I contend that mistakes

---

[85] *N.J. Stat. Ann.* §2C:18-2(a)(2).
[86] 18 *P.A. Cons. Stat.* §3503(a).
[87] *N.J. Stat. Ann.* §2C:14-9(a).

of law should not be treated differently from mistakes of fact *even if* the contrast can be drawn satisfactorily—as I have argued to be the case. Consider perhaps the most famous hypothetical example used to illustrate the oddity of supposing that ignorance of fact exculpates whereas ignorance of law does not. In Sandy Kadish's celebrated case, Mr. Fact and Mr. Law both violate the law by hunting out of season. They are hunting on June 16, but the season has ended the previous day. For different reasons, however, neither hunter is aware he is violating the law. Mr. Fact has somehow lost track of the calendar, and mistakenly believes the date to be June 15. Mr. Law, however, knows today's date to be June 16, but mistakenly believes the hunting season extends an extra day. Because mistakes of fact exculpate, Mr. Fact will not be subject to liability for hunting out of season. Because mistakes of law do not exculpate, Mr. Law will be subject to liability for the same act.

Kadish's hypothetical case can be used for at least three purposes. First, on the level of intuition, nearly all commentators concur that it would be unjust to exculpate Mr. Fact but not Mr. Law for the same offense. When first-year law students initially encounter this hypothetical, they almost all agree that existing law is absurd as applied here. A defense of current law must either demonstrate why Mr. Fact but not Mr. Law deserves exculpation after all, or show why this particular example should not be used to challenge the entire basis for drawing a distinction between the exculpatory significance of mistakes of fact and mistakes of law in the first place.[88] Second, this hypothetical case casts doubt on some of the rationales used to support the rule of *ignorantia juris.* Consider, once again, the allegation that everyone is presumed to know the law. No commentator, of course, contends that everyone is presumed to know the facts. As an empirical generalization, however, a given hunter is probably more likely to be mistaken about the duration of the hunting season than about the date. Moreover, the latter mistakes are easier to rectify than mistakes about the period of time in which hunting is allowed. If so, why should the foregoing presumption apply only to law and not to fact? Third, it is noteworthy that this hypothetical case does nothing to support the alleged difficulty of drawing the contrast between fact and law. *That* contrast seems crystal clear in this case, however elusive it may seem

---

[88] See Simons: *Op. Cit.* Note 83.

to be elsewhere. This example suggests that any problem in justifying the current doctrine of *ignorantia juris* is unlikely to derive from the supposed difficulty of contrasting fact from law.

Nonetheless, I readily concede that the border between mistake of fact and mistake of law *can be* tricky, as it seemingly shifts depending upon exactly what we suppose defendants must *know* or *suspect* (or be ignorant of) in order to be blameworthy. Recall the example of Jacob, the camper who is uncertain about whether his batteries should be recycled. Although I do not understand why it should be relevant to his blameworthiness that his mistake is about whether his batteries are alkaline or about whether alkaline batteries are the type of objects that must be recycled because they harm the environment, let me now stipulate that Jacob makes only the latter mistake. If so, he clearly seems to be uncertain about the law. He knows he is not recycling, knows the objects he is not recycling are alkaline batteries, but is uncertain about whether the environmental laws prohibit him from throwing them away. Suppose, however, that a defendant becomes eligible for exculpation not because he is ignorant of law, but rather because he is ignorant of the morality that underlies it. On this supposition, the nature of Jacob's mistake begins to look different. I originally stipulated that Jacob knows it is wrong to harm the environment; he is uncertain about whether the batteries he throws into the garbage will do so. *This* mistake appears to be factual, involving the effects of discarded objects on the environment. Even though Jacob has made a mistake of law, what seems to matter to his blameworthiness is his mistake of fact. Expressed in terminology I will employ later, he is mistaken about the specification of a *malum in se*.

Realizing that exculpation is owed to persons who make mistakes about the morality that underlies law rather than about the law per se adds new potential complexities to the familiar uncertainties about contrasting mistake of law from mistake of fact. Nomy Arpaly discusses a Nazi who explains his role in the extermination of Jews by insisting they have a secret plot to take over the world.[89] Is this Nazi simply mistaken about the facts? Perhaps. More plausibly, however, this Nazi is guilty of what Arpaly calls *motivated irrationality*. Those who care about treating people decently are loath to believe a fantastic, incriminating story about a third party, even if that third party is someone of whom they would like to think badly. In cases such as the above, it is doubtful

---

[89] Nomy Arpaly: *Unprincipled Virtue: An Inquiry into Moral Agency* (Oxford: Oxford University Press, 2003), esp. p.102.

that a sound refutation of the tale of the supposed Jewish conspiracy would have made much of a difference to the Nazi's genocidal behavior. In all probability, he believes a silly proposition of fact because he has a warped conception of morality. His *material* mistake, in other words, involves the content of morality.

In any event, it is a great advantage of my theory that a sharp contrast between fact and law, or between facts and the morality that underlies the law, need not be drawn. Why has my straightforward proposal to treat mistake of fact and mistake of law symmetrically been resisted? I am unsure. *One* of many possible answers focuses on the controversial meta-ethical commitments on which this symmetry depends. Propositions of fact are capable of being true or false, and propositions of law are almost certain to be capable of being true or false as well.[90] But it is at least respectable to hold that moral judgments are incapable of being true or false, so it is less clear what it would mean to be *mistaken* about them. If mistakes are false beliefs, and moral judgments are neither true nor false, mistakes (in this sense) become impossible.[91] In what follows, I will presuppose a cognitivist account according to which moral claims have truth values, like propositions of fact or propositions of law. Thus no special account is needed to explain how it is possible to be mistaken about them. Yet again, however, these meta-ethical inquiries are beyond the scope of my project.

A far more common (if less philosophically sophisticated) reason to reject the symmetry I favor has already been discussed at length. Existing policy about *ignorantia juris* is a testament to the influence of consequentialist thought on criminal law doctrine; the specter of exculpating perpetrators of serious crimes who are ignorant their conduct is wrongful is supposedly too horrific to contemplate. But we should not reject my theory because it threatens to "let our worst politicians off the hook far too easily."[92] As I have indicated,

---

[90]   For some subtleties, see Kevin Toh: "Legal Judgments as Plural Acceptances of Norms," in Leslie Green and Brian Leiter, eds.: *Oxford Studies in the Philosophy of Law* (Oxford: Oxford University Press, Vol. 1, 2011), p.107.

[91]   Even if this cognitivist presupposition turns out to be indefensible, and no belief about a moral claim can be true or false, noncognitivist accounts of morality may contain the resources to explain how mistakes about moral judgments are possible. See, for example, Simon Blackburn: "AntiRealist Expressivism and Quasi-Realism," in David Copp, ed.: *The Oxford Handbook of Ethical Theory* (Oxford: Oxford University Press, 2006), p.146.

[92]   See William J. Fitzpatrick: "Moral Responsibility and Normative Ignorance: Answering a New Skeptical Challenge," 118 *Ethics* 589, 610 (2008).

we lack reliable intuitions about such matters. In addition, as I will recount in more detail in Chapter 4(A) and 4(C), we need not be too worried that my theory will free monstrous villains to prey upon us.

A final clarification of my view is needed. As I have said, no *deep* disparity exists between the exculpatory significance of mistake of fact and mistake of law. But a surface disparity *might* exist nonetheless. That is, as a matter of contingent empirical fact, persons might make mistakes of fact more often than they make mistakes of morality. For example, we are more likely to lack responsibility for killing a human being because we are unaware that the substance we administered is a poison than because we are unaware that poisoning a human being is wrongful. Perhaps we should not generalize from such examples to support any sort of disparity between mistakes of fact and law. We all recognize that moral uncertainty is pervasive, both in our profession and in society at large; only the most arrogant and self-deceived philosopher would profess to have an extremely high level of confidence in the matters about which we disagree. Even my dismissal of a consequentialist theory of morality is bitterly contested. Apart from the clearest cases, we are not entitled to be smug that our moral intuitions are correct. If uncertainty about morality is ubiquitous, persons may make mistakes about morality just as frequently as they make mistakes of fact. But why should we care for normative purposes? Fortunately, I need take no firm position on the contingent empirical question of whether mistakes of fact are more common than mistakes of morality.

I conclude that it is not especially difficult to contrast mistakes of fact from mistakes of law—or of the morality that underlies it. If I am correct, it becomes easier to infer that the two kinds of mistake should differ in their exculpatory significance. This inference, however, would be mistaken. To my mind, the amount of scholarly angst about the supposed difficulty of contrasting matters of fact from matters of law is something of a distraction. Like an obsession with notice, these supposed difficulties threaten to blind us from confronting the deeper normative problem of whether the law *should* be sensitive to the kind of mistake a defendant makes. As we will see, the underlying theory of responsibility I invoke in Chapter 3(B) supports a presumptive symmetry between the exculpatory significance of both kinds of mistake.

D. The Structure of Exculpatory Claims: Ignorance of Law as a Denial of Mens Rea

Only a handful of defendants who are ignorant of law succeed in exculpating themselves on either of the grounds discussed in Part B. Few are able to show that notice was somehow deficient, or that they relied to their detriment on authoritative advice. Although discussions of these two bases of exculpation are typically included in every textbook, they have only a marginal impact on the real world of criminal justice. The most significant qualification of the rule that ignorance of law is no defense has yet to be examined. In a surprisingly wide range of cases, a person who is unaware her conduct violates the law is exculpated not because she possesses a true defense, but rather because she commits no crime in the first place. In the examples to which I will refer, defendants who make mistakes of law are exculpated by denying mens rea—the mechanism I described in Part C through which all defendants are exculpated when they plead ignorance of fact.

When ignorance of law precludes a person from committing the crime charged, it is inaccurate to describe her plea as an *exception* to the general rule of *ignorantia juris*. Instead, it should probably be called a *qualification*. It surely represents an important escape from liability that is inconsistent with what both laypersons and specialists regard as the spirit of that harsh rule. It is also surprisingly prevalent, so no examination of existing law can afford to neglect it. For these reasons alone, this qualification merits close scrutiny. But my purposes extend further, as careful thought about this intricate body of law yields a number of important insights. Thus this investigation, initially presented as a mere part of a survey of positive law, is crucial for my normative purposes, allowing us to better appreciate what is at stake in proposals to treat ignorance of fact and law symmetrically. In addition, this body of law will enable us to understand that it is not exactly ignorance of *law* that exculpates. Courts frequently spare defendants from *legal* liability when their conduct is *morally* innocent. These conclusions play a major role in my subsequent theory of how ignorance of law bears on responsibility.

Once we decide *that* ignorance of law should exculpate, we will have to determine *how* it should do so—that is, what *kind* of exculpatory claim it should be.[93] This determination is not as obvious as one might think. I introduce a basic (but regrettably complex) taxonomy of exculpatory claims to understand the multiplicity of options that are available. In order to grasp the basic framework in which exculpatory pleas are situated, we must start not with a crime, but rather with an *accusation, charge,* or *allegation* that a particular person has committed a crime. Someone accused of an offense can seek to avoid liability in several conceptually distinct ways, each of which can be subdivided further. Although they are potentially available in all cases, I will illustrate these possibilities by supposing the defendant responds by pleading ignorance of law. Suppose, in other words, that a defendant believes (correctly or incorrectly) that she does not deserve to be punished because she did not realize her conduct was illegal. Thus far, I have tended to uncritically suppose this defendant alleges an *excuse.* Along with justifications, excuses are a type of *defense.* Both types of defense are *substantive* in that they bear on the *desert* of the defendant. That is, they show the defendant does not deserve to suffer the punishment the state would otherwise be authorized to impose. Of course, not all defenses are substantive. Some defenses, such as those involving exclusionary rules, are designed to deter police misconduct. Thus they have an ulterior purpose and do not purport to contest that the defendant is blameworthy. Non-substantive defenses may result in the acquittal of a defendant who is fully deserving of the sentence the state would otherwise be authorized to impose.

Justifications and excuses are the two most well-known (and arguably the only) substantive defenses; a defendant who is justified or excused does not deserve liability or punishment.[94] Countless conferences and workshops have been convened to draw the elusive boundary between justification and excuse. Fortunately, many of the details of these debates need not detain us here.[95] As usually conceptualized, a defendant who pleads a justification concedes that he breached a

---

[93] For further thoughts in this direction, see Re'em Segev: "Moral Rightness and the Significance of Law: Why, How, and When Mistake of Law Matters," 64 *University of Toronto Law Journal* 33 (2014).

[94] For an argument that at least one additional kind of defense is needed, see Duff: *Op.cit.* Note 76, especially chapter 11.

[95] See Douglas Husak: "On the Supposed Priority of Justification to Excuse," in Husak: *Op.cit.* Note 74, p.287.

statute, but alleges that his conduct is legally permissible (all things considered) in the circumstances in which it occurred. A defendant who knowingly kills in a paradigm case of self-defense, for example, contends that the law allows him to knowingly kill in the situation in which he acts. Excuses are different. As usually conceptualized, a defendant who pleads an excuse concedes that he breached a statute impermissibly, that is, without justification, but alleges that he is not blameworthy for having done so. A defendant who causes a greater evil under duress, for example, typically contends that the law withholds blame, liability, and punishment from him, even though his conduct is impermissible.

Most legal philosophers concur that *if* ignorance of law is to serve as a defense, it must be construed as an excuse rather than as a justification. Ultimately, they may be correct. After all, as Fletcher assumed in his refutation of Hall, mistaken defendants do not maintain they are *permitted* to breach the law. Unlike the fictional James Bond, those who are ignorant of the law of homicide do not imagine themselves to possess a "license to kill." More plausibly, the ignorant defendant should be understood to argue that she is blameless and therefore ineligible for liability, despite having performed an impermissible and unjustified act. Even if ignorance of law is construed as a plea of mitigation that warrants a reduction in the severity of punishment rather than as a complete defense that mandates an outright acquittal, most legal philosophers would construe it as a partial excuse rather than as a partial justification.[96] To this point, I have implicitly understood the plea in this way. At the end of the day, I will agree that this conceptualization is the best option—but only after a critical examination of its several alternatives.

Conventional wisdom about the nature of the plea of *ignorantia juris* has been challenged from several directions. According to Michael Cahill, for example, the plea should not be conceptualized as what I have called a substantive defense at all.[97] Why should a defendant who is ignorant of law ever be acquitted if we concede she deserves penal liability and punishment? Cahill responds that ignorance of law might function as a non-substantive public policy defense roughly akin to entrapment or a statute of limitations. I believe Cahill is correct to argue that granting this defense is likely to produce a number of

---

[96] See Douglas Husak: "Partial Defenses," in Husak, *id.*, p.311.
[97] Michael Cahill: "Mistake of Law as Nonexculpatory Defense," (forthcoming).

beneficial consequences. Thus the state should sometimes accept this plea even if we agree (as I do not) that a given defendant who is ignorant of law deserves just as much punishment as a defendant who is aware her conduct is illegal. Because I am primarily interested in the connection between ignorance of law and the punishment defendants *deserve*, however, I do not address Cahill's position further until I turn to questions of implementation in Chapter 5(B). Here we will see that Cahill is (at least) correct about a limited class of cases—those in which defendants commit what they know to be moral wrongs that have not been proscribed by the legislature ex ante.

Thus I narrow my present focus to substantive defenses: those that bear on the desert of the defendant. Even so, it is noteworthy that not all criminal theorists who treat ignorance of law as a substantive defense agree it is best conceptualized as an excuse. In a provocative paper, Re'em Segev argues that ignorance of law should often be treated as a *justification*.[98] An argument for this conclusion is easy to formulate. An act is justifiable when it is permissible, all things considered. Suppose we construe the scope of the permissible to encompass conduct that would be allowed pursuant to the best evidence available to the agent at the time. On most accounts, conduct that is responsive to the best evidence available to the agent is *reasonable*. Medieval doctors, according to this train of thought, acted reasonably when they drained blood from their diseased patients, even though we now realize that their treatments did far more harm than good. After all, the best medical science of the day recommended that patients be bled when they were stricken with given kinds of afflictions. Hence, this line of thought continues, these doctors acted permissibly by conforming to the best medical practice of their era. Suppose these doctors were (posthumously) accused by contemporary moral philosophers of committing the wrongful act of killing their patients. Their plea might well be a justification ("I acted permissibly under the circumstances") rather than an excuse ("I should not be blamed despite acting impermissibly under the circumstances"). Although the medieval doctor is alleging ignorance of the facts about medical science, a parallel argument can be constructed for persons who allege ignorance of law. According to the same rationale, a person who conforms to the best available evidence about the law acts reasonably, and thus permissibly, and thus justifiably. Hence Segev concludes that

[98] Re'em Segev: "Justification, Rationality and Mistake: Mistake of Law Is No Excuse? It Might Be a Justification!" 25 *Law and Philosophy* 31 (2006).

at least some persons who plead ignorance of law should be construed to offer a justification rather than an excuse.

Unquestionably, the premise equating justifications with the reasonable, thereby construing them to encompass conduct that conforms to the best evidence available to the agent at the time, is the most vulnerable part of this argument. We may or may not accept this premise. For present purposes, however, we need not resolve this deep and divisive dispute; it mostly involves the nature of justification and only indirectly involves the topic of ignorance of law itself. As a normative matter, we can decide whether and under what circumstances ignorance of law should exculpate without settling controversial issues about the concept of justification. More important for the topic at hand, the basis of exculpation on which I will eventually focus in this part introduces a very different kind of qualification to the general rule of *ignorantia juris*—whether or not Segev's views about the nature of justification are sound. Both justifications and excuses are a type of substantive defense, and the exculpatory consideration I examine below is not a true defense of *any* kind. A defense is needed only if the defendant has committed an *offense*—that is, a crime. Offenses, as I have indicated, are comprised of their various elements. These elements include mens rea. The qualification of the rule of *ignorantia juris* I purport to discuss in the remainder of this part construes this plea as a denial of an offense—more specifically, as a denial of a mens rea element of the offense charged. Even though Section 2.04(1)(b) uses the word "defense," a defendant who makes this kind of plea has no need for a true defense. He does not literally invoke a defense because he alleges that the crime did not occur in the first place. The crime did not occur because at least one of its elements—its mens rea—is not satisfied.

Although legal philosophers should be familiar with this type of plea by some guise or another, denials of mens rea seem paradoxical in the context of mistake of law. As a result of ignorance, a belief that one is not violating the law turns out to be *correct*. But if a mistaken belief that one is not violating the law turns out to be correct, where is the *mistake*? The very existence of this plea goes right to the heart of my project, even requiring a reformulation of my basic question. To this juncture, I have supposed (Q) asks what the law ought to be if A and B commit the same act Φ that violates the same law L, when A but not B knows Φ violates L. It should now be apparent that this description needs to be modified. If the content of law L allows the ignorant defendant to plead a denial of mens rea, B's ignorance of L entails he *cannot* breach it. And as we will see, a great many penal laws *do* allow denials of mens rea to exculpate. In these cases, the schema to which (Q) responds is literally incoherent. To be precise, we would need to recast the basic question (Q) to ask what the law ought to be if A and B commit the same act Φ, when A's act violates L and B's act *would have* violated L *but for* his ignorance. For the sake of simplicity, I have ignored this complication, and will continue to do so. For at least two reasons, however, it should not be forgotten. First, this incoherence passes under the radar screen; I am unaware of a single criminal theorist who has written about ignorance of law and has discussed it. Second, it threatens to make my inquiry too easy to resolve. How could the principle of legality allow anyone (e.g., B) to be punished just because his act *would have* amounted to a crime *if* he had possessed a mens rea he did not actually have? When B successfully pleads a denial of mens rea, the only possible outcome is acquittal.[99] In this range of cases, the basic question (Q)—which appeared to be difficult—has an obvious solution: B must not be punished for L at all. He must not be punished for L because he did not breach it, and he did not breach it because he did not satisfy each of its elements.[100]

In what follows, I return to positive law and cite several specific statutes and cases to illustrate a few of the many confusions that may result from efforts to categorize an exculpatory claim. In the first place, the very contrast between denials and other bases of exculpation can be very difficult to draw; the proper classification of a given plea is often uncertain. Clearly, a clause or term contained in the offense itself sometimes provide the basis for a true defense, including a defense of ignorance of law. When a legally ignorant defendant is acquitted by the application of such language, should she be understood to deny criminality by contesting a mens rea element of the offense charged? Often, the answer is no. Instead, she invokes a true defense that just happens to appear in the text of the statute. Although justifications and excuses typically are found in sources extrinsic to the offense charged, the statutory basis for a true defense need not lie outside the parameters of

---

[99] Or so it would seem. For some complexities, see Paul H. Robinson: "Imputed Criminal Liability," 93 *Yale Law Journal* 609 (1984).

[100] Because I am interested in liability *for* L, I leave aside the enormous perplexities involving liability for *attempts* to commit L. For a taste of these perplexities, see R.A. Duff: *Criminal Attempts* (Oxford: Clarendon Press, 1996); and Gideon Yaffe: *Attempts* (Oxford: Oxford University Press, 2010).

the statute. In short, the fact that the basis of exculpation cites language in the text of a statute is not itself decisive in categorizing the plea as a defense or as a denial of mens rea. This important point is easy to overlook. I will return in Chapter 5(A) to the significance of my claim that the particular manner in which a statute *affords* exculpatory significance to a given plea is not dispositive as to the *kind* of plea it is.

If the proper classification of a given plea can prove to be so problematic, we should pause to ask whether the task is worth the bother. Conceptual clarity aside, why is categorization important? Distinctions are valuable only if they help to resolve tangible disputes. Important consequences *do* follow, however, when a person responds to a charge by pleading a denial of mens rea rather than a genuine defense. Most notably, constitutional law in the United States includes a presumption of innocence.[101] To oversimplify only a bit, this presumption requires the prosecution to bear the burden of proving guilt in a criminal trial beyond a reasonable doubt. But what is *guilt*? For present purposes, the answer is that guilt amounts to the commission of a crime by the defendant. Guilt in this sense does not entail liability; the defendant still may possess a defense. But what, then, is a *crime*? I repeat the answer already given. Crimes are exhaustively composed of the conjunction of their several elements. Thus the state has the burden of proving a consideration relevant to liability if it is an element of the crime charged.[102] But if the consideration relevant to liability is *not* an element of the crime charged but rather a true defense, the state does not have the burden of (dis)proving it.[103] In any event, the state does not have the burden of disproving all defenses by the same high standard that pertains to elements of offenses—that is, the standard of proof beyond a reasonable doubt. Thus the categorization of an exculpatory consideration as a defense or as a denial of a mens rea element has crucial implications for the allocation of the burden of proof in criminal trials. The particular defenses in a number of federal offenses discussed below do not contest any of the elements

---

[101] For an extended discussion of the presumption of innocence and its philosophical significance, see the special issue in 8 *Criminal Law and Philosophy* 283–525 (2014).

[102] For present purposes, I construe the presumption of innocence *formally*. For a discussion of the contrast between formalistic and substantive interpretations of the presumption of innocence, see Duff: *Answering, Op.cit.* Note 76.

[103] Admittedly, this generalization is subject to exceptions. Moreover, many legal philosophers are likely to regard it as excessively formalistic, allowing offenses to be gerrymandered so that issues that bear on presumptive wrongs are artificially treated as defenses.

of these crimes—even though they appear in the texts of the statutes charged. Inasmuch as the defendant who pleads one of these defenses does not dispute that he committed what I have defined as a crime, the burden of proof with respect to his plea may be allocated to him. I will return to a discussion of burdens of proof in Chapter 5(A).

Quite a few offenses contain language that explicitly requires a defendant to have knowledge of the law he is alleged to have breached, even though the basis of exculpation may not be a denial of mens rea. The use of this language has obvious advantages, removing all guesswork about whether ignorance of law exculpates. Commentators recognize that these offenses exist, but even seasoned criminal theorists may be surprised to learn how common they prove to be. Perhaps the fact that most of these statutes appear in the United States Code (USC) has led many commentators to underestimate their number; the majority of legal philosophers are probably more familiar with the *Model Penal Code* and the state codes that (more or less) adopt it. In the *Model Penal Code*, statutes explicitly requiring a defendant to possess knowledge of the law he is accused of breaching are unusual.[104] In any event, I offer several examples of this kind of statute from federal law.[105] As we will see, they represent only one device by which ignorance of law is given exculpatory significance.

Statutes use different locutions to explicitly provide that knowledge of illegality is needed for liability. 18 USC Section 1902 provides the best example, serving as a model for how offenses should be drafted if ignorance of the law is to preclude punishment. This offense prohibits government officials from buying and selling agricultural commodities, and further provides: "No person shall be deemed guilty of a violation of any such rules, unless prior to such alleged violation he shall have had actual knowledge thereof." One can only wonder why the clarity of this provision is not replicated more frequently. Other statutes achieve the same result a bit less directly, by the operation of an "unless" clause: " . . . [unless he] had no knowledge of the rule" or, in lengthier prose, " . . . unless prior to such alleged violation he shall have had actual knowledge thereof." 15 U.S.C. Section 80a-48, for example, employs

---

[104] For some examples, see Simons: *Op.cit.* Note 83, pp.536–537.

[105] Commentators on federal law have noted that "the *ignorantia legis* principle has been seriously eroded over the last century, and in recent years, this erosion has threatened to become a landslide." Sharon Davies: "The Jurisprudence of Willfulness: An Evolving Theory of Excusable Ignorance," 48 *Duke Law Journal* 341, 343 (1998). Since the time her article was written, I doubt she would continue to describe the erosion as a landslide.

this language to require awareness of the regulation as a precondition of liability for violating securities rules. Other federal statutes specify that defendants must act "with the intent to evade" the law. For example, 21 U.S.C. Section 960(d)(5) criminalizes false statements made in regard to the import or export of given chemicals if those statements were made with the intent to evade record- keeping or reporting requirements. 31 U.S.C. Section 5332(a) proscribes bulk cash smuggling with the intent to evade a currency reporting requirement under 31 U.S.C. Section 5316, and 18 U.S.C. Section 228(a)(2) criminalizes travel in interstate or foreign commerce if a person intends to evade a child support obligation. Although this language does not unambiguously indicate that knowledge of illegality is a material element of the offense, it is hard to imagine how a person could act with the intent to evade an obligation she did not realize she had.

Unfortunately, legislators deviate from the clarity these devices involve. Sometimes a statute creates the appearance of requiring knowledge of criminality only to withdraw it by adding a disjunctive clause that allows liability to be imposed through a weaker standard. 18 U.S.C. Section 922(f)(1), for example, which prohibits transporting firearms in interstate commerce, seemingly mandates awareness that the conduct is illegal. 8 U.S.C. Section 1185(a)(2), to cite another example, prohibits the transporting of illegal aliens, and apparently requires knowledge that the transport is unlawful. But a second disjunct in these two statutes allows liability to be imposed when the defendant has "reasonable cause" to believe his conduct is illegal. The latter clause creates a negligence standard, a far cry from the actual knowledge mentioned in the first disjunct. This statutory language is bound to cause confusion; the second disjunct renders the first all but irrelevant.

The above statutes allow a defense of ignorance of law. Henceforth, I will focus on the defendant whose plea of ignorance of law does not cite a true defense that appears in the text of the statute, but alleges the absence of a mens rea element in the offense charged. Her argument that no crime occurred because she is ignorant of law can be sound only if one or more mens rea elements require her to be aware of the law she is said to have breached. *How* might a mens rea element of a statute make such awareness a necessary condition of liability? Positive law includes at least two distinct devices to allow defendants to deny mens rea by pleading ignorance of law. In what follows, I will describe and provide examples of each such mechanism. The uncertainty caused by these devices is an invitation to clean up positive law to prevent confusion among laypersons and legal scholars alike. In Chapter 5(A) I will suggest possible ways to do so. Before we can be expected to feel the urgency to improve positive law, however, we must understand the mess that legislatures and courts have created.

At least two devices are used to allow legally ignorant defendants to deny mens rea. In each of these situations, it should be clear that exculpation could have been achieved with less controversy had legislators done a better job drafting criminal statutes. The first mechanism that allows the plea of ignorance of law to function as a denial of mens rea is employed whenever a mens rea term of uncertain meaning in a statute is construed to require knowledge of the offense. The notoriously troublesome adverb *willfully* is often given this interpretation. In a great many cases, courts construe this statutory requirement to entail that the defendant must know the law before she can breach it. Several commentators have examined these statutes at length, so my treatment can be brief.[106] *Cheek v. United States* is the most well-known case in which courts held that a "willful" federal tax evasion under I.R.C. Section 7201 requires the prosecution to prove the defendant voluntarily and intentionally violated a "known legal duty."[107] Since *Cheek* was decided in 1991, numerous federal tax cases have followed suit. In *United States v. Gurary*, for example, to support conviction under I.R.C. Section 7206(2), a complicity prosecution requiring the defendant to "willfully" aid and assist the filing of false federal corporate income tax returns necessitated proof of a "known legal duty".[108] Knowledge of illegality is also a precondition of guilt for evading business receipt reporting requirements under I.R.C. Section 6050I.[109] The same result is typically reached under statutes governing false statements. Defendants must know their conduct is unlawful to allow a conviction for causing campaign treasurers to submit false reports to the Federal Election Commission in violation of 18 U.S.C. Section 1001.[110] The anti-structuring provisions in securities law are construed similarly. *Ratzlaf v. United States* famously held that a violation of 31 U.S.C. Section 5322, which prohibits the willful structuring of transactions to avoid bank reporting requirements,

---

[106] *Id.*
[107] 498 U.S. 192 (1991).
[108] 860 F.2d 521 (2d Cir. 1988).
[109] *United States v. Rogers*, 18 F.3d 265 (4th Cir. 1994).
[110] *United States v. Curran*, 20 F.3d 560 (3d Cir. 1994).

requires knowledge the act was unlawful.[111] Firearms offenses provide additional examples. 18 U.S.C. Sections 922(a)(1)(A) and 924(a)(1)(D), which prohibit willfully dealing firearms without a federal license, is interpreted to require proof that the defendant knew his conduct was unlawful.[112] Similar examples can be found in health law, employment law, international trade law, the law governing student loans, and myriad additional areas.

In quite a few other situations, however, courts construe willfulness *not* to require knowledge of illegality. One would hope to find fairly clear principles to determine when courts would or would not construe an ambiguous mens rea term to entail knowledge of the offense. In the absence of these guidelines, even the most diligent citizens and attorneys must pore over precedent in addition to statutory text to determine whether persons must know the law in order to breach it. Unfortunately, no clear principles can be found. I do not mean to say that no principles have ever been *articulated*. Instead, I mean to suggest, first, that the articulated principles are not especially helpful in making predictions about how courts will interpret (or ought to interpret) statutes containing unclear culpability terms. Second, some or perhaps all of the considerations mentioned in these principles appear to be relevant only because they correlate imperfectly with other variables that are more basic.

Complexity is among the most familiar reasons to construe the mens rea term *willfully* to require defendants to know their conduct breaches a legal duty. This rationale is invoked, for example, in the context of tax evasion. Because the tax code is so complex, courts contend that the statute used to prosecute Cheek must be interpreted to allow a denial of mens rea. But the difficulties with this argument— some of which I will mention later—were immediately evident to the dissenting justices. Two mistakes of law provided the source of Cheek's plea for exculpation. Under the influence of anti-income tax zealots, he alleged, first, that the income tax is unconstitutional, and, second, that his salary as an airline pilot does not constitute taxable income. The Court found only the second of these mistakes to be exculpatory. But even though no one would dispute that the tax code as a whole is complex, Cheek's particular mistake—that income is not taxable— is hardly a product of that complexity. Why should the complexity

---

[111] 510 U.S. 135 (1994).
[112] *Bryant v. United States,* 524 U.S. 184 (1998).

of an entire statutory scheme matter if the particular mistake of law committed by the defendant is elementary? Moreover, constitutional law is also unquestionably complex. Why, then, was not Cheek's first mistake—about the constitutionality of the income tax, which the majority held to lack exculpatory significance—just as exculpatory as his second?

As I have indicated, these issues have been debated by legions of commentators.[113] Less frequently asked, however, is *why* the complexity of a law or a statutory scheme should count in favor of awarding exculpatory significance to a mistake. Of course, any number of objections can be brought against the enactment of impenetrable statutory schemes. Presumably, however, complexity matters to the blameworthiness of an offender because persons are far more likely to be mistaken about complex matters than about those that are simple. Even reasonable people are prone to error when a topic is difficult. Can perplexed taxpayers baffled by statutory legalese really merit the condemnation and stigma heaped on criminals? But this rationale, although correct as far as it goes, fails to explain why courts do not take the more direct route of allowing a mistake of law to exculpate when it is reasonable. Complexity could have functioned as one of the considerations used to identify which mistakes *are* reasonable. In fact, however, courts have not taken this approach. They do not admit that complexity counts in favor of a defense of reasonable ignorance of law, but rather invoke complexity as a basis to construe a mens rea term to require offenders to be aware of the law they violate. In short, courts seem to prefer an approach that construes mistake of law to function as a denial of mens rea rather than as a true defense. Here, as elsewhere, the ancient doctrine of *ignorantia juris* is preserved even while its spirit is circumvented.

A second and superficially similar device is utilized when courts construe an explicit mens rea term of uncertain scope in a statute to modify a subsequent element in order to require a defendant to be aware she is violating the law as a precondition of her liability. *Knowledge* is the most notable term construed in this way, and *United States v. Liparota* is the most well-known such case.[114] The defendant

---

[113] See, for example, Richard Singer and Douglas Husak: "Of Innocence and Innocents: The Supreme Court and Mens Rea since Herbert Packer," 2 *Buffalo Criminal Law Review* 859 (1999).

[114] 471 U.S. 419 (1985).

was charged with a violation of 7 U.S.C. Section 2024(b)(1): "whoever knowingly uses, transfers, acquires, alters or possesses [food stamps] . . . in any manner not authorized [by the statute or regulations]." Liparota was not mistaken about the facts. He knew he was acquiring food stamps, but was unaware that his purchase was contrary to law. The Court construed the adverb *knowingly* to "travel all the way down the statute" to modify the clause " . . . in a manner not authorized," so that a person who is unaware his mode of acquisition is contrary to law does not commit the offense. Why adopt this controversial construction of the statute? Rules of grammar hardly dictate this result, and probably oppose it. To underscore the novelty of such an interpretation, consider the gloss supplied elsewhere by an English judge: "The principle that ignorance of the law is no defence in crime is so fundamental that to construe the word 'knowingly' in a criminal statute as requiring not merely knowledge of the facts material to the offender's guilt but also knowledge of the relevant law would be revolutionary and to my mind wholly unacceptable."[115] What led the *Liparota* Court to its "revolutionary" and "wholly unacceptable" construction? The answer, cryptic though it may be, turns out to be enormously important for my overall normative purposes. The Court reasoned that a contrary interpretation, requiring only that the defendant knows he is acquiring food stamps but not that his acquisition is unlawful, would "criminalize a broad range of innocent conduct."[116]

Time and time again, when interpreting federal criminal offenses that are silent or ambiguous about the required mental state or its scope, courts construe the statute in whatever way is necessary to separate wrongful from innocent conduct.[117] I suspect most commentators agree with the outcome in many of these cases. The difficult issue, of course, is to decide what makes a given person *innocent*. Unless we understand what constitutes innocence, we cannot make sense of this line of precedents or decide how they apply to future scenarios.[118] Regrettably, courts provide little insight into what they mean. Still,

[115] *Grant v. Borg* (1982) 1 WLR 638, 646B.
[116] *Op.cit*. Note 114, p.426.
[117] More recently, see *Elonis v United States*, 572 U.S. ___ (2015).
[118] Consider a recent attempt: "The more the element is the core of the crime, the more it seems like the norm that ignorance of the law is no excuse should apply. On the other hand, the more the legal question raised by the element is distinct from the definition of the crime, the more it seems like knowledge of a legal status can be incorporated without running afoul of that principle." Orin Kerr, *The Volokh Conspiracy* (June 18, 2015) http://lawprofessors. typepad.com/crimprof_blog/2015/06/ignorance-of-the-law-is-no-excuse-or-is-it.html.

one point is crystal clear: courts cannot simply be referring to *legal* innocence. After all, the act of the defendant *would* have breached the applicable regulations if the court had construed the statute differently. Presumably, then, the conception of innocence in question is *moral*. As one commentator expresses this point, judges interpret these statutes by consulting an "unwritten moral code ... To interpret the statute that is written by Congress the Court has used a moral code that is not."[119] As I have insisted all along, moral wrongfulness and blameworthiness are preconditions of justified liability and punishment, and the cases I survey in this part support this conclusion.

Even though they do not advance a general account of innocence itself, courts usually supply illustrations. In *Liparota,* for instance, examples of innocent behavior include "a nonrecipient of food stamps who 'possessed' stamps because he was mistakenly sent them through the mail due to administrative error, 'altered' them by tearing them up, and 'transferred' them by throwing them away."[120] It is important to note that no evidence indicated that Liparota himself was innocent in any of these ways; each of these illustrations involves a hypothetical situation. Thus the Court construed a statute to avoid convicting a defendant in order to protect *other* persons who *might* be charged with a violation of the same law but are allegedly innocent, even without suggesting the defendant *himself* qualified under this rationale. The Court's reasoning seemingly allows all defendants who are unaware their handling of food stamps violates the applicable regulations to deny mens rea and thereby evade liability and punishment.

The goal of protecting so-called innocence plays a major role in a wide range of cases involving defendants who are ignorant of law. It is cited (along with familiar worries about statutory complexity) in favor of judicial constructions of the mens rea term *willfully* that permit defendants to deny criminality when they are unaware of the law they breach. I have already mentioned the leading such case of *Ratzlaf v. United States.*[121] *Ratzlaf* held that any mistake of law, no matter how unreasonable, exculpates a defendant charged with willfully structuring a monetary transaction to avoid reporting obligations. As in *Liparota,* the Court reasoned that a contrary interpretation would

---

[119] John Shepard Wiley, Jr.: "Not Guilty by Reason of Blamelessness: Culpability in Federal Criminal Interpretation," 85 *Virginia Law Review* 1021, 1046 (1999).

[120] *Op.cit.* Note 114, pp.426–427.

[121] *Op.cit.* Note 111.

allow persons to be punished who had "non-nefarious" reasons not to tell the government about their monetary transactions involving large sums of money. Did Ratzlaf himself have such a reason? The Court did not say, but might have been expected to do so had it regarded him to be innocent. Again, examples of the alleged innocence of hypothetical defendants are given in lieu of a substantive account. Many of these examples are peculiar at best, and obfuscate more than they illuminate. They include taxpayers seeking to avoid an IRS audit and husbands trying to avoid an increase in their alimony payments.[122] The crucial point, however, is that the Court managed to exculpate a defendant who was ignorant of his legal duty without purporting to expand the scope of a true defense of ignorance of law. In case there is doubt I have characterized the Court's achievement accurately, it explicitly stated that its decision did "not dishonor the venerable principle that ignorance of the law generally is no defense to a criminal charge."[123]

Statutory terms other than "knowingly" and "willfully" allow courts to protect innocence by permitting ignorant defendants to deny mens rea. Another such word is *corruptly*, contained in quite a few bribery statutes, including 18 U.S.C. Section 201. Bribery laws must be read narrowly because they threaten to capture a great deal of benign political activity, such as logrolling, vote-trading, and campaign contributions by special interest groups. According to some commentators, interpretations of this term require the jury to summon its moral intuition to determine whether the behavior that satisfies the other elements of the offense is performed with an evil intent. Thus the corrupt intent element functions to effectively narrow these potentially overinclusive anticorruption laws to allow the conviction of only those whose conduct is deemed to be wrongful.[124]

Courts also invoke the goal of protecting innocence in the handful of cases that cite *Lambert v. California* as authority for overturning statutes that stretch the boundaries of state authority. In *Conley v. United States*,[125] for example, the court invalidated a law in the D.C. Code making it felonious for a person to be present in a motor vehicle he knows to contain a firearm. According to the court, due process precludes convicting a person of a crime of omission if he had no

---

[122] *Id.,* at 144.

[123] *Id.,* at 149.

[124] See Brennan T. Hughes: "A Statutory Element in Exile: The Crucial 'Corrupt Intent' Element in Federal Bribery Laws," (forthcoming).

[125] *Op.cit.* Note 14.

reason to believe he had a legal duty to act. The court went on to characterize the "fundamental constitutional vice" of the statute to be its proscription of entirely innocent behavior: merely remaining in the vicinity of a firearm in a vehicle. The average citizen would not suppose this conduct to be wrongful unless the government proved the defendant had notice of a legal duty to behave otherwise. Once again, the court did not examine whether the defendant himself was ignorant of the law in question; his "personal situation" was said to be "irrelevant." The court parroted the usual adage that ignorance of law does not excuse. It continued, however, "in unusual circumstances, that maxim conflicts with 'one of the bedrock principles of American law'": the principle that "[i]t is wrong to convict a person of a crime if he had no reason to believe that the act for which he was convicted *was* a crime, or even that it was wrongful." This rationale is potentially broad, but the court tried to distinguish other cases in which ignorance of law was rejected as a defense—such as ordinances prohibiting the owning of dangerous pit bulls—by alleging that these defendants had duties to inquire about the law. Although the concurring judge disagreed on this very point, the court denied that persons who simply ride in vehicles in which they know guns to be present have a comparable duty to inquire. I will return to the role supposedly played by alleged duties of inquiry in Chapter 3(C).

"Innocent" persons who are ignorant of law can be spared from liability and punishment even though courts do not construe a mens rea term at all. *Skilling v. United States,* also mentioned above, is illustrative.[126] The issue in *Skilling* is whether a corporate executive violated the federal "honest service wire fraud" statute, 18 U.S.C. Sections 371, 1341, 1343, and 1346. The statute itself seemingly proscribed an extraordinarily broad range of conduct, literally prohibiting any "scheme or artifice to deprive another of the intangible right of honest services." Might an employee commit this offense by making a personal call on the company phone during working hours? Surely this behavior is "innocent"; no reasonable person would believe it to be wrongful and prohibited by law. To avoid this absurd result, the Court construed the statute to prohibit only bribes and kickbacks—even though nothing in the statute itself supported this narrow reading. The dissenting opinion forcefully argued that the construction by the Court did not so much interpret

---

[126] *Op.cit.* Note 70.

the statute as to define an altogether new federal crime.[127] We need not decide which side has the better argument. For present purposes, the important point is that the mode of statutory interpretation adopted in *Skilling*—which construes an overbroad statute to reach only the most egregious kinds of behavior—protects defendants who are unaware that less egregious conduct is potentially criminalized. Thus it allows persons accused of "innocent" behavior to deny they are breaching the statute at all.

To summarize, courts use at least three distinct devices to exculpate defendants who are ignorant of law, only the second and third of which clearly involve a denial of mens rea. First, some offenses contain language that *explicitly* requires a defendant to possess knowledge of the law he is alleged to have breached. Second, a mens rea term of uncertain *meaning* in a statute, such as *willfully,* is construed to require knowledge of the offense. Finally, a mens rea term of uncertain *scope* in a statute—most notably, *knowingly*—is interpreted to modify a subsequent element in order to protect the innocence of a defendant by requiring her to be aware of the law she is violating.

I now make three general observations about the complex body of law I have just surveyed. First, ignorance of law exculpates far more frequently in positive law than many theorists concede. The sheer number of statutes that allow ignorant defendants to be acquitted is ample indication of the strain caused by the harsh rule of *ignorantia juris.* Second, interpretive disagreements are inevitable unless a statute explicitly indicates that its mens rea element should be construed to provide that a defendant is not liable unless she realizes her conduct is unlawful. As it would be easy to expressly indicate in a statute that ignorant defendants should not be liable, one wonders why clarity is not achieved more often. Third, we should ask *why* courts go to such lengths to acquit legally ignorant defendants by construing a mens rea term to allow this result. Why resort to a convoluted interpretation of a statute when it would have been simpler to candidly enlarge the scope of the defense of ignorance of law itself? Any answer is speculative. I admit that courts have *not* made so sweeping a claim, struggling instead to preserve the doctrine of *ignorantia juris.* Yet again, we see the grip of this adage on judicial reasoning is nearly impossible to dislodge. Of course, the philosopher of criminal law—who aspires to improve the content of the substantive criminal law even though his

[127] *Id.,* p.2935.

recommendations do not satisfy an alleged desideratum of *fit* with the relevant precedents—need not be so reticent.

Samuel Buell and Lisa Griffin offer what might be a unique perspective on the above cases—those in which courts purport to protect innocent persons by construing (or inserting) a mens rea provision in the statute.[128] Instead of regarding ignorance of law as *exculpatory* and a basis for acquittal, Buell and Griffin suggest it is more perspicuous to construe knowledge of law as *inculpatory* and a basis for conviction. Ignorance of the law is not a condition that *precludes* blameworthiness as much as knowledge of the law is a condition that *confers* blameworthiness.[129] Expressed in the terminology I adopt here, ignorance of the law does not deny mens rea; instead, knowledge of the law affirms it. The ingenious twist provided by Buell and Griffin is helpful in focusing our attention on a problem that is easy to overlook but needs to be confronted squarely. As these authors recognize, it may not be so hard to show why persons who are *ignorant* of law are blameless. What is more difficult, however, is to show why persons who are *knowledgeable* of law are blameworthy.

Why should we concede that persons are morally blameworthy just because they violate a law knowingly? The answer may seem clear when the law in question is a *malum in se*. Committing these crimes is wrongful. But matters become more difficult when a *malum prohibitum* is involved. Do persons commit a moral wrong when they perpetrate a *malum prohibitum,* knowingly or otherwise? Always? Sometimes? Never? The law itself, I have claimed, does not create obligations of compliance. It is hard to see how mere knowledge of illegality can transform what is innocent into something that is wrongful and thus eligible for blame. We may be unsure why a defendant who is ignorant of law is morally innocent and deserves to be acquitted. The bigger problem, however, is to explain why a defendant who knows the law *lacks* moral innocence and deserves to be convicted. If I am right that moral wrongfulness and blameworthiness are preconditions of liability, mere awareness of the law does not show that punishment is deserved. What helps to show punishment is deserved, I have alleged, is awareness that conduct is morally wrongful.

---

[128] Buell and Griffin: *Op.cit.* Note 66.

[129] Admittedly, Buell and Griffin purport mostly to recommend how police and prosecutorial discretion should be exercised.

In this part I have covered a fair amount of complex conceptual ground while purporting merely to describe existing law. I began by distinguishing a variety of ways positive law attaches exculpatory significance to the plea of ignorance of law. I eventually focused on one such mechanism in particular: a denial of mens rea, that is, a denial the defendant violated the law at all. This device is used with surprising frequency, indicating yet again the strain *ignorantia juris* inflicts on our system of criminal justice. But the state pays a steep price when it affords exculpatory significance to ignorance of law as a denial of mens rea rather than as a defense. First, persons avoid liability and punishment even when their mistake of law is manifestly *un*reasonable. Although many commentators join me in believing our criminal justice system is too punitive when defendants are ignorant of law, few have contended that exculpation should be granted even to those (such as Cheek) whose mistake is unreasonable. On this matter, courts are in the unusual position of being more lenient than most legal philosophers (although not, we will see, than I). Moreover, the mechanism we select has implications for burdens of proof. If exculpation is extended because those who are ignorant of law do not satisfy an element of the offense, states must assume the burden to prove defendants are aware of the law they violate. Again, this result is more favorable to defendants than most of the reforms urged by commentators (although I am ambivalent on this point). Even those criminal theorists who advocate a more generous defense of ignorance of law typically recommend that defendants should bear the burden of proving their mistake. I do not claim that either of these implications is fatal to the proposal that ignorant defendants should escape liability by denying mens rea. Perhaps the price of construing the plea as a denial of mens rea rather than as a true defense is worth paying. At the very least, however, we need to be clear about the nature of our commitments before we decide whether a given exculpatory consideration such as ignorance of law should be afforded significance as a denial of mens rea or as a true defense.

One would hope that theorists who aspire to reform the law would have much to learn by examining the conditions under which legislators or judges allow defendants who are ignorant of law to be exculpated by pleading a true defense or by denying mens rea. Too often we are given no clear principles to decide when a particular offense should be construed so that a defendant cannot be liable unless she knows her conduct is illegal. Legislation is notoriously ambiguous on this matter.

One such principle, although cryptic, is especially important for our normative purposes: the state should not impose liability on persons who are innocent. A suitable explication of this principle confirms my assumption that moral wrongfulness is a precondition of deserved punishment. In any event, the above survey illustrates some of the many possible devices for implementing into positive law a theory that affords a greater degree of exculpatory significance to the plea of ignorance of law. In particular, a device surprisingly prevalent in positive law entails that defendants who are unaware they are violating the law must be acquitted because they do not violate the law at all. This is the position to which we should gravitate if we aspire to treat mistakes of fact and mistakes of law symmetrically.

Conclusion

In this chapter I have described how existing law treats defendants who are ignorant of law. The story is complex. My objective has not been merely to summarize the current state of the law, but to suggest what legal philosophers might learn from the survey. It is easy to detect the normative strains this description repeatedly reveals. Case law reaches results that seem unjust, although the relative paucity of cases indicates this injustice is often recognized and mollified informally. In any event, commentators have been unable to provide an adequate rationale for the status quo, and sometimes fail to appreciate the full implications of the arguments they offer. Their efforts reveal the work that remains to be done in crafting an acceptable approach to the problem of *ignorantia juris*.

Casebooks and commentators tend to focus on two issues. First, they suggest that notice plays a major role in understanding the conditions under which ignorance of law is exculpatory. Inasmuch as the bar has been set low for how the demands of notice can be satisfied, few defendants succeed in passing under it. We should applaud greater efforts by our criminal justice system to inform citizens of their legal duties, but these endeavors are unlikely to remedy the injustice I believe is created by our current doctrine. Second, much has been written about the disparate treatment our codes afford to mistake of fact and mistake of law. In my judgment, the contrast itself is not too difficult to draw once the propositional content of beliefs is disambiguated. But the more important issue is why the distinction between these two kinds of mistake should matter for the normative purpose of inflicting punishments that are deserved. I anticipate that our best theory of responsibility will turn out to afford the same degree of exculpation to defendants who make either kind of mistake.

Finally, I have provided the conceptual spadework to situate the plea of ignorance of law in a broader taxonomy of exculpatory claims. Although many classifications of this plea are possible, positive law often allows this claim to preclude liability by denying mens rea, that is, to preclude liability without invoking a true defense. A growing number of statutes contain a *mens rea* element that entails that defendants who are ignorant of law do not breach the law at all. This device should not be implemented in a piecemeal fashion or as a product of strained judicial interpretations of poorly crafted statutes. The frequent use of this device to exculpate "innocent" defendants is perhaps the best evidence of the strain the rule of *ignorantia juris* places upon our system of criminal justice—even though courts prefer not to admit it.

Case law, scholarly commentary, and the foregoing developments are ample testimony of the deficiencies in existing law. What changes should be made? Fortunately, a number of contemporary moral philosophers have been working on parallel problems and have helped to identify an approach I believe to be preferable. I finally turn from penal theory to moral philosophy in the hope of finding a better solution—one that furthers the central objective of criminal theory by improving the content of the substantive criminal law.

3

Responsibility

My description of background assumptions and subsequent survey of existing legal practice has set the stage for a normative theory of the exculpatory significance of ignorance of law. Unless we rely solely on intuitions—which I have argued to be especially unreliable in this context—any such account must invoke a general theory of responsibility. In this chapter I examine the conditions under which it is plausible to hold persons blameworthy, and discuss how these conditions apply to those who are mistaken about whether their conduct is wrongful. My views about the exculpatory significance of mistake of *law* invoke two presumptions from Chapter 1: I draw heavily from the best treatments of the exculpatory significance of mistake of *fact,* and also from the most persuasive work done by philosophers on *moral* responsibility. Although I try hard to defend my theory, I am painfully aware that my support is unlikely to convince those many legal philosophers whose views about the foundations of responsibility are unlike my own. As I repeatedly indicate, few topics in contemporary philosophy are in such a state of turmoil and flux. But even competitive theories, I argue, afford far greater exculpatory significance to ignorance of law than our current practice.

The concept of responsibility is multiply ambiguous, and I begin by discussing two of its several senses. In Part A of this chapter, I examine the conditions under which someone has the *capacity* for responsibility. No single feature differentiates those who possess this capacity from those who do not, so problems can be expected when an individual satisfies some but not all of these criteria. Nonetheless, I follow a great many philosophers in thinking that *rationality,* that is, our ability to conform our behavior to reasons, is the most important such property. We are apt subjects of moral blame when we possess the capacity to conform to *moral* reasons. Part B is the most speculative and inconclusive in the entire book. I borrow the property of being responsive to moral reasons from Part A to resolve questions about whether and to what extent persons are responsible for their wrongful acts. I argue that reason-responsiveness should be construed internally or subjectively in order to justify holding wrongdoers fully blameworthy for their conduct Φ that violates law L. As it is hard to see why rational persons should respond to reasons of which they are unaware, this theory supports the conclusion that defendants deserve *complete* exculpation in nearly every case in which they are totally ignorant of the wrongfulness of their behavior. Some of the most well-known competitive theories— in particular, the most plausible versions of quality of will theories— can also be construed to support a reduction in the punishment of such persons, although their support may be more tenuous. Following my proposal to model the culpability of defendants who are mistaken about the law according to the familiar principles of exculpation that apply to defendants who are mistaken about the facts, I distinguish different degrees of blameworthiness among wrongdoers who merit some quanta of responsibility for their conduct. The person who is reckless—who consciously disregards a substantial and unjustifiable risk her conduct is wrongful—deserves some amount of blame for her wrongdoing, but less than that of the person who fully appreciates his conduct is wrongful.

Several philosophers who sympathize with my claim that many morally or legally ignorant wrongdoers are entitled to some degree of exculpation allow a reduction in blame only when such persons are *non-culpably* ignorant, that is, only when they are not culpable *for* their ignorance. Some ignorant persons, however, *are* culpable for their ignorance, alleged to merit no exculpation, and thus are held to be just as responsible as those who are aware their conduct is wrongful. Ignorance is culpable, these philosophers continue, when it can be *traced* to a prior culpable act consisting in a failure to inquire. In Part C, I critique tracing strategies. I argue that ignorant defendants are seldom if ever culpable for Φ because they failed to discharge an alleged duty to inquire about the wrongfulness of Φ at an earlier time. I describe five distinct hurdles tracing strategies must surmount before they succeed in showing A and B are equally culpable for Φ. I argue that few if any cases meet this burden.

A. The Capacity for Responsibility

If I am correct that we have special reasons to suspect our intuitions are unreliable when asked to make judgments about the basic question (Q), it is tempting to try to dispense with them. We might put intuitions aside and move directly to an examination of the more general considerations at stake. Again, (Q) asks about the relative amount of punishment that should be imposed on A and B for engaging in the same conduct Φ that violates the same law L. I have interpreted this question to ask about the degree of moral desert, blameworthiness, or responsibility of A relative to that of B. To answer this question, we cannot avoid commitment about the underlying conditions of responsibility. It is facetious to suppose we can determine whether or to what extent A and B differ in their responsibility for Φ without a general idea of what makes anyone responsible for anything.

Theoretical disagreement about the exculpatory force of ignorance of law derives from deeper disagreement about whether A and B satisfy the conditions of moral responsibility to a comparable degree. As I will explain in more detail in Part B, different conceptions of responsibility may have radically different implications for the culpability of persons who are ignorant their behavior is wrongful. At the same time, however, I confess to serious reservations that abstract arguments will advance the inquiry as far as we might hope. My misgivings stem from the fact that the criteria that underlie moral responsibility are enormously controversial—as much so, perhaps, as any topic in the whole of philosophy. These criteria have divided philosophers since the time of Aristotle, although my survey of the landscape suggests that disagreement is even more vehement today. We live in an era that has seen an explosion of interest in questions about the foundations of blameworthiness; new books or articles seem to appear nearly every week. Even specialists fall quickly behind in their attempts to stay abreast of the latest developments. It is safe to say, however, that no argument in favor of one conception over another has begun to attract anything approaching a consensus. Because this topic is so difficult and yet so central, it is bound to be the least definitive part of *any* philosophical investigation of ignorance of law—including my own. We should not be optimistic about the prospects of applying a theory to illuminate a problem when that theory is every bit as uncertain as our intuitions about the problem itself. We have come full circle.

If I am correct, we are at sea in trying to identify a methodology that will move our inquiry forward. Intuitions are conflicting, contaminated, and unreliable, but no consensus comes close to favoring a general theory. Despite these formidable obstacles—which help to make the topic of *ignorantia juris* so intractable and challenging—I will sketch the theoretical foundations of the approach I will adopt. I do so in two parts. This subdivision is needed because *responsibility* is multiply ambiguous, and two of its several meanings are of special significance.[1] Ultimately, we will be interested in the conditions that must be satisfied to determine whether and to what extent a particular defendant is responsible for a specific act-token Φ. First, however, we should try to state the criteria that must be satisfied before someone qualifies as a *responsible agent,* that is, a being who is *capable* of being blameworthy for what he does or fails to do, a being about whom claims of responsibility are intelligibly predicated, a being who is the appropriate target of our reactive attitudes.[2] I hope that normal human adults are responsible agents, and skunks are not. But why is this so? What property do sane adult humans possess that skunks lack in virtue of which we but not they are able to be responsible for at least some of what we do? I address this question in this part.

Some philosophers famously believe that normal human beings are *not* responsible agents and thus we need not attend to further details about A, B, Φ, or L. The most well-known objection to the claim that we are capable of being blameworthy for our conduct derives from worries about the relevance of universal causal determinism. It is plausible to suppose that no person can be responsible for wrongful conduct unless she could have done otherwise.[3] But no one could have done otherwise, determinists continue, given our anteced-ent causal histories. Like every other entity in a naturalistic universe, we are subject to causal laws. Some determinists—typically called *hard* determinists—conclude that we are not responsible agents and thus can never be blameworthy for any act we perform. As every

---

[1] See Michael J. Zimmerman: "Varieties of Moral Responsibility," in Randolph Clarke, Michael McKenna, and Angela M. Smith, eds.: *The Nature of Moral Responsibility: New Essays* (New York: Oxford University Press, 2015), p.45.

[2] For an argument that persons can be apt subjects of moral assessment without satisfying the requirements of moral agency, see Julia Driver: "Appraisability, Attributability, and Moral Agency," in *id.,* p.157.

[3] For the most well-known challenge to this "plausible supposition," see Harry G. Frankfurt: "Alternate Possibilities and Moral Responsibility," 66 *Journal of Philosophy* 829 (1969).

philosopher is well aware, the volume of critical commentary about the challenge to our capacity for responsible agency posed by universal causal determinism could fill a small library. I make no effort to join this debate. When I later say that we are responsible agents in virtue of our ability to respond to moral reasons, I do not mean to deny that our behavior is caused.[4] But my views do not depend on the truth of compatibilism. I hope libertarians will support my conclusions too, even though I tend to believe our capacity to respond to reasons exists within a framework of universal causal determinism.[5]

Skepticism that any of us is ever blameworthy for anything we do is not confined to hard determinists. Additional global doubts about responsibility stem from many sources, most notably the pervasiveness of *luck*.[6] We lack control over what is due to luck, and it is tempting to believe that control is a prerequisite for blameworthiness. After all, whether persons succeed in altering the world as they intend is often a matter of causal luck. Moreover, constitutive and situational luck—luck about *who* we are, about the beliefs and desires we happen to have, and about the predicaments and circumstances in which we find ourselves—is ubiquitous. If we lack control over and thus are not responsible for each of these variables, how can we be responsible for the actions that are contingent upon them? To blame us for what is beyond our control would seem to be profoundly *unfair*. As Alex Guerrero laments:

For any action, X, performed by some person, Q, there are a host of factors that led Q to do X. Some of these have to do with what Q believes and values, some of them have to do with how Q deliberates. And there are likely other subconscious or non-rational factors that led Q to do X. For all of these factors, there is a causal story about how they came to obtain . . . The old and familiar question is *how much of all this must one have had control over, or be responsible for, or have caused, in order for one to be morally responsible for doing X?*[7]

---

[4] Those who reject determinism disagree about the conditions needed to make us responsible agents, and whether these conditions ever are satisfied. See David Palmer, ed.: *Libertarian Free Will: Contemporary Debates* (New York: Oxford University Press, 2014).

[5] For healthy skepticism, see Adam J. Kolber: "Free Will as a Matter of Law," in Michael Pardo and Dennis Patterson, eds.: *Philosophical Foundations of Law and Neuroscience* (Oxford: Oxford University Press, forthcoming, 2016).

[6] See Neil Levy: *Hard Luck* (Oxford: Oxford University Press, 2011).

[7] Alexander A. Guerrero: "Deliberation, Responsibility, and Excusing Mistakes of Law," 11 *APA Newsletter on Philosophy and Law* 2 (2011) (emphasis in original).

Requiring us to have control over *each* of the many factors that plays a causal role in our conduct is a short step from holding none of us responsible for anything. But where should we draw the line to which Guerrero alludes? No one should be confident in her answer.

It is a gross understatement to admit that the foregoing worries have devastating implications for my project. I aspire to describe what the law ought to be when persons are ignorant of law. My position rests on the theory of moral responsibility I sketch. Skeptics about moral responsibility will of course reject my foundational theory. Where does this reasonable disagreement leave my project? Even if we are ultimately persuaded that those philosophers who believe we possess the capacity for moral responsibility have the better arguments, the case for concluding that none of us is ever responsible for anything is too powerful to reject out of hand. It is not akin, for example, to epistemological skepticism that we might be brains in vats or manipulated by evil demons. In positive law, the presumption of innocence is narrowly applied to the proposition that persons should not be punished unless they have been proved to commit a criminal offense beyond a reasonable doubt. But the rationale that supports this presumption is not so easily confined. It can reasonably be extended, for example, to ensure that the crimes for which persons are punished are a legitimate exercise of state authority in the first place.[8] But why stop here? The presumption might also be extended to require proof beyond a reasonable doubt that anyone subjected to penal sanctions is a responsible agent. I am uncertain whether this last burden can be met. Either we produce good reasons not to extend the presumption of innocence so far, or we try to show that those of us who are subject to penal liability possess the capacity for moral responsibility beyond a reasonable doubt.

These challenges must eventually be confronted, although attempts to do so here would take us too far afield. Clearly, arguments for a wholesale rejection of blameworthiness must be unsound if my project is to be salvaged. If no one is ever responsible for anything because of the ubiquity of luck or our inability to do otherwise, there is no need to ask whether ignorance of morality or law poses any special

---

[8] See Patrick Tomlin: "Extending the Golden Thread? Criminalisation and the Presumption of Innocence," 21 *Journal of Political Philosophy* 44 (2013). For a forceful defense of the contrary view, see Ricahd L. Lippke: *Taming the Presumption of Innocence* (Oxford: Oxford University Press, 2016).

problem for the desert that underlies liability and punishment. On more than one occasion I have struggled to resist the urge to write a book about responsibility and to respond in detail to the many objections to the view I eventually formulate.[9] Along with the vast majority of philosophers and legal theorists, however, I will simply presuppose we are agents to whom responsibility can be predicated so that we *sometimes* are blameworthy for our conduct. It remains to be seen, of course, whether and to what extent we are responsible and blameworthy for Φ when we are unaware it is wrongful.

Before proceeding, I should mention an additional respect in which my preferred approach may not be taken for granted. Even those theorists who concur that a viable position on ignorance of law depends on a general theory of moral responsibility may disagree about what is needed to produce such a theory. According to Peter Strawson, being morally responsible is simply a matter of being an appropriate target of a particular set of reactive attitudes—such as gratitude, indignation, resentment, and the like.[10] Significantly, Strawson maintains it is appropriate for us to direct these reactive attitudes to agents even without supposing them to satisfy any specific set of conditions. In other words, our justification for holding A or B responsible does not depend on whether they have any particular property. Instead, the reactive attitudes are simply a natural expression of an essential feature of our form of life: the *interpersonal* way of life. Thus the practice of holding persons responsible—embedded as it is in our interpersonal way of life—cannot be abandoned, and does not stand in need of an external rational justification.[11] I admire much of the Strawsonian project and agree that our reactive attitudes play a huge role in a viable theory of blameworthiness.[12] Nonetheless, I believe the foregoing aspect of his approach is misguided. If persons are responsible, there must be something about them that makes them so; when our reactive attitudes are applied appropriately, they track some feature of the person toward

---

[9] In particular, I do not respond to worries about *manipulation* that have long troubled compatibilists. See Derk Pereboom: *Living without Free Will* (Cambridge: Cambridge University Press, 2001). For a retort, see Shaun Nichols: *Bound: Essays on Free Will and Responsibility* (Oxford: Oxford University Press, 2015), especially chapter 4.

[10] See Peter F. Strawson: "Freedom and Resentment," 48 *Proceedings of the British Academy* 1 (1962).

[11] *Id.,* p.23.

[12] For a critical discussion of many aspects of this project, see Michael McKenna and Paul Russell, eds.: *Free Will and Reactive Attitudes: Perspectives on P.F. Strawson's Freedom and Resentment* (Burlington, VT.: Ashgate, 2007).

whom these attitudes are directed.[13] If A is more responsible and blameworthy than B, there must be something morally dissimilar between them. In order to make progress on the topic at hand, we need to identify what that something is.

It is doubtful that any *single* criterion distinguishes responsible from non-responsible subjects. Several criteria mark this contrast. The clearest cases of responsible agents—you and I—possess each of them. The clearest cases of non-responsible things—sticks and stones—possess none. Michael Moore helpfully summarizes eight of these criteria.[14] First, the possession of mental states: responsible agents have beliefs, desires, and intentions; trees and mollusks do not. Second, phenomenal experience: agents are unlike robots because they have conscious experiences. Although quite a few of these mental states are inaccessible to us, we would be very different creatures if none were the objects of our conscious experience. Third, intentionality: many of our mental states have content; we believe we are guided by our representations of the world. Fourth, the possession of cognitive and conative states: these states guide our actions and constitute our agency. Fifth, practical rationality: we represent the world as we *desire* it to be, as we *believe* that it is, and as we *intend* to make it. Sixth, emotion: the absence of feelings makes a being less than a person and might compromise his responsible agency. A recognizable agent is passionate about certain projects and empathizes with those who suffer. Seventh, stability of character over time: the entire constellation of an individual's intentional states instantiate an intelligible character structure. Fractured personalities and temporally disjointed chameleons are not the kind of beings we take ourselves to be. Finally, autonomy: responsible agents have the power to alter moral relations in the world through voluntary acts of will. Our ability to consent and to make commitments expresses our autonomy most directly. The absence of any of these eight characteristics would jeopardize our status as responsible agents. Matters become more contentious, of course, when a given subject has some but not all of these features, or has each to only a rudimentary degree.

---

[13] Thus I tend to favor *alethic* conceptions of the grounding of responsibility claims. See Gideon Rosen: "The Alethic Conception of Moral Responsibility," in Clarke et al., *Op.cit.*, Note 1, p.65. But I would prefer to remain as neutral as possible on grounding questions.

[14] See Michael S. Moore: "The Quest for a Responsible Responsibility Test—Norwegian Insanity Law after Brevik," 10 *Criminal Law and Philosophy* (forthcoming, 2016).

Notwithstanding the length of this list, I believe a single capacity is especially significant in making persons responsible. This capacity is central because its existence is presupposed by most of the criteria Moore describes. This capacity, I submit, is *rationality* understood as *reason-responsiveness:* our ability to respond to and be guided by reasons. As we are interested in the capacity for *moral* responsibility in particular, our responsiveness to *moral* reasons is what concerns us. Quite simply, we persons are able to conform our behavior to the moral considerations that are available to us when we deliberate about what to do and act accordingly.[15] That is, we are suitable candidates for attributions of blame when we possess the capacity to respond to moral reasons. A great many philosophers endorse this model in some form or another, and have spent the better parts of their careers explicating it. It probably represents the single most popular kind of position among those who specialize in the foundations of moral responsibility. The details of a "moral reason-responsive" account, however, are enormously controversial. Which reasons are moral reasons? Might we be guided by some subset of moral reasons but not by others? In what does this alleged capacity consist? What exactly is meant by guidance, and what exactly is meant by responsiveness? What should we say when these capacities are temporarily diminished? Under what circumstances must we be capable of changing our behavior in light of these reasons? To what extent must our account incorporate the empirical findings of social psychologists that indicate that our rational capacities are sensitive to changes in our circumstances? Are additional considerations required for this account to *suffice* for responsibility? Do manipulative interferences (for example, hypnotism, brainwashing, or duress) undermine responsibility? Is this account symmetrical between praise and blame? I will not delve into these fascinating puzzles, despite their obvious relevance. Yet again, the complex details of responsibility are beyond the scope of my project. Still, I must at least comment briefly on a characteristic of responsible agency that may *not* be captured by a reason-responsive account. I have said that a being lacking in emotions is less of a person. Is such a being less reason-responsive and thereby less responsible? Moreover, I must say something about what it means for a reason to be available to an agent. Under what circumstances, if

---

[15] See the account provided by John Martin Fischer and Mark Ravizza: *Responsibility and Control: A Theory of Moral Responsibility* (Cambridge: Cambridge University Press, 1998).

any, are matters of which we are unaware available to us? I will address the second of these questions in Part B.

The need to adopt a position on the first question is starkly presented by the case of psychopaths. Psychologists disagree about the exact nature of psychopathy. Suppose, however, that the following crude story is roughly correct: psychopaths are able to parrot moral considerations but cannot fully grasp or feel their emotional tug qua reasons. Is their cognitive grasp of morality sufficient to allow us to conclude they are capable of being *guided* by these reasons? Once again, this issue has generated a voluminous literature; reasonable minds can and do differ.[16] Although nearly every crucial empirical finding about psychopathy is contested, uncertainty about the responsibility of psychopaths frequently is due to disagreement about the foundations of responsibility itself. Inasmuch as the wrongful behavior of psychopaths often reveals utter disregard for the value of other persons, many philosophers who accept what I call a quality of will theory have little hesitation pronouncing them to be responsible for their crimes.[17] But the challenge posed by psychopaths is acute for the view of responsibility I presuppose here. If the phenomenological ability to *experience* moral feelings (sometimes described as *sentimentalism*) is a necessary condition for the capacity to be *guided* by moral reasons, for the capacity to be truly *responsive* to them, psychopaths may be exempt from the responsibility conferred by my theory. This possibility is not a reductio of my position. In my judgment, psychopaths should be regarded as borderline cases for deserved punishment.[18] For good reason, I do not take a firm side on this divisive issue.

Whatever the correct position about psychopaths, the criminal law recognizes a number of less controversial exceptions to the generalization that human beings possess the capacity for moral responsibility. Infants and the insane are the clearest examples of non-responsible humans. Addicts also present an especially troublesome case; different models of moral responsibility appear to have different

---

[16] See Luca Malatesi and John Mcmillan, eds.: *Psychopathy and Responsibility* (Oxford: Oxford University Press, 2010); and Thomas Schramme, ed.: *Being Amoral: Psychopathy and Moral Incapacity* (Cambridge, MA: MIT Press, 2014).

[17] See Samuel H. Pillsbury: "Why Psychopaths are Responsible," in Kent Kiehl and Walter Sinnott-Armstrong, eds.: *Handbook on Psychopathy and Law* (New York: Oxford University Press, 2013), p.297.

[18] See Stephen J. Morse: "Psychopaths and Criminal Responsibility," 1 *Neuroethics* 205 (2008).

implications for their blameworthiness.[19] Debate about the nature of addiction itself—whether to conceptualize it as a *disease* or a *choice*—has nearly come to resemble disagreement about religion, and seems all but immune to empirical verification or falsification.[20] In what follows, I have virtually nothing to say about these actual or possible exceptions. Instead, I propose to deal with relatively easy cases. Each of my subsequent examples should be taken to presuppose that the agents in question are sane, non-addicted, non-psychopathic adults. If we cannot agree about even the simplest examples, we have no prospects for resolving the larger project at hand. A theory of ignorance of law is hard enough to defend without the inevitable difficulties of applying it to tricky cases of creatures on the borderline of responsible agency. I will be satisfied if my analysis works tolerably well for clear examples, and leave to subsequent study the wrinkles that are bound to arise when extending it elsewhere.

I am *mostly* uninterested, however, in our general capacity for moral agency or how to decide whether borderline cases possess or lack it. In what follows, I focus on a different but related issue about responsibility: *given* that we have the *capacity* for moral agency, what conditions must be satisfied before we actually *are* responsible for our conduct? In particular, to what extent are A and B responsible for Φ despite differing in their awareness that it violates a moral or legal norm L? It would be odd (but not incoherent) if a capacity were the basis of our responsible agency, but its exercise were irrelevant to whether we are responsible for what we do. Therefore, as we will see, I appeal to a theory of moral reason-responsiveness to answer this question as well.

B. Responsibility for Conduct

Our ability to be guided by moral reasons is the single most important of the several variables that give us the capacity for moral responsibility. I presuppose a general understanding of this capacity in order to move directly to the specific topic at hand: *given* that we possess the *capacity*

---

[19] See the several essays in Neil Levy, ed.: *Addiction and Self-Control* (Oxford: Oxford University Press, 2013).

[20] See Gene H. Heyman: *Addiction: A Disorder of Choice* (Cambridge, MA: Harvard University Press, 2009).

for moral responsibility, and thus are moral agents who are proper objects of blame, what conditions must be satisfied before we actually *are* morally responsible for what we do? In particular, to what extent is B morally responsible for conduct Φ that violates law L when she is unaware of the moral status of her breach? How does her degree of blameworthiness compare with that of A, who is identical in all respects except that he understands Φ to be wrongful? These questions cannot be answered in the absence of a commitment to a general theory of moral responsibility. In this part I sketch and apply such a theory. According to the account I prefer, agents are rarely *fully* responsible for Φ unless they are actually aware Φ is wrong. According to the main competitor to this theory—an alternative I do not pretend to refute— such agents deserve quite a bit of exculpation when they are unaware Φ is wrongful, although their degree of exculpation is probably less than total. In any event, I recognize that the effort to ground an answer to (Q) in a theory of moral responsibility is the weakest link in my overall position about the blameworthiness of defendants who commit wrongful acts in ignorance. I draw solace from the fact that the underlying theory of responsibility is bound to be the weakest link in *any* position about the exculpatory significance of a given factor such as ignorance of law.

I begin by noting a chasm between the quantity and quality of the scholarly work on this topic generated by moral philosophers as opposed to that produced by criminal theorists. The very existence of this gulf is puzzling. As I have indicated, many commentators share my view that the criminal law should conform to morality presumptively. Thus one would expect to find a convergence between the particular controversies about responsibility debated by philosophers of criminal law and those examined by moral philosophers. Each discipline has produced a wealth of recent literature, for example, on the conditions that must be satisfied before persons are justified in using force in self-defense, or on the normative relevance of findings from neuroscience. By contrast, serious work on the preconditions of responsibility for conduct is an exception to the convergence one would anticipate. The past several years have witnessed an explosion of interest among moral philosophers about the foundations of blameworthiness, and several of the theories that have been defended support the conclusion that wrongdoers deserve some degree of exculpation when they violate norms of which they are unaware. Yet few parallel treatments have been undertaken by philosophers of criminal law. Most of the contemporary scholarship on criminal responsibility evades this topic altogether or confines its focus to what I call *narrow* culpability: the particular kind of mens rea needed to impose liability under given statutes. Scholars rarely draw systematically from the wealth of literature produced by moral philosophers to challenge orthodoxy about *ignorantia juris*.[21] Although I have no hypothesis to explain why criminal theory on this topic has been so unaffected by recent developments in moral philosophy, I hope to take a modest step to bridge this divide. As I emphasize repeatedly, we cannot begin to decide whether and to what extent A and B are responsible for Φ without making a commitment about whether and to what extent anyone is ever responsible for anything she does.

It is natural to suppose that questions about whether persons are responsible for conduct Φ should be resolved by invoking the same framework that shows why they possess the capacity for responsibility in the first place.[22] That is, agents become eligible for attributions of responsibility for a given act by exercising (or failing to exercise) their capacity to be reason-responsive with respect to it. Roughly, we become blameworthy for wrongful conduct when our capacity is intact but we utilize it incorrectly. I propose to briefly elaborate on this position before turning to a critical examination of what I take to be its main rival. Although my explication is woefully short of the nuance and detail that philosophical specialists would prefer, I hope to say enough to motivate my conclusion that a reason-responsive account of responsibility—when construed most plausibly—shows why offenders who act in total ignorance of law typically deserve complete exculpation. I will also argue—even more tentatively—that this conclusion does not depend entirely on accepting a reason-responsive account. Even the most well-known competitors to this view—quality of will theories—should be interpreted to support some degree of exculpation for persons who are ignorant of wrongdoing. For present purposes, the most important difference between these rival theories is not *whether,* but *to what extent* they exculpate B relative to A.

---

[21] For a recent exception, see Stephen P. Garvey: "Authority, Ignorance, and the Guilty Mind," 67 *Southern Methodist University Law Review* 545 (2014).

[22] As I survey the landscape, theories that ground responsibility for conduct in defective deliberation are prevalent among contemporary moral philosophers. According to the influential account of John Fischer, for example, persons are responsible when they exhibit moderate reasons-responsiveness, which involves being normally reasons-receptive (able to recognize reasons as such) and at least weakly reasons-reactive. See John Martin Fischer: *Deep Control: Essays on Free Will and Value* (Oxford: Oxford University Press, 2012).

I hope an account of responsibility in terms of moral reason-responsiveness is compatible with *any* framework for conceptualizing the nature of wrongfulness in first-order morality. In what follows, however, I invoke what often is called an *objective* account of obligation. Although many different conceptions of wrongfulness have been proposed for different purposes,[23] I tentatively invoke the following view: in any given situation, what a person ought to do is a function of the *reasons* for or against the alternative courses of action she could perform. Conduct Φ is wrongful when the moral reasons against it are stronger than the reasons in favor of performing it. What these reasons are and how they are balanced does not depend on the beliefs of the defendant herself; the determination of whether Φ is wrongful (unlike the position I favor regarding responsibility for Φ) is thoroughly *objective*.[24] I recognize that this particular conception of objective wrongfulness, like any other with which I am familiar, is problematic.[25] I acknowledge that reasons are notoriously difficult to identify and to balance, that some appear to be incommensurable with one another, and that some might be outweighed while others are excluded. Moreover, this objective conception offers almost no assistance in guiding action. I hope the essentials of my view about ignorance of law are not undermined if an objective conception of wrongfulness turns out to be misguided.

We routinely exercise our capacity to respond to moral reasons, but sometimes deserve blame when we do so incorrectly. Consider the following example, which I hope to be straightforward. Imagine Sabine notices that her neighbor leaves his expensive bicycle unlocked on his porch when he returns home from school. When he is fast asleep at night, she sneaks onto his porch, steals his bike, and sells it to her friend, who she knows will be happy to buy a nice bicycle below its market value. Sabine is virtually certain her theft will be undetected. On a purely prudential calculus, she increases her expected utility by taking the bike. Nonetheless, she recognizes the existence of moral reasons against her act of theft, and knows these reasons outweigh her prudential reasons to steal. But she takes the bike anyway. No excuse (e.g., duress) or justification (e.g., necessity) applies to her behavior. In

---

[23] The various candidates are nicely described in Michael J. Zimmerman: *Ignorance and Moral Obligation* (Oxford: Oxford University Press, 2014).

[24] See T.M. Scanlon: *Being Realistic about Reasons* (Oxford: Oxford University Press, 2014).

[25] Among other problems, this conception has difficulties accounting for supererogation.

the event my example is under-described, and more detail is needed, I stipulate that Sabine's motive for stealing the bicycle is solely to obtain money to finance her vacation to Las Vegas where she plans to indulge her penchant for gambling. But she is not an addict suffering from an overwhelming compulsion to gamble. She simply enjoys it. If *anyone* is blameworthy for *any* act Φ, Sabine is blameworthy for her act of theft. I see little point in proceeding further and trying to make headway on the topic at hand if we cannot agree about attributions of responsibility in this simple case.

Would anyone other than responsibility-abolitionists disagree with my judgment about this case? Even Gideon Rosen, a notorious skeptic about impositions of blame, would concede Sabine's bicycle theft presents an easy case. The basis of his skepticism about this example would be entirely epistemological.[26] That is, Rosen denies we can ever be sure that a wrongdoer acts contrary to the balance of moral reasons she herself understands and appreciates. To *some* extent, Rosen's worries about evidence can be put aside. As I have stipulated the relevant facts about our bicycle thief, we can meaningfully inquire about her blameworthiness while remaining agnostic about whether we could have much certainty these facts actually obtain in the absence of stipulation. Nonetheless, any theory of responsibility we hope to apply to real cases in the law had better be able to overcome this difficulty. Thus I join those critics who suspect Rosen's epistemological reservations are exaggerated.[27] In some cases, I think, we *can* be confident that persons act contrary to the reasons they themselves recognize. Credence is highest when we take the first-person perspective. If most of us were to steal a bike to bankroll our vacation, we would experience the emotions characteristic of healthy agents who commit wrongful acts knowingly: the guilt and remorse that follows our awareness of what we have done. These psychological reactions are (admittedly inconclusive) evidence that we acted against the balance of moral reasons as we ourselves understood them. I suspect that Rosen's skepticism about the epistemological basis for attributions of responsibility say as much about Rosen himself as about the view he defends. I would be surprised to learn that he has

---

[26] Gideon Rosen: "Skepticism about Moral Responsibility," 18 *Philosophical Perspectives* 295 (2004).

[27] See William J. Fitzpatrick: "Moral Responsibility and Normative Ignorance: Answering a New Skeptical Challenge," 118 *Ethics* 589 (2008).

ever stolen anything. But persons whose past is more checkered may be in a better position to appreciate the phenomenology I have just recounted. Even so, I will eventually agree that Rosen is correct when he contends that each of the several criteria needed to impose *full* responsibility for wrongdoing are satisfied rarely—especially when we are required to *prove* that others satisfy them.

As stipulated, however, Sabine's case is *so* easy that it does little to support a particular conception of responsibility; *any* non-skeptical theory, including those I reject, had better succeed in finding this case to be unproblematic. Still, it is instructive to investigate *what* is so easy about it. Different answers would be given. On my view, Sabine's case is straightforward because she herself is fully cognizant her conduct is wrongful. Expressed more colloquially, Sabine *knows better* than to steal the bicycle. In the simplest, clearest, and least controversial examples in which persons are blameworthy, agents act with what might be called *akrasia* or *weakness of will*. Nothing depends on my use of this notorious term.[28] I simply mean that the clearest cases of blameworthiness involve persons who understand their moral reason against doing Φ, agree that the balance of reasons require them not to Φ, but decide to Φ anyway, that is, to act contrary to the balance of reasons they recognize.[29] As far as I can see, the only meaningful (and non-epistemological) point of contention among moral philosophers (who do not advocate the abolition of responsibility altogether) is whether persons are ever blameworthy for wrongful actions *other* than those that correspond to this description. But unless at least some agents are responsible when they commit actions they recognize to be wrongful, I doubt we will agree that anyone is ever responsible for anything.

To be sure, *some* akratic defendants have a plausible claim for at least a partial excuse from blame on other grounds. Exculpation may be deserved in those situations in which the akratic defendant battles mightily but unsuccessfully against the temptation to offend. Consider, for example, a stereotypical kleptomaniac. He realizes theft

---

[28] The nature and even the possibility of akrasia present a deep puzzle in philosophy I make no effort to unravel. See Alfred R. Mele: *Backsliding: Understanding Weakness of Will* (Oxford: Oxford University Press, 2013).

[29] I count agents as making an error in practical reasoning when they do not actually *do* what they believe they have most reason to do, although other accounts of akrasia differ on this matter. Practical deliberation, on my view, concludes with the judgment "I will do Φ" rather than "I ought to do Φ."

is wrongful, would prefer not to accede to his impulse to steal, but eventually surrenders after an internal struggle. Perhaps he merits some degree of exculpation because his desire, although probably not literally irresistible, makes conformity with the law too onerous. Stephen Garvey would afford this agent a partial excuse, [30] and Stephen Morse would concur[31]—even though they disagree about whether the defect in such agents is located in their will or in their reason. Of course, a problem in any proposal to allow some degree of exculpation for these "hard choices" is to differentiate between those whose desires are difficult and those whose desires are not-so-difficult to resist. But equally problematic lines must be drawn for defendants who plead *any* excuse, including duress or provocation. In any event, in what follows I will confine my attention to akratic offenders whose temptation to act wrongfully is not so strong to warrant a partial excuse. I do not believe the defendants I have in mind are exceptionally unusual: many individuals are aware their acts are wrongful, could desist with minimal effort, but decide to offend anyway. I take Sabine to be an example.

Notice that exculpation would be deserved if the wrongdoer made a material mistake of *fact*. We would not hold persons *fully* responsible (the adverb is important) for wrongful conduct unless their actions would be wrongful on the facts as they believe them to be. Suppose that Juan routinely turns on the light to illuminate his office when he arrives at work in the morning. Unbeknownst to him, a terrorist has secretly rewired the mechanism so that a bomb will detonate in the building when the switch is flipped, causing the deaths of innocent victims. In other words, Juan does not know the following factual proposition

p1: Throwing this switch will kill innocent people.

Suppose further, in case the additional information is relevant to our judgment, that no evidence of this plot is detectable to Juan or even to expert electricians who examine the outside of the mechanism. When he enters and turns on the light, an explosion produces the deadly result. Does Juan merit *any* blame whatever for causing

[30] Stephen P. Garvey: "Dealing with Wayward Desire," 3 *Criminal Law and Philosophy* 1 (2009).
[31] Stephen J. Morse: "Diminished Rationality, Diminished Responsibility," 1 *Ohio State Journal of Criminal Law* 298 (2003).

death? Of course not. I hope the explanation is obvious. Although p1 is a decisive moral reason not to Φ (viz., to throw the switch), it could not have played a role in Juan's practical reasoning. Subject to an important qualification I mention below, no rational person can be faulted for failing to respond to a reason he is unaware applies to his conduct. Juan's practical reasoning or reason-responsiveness is not the least bit defective when he is unresponsive to a factual proposition he does not have the slightest reason to believe to be true.

Some philosophers would object that Juan's case is easy not because the harm he causes is *unforeseen*, but rather because the harm he causes is *unforeseeable*. I have stipulated that a reasonable person in Juan's circumstances would have no inkling the switch had been altered. But suppose we relax this stipulation so that a reasonable person in his situation *would* have foreseen the explosion; the rewiring is clumsy, and Juan himself would have noticed it had he been more attentive. On this revised stipulation, a number of commentators would conclude that Juan becomes responsible. The reason would now be *available* to him, and I used this term in my earlier description of the capacity needed for responsibility. But legal philosophers should know better than to be persuaded. Even if they would hold a person to be blameworthy for foreseeable but unforeseen harms, they would not do so *to the same extent* as a person who actually foresees them. The former standard involves negligence whereas the latter involves knowledge, and no respectable criminal theorist equates these two culpable states. Even if Juan is somewhat blameworthy for foreseeable (that is, negligent) harms, he clearly is not *as* blameworthy as if he had actually foreseen (that is, known) them. The controversial issue of whether a wrongdoer is blameworthy *at all* for his negligence is sufficiently complex to warrant a separate (but unfortunately inconclusive) treatment in Chapter 4(D). What does *not* require an extended defense, however, is the judgment that negligent actors are less culpable than those who foresee those very harms.

If this account is correct thus far, the pressing matter for my inquiry is whether a different standard of assessment should be invoked when persons make mistakes about the *moral* rather than about the *factual* status of their conduct. To illustrate how potentially radical my position seems to be, I now introduce a second (thankfully unusual) agent: Carlos, an otherwise identically situated person who is *not* mistaken about p1; he is aware the mechanism has been altered and knows innocent people will be killed if he throws the switch. Instead, Carlos is mistaken about the following moral proposition

p2: Killing innocent people is wrong.

Clearly, p2 is an overwhelmingly powerful moral reason not to Φ. As with p1 in the case of Juan, however, p2 could not enter into Carlos's rational deliberations about what to do. If Carlos does not believe p2, he has no more moral reason (from his internal point of view) not to Φ than Juan, who does not believe p1. Subject to a very important qualification I mention below, the rational deliberation of agents such as Carlos is not defective when their reasoning involves only those propositions they believe to be true. According to the theory of responsibility I favor, neither Juan nor Carlos merits any blame for conduct they perform in complete ignorance of propositions that play no role in their rational calculations. The same explanation that shows why Juan is not blameworthy for failing to be responsive to a factual proposition of which he is unaware applies with equal force to show why Carlos is not blameworthy for failing to be responsive to a moral proposition of which he is unaware. Mistakes of fact and mistakes of morality have the very same effect on practical reasoning and a theory of responsibility that is constructed upon it.

Juan and Carlos lack blame for Φ because their deliberation or practical reasoning is unassailable from the standpoint of internal rationality. The same cannot be said of Sabine. The difference between the examples is clear: Sabine, unlike Juan or Carlos, exhibits a clear deficiency in rational deliberation, that is, in her internal response to moral reasons. Gideon Yaffe uses the term *corruption* to describe the deficiency in practical reasoning that renders wrongdoers responsible. Although I have no quarrel with this term and occasionally borrow it, my account of corrupt deliberation is unlike his. According to the conception I believe is most relevant to moral blameworthiness, deliberation is corrupt when an agent (such as Sabine) responds incorrectly to the balance of moral reasons *according to her own lights*. Of course, philosophers have distinguished numerous conceptions of rationality. Many of these conceptions are wholly objective or externalist; rationality consists in responding to whatever reasons actually exist. Why, then, should the standard of assessment be subjective or internalist when we make judgments of responsibility? Clearly, this part of my theory is the most controversial to date. Neil Levy defends this requirement as follows: "It is only reasonable to demand that someone perform an action if performing that action is something they can do rationally; that is, by means of a reasoning procedure that operates over their beliefs and desires. But what agents can do rationally in this sense is a function of their internalist reasons."[32] Consider the contrary view—the (absurd) claim that would hold both Juan and Carlos to be blameworthy because they fail to act as they have most reason to do from an externalist perspective, that is, from the vantage point of the reasons they objectively have, despite being unaware of them. Levy continues:

Suppose that there is a divergence between internalist and externalist reasons: what I have most reason to do, externalistically, is not something that I take myself to have any reason at all to do. In that case, if I do what I have most (externalist) reason to do, I do so not as a result of weighing reasons or any other reasoning procedure. I do so by chance, or through a glitch in my agency, or what have you.[33]

Thus I believe judgments of moral responsibility should require an *internal* assessment of the reason-responsiveness of agents, that is, should proceed from the subjective perspective of the agents themselves. Internalism or subjectivism about reason-responsiveness is the applicable standard of responsibility even though assessments of the reasons that make conduct wrongful proceed externally, according to the facts that govern the situation. Despite my contention that all three agents perform wrongful actions, Sabine is blameworthy but Juan and Carlos are not, because only she acts irrationally in the relevant sense by exhibiting a defect or corruption in her response to moral reasons. Only Sabine performs an action that is akratic, that is, contrary to her own all-things-considered judgment about what would be best for her to do morally.

As I have indicated, no contemporary penal theorist openly embraces a subjectivist theory of rationality to undermine conventional wisdom about *ignorantia juris*. But is this account of blameworthiness completely alien to philosophers of criminal law? It is hard to be sure. I have scolded legal philosophers for failing to develop a theory of the foundations of criminal responsibility. Of course, penal theorists have not been completely silent about this matter. They overwhelmingly

---

[32] Levy: *Op.cit.* Note 6, p.128.
[33] *Id.*

favor a *choice* theory of culpability. It has never been entirely clear what a "choice theory" is supposed to involve; it is typically invoked in opposition to a *character* theory. In any event, no philosopher of criminal law, as far as I am aware, has worked out the details of a choice theory, even though they almost uniformly pledge their allegiance to it.[34] My reason-responsive account certainly qualifies as a choice theory, as defendants would not be blameworthy unless they chose to do wrong. For all I know, my account *just is* a choice theory. Juan, after all, *chooses* to throw the switch that detonates the bomb, but no one would hold him responsible for the devastation. Responsibility is withheld because he does not choose to kill and act wrongfully *under that description*. Carlos, of course, *does* choose to kill. But it would be strained to say he chooses to commit the *moral wrong* of killing. Choice theorists owe us an account of the *content* of choice, of what must be known by the agent before his choice renders him blameworthy. Here is where a reason-responsive theory comes to the rescue. Carlos did not choose to commit a wrong under that description. He is not morally blameworthy because the moral reason not to kill (p2) could play no more of a role in his rational deliberation than the factual reason (p1) could play for Juan.

I have said that Juan is not blameworthy for performing Φ because the reason not to do so could not have entered into his rational calculation. Many of those who share my conclusion about Juan's lack of blame will exculpate him through a different route: they will deny his act Φ is wrongful in the first place. Their motivation is easy to appreciate. According to a prominent train of thought, the function of morality is to guide conduct. Moral wrongs must have whatever content enables them to play this role. As no one could be guided by a moral norm against causing a deadly explosion he has no inkling will occur when he flips a switch, philosophers who subscribe to this school of thought will conclude that Juan's act is not wrongful, even though it causes many deaths. If these philosophers are correct, questions about Juan's blameworthiness would not arise, because I have conceded that such issues are presented only when agents act wrongfully. I cannot deny that I feel the attraction of this position. Perfectly coherent accounts of wrongfulness and permissibility can be derived from the

---

[34] For an account of the relevance of choice, see T.M. Scanlon: "The Significance of Choice," Lecture I in *The Tanner Lectures on Human Values* (Salt Lake City: University of Utah Press, 1988), p.151.

desideratum of guiding conduct. We all sympathize with the distraught Juan, who is devastated when he learns he has been used as a dupe in the terrorist plot. Still, I hold our sympathy is better expressed by withholding responsibility than by denying his conduct is wrongful. In what follows, I will proceed as though my initial description is correct. In other words, I will suppose that Juan's conduct Φ is wrongful so that meaningful questions about his blameworthiness can be raised (and subsequently denied). Even so, I admit that the division I have tried to preserve—between conceptions of wrongfulness and theories of responsibility for wrongful conduct—is easily eroded.

In any event, many moral philosophers disagree with my externalist or objective account of how wrongs should be conceptualized. I hope my mixture of objectivism about wrongdoing with subjectivism about blameworthiness is not toxic. I cite only one advantage of this combination. Our judgments of blameworthiness can be sensitive to empirical findings in social psychology if they are dependent on the reasons grasped by individuals themselves. We rational agents can only respond to reasons we recognize, and the causal factors that promote or inhibit this recognition thus play a role in assessing our responsibility. I have simply stipulated that none of these factors is present in Sabine's case, but we should be attentive to whether examples in the real world conform to this stipulation. Countless studies support *situationalism,* that is, the idea that our tendency to recognize moral reasons fluctuates wildly with alterations in the environments in which we are placed.[35] These studies also demonstrate an enormous amount of variation from one individual to another. Quite often we are not conscious of the effect these factors cause, despite their demonstrable influence on us. I do not try to summarize this rapidly growing body of empirical literature. But suppose it is true, for example, that a high volume of ambient noise in an environment plays a nontrivial role in our ability to detect morally relevant considerations. If so, a subjective theory of reason-responsiveness is well equipped to take this empirical finding into account in assessing whether and to what extent persons are blameworthy—even though such findings are immaterial to wrongfulness itself. Theories that deem these environmental variables to be irrelevant to our moral responsibility are in danger of casting the net of blame too widely.

---

[35] John Doris: *Talking to Our Selves: Reflection, Ignorance, and Agency* (Oxford: Oxford University Press, 2015).

Of course, I am not the first philosopher to argue that the class of wrongful actions for which persons are fully morally responsible consists of those that are contrary to the agent's own subjective judgment of what is best. Most notably, variations of this position have been elegantly defended by Gideon Rosen[36] and Michael Zimmerman,[37] and I readily acknowledge my enormous debt to each of them.[38] Even though the similarities between our respective positions are far more significant than the dissimilarities, I want to highlight two points of disagreement.[39] In one respect, my position is even more radical than theirs. Both Rosen and Zimmerman develop an account that purports to hold persons blameworthy for Φ pursuant to what moral philosophers typically call *tracing* strategies. That is, they contend that a person can be responsible even for wrongful actions committed in factual or moral ignorance if her blameworthiness can somehow be traced to a prior ("benighting") act for which she was *not* ignorant. If a tracing strategy can be successfully deployed in a given case, both Rosen and Zimmerman would hold the agent culpable *for* his ignorance, and they contend that only non-culpable ignorance exculpates. I tend to reject tracing strategies insofar as they purport to hold wrongdoers fully responsible for Φ, and thus conclude that wrongdoers merit exculpation even when Rosen or Zimmerman would deem them to be culpable for their ignorance. My basis for skepticism about tracing strategies is sufficiently important and complex to merit its own treatment in Part C of this chapter.

In another very important respect, however, my position is *less* radical than that of either Rosen or Zimmerman. *Far* less radical, in fact. The conclusions I have defended admit of a crucial qualification: I hold a class of persons to be *somewhat* blameworthy even when they do *not* know they are acting contrary to the balance of moral reasons. I have sometimes denied that a given agent is *fully* responsible, or eligible for the *full* amount of punishment that may be imposed for his wrongful act Φ, and this adverb hints at the important qualification

---

[36] Gideon Rosen: "Culpability and Ignorance," 103 *Proceedings of the Aristotelian Society* 61, 83 (2003).

[37] Michael Zimmerman: *Living with Uncertainty: The Moral Significance of Ignorance* (Cambridge: Cambridge University Press, 2008).

[38] Many of the philosophers on whom I rely disagree with each other. Zimmerman has expressed these differences in a manner that sounds far from trivial. See Michael Zimmerman: "Review of Levy," −10 *Criminal Law and Philosophy* (forthcoming, 2016).

[39] I discuss other points of disagreement in Chapter 4(A).

of my position. This important qualification is best introduced in the context of mistake of fact. Return again to Juan, the unsuspecting employee who throws the switch that has been rewired to kill innocent victims. I am sure no one will blame Juan to any extent for what I have stipulated to be an objectively wrongful act. Nonetheless, we should not be quick to conclude that a person cannot bear *any* quantum of blame unless he actually believes the switch has been altered. A simple modification of the original example should suffice to show that a person may be somewhat responsible despite not believing p1, viz., the act will kill innocent people. Suppose Juan★ (distinguished from the original Juan by an asterisk) is aware that terrorists are lurking in the vicinity and have rigged a number of devices to dupe law-abiding citizens into causing death. He attaches, say, a 10 percent probability to the proposition that the switch has been rewired and will cause an explosion when it is flipped. His degree of credence in p1 is fairly low; we would not say he *believes* it to be true. Nonetheless, given his suspicion that his act might cause serious harm, Juan★ bears some degree of blame for throwing the switch and killing the victims.

I do not venture a detailed opinion about what Juan★ should *do* to alleviate his suspicion in the modified example. A number of contemporary moral philosophers have examined at length how persons should behave when they are uncertain of important factual or moral properties of the alternative courses of action available to them.[40] Clearly, they should take precautions when the stakes are sufficiently high.[41] But this problem in first-order morality is not my immediate concern. I ask only what quantum of blame a person merits when she does *not* do whatever she ought to have done and acts wrongfully in the kind of circumstance I have described. A defendant who causes harm after failing to take precautions does not deserve the same quantum of blame as someone who knows that very harm will occur. In the original example, Juan lacks *any* degree of responsibility for his conduct. In the modified example, Juan★ deserves *some* degree of blame for acting wrongfully by taking a risk that turns out to cause a massive harm. Criminal law theorists will have no difficulty invoking familiar culpability terms to describe these two judgments. In the original

---

[40] For example, see Andrew Sepielli: "What to Do When You Don't Know What to Do When You Don't Know What to Do . . . ," 48 *Nous* 521 (2013); and Holly M. Smith: "The Subjective Moral Duty to Inform Oneself before Acting," 125 *Ethics* 1 (2014).

[41] See Alexander A. Guerrero: "Don't Know, Don't Kill: Moral Ignorance, Culpability, and Caution," 136 *Philosophical Studies* 59 (2007).

case, Juan is not even negligent for causing the explosion; a reasonable person in his situation would have acted similarly. Only the application of a standard of strict liability would subject him to punishment, and the use of this standard in the context of homicide would be a normative abomination.[42] In the modified example, however, Juan★ is reckless. He consciously disregards a substantial and unjustifiable risk his act will cause death. Responsibility is greater when a person knowingly acts contrary to the balance of moral reasons than when he suspects he might be acting contrary to the balance of moral reasons. Criminal theorists will readily agree that Juan★ is reckless and thus culpable in the modified example, but less so than if he had actually known the switch would activate the bomb. In the context of matters of fact, nearly all philosophers of criminal law concur that at least two different culpable states (viz., knowledge and recklessness) must be distinguished to adequately capture the possible quantum of blame (if any) persons may deserve for their wrongful behavior.[43]

These same judgments should be replicated in the domain of mistake of morality. Return to Carlos, the unusual agent who does not believe p2: killing innocent people is wrong. I have said he is not morally blameworthy for doing what he believes he lacks a moral reason not to do. Suppose, however, that Carlos★ *suspects* p2 to be true. More precisely, he is aware of the substantial and unjustifiable risk that killing human beings is wrongful. He attaches, say, a 10 percent probability to the proposition that he would commit a wrongful act by throwing the switch he knows will cause an explosion. In this modified example, Carlos★, like Juan★, is *reckless.* His recklessness derives from his suspicion about a matter of morality rather than about a matter of fact. On this supposition, Carlos★, like Carlos, acts wrongfully by throwing the switch. But Carlos★, unlike Carlos but like Juan★, bears some degree of blame for doing so. None of these characters, however, is as blameworthy as A, who makes no mistake at all about Φ.

Thus a defendant B who is ignorant of the morality that underlies the law but is aware his conduct Φ creates a substantial risk of being wrongful is responsible and subject to punishment for her act, albeit to

---

[42] Unfortunately, strict-liability homicide statutes are hardly unknown. See the example criticized in Douglas Husak: "Strict Liability, Justice, and Proportionality," in Douglas Husak, ed.: *The Philosophy of Criminal Law* (Oxford: Oxford University Press, 2010), p.152.

[43] I say *nearly* all philosophers contrast knowledge from recklessness because some hold the former to be a special case of the latter. See Larry Alexander and Kimberly Kessler Ferzan with Stephen Morse: *Crime and Culpability* (Cambridge: Cambridge University Press, 2009).

a lesser extent than A, who knows his conduct violates L. How *much* less punishment should be inflicted on defendants who are reckless about whether their conduct is wrongful, relative to defendants who know their conduct is wrongful? Judgments of relative proportionality are notoriously problematic in any context. Still, codes have ample experience dealing with similar problems; a clue might be gained from the way jurisdictions grade the seriousness of inchoate offenses such as attempt, solicitation, or conspiracy. Perhaps the severity of the sentence deserved by the reckless defendant should be a specified fraction of the punishment to which the fully culpable, knowledgeable defendant is subject: one-half, for example. If this proposal is adopted, Jacob, who is reckless about his wrongful disposal of batteries, would be eligible for half of the sentence imposed on a camper who commits the same offense knowingly.

But B is subject to punishment for her mistake of law only when Φ actually *does* violate L or the morality that underlies it. What about the situation in which Φ turns out *not* to violate L? Jacob, our confused camper, might fortunately be correct that he commits no wrong by throwing his batteries into the garbage. Quite a few philosophers would say that the difference between his culpability when he happens to be correct and his culpability when he happens to be incorrect is simply a matter of luck, and luck should not infect our judgments about his degree of blameworthiness. The general topic of moral luck has spawned an enormous literature, and (once again) is well beyond the scope of this book.[44] But whatever position we adopt about the phenomenon of luck, I see little ground to punish the legally ignorant B *for* L when his conduct Φ happens not to breach it.[45] As far as I can see, the only basis for imposing liability on B when he happens to guess correctly that his conduct is not a wrongful violation of L would require the enactment of an analog of the offense of reckless endangerment in positive law.[46] Thus B would bear some blame and liability *whenever* she believes her conduct creates a substantial and unjustifiable risk of being wrongful. If her fears materialize and Φ *is* wrongful and *does* breach L, she is liable for recklessly breaching

---

[44] See, for example, Alfred R. Mele: *Free Will and Luck* (Oxford: Oxford University Press, 2006).

[45] Nor should B be liable for an *attempt* to breach L, although attempts are also beyond my purview See R.A. Duff: *Criminal Attempts* (Oxford: Clarendon Press, 1996); and Gideon Yaffe: *Attempts* (Oxford: Oxford University Press, 2010).

[46] *Model Penal Code* §211.2.

L. If her fears do *not* materialize and Φ is *not* wrongful and does *not* breach L, she would be liable for a different offense: a crime akin to reckless endangerment in existing law, committed when a defendant is reckless but causes no harm. I tend not to favor the creation of this new offense, probably because of my minimalist sympathies about the scope and limits of the substantive criminal law.[47] But I have no decisive objection to enacting such a statute: an analog of reckless endangerment for defendants who make mistakes about the morality that underlies law, punishing them whenever they believe their conduct creates a substantial and unjustifiable risk of causing harm.

Let me summarize my position thus far. Applications of the culpability hierarchy in the *Model Penal Code* would hold a defendant to be fully responsible for Φ if he knows it will detonate the bomb, responsible to a lesser extent if he is reckless about whether Φ will do so, probably not responsible if he is negligent about whether Φ will do so, and clearly not responsible at all if he is not even negligent about whether Φ will detonate the bomb. I propose to treat mistakes of fact and law *symmetrically* by replicating the same normative structure in each context. That is, a somewhat oversimplified statement of my theory of ignorance of law is that it applies to mistakes of law the same culpability framework that is familiar in the domain of mistakes of fact. I say this statement is oversimplified because the symmetry I defend is only presumptive—much like the presumption that the penal law should conform to morality. I will spend a good deal of time in Chapter 5 discussing whether this presumption is overcome when we determine how my theory of legal ignorance should be codified in the real world of positive law. Still, the objective to which we should aspire—from which retreats require a special justification—would produce a perfect symmetry. Thus it would hold a defendant fully culpable for Φ if she knows her act is contrary to the balance of moral reasons and is wrong, culpable to a lesser extent if she is reckless about whether Φ is contrary to the balance of moral reasons and is wrong, and not culpable at all if she is not even negligent about whether Φ is contrary to the balance of moral reasons and is wrong. Even though it may be controversial, I regard my proposal to apply the same normative framework about the exculpatory significance of ignorance of fact to judgments about the exculpatory significance of

---

[47] See Douglas Husak: *Overcriminalization* (Oxford: Oxford University Press, 2008).

ignorance of law to be relatively straightforward. Criminal theorists have long wrestled with the distinctions between these culpable states in the context of mistakes of fact, and can draw from their accumulated wisdom to reach insights about mistakes of law.

The usefulness of these distinctions is not merely the product of a fertile philosophical imagination. Recklessness with respect to the wrongfulness of conduct is not merely a *possible* culpable state; it has become remarkably common in cases we are likely to encounter every day. As I repeatedly emphasize, the complete absence of suspicion that a *malum in se* is wrongful is exceptionally rare among sane adults. But a suspicion that falls short of knowledge is not the least bit unusual when a *malum prohibitum* is involved. Jacob, the camper who throws away batteries that should be recycled, offers a realistic example of someone who is reckless about the wrongfulness of his act. If we treat mistakes of fact and mistakes of law symmetrically, the quantum of blame Jacob deserves is somewhere between the amount deserved by the wrongdoer who *knows* his batteries should be recycled and the amount deserved by the wrongdoer who is not even cognizant of the risk that his batteries should be recycled. Current doctrine about *ignorantia juris* is woefully deficient because it is all-or-nothing, and does not contain the resources to allow us to adequately represent Jacob's degree of blame. A major advantage of my theory that treats mistakes of fact and law symmetrically is that it allows us to do so.

The culpability hierarchy of the Code as it applies to mistakes of fact is perfectly suited to capture distinctions that should be applied to mistakes of law. But criminal theorists will notice that I have achieved symmetry by oversimplifying the culpability structure of the Code. In the domain of fact, a defendant who *intends* or has the *purpose* to violate L is often regarded as more blameworthy than one who merely *knows* he is doing so. If fact and law are treated symmetrically, shouldn't the contrast between intention and knowledge play the same role in a theory of ignorance of law that it plays in a theory of ignorance of fact? If so, a defendant who intends to break L would be more culpable than a defendant who knows (or is reckless about whether) he is breaking L. Admittedly, some criminal theorists and moral philosophers have challenged the moral significance of the contrast between intention and knowledge. Is it really true that a defendant who acts intentionally with respect to the facts that comprise a wrongful action is more blameworthy than a defendant who acts knowingly, that is, is practically certain that these facts obtain? I am inclined to answer this question affirmatively, but my present point is different. Although the debate about the moral significance of the contrast between intention and foresight is crucial for any number of controversies about matters of fact—especially in the domain of inchoate crimes such as attempt and solicitation—it appears to have little practical application to mistakes of law or morality. Cases in which wrongdoers *intend* or have the *purpose* to commit a wrongful act qua wrong as opposed to merely *knowing* they are committing that wrongful act will be fairly rare. Perhaps the membership of an initiate into a criminal gang, for example, depends on whether he intends to commit an act that is wrong. Everyone has encountered defiant children who are determined to test the bounds of parental authority. And one can imagine a rapist who would be uninterested in sexual penetration if he thought his victim consented. These individuals would have no motivation to perform their acts unless they were wrongful. These kinds of case, however, do not seem to me to mark a very important difference in blameworthiness relative to wrongful acts performed knowingly.[48] If my judgment about this matter is incorrect, the culpability structure I invoke can easily be supplemented to include purpose or intention. But if I am correct, the culpable states that are needed with respect to ignorance of law can be limited to three: knowledge, recklessness, and negligence. Or perhaps this list can be pared to two: knowledge and recklessness. Negligence is a highly controversial mode of culpability in the domain of matters of fact, and we should not be surprised to discover that controversies about it resurface in the domain of matters of law. As I have indicated, the issue of whether persons are blameworthy when they make negligent mistakes of law is sufficiently complex to merit its own (unfortunately inconclusive) treatment in Chapter 4(D).

I now return to the underlying philosophical theory of responsibility that exculpates wrongdoers who are morally ignorant. We can understand the strengths and weaknesses of a subjectivist reason-responsive theory more easily by evaluating its main rival. Many moral philosophers who agree that persons are responsible for much of what they do offer competitive criteria of when this is so, and some of the plausible options have different implications for the blameworthiness of persons who are unaware their acts are wrong. In what follows, I provide a brief description of the single most popular alternative,

---

[48] But see the contrast between attacks and endangerments described in R.A. Duff: *Answering for Crime* (Oxford: Hart, 2007).

ignoring the vast array of novel theories that have recently been defended.[49]

The most serious rival to the conception of responsibility I have defended involves a family of views that might be called *quality of will* theories. These views do not locate moral responsibility in an agent's defective or corrupt practical reasoning—at least as I understand these terms. Nor do they require choice or control. Instead, they purport to ground responsibility for a wrongful action Φ in the *will*: agents are blameworthy when their acts proceed from a will that is morally objectionable. Expressed somewhat differently, an individual is responsible when her action expresses negative attitudes that reveal something bad about her as a person. Countless variations and permutations of quality of will theories have been proposed,[50] but a sustained evaluation of this family of views is, yet again, well beyond my scope. Suffice it to say that their central differences consist in the accounts they offer of the exact factors that make the quality of a given will objectionable.[51] The candidates mentioned most often include malice, contempt, hostility, indifference, lack of consideration for the welfare and interest of others, and even disrespect for law.

I quickly cite just three representative examples of a quality of will theory.[52] Nomy Arpaly holds an action to be blameworthy when it results from an agent caring too little about what is morally significant—which is not a matter of de dicto caring about morality (under that description) but rather a matter of de re caring about what is actually significant morally.[53] As the fact that my action will cause others to suffer is morally significant, for example, I can be blameworthy for acts that have this effect, even if I (like Carlos) do not believe that suffering matters. Holly Smith contends that persons are

---

[49] In particular, I ignore what might be called *hierarchical, structuralist,* or *mesh* accounts. The most well-known representatives of this school of thought are inspired by Harry Frankfurt: "Freedom of the Will and the Concept of a Person," 68 *Journal of Philosophy* 5 (1971).

[50] For some details, see Michael McKenna: *Conversation and Responsibility* (Oxford: Oxford University Press, 2012).

[51] For example, we might contrast quality of character, quality of judgment, and quality of regard. See David Shoemaker: "Qualities of Will," 30 *Social Philosophy and Policy* 95 (2013).

[52] For additional examples, see T.M. Scanlon: *What We Owe to Each Other* (Cambridge: Harvard University Press, 1998); Angela Smith: "Control, Responsibility, and Moral Assessment," 138 *Philosophical Studies* 367 (2008); and Pamela Hieronymi: "Reflection and Responsibility," 42 *Philosophy and Public Affairs* 3 (2014).

[53] Nomy Arpaly: *Unprincipled Virtue: An Inquiry into Moral Agency* (Oxford: Oxford University Press, 2003), chapter 3.

responsible for a wrongful act when they have a morally objectionable configuration of desires and aversions that give rise to it.[54] Elizabeth Harman contends we can be responsible for acts that are a product of false moral beliefs because we have obligations to believe many of the moral truths that govern our actions. She holds mistaken beliefs to be "blameworthy if they involve inadequately caring about what is morally significant."[55] Obviously, each of these diverse views confronts a number of challenges I make no effort to press.

Analogs to quality of will theories have been proposed by legal philosophers as well. Peter Westen, for example, correctly contends that the fate of wrongdoers who are ignorant of law depends on whether they satisfy whatever conditions are contained in the correct theory of responsibility. When wrongdoers are ignorant of the statute they break, Westen holds that they ought to be excused unless they were "motivated by attitudes of malice, disinterest, callousness, disregard or neglect toward the legitimate interests of others that the act of punishing them invariably ascribes to them."[56] But why is *this* the correct theory of responsibility by reference to which an excuse should be granted or withheld?[57] What subjective reason do *I* have not to be disinterested in others if I do not believe their welfare is my legitimate concern? Of course, quality of will theorists will reply that I *need* no such subjective reason in order to be blameworthy. But why?

The lure of these accounts should be evident: quality of will theorists have a basis for holding Carlos responsible without simultaneously blaming Juan. No one would say that Juan manifests disregard for the welfare of others when he flips a switch he has no idea has been rewired to kill innocent victims. But Carlos manifests extreme indifference for the lives of others, even if he is unaware that doing so is wrong. Hence these accounts provide a clear basis for denying the presumptive symmetry I favor and distinguishing the exculpatory significance of *fact* from that of *law* or the morality that underlies it. I am convinced that the majority of philosophers of criminal law who deny any degree of exculpation to offenders who are ignorant of morality presuppose a quality of will theory of responsibility—even if they do not recognize

---

[54] Holly Smith: "Dual-Process Theory and Moral Responsibility," in Clarke et al., eds.: *Op.cit.* Note 1, p.175.

[55] Elizabeth Harman: "Does Moral Ignorance Exculpate?" 24 *Ratio* 443 (2011).

[56] Peter Westen: "Two Rules of Legality in Criminal Law," 26 *Law and Philosophy* 229, 262 (2007).

[57] See Peter Westen: "An Attitudinal Theory of Excuse," 25 *Law and Philosophy* 289 (2006).

their commitment explicitly. I have already provided examples of legal philosophers who make such commitments,[58] and further illustrations will follow.[59]

Philosophers who hold a quality of will theory of responsibility will agree that Sabine's example is easy, but will tell a different story about why this is so. What makes her blameworthy for her theft of the bicycle, they will insist, is that her behavior manifests whatever quality of will grounds her responsibility. Because Sabine elevates her own interests over those of others, her act exhibits the very attitudes that any quality of will theorist would cite as the locus of blameworthiness. As I have said, many of these theories deny that her beliefs about morality are relevant to her responsibility. According to these accounts, Sabine exhibits an objectionable quality of will regardless of what she happens to think about the morality of theft. Philosophers who hold such theories of blameworthiness sometimes express bafflement (or even outrage) about criteria that take seriously the possibility that ignorance of wrongfulness might exculpate as widely as my own account allows.

Before saying more about quality of will theories directly, it is worthwhile to point out that legal philosophers who hold such views have a difficult time preserving the doctrine of *ignorantia juris* in anything resembling its current form. The reason is that the particular negative characteristics most often mentioned that make a will objectionable—such as contempt, hostility, indifference, and disrespect for the welfare of others—are not clearly displayed when wrongdoers commit a great many penal offenses, especially those that are *mala prohibita. Perhaps* these traits are exemplified when defendants print counterfeit bills or evade their taxes. But it is a stretch to say that these traits are manifested when defendants commit money laundering or drive an unregistered vehicle. And few would allege with a straight face that Battersby's act of caring for children for more than thirty consecutive weekdays without a license exhibits *any* defective traits of will. If the foregoing cases involve wrongful acts for which defendants can be blamed and punished, we need a more illuminating account of the reprehensible traits of will they are alleged to manifest. In the absence of such an account, it would seem that quality of will theorists are also committed

---

[58] See Dan M. Kahan: "Ignorance of Law Is a Defense: But only for the Virtuous," 96 *Michigan Law Review* 127 (1997); and Alexander and Ferzan with Morse: *Op.cit.* Note 43.

[59] See Michelle Dempsey: "Book Review: Michael J. Zimmerman, *The Immorality of Punishment*," 32 *Law and Philosophy* 333 (2013).

to a massive reform of the practices of punishment in our systems of criminal justice.

Moreover, criminal theorists need to be cautious before uncritically adopting any version of a quality of will theory. If the ultimate basis of responsibility inheres in the will, and the will enjoys this status because it represents the core of who we are as persons, quality of will theories become dangerously close to those that ground responsibility in our *character*—in *who* we are. My skepticism notwithstanding, I do not insist that quality of will theorists cannot possibly succeed in explaining why they do *not* locate responsibility in our character. Unless they are able to do so, however, they are bound to encounter stiff resistance from criminal theorists, many of whom go to great lengths to explain that responsibility attaches to a particular choice made by a defendant rather than to the character of the defendant who makes it.[60] My reason-responsive theory preserves the significance of choice—the choice to do wrong. Quality of will theorists attach less significance to choice. After all, no one chooses the quality of her will or whether it manifests objectionable features when wrongs are perpetrated. In addition, do we really gain deep insights into the will of a person by directing our focus on a single action she performs—as the penal law is prone to do? If our ultimate concern is with the will, why afford such importance to a particular crime? These questions should give pause to penal theorists who are tempted to embrace a quality of will theory. Most philosophers of criminal law explicitly repudiate character theories, and it would be troublesome indeed if the kind of theory they reject could not be distinguished from the kind of theory they accept.[61]

These reservations notwithstanding, if a quality of will theory really provides a better foundation of moral responsibility, the case for affording broad exculpatory significance to ignorance of law all but evaporates. Or does it? Although I initially presented quality of will theories as *rivals* to a reason-responsive account, they need not be construed as competitors. They might be combined (conjunctively or disjunctively) in various ways, suggesting different bases for holding wrongdoers to be blameworthy. Admittedly, several quality of will

---

[60] Alternatively, criminal theorists could point to the many places in which the penal law already seems to attach significance to who we are rather than (or in addition) to what we do.

[61] For a discussion of character theories and how they might be improved, see Victor Tadros: *Criminal Responsibility* (Oxford: Oxford University Press, 2005).

theorists expressly advertise their ability to resist proposals to exculpate wrongdoers who act in moral ignorance. I suspect that the difficulty of demonstrating why ignorance of morality does *not* exculpate has boosted the popularity of these theories; philosophers frequently appeal to quality of will accounts in the course of their efforts to refute views they regard as highly counterintuitive, such as those of Zimmerman and Rosen. They are bound to do so when they respond to my own theory. But I am unmoved. A number of these theorists agree that the agent's beliefs about the wrongfulness of her conduct *should* be included among those factors from which the quality of her will is inferred. To decide whether they are correct, we need to begin by recalling that our basic question (Q) is essentially comparative. Consider two bicycle thieves; the first but not the second is aware theft is wrongful. Clearly, the wills of these individuals *can* be distinguished: their actions express something significantly different about who they are as persons. Sabine, the first thief, manifests a willingness to act contrary to what she knows to be the demands of morality. But the thief who is unaware of the wrongfulness of his act manifests nothing remotely comparable. On what ground should this difference be regarded as wholly immaterial to an assessment of the quality of their respective wills? On the level of intuition—in which I admit to having little confidence—the will of the first thief is far more reprehensible. If I am correct, quality of will theorists who reject my invitation to differentiate between the responsibility of A and B need to establish not only that the will is the locus of blameworthiness, but also that ignorance of wrongdoing is immaterial to judgments about the quality of the will. Even if we agree that Carlos is *more* blameworthy than Juan, we should not infer that Carlos is just as blameworthy as the villain who throws the switch and makes *neither* a factual mistake about p1 *nor* a moral mistake about p2. The quality of *his* will seems worst of all. If so, quality of will theorists should agree that only he deserves the *full* quantum of blame the criminal law authorizes for his offense.

Thus the two kinds of theories I introduced as competitors need not be conceptualized as rivals at all. They can be used in tandem to undermine the doctrine of *ignorantia juris*. Perhaps corrupt deliberation or a deficiency in reason-responsiveness *just is* (or at least *involves*) a defect in the will that manifests a failure to assign a proper weight to considerations recognized as moral. If so, even philosophers who hold a quality of will theory should afford quite a bit of exculpation to persons who act in ignorance of the morality that underlies law. This point requires additional emphasis, as it is among the most important issues on which my theory of ignorance of law depends. Especially when so-called *thick* moral concepts are involved, it would seem preposterous not to allow awareness of wrongdoing to count toward an assessment of the quality of will and the degree of blame the agent merits. To illustrate, imagine persons who treat others unkindly or cruelly. Surely we distinguish between cases in which the wrongdoer is *unknowingly* unkind or cruel from those in which she *knows* her behavior is unkind or cruel. We respond to persons who make unkind or cruel remarks without knowing they have done so very differently from how we respond to persons who make the same remarks while fully aware of what they are doing. Admittedly, unlike the view I favor, theories that take awareness of wrongdoing into account in assessing the quality of a will might still direct *some* amount of blame toward the individual who is completely clueless her conduct is wrongful. In the absence of further detail, it is impossible to determine *how much* of a distinction quality of will theorists should recognize between the relative blameworthiness of each wrongdoer. But even if the person is blameworthy in both instances, the amount of blame she deserves is greater in the latter than in the former case.

A final factor should be mentioned before we decide to punish ignorant wrongdoers simply because something is objectionable about their wills. Even if we believe morally mistaken persons *do* deserve a substantial amount of blame, we might have serious misgivings about actually *treating* them as they deserve. Consequences play a crucial role in such decisions.[62] If *punishment* is something close to a last resort,[63] we might decide that *moral education,* rather than blame, is the more appropriate response to wrongdoers who are morally ignorant—the response we should prefer notwithstanding the desert conferred by the quality of their wills. *Instruction,* rather than *punishment,* is the more humane and productive option for those who are mistaken about morality, even if we hold such persons to be blame*worthy.*

I have argued that the case for affording complete exculpation to persons who are ignorant of law may not depend on which of the two kinds of theory we accept. The only theories of responsibility that grant *no* exculpation to defendants who act in moral ignorance *either*

---

[62] See Douglas Husak: "Why Punish the Deserving?" in Husak: *Op.cit.* Note 42. p.393.
[63] For critical discussion, see Douglas Husak: "The Criminal Law as Last Resort," 24 *Oxford Journal of Legal Studies* 207 (2004).

construe a quality of will theory to hold beliefs about wrongdoing to be irrelevant to assessments of the will *or* invoke an altogether different ground of responsibility than I have heretofore discussed. I do not pretend to have mounted a fatal objection to the former alternative. However implausible their position may appear to me, I am aware that several prominent moral philosophers steadfastly deny that awareness of wrongdoing is material to judgments about the quality of an agent's will. I also concede that the latter alternative should be taken seriously, even though I have neglected to discuss it. As I repeatedly indicate, this topic is presently in a state of flux; new theories of responsibility appear almost weekly, and substantial refinements of old theories are ubiquitous as well. The proliferation of novel views indicates a profound philosophical dissatisfaction with existing efforts. It would be absurd to suppose the last word on this topic has been written. Even so, I conclude that we have a powerful theoretical basis to afford quite a bit of exculpation to B relative to A when both commit Φ in violation of L. We may still be uncertain about exactly *how much* exculpation should be extended. According to the view I ultimately prefer, however, persons who are totally ignorant their conduct is wrongful should typically be absolved from blame and punishment altogether.

C. Culpable Ignorance and a Duty to Inquire

My two most important claims thus far in this chapter are as follows: First, a person A is fully responsible for Φ when he knows it to be wrongful, that is, when he recognizes it to be contrary to the balance of moral reasons. Only such persons should be subject to the maximum degree of punishment the criminal law should allow for their offense. Second, a person B can be responsible for Φ to a lesser degree than A, even though she does not know it to be wrongful and contrary to the balance of reasons. My account of the degree of blame B deserves in the latter scenario borrows heavily from the positive law of recklessness in the context of mistake of fact. Thus B is responsible for Φ when she is aware that she might be acting contrary to the balance of moral reasons, that is, when she is aware she creates a substantial and unjustifiable risk she is acting contrary to the balance of reasons. Such a person is responsible, albeit to a lesser amount than A. The conjunction of these two claims might be challenged from any number of directions. One might hold that neither of the foregoing persons is responsible to any degree: even those who perform akratic actions lack responsibility. Alternatively, one might impose responsibility on the person who acts akratically while withholding it from anyone else, including the person who suspects she is acting wrongly. In my judgment, each of these challenges casts the net of responsibility too narrowly.

In this part I will critique a very different challenge—a challenge with the potential to dramatically *expand* the scope of responsibility. I propose to examine the allegation that some persons *other* than A, that is, other than those who act akratically, can be *fully* responsible and blameworthy for Φ. Like A, such persons should be subject to the maximum degree of punishment the criminal law should authorize for their offense. According to the strategy I will consider, B bears the *same* degree of responsibility as the akratic agent A when she is *culpable for her ignorance*. B may bear this amount of blame even though she need not (although she might) suspect that Φ is wrongful. The strategy I will evaluate enlarges the scope of responsibility beyond the limits I allow by holding some individuals to be fully responsible for Φ who I believe bear no responsibility for Φ whatever. In other words, it holds such persons to be responsible for Φ to the *same* degree as A, the fully responsible akratic agent. I am sure a great many philosophers will welcome this invitation to expand the scope of responsibility from the narrow parameters I impose. Indeed, quite a few *have* welcomed it. In one form or another, those who mount challenges of this form can be found as far back in history as Aristotle and Aquinas.

When is it plausible to think that a person who performs a wrongful act Φ that she does not know or even suspect to be wrongful is just as responsible *for* Φ as A, who performs Φ while aware of its wrongfulness? I place special emphasis on the *for* relation. An argument to show that a person deserves blame for breaching a law of which she is ignorant had better succeed in explaining why she becomes subject to punishment *for* the very law she breaks. The answer I propose to explore (and ultimately to criticize) is that this person bears the same degree of blameworthiness for Φ as A despite failing to recognize its wrongfulness when she is *culpable* for her failure to recognize its wrongfulness, that is, when she is responsible for *not* knowing Φ is wrongful. Henceforth I will call this culpably ignorant wrongdoer C to distinguish him both from the akratic defendant A and the ignorant defendant B (whose ignorance may be culpable but need not be). According to the strategy

I will discuss, if C is responsible for *not* understanding Φ is wrongful, he is just as blameworthy for Φ as A, who *does* appreciate its wrongfulness. When *is* someone responsible for not understanding his conduct to be wrongful? The most familiar answer to *this* question is that C is culpable for his lack of knowledge when he is blameworthy for performing or failing to perform some *earlier* act or omission Ω that he *could* and *should* have performed to which his subsequent ignorance can be traced.[64] After all, this train of thought continues, C cannot be heard to protest attributions of fault for not knowing something when he is at fault for not knowing it. And he is at fault for not knowing it if there is something Ω he could and should have done in the past that would have rectified his ignorance in the present, that is, at the moment he commits Φ. Recall that I let the symbol μ represent the *difference* in the quantum of punishment that A and C deserve for violating L. When C breaches a duty to Ω, μ is said to be equal to o. That is, when C does not discharge his duty to Ω, his failure supposedly renders him culpably ignorant and thus blameworthy to the same extent as A for Φ.

I say that those philosophers who hold persons to be blameworthy for acting in moral ignorance when they are culpable for their ignorance create the *potential* for a dramatic increase in the number of persons who merit blame. It is not at all clear, however, how frequently the ignorance of such persons is due to a prior culpable act Ω they should have performed. Philosophers who invoke these strategies divide among themselves about *how much* moral ignorance is culpable. Some purport to detect culpable ignorance nearly everywhere; others find it sparingly. This question is partly empirical. It also derives, of course, from competing normative accounts of the conditions under which ignorance is culpable.

I will spend a fair amount of time discussing terminology and setting up the position I will ultimately attack, as distinct locutions are typically employed to express the above strategy in different academic disciplines. Many *moral* philosophers tend to describe the above approach as a *tracing* strategy. In order to decide whether ignorant persons are fully blameworthy for committing a wrongful action Φ, those who invoke tracing strategies appeal to a different, prior wrongful act or omission Ω to which their ignorance about Φ can be traced. As I construe tracing strategies, they need not be reserved for cases

---

[64] This previous act Ω is helpfully called a *benighting* act by Holly Smith: "Culpable Ignorance," 92 *Philosophical Review* 543 (1983).

of ignorance; they also may be invoked to explain why, for instance, someone may be blameworthy for an act even though he could not have been expected to do otherwise at the moment he performs it. If this person placed himself in the predicament in which viable alternatives became unavailable—say, by voluntarily joining a criminal gang—he is said to be blameworthy for the subsequent wrongful act he performs because he wrongfully placed himself in that very predicament. As so construed, tracing strategies purport to show why persons should not be permitted to profit from culpably creating the conditions of their own defense.[65] But even though tracing strategies have a more general application, I will confine their scope to cases of ignorance. Thus, according to versions of the tracing strategy I will discuss here, defendants who are ignorant that Φ is wrongful are fully blameworthy for engaging in it when there is a previous wrongful act Ω to which their ignorance can be traced. More precisely, those persons who act in ignorance by breaching their duty not to commit a wrongful act Φ at t2 are *fully blameworthy* for their breach if they had a prior duty Ω at t1 that they failed to discharge to which their subsequent ignorance can be traced.

Even when confined to cases of ignorance, tracing strategies have generated a wealth of commentary. Much of this literature examines whether ignorant persons might be blameworthy for Φ even *without* a prior wrongful act Ω to which their responsibility is plausibly traced. Some philosophers present imaginative examples in which we allegedly intuit that ignorant persons are blameworthy in the absence of tracing;[66] others critique each such example either by withholding responsibility or by finding a prior wrongful act to which responsibility can be traced after all.[67] I will not discuss these alleged examples and counterexamples. Many such cases depend on the general reliability of our intuitions about whether and under what conditions persons are blameworthy—a presupposition I contested in Chapter 1(C). In any event, the controversial point I examine here is not whether ignorant persons are ever responsible *without* recourse to tracing. Instead, I will raise hurdles that must be surmounted before tracing strategies can

[65] See the Symposium on "Actio Libera in Causa," 7 *Criminal Law and Philosophy* 549–636 (2013).

[66] See, for example, Manuel Vargas: "The Trouble with Tracing," 29 *Midwest Studies in Philosophy* 269 (2005).

[67] See, for example, John Martin Fischer and Neil A. Tognazzini: "The Triumph of Tracing," 43 *Nous* 531 (2009).

succeed in establishing responsibility *for* Φ. In particular, I will examine whether tracing strategies ever succeed in showing that an ignorant person C bears the same degree of responsibility for Φ as A, who knows Φ is wrongful.

The term *tracing* has not found its way into the writings of many criminal theorists. Instead, philosophers of criminal law tend to employ a different locution to contrast culpable from non-culpable ignorance. They frequently couch their position by positing a *duty to inquire*. That is, they suppose that A and C are equally responsible for conduct Φ, which violates law L, when A knows of the violation and C does not, but C is culpable for his ignorance because he failed to discharge his duty to inquire and learn the content of L. According to this train of thought, when we have a duty to inquire but fail to discharge it, we are just as responsible for performing Φ in ignorance as if we had performed Φ fully aware of its relevant legal properties. On the other hand, defendants (if they exist) who do not have a duty to inquire about L are *non-culpable* for their ignorance. When defendants are non-culpable for their ignorance that Φ is wrongful, they are exempted from any quantum of blame in law. Obviously, alleged duties of inquiry have played a major role in scholarly commentary about *ignorantia juris*. That is, many legal philosophers contend that the supposed existence of a duty to inquire, and the corresponding contrast between culpable and non-culpable ignorance offers a major part of a solution to our basic question (Q).

Regardless of the terminology invoked to mark the contrast, an application of the distinction between culpable and non-culpable ignorance is often used to shed light on such cases as the following. Consider three individuals who engage in the same wrongful conduct Φ: the owning of slaves. Person #1 is Heather, who lives in South Carolina in 1850. Abolitionists preach against the evils of slavery and distribute pamphlets that circulate widely, which argue cogently that owning slaves is wrongful. Heather has considered these arguments and has become persuaded they are sound. But she does not want to do the hard work her slaves perform on her plantation, so she persists in her ownership despite her moral conversion. Person #2 is Hazel, who lives in the same time and place as Heather. Hazel has access to the same sources of information as Heather, but fails to pay much attention to them. Abolitionists knock on her door and preach at her church, but she blissfully ignores them and happily continues to use slaves on her plantation. Person #3 is Hernan, a character we have met before. He is now an otherwise conscientious slave-owner who lives in the Middle East in the second century B.C. The few scholars he could have consulted (including Aristotle) agree that owning slaves is morally permissible when they are conquered in war. The tiny handful of dissenters who regard slavery as immoral are widely regarded as crackpots. Although Hernan concedes that many ways of treating slaves are immoral—torture and sexual abuse, for example—he categorically denies he breaches a duty simply by owning them. How does the quantum of blame each of these individuals deserves for owning slaves differ, if at all?[68]

Heather's action exemplifies akrasia; if anyone deserves the full quantum of blame for owning slaves, she is the perfect candidate. But what about the relative blameworthiness of Hazel and Hernan? It is tempting to suppose their blameworthiness *is* different, and recourse to the concept of culpable ignorance may explain why. Although we now have no doubt about the immorality of slavery, it seems unfair to blame Hernan for lacking the moral wisdom shared by none of his contemporaries but that is feely available to us today. As his ignorance of the immorality of Φ is non-culpable, he is not blameworthy for it. Not so with Hazel. Although she differs from Heather in being ignorant of the immorality of her actions, she seemingly differs from Hernan in being culpable for her ignorance because she failed to discharge a duty to inquire that it is reasonable to suppose she had. Because she is culpable for her ignorance, many moral and legal philosophers would conclude that the quantum of blame she deserves for Φ is equal to that of Heather.

The above positions are seductive, but my own verdicts differ. I concur that Heather, the akratic slave-owner, is fully culpable for her wrongful acts; she is blameworthy regardless of how she came to know slavery is wrongful. Hernan is not culpable at all. A determination of Hazel's blameworthiness, however, is contingent on a further detail: whether she is aware of the risk she is acting wrongfully. Thus she might or might not bear any blame, depending on additional information. In either event, she is less blameworthy than Heather, despite her culpable ignorance. Notice that no previous act Ω is needed to explain any of these three judgments. All we need to do to ascertain

---

[68] Discussions of whether ancient slave-owners are blameworthy have been a staple of treatments of moral ignorance since the example was introduced by Michael Slote: "Is Virtue Possible?" 42 *Analysis* 70 (1982).

the blameworthiness of these three slave-owners is to examine their mental state at the moment they engage in Φ. I hasten to add, however, that not all cases are analogous. On a *few* occasions, those who merely suspect but do not know they are acting wrongfully *are* just as blameworthy as those who act knowingly. To oversimplify a bit, if C fails to inquire precisely because he fears what he would learn if he did, and prefers to remain ignorant about the possible wrongfulness of Φ to insulate himself from the full quantum of blame he would otherwise merit, he is as blameworthy for Φ as A. I postpone until Chapter 4(A) my discussion of these cases of *willful blindness* (or *willful ignorance*). What I critique in the remainder of this part is the general strategy that purports to show that a person C who commits a wrongful act Φ not knowing it to be wrong but who has failed to do something Ω he could and should have done—that is, discharge his duty of inquiry—is just as culpable as A, who performs Φ knowing it to be wrongful.

I hope to have offered a tolerably clear formulation of the general strategy to be discussed. In the remainder of this part, I will argue that applications of the distinction between culpable and non-culpable ignorance are not especially helpful in developing a theory of the conditions under which ignorance of law or morality has exculpatory significance. I will contend that five distinct conditions must be satisfied before A and C are equally responsible for their wrongful act Φ, and that these conditions are almost never met. First, C must *have* a duty of inquiry. But no *general* duty to inquire exists, regardless of whether p—the proposition of which she is ignorant—involves a law or a fact. Second, if such a duty exists, C must be aware of it. Otherwise, it is question-begging to invoke this duty to show that C is culpable for the subsequent act he does not know to be wrong. Third, discharging this duty must rectify C's ignorance that his conduct is wrongful. But the content of this alleged duty is very hard to identify in any detail; when its content is specified adequately, C's ignorance may not be rectified by discharging it. Fourth, the analysis that purports to show that culpable ignorance renders persons fully blameworthy for what they would have known had they discharged their duty of inquiry is vulnerable to counterexamples. If C is just as blameworthy as A, his case cannot fall under these counterexamples. Finally and perhaps most important, I will argue that even if the previous four reservations misfire, those who breach a duty to inquire rarely if ever are *equal* in blameworthiness to those who commit the same wrongful act knowingly.

First, I contend that no account of culpable ignorance that depends on a duty of inquiry is likely to be helpful in answering my basic question (Q) for the simple reason that no general, stand-alone duty to inquire exists. Let us examine further the nature of this alleged duty Ω. Is it supposed to be a moral duty, a legal duty, or both? Neither alternative is promising. No person has a general moral or legal duty to become more knowledgeable about the content of morality or law. If such a duty were to be countenanced, persons would commit a moral or legal wrong merely by failing to inform themselves of their moral or legal duties—quite apart from how their ignorance affects their subsequent conduct. Although moral philosophers notoriously disagree about what duties we have, we rarely hear them allege that ignorance of these matters is wrongful per se. Does anyone think, for example, it is wrongful simply to be uninformed about the law governing battery disposal? Such a duty is posited only when theorists struggle to explain why someone might be blameworthy for his failure to discharge a *different* duty—a duty involving Φ, that is, to properly recycle the batteries. In almost no other context is moral or legal ignorance *itself* condemned as a dereliction of duty.

If a general duty to learn our moral and legal duties were to exist, each and every one of us—including the most sophisticated academic philosophers as well as the most experienced practitioners and teachers of criminal law—would breach it routinely. Any candid philosopher would admit she is unaware of many of her duties, despite having spent her entire professional career in the study of moral theory. Ethics is hard![69] The parallel point about law is even more apparent. Even the most learned professor of criminal law would concede he is aware of only a tiny fraction of the enormous number of penal laws to which he is subject. This point applies even more obviously to ordinary citizens. The supposition that each of us is under a general duty to learn the law is absurd. Presumably, then, to be at all plausible, this alleged duty cannot be universal in scope, and is probably best construed as a conditional; it cannot extend indiscriminately over the entire universe of our moral and legal duties. No one can possibly be expected to conduct a fishing expedition by combing through penal codes in legal jurisdictions or essays by moral philosophers to discover new duties they did not imagine themselves to have.

---

[69] Elizabeth Harman: "Ethics Is Hard! What Follows?" (forthcoming). I agree with her first sentence but disagree with the implications she draws from it.

A clarification of this first point is needed to avoid possible misunderstandings. In the first place, I readily concede that persons sometimes *do* have duties to inquire—especially in the domain of fact. It is obvious, for example, that a person is obligated to determine if a gun is loaded before he handles and points it. We also may have duties to ascertain the content of the law. These duties may not be quite as common as some theorists would lead us to believe, but they undoubtedly exist nonetheless. When we fail to discharge these duties, we often are culpably ignorant; culpable ignorance is a genuine phenomenon I do not mean to deny. Nor do I mean to deny that the contrast between culpable and non-culpable ignorance may have moral significance. Suppose, for example, I am able to benefit only one of two persons: Karen and Kathy are trapped in a flood they did not expect to occur, and I can only rescue one. Karen ignored warnings that the waters would rise above her rooftop. Kathy received no such warnings. The fact that she is culpably ignorant she would be trapped is a decisive reason to prefer Kathy. What I contest, however, is a particular normative *use* to which criminal theorists often *put* the concept of culpable ignorance. I claim that persons who have a duty to inquire but fail to discharge it are rarely if ever as blameworthy for their subsequent wrongdoing as those who realize Φ is wrong.

So much for possible misunderstandings. If I am correct that no *general* duty to inquire exists, under what specific circumstances *does* such a duty arise? How would an objectivist theory of moral wrongfulness answer this question? I suppose that persons have a duty to make inquiries up to the point where further investigation would do more harm than good. Different individuals would reach this point at different times, depending on the opportunity costs of additional inquiries. If more investigation by a tenured professor would simply delay completion of his magnum opus, perhaps he should conduct further inquiries. But if more investigation by a surgeon would prevent her from saving additional lives, she should terminate her inquiries at an earlier time. More generally, it is hard to see how it could be an efficient use of anyone's time to inquire whether Φ is wrongful if he does not intend to Φ and almost certainly never will Φ.

Because C has no general duty to inquire about L, it is crucial to note that the strategy I discuss here cannot possibly succeed in showing why nearly *all* persons are alleged to be blameworthy despite their ignorance of law. Any attempt to invoke this line of thought as a *global* solution to our basic question (Q) is far too ambitious. In many cases in which a person has such a duty, however, she is likely to be *reckless* for her failure to discharge it. If she is in the business of dumping chemicals into water, for example, she is almost certain to be aware of the risk that what she is doing might be harmful. Thus this strategy probably applies only to persons who are responsible on the second ground I defend, that is, only to those who are aware of the risk that their actions are wrong. I have already conceded that recklessness about wrongdoing is a culpable state that makes a defendant somewhat blameworthy when he commits an offense. As I have also contended, however, the culpability of these persons can be established *without* the need to posit a duty to inquire. Thus duties of inquiry are not needed in the very cases in which it is plausible to suppose that persons are responsible despite their lack of knowledge their acts are wrongful.

I move now to my *second* objection to the claim that duties of inquiry are helpful in answering my basic question (Q). Suppose we are in a circumstance in which persons *do* have a duty to inquire—a duty to Ω. The existence of this duty, it should be recalled, is designed to explain how C can be blameworthy for breaching a different, subsequent duty—a duty not to Φ—of which (ex hypothesi) he is unaware. In order to provide the needed explanation, we had better stipulate that C is *aware* of his duty to Ω, that is, to inquire about Φ. My basis for this stipulation is that tracing strategies or duties to inquire are needed only if it is plausible to suppose that ignorance of law has exculpatory force in their absence. Several kinds of theories about the preconditions of responsibility—such as some quality of will theories—deny exculpation to persons ignorant of wrongdoing. Tracing strategies or duties to inquire play no role in these theories.[70] We should note that the very popularity of these strategies is a powerful reason to acknowledge the strong appeal of exculpation for ignorant defendants. Criminal theorists and moral philosophers alike tend to recognize that *some* account of why ignorance of law does not exculpate is needed.

But if we fear that a person is not blameworthy for breaching a duty Φ of which he is unaware, it can only be question-begging to posit an *additional* duty Ω of which he is unaware to explain how he can be blameworthy for breaching his original duty. Expressed somewhat differently, we make no progress in explaining how persons

---

[70] See Angela M. Smith: "Attitudes, Tracing, and Control," 32 *Journal of Applied Philosophy* 115 (2015).

can be blameworthy for breaching duties of which they are unaware by multiplying further duties of which they are equally unaware. If persons are not already blameworthy for breaching a duty Φ of which they are unaware, any rationale that posits an additional duty Ω of which they are also unaware to explain why they are blameworthy for Φ would be question-begging. Thus we need to assume that C *knows* he has a duty to inquire if we are to succeed in establishing his responsibility for Φ. In a great many cases, however, C will *not* be aware he has this duty. He will not realize he has this duty even if we concede, as often I do not, that it exists in his particular circumstance. It is for this reason that recourse to a supposed political obligation—to an alleged obligation to obey the law per se—is not especially helpful in resolving (Q). Before political obligations can be employed in our inquiry, persons must be aware of their existence—as many of us are not. In any event, the supposition that persons have one or more additional duties is often unhelpful in explaining why they are blameworthy for breaching a different duty of which they are unaware.

I illustrate this second difficulty with an example. Suppose that White is exercising in a health club, and curses after he fails to lift a heavy weight. Black blames him for cursing. White denies he had an obligation not to curse. After all, he replies, he is exercising in a gym, not a church. Black responds by pointing to a sign on the wall that White had not noticed. The sign lists fifteen "rules of the health club," the seventh of which prohibits cursing. White now shifts his ground. He concedes he had an obligation not to curse, but alleges he is not blameworthy for breaching this obligation, as he was unaware of its existence. Black remains unimpressed. He does not simply insist that "ignorance of the rules is no excuse." Instead, he offers a more sophisticated response: White is culpable for his ignorance. Black insists that the list of rules on the wall should be construed to contain an implicit, unarticulated rule that creates a duty to know all of the other rules, and White's failure to know *that* rule provides a reason to blame him for cursing. To make Black's case stronger, suppose the additional rule to which he alludes actually appears on the sign. In other words, suppose the final rule is: "Members have a duty to know all of the foregoing rules." Should White finally be persuaded he is to blame for cursing? Does he have a better reason to accept blame than if the sign had not contained such a rule? Surely White will protest that he was equally ignorant of the final rule. If he is not to blame for conduct that violates a rule of which he is unaware, the existence of additional rules of which he is equally unaware can hardly provide a rationale for blaming him.[71]

It will not do, of course, to resort to the familiar standard of the reasonable person and insist that White *should* have read the sign he did not read. This answer, of course, invokes a negligence standard. If C's degree of culpability in failing to discharge his duty of inquiry consists in mere negligence, it is hard to see how he could possibly be as culpable for Φ as A, who knows cursing to be wrong. No criminal theorist equates the blameworthiness of defendants who act knowingly with those who act negligently when mistakes of *fact* are involved, and we should be just as quick to reject this alleged equivalence when mistakes of law are involved. More than mere negligence in failing to inquire is needed.

My *third* objection might more precisely be characterized as a reservation. It centers on the *content* of this supposed duty Ω. That is, *what* exact inquiries do persons have a duty to undertake, and how is this alleged duty to be discharged? Suppose C suspects Φ to be wrong. If so, how would he discharge his alleged duty to inquire before proceeding to Φ? Consider again the plight of Jacob, our camper who throws his dead flashlight batteries into the garbage despite his uncertainty about whether the law requires recycling. Suppose we are inclined to think that persons in his situation have a moral duty to inquire, and cannot be exculpated unless they discharge it. What *exactly* do we think Jacob must do in the real world to conform to this supposed moral duty? No lawyer is around on his camping trip, and we cannot really think he should have consulted a lawyer before leaving his home. Perhaps the answer would be easy if Jacob's jurisdiction sent him annual notices about the local recycling laws. In this event, he need only read the information made available to him. But what if accurate information is not so easy to obtain? In everyday situations, I assume that most conscientious individuals try to rectify their uncertainty about their legal duties by asking friends they believe to be knowledgeable or authoritative. Unfortunately, our acquaintances may be equally clueless—or unavailable for consultation on our camping trips. What if Jacob makes inquiries of a few such persons, but emerges no more certain than before? What else do we demand he do before exculpation is granted if he eventually acts wrongfully?

---

[71] I originally presented this response in Douglas Husak: "Ignorance of Law and Duties of Citizenship," 14 *Legal Studies* 105 (1994).

Commentators who posit a duty to inquire as a general solution to the problem of *ignorantia juris* tend to be woefully short on details about this matter. That is, they offer few specifics about the precise content of the supposed duty Ω they invoke. Most of their advice comes from the domain of fact, where it is often easier to say what persons should have done (e.g., put on their glasses, or look inside their gun) to rectify their ignorance. In morality or law, however, advice is harder to give. Generalizations are perilous; what diligent persons are expected to do to learn about one law may differ greatly from what they are expected to do to remedy their uncertainty about another. Still, accurate information about many laws can be surprisingly difficult to acquire. Skeptical readers are invited to surf the Internet to try to discern the local rules governing battery recycling. The apparent assumption is that discharging a duty to inquire would typically rectify ignorance about Φ. The counterfactual dependence on which this assumption rests, however, may turn out to be false more often than it is true. If I am correct about this difficulty, a great many defendants will be exculpated for Φ, even if we posit a duty Ω to inquire about its wrongfulness.

This problem is most acute when we suppose that persons have duties to inquire about the *moral* status of their conduct. Neil Levy persuasively argues that often there is nothing agents can reasonably be expected to have done that would have removed their ignorance that Φ is morally wrongful.[72] He considers, for example, an unscrupulous corporate officer who engages in unethical business practices out of greed and arrogance. What duty of inquiry can we sensibly impose on him that would have alerted him to the wrongfulness of his behavior? Should the officer have been made to attend a course in business ethics? Enter graduate school in philosophy? Surely these demands are far-fetched. But even if our businessman had taken such extreme steps, it is unlikely he would have come to recognize the error of his ways. Levy's realistic example of moral uncertainty is helpful—although nothing should depend too much on any particular selection. Still, the controversy about vegetarianism may be instructive. Obviously, philosophers are deeply divided about the moral status of eating nonhuman animals. It would be presumptuous for anyone to be supremely confident that

---

[72] Neil Levy: "Culpable Ignorance and Moral Responsibility: A Reply to Fitzpatrick," 119 *Ethics* 729 (2009). Some of the difficulties of rectifying moral ignorance are also described by Jan Willem Wieland: "What's Special about Moral Ignorance?," 28 *Ratio* ___ (2015).

her own position represents the last word. What should a conscientious carnivore do to rectify her uncertainty? The answer is hardly clear. Suppose she had enrolled in a course led by Peter Singer as well as in a course taught by a well-known philosopher on the other side. I predict our carnivore would emerge as confused as ever. If moral uncertainty were easy to resolve, it would not be so pervasive—even among those philosophers who have spent their lives deliberating about the content of morality.

I do not allege that no progress on such issues has been made. Contemporary philosophers have shown an increasing interest in the topic of what persons should do when they are uncertain about the demands of morality. Many have suggested that the answer depends largely on the stakes of being wrong.[73] Moral mistakes about life and death are more momentous than moral mistakes about the disposal of batteries. But it is crucial to recognize that this plausible response is not directly germane to my inquiry. I stipulate that Φ is wrongful, and do not ask what persons should do when they are uncertain of its wrongfulness. I ask instead about the blameworthiness of persons who go on to perform Φ. Blame for failure to discharge a duty to Ω—that is, to have inquired about Φ—is not equivalent to the blame merited for knowingly violating a duty not to Φ, whether or not the costs of being mistaken turn out to be exorbitant.

Suppose, however, that each of the three foregoing hurdles can be overcome. Imagine, that is, that a person C *has* a duty Ω to inquire, the content of which can be specified with reasonable precision. C *knows* he has this duty, fails to discharge it, subsequently performs wrongful action Φ, and would not have remained ignorant about his duty not to Φ had he discharged his duty to Ω. Can we then attribute blame to C for Φ? I adapt a counterexample from Holly Smith to provide a fourth reason we cannot.[74] Suppose a secretary is ordered by her supervisor to tabulate information from all office employees about their allergies as part of a school project for the supervisor's young daughter. The secretary deliberately fails to do as she is instructed. Later, an office employee suffers a seizure and dies—a death that would have been prevented had the secretary discharged her duty to collect information, learned that the victim had a deadly allergy, and known that life-saving medicine is widely available. Intuitively, I hope, we would not hold the secretary

---

[73] See the defense of moral epistemic contextualism in Guerrero: *Op.cit.* Note 41.
[74] Smith: *Op.cit.* Note 64.

responsible *for* the death of the victim. Why not? The answer must be that an additional condition must be satisfied before it is plausible to hold a person responsible for Φ because she fails to discharge a duty to inquire Ω. Smith herself speculates that the subsequent unwitting act must "fall within the risk" of the prior benighting act.[75] This condition, however, is notoriously difficult to explicate. If we construe *types* of risk narrowly, few unwitting acts will be within the risk of benighting acts, and Φ almost always will be excused. I will make no further effort, however, to embellish this additional but heretofore unspecified condition. Legal philosophers who regard culpable ignorance as a more integral part of a theory of ignorance of law should be encouraged to meet this challenge.

I offer a *fifth* and final objection to those who believe the existence of a duty to inquire is crucial in resolving our basic question (Q). How and why does a breach of duty Ω provide any reason to punish or blame a person *for* Φ—an entirely different duty? I contend that a breach of the alleged duty Ω—the duty to inquire—does not provide the needed explanation. Recall that we are not trying to decide whether C is blameworthy to *any* extent, but whether C deserves a quantum of blame or punishment *comparable* to that deserved by A for committing Φ. But is hard to see how a breach of this alleged duty Ω can render C just as blameworthy as A. How does the amount of blame merited for breaching Ω *substitute* for, or *transfer* to, a knowing violation of Φ—in precisely the exact amount needed? Let me describe the general difficulty abstractly by assigning two new symbols to quantify degrees of blame. First, how blameworthy is A, our knowing wrongdoer, for Φ? Call his unit of blameworthiness ¥. Now, let us assign a quantum of blame to C, who has a duty Ω to inquire about L, but fails to discharge it. Call this unit of blameworthiness €. The general problem is: *Why suppose that* ¥ *equals* €? If A and C are to be equally culpable for the same act Φ that violates the same law L, it had better be true that ¥ and € are equal. If € were less than ¥, C would be less culpable than A for their wrongful act Φ. If € were greater than ¥, C would actually be more culpable than A for Φ. Thus ¥ must equal €. But why suppose this equality holds? In all probability, € will rarely equal ¥. When they *are* equal, the result is likely to be coincidental. To suppose that the blame C deserves for failing to discharge his duty of inquiry Ω must always

---

[75] *Id.*, p.551.

be exactly the right amount needed to make him as culpable as A for Φ is an article of faith. In other words, what is conspicuously absent from strategies that rely on a duty to inquire to solve the basic question (Q) is a reason to suppose that ¥ equals €.

Let me now describe much the same general difficulty a bit more concretely. A failure to discharge the very same duty of inquiry Ω can lead to many very different wrongs—Φ1 or Φ2. Suppose C fails to discharge a single duty of inquiry Ω. For example, he fails to consult the Oracle at Delphi at t1, who would have rectified his moral ignorance about any subsequent wrongful act Φ he will perform at t2. Suppose one such wrongful act Φ1 he will perform at t2 is the owning of slaves. The Oracle would also have rectified his moral ignorance about another wrongful act Φ2 he will perform at t2—say, the breaking of a promise. The problem is that any blame he merits for his failure to inquire Ω would seem to be a constant, as it breaches one and the same duty. But Φ1, the owning of slaves, is significantly worse than Φ2, the breaking of a promise. Person A, who performs both Φ1 and Φ2 knowing they are wrong, is more blameworthy for Φ1 than for Φ2. How can the blame C deserves for his failure to discharge Ω, which is a constant, explain why his subsequent blame varies, and he would be significantly more blameworthy for owning slaves than for breaking a promise? Unless this question can be answered, C's blame for owning slaves and for breaking a promise would seem to be a constant, and cannot be equal to that of A, who is more blameworthy for Φ1 than for Φ2.

Consider an example that is easier to imagine. Suppose C is driving and fails to read a sign instructing him to slow down because dangerous curves are ahead. His wrongful act Ω creates risks of very different harms. Suppose his excessive speed leads him to commit wrongful act Φ1 and kill a child. Or suppose his excessive speed leads him to commit wrongful act Φ2 and kill a cat. Surely a wrongdoer A who knowingly performs Φ1 and kills a child is more blameworthy than if he performs Φ2 and kills a cat. How can C, who violates the same duty of inquiry Ω, be just as culpable as A? The blame A deserves is highly variable; the blame C deserves seems to be a constant. Again, how does the amount of blame C merits for breaching Ω *substitute* for, or *transfer* to, a knowing violation of any wrongful act Φ—in precisely the exact amount needed? I am dubious an adequate answer can be given.

I digress briefly to mention that the five objections I have raised against the supposition that C is typically as blameworthy as A when the former is culpable for his ignorance can be cited with only a few modifications in several other contexts in which the contrast between culpable and non-culpable ignorance is invoked. Most important, most of these objections apply to the parallel supposition that persons lack a *defense* from penal liability when they have culpably caused the conditions of their own defense. Suppose, for example, an intoxicated defendant is charged with a crime that requires recklessness. He defends on the ground that his level of intoxication prevented him from being conscious of the risk he created. Nearly all jurisdictions reject his plea.[76] Many commentators disallow this defense because they trace the defendant's blameworthiness to his prior act of voluntarily becoming intoxicated. But this ground for rejecting the defense encounters many of the difficulties I have presented in the context of ignorance of law. The fifth such difficulty is especially salient. Why suppose that any culpability in becoming intoxicated is equivalent to and thus can transfer to or substitute for the culpability this drunken defendant would have possessed had he committed the crime while sober? Treating the drunken offender *as if* he were sober is no more defensible than treating the ignorant defendant *as though* he knew the law. Here, as elsewhere, careful thought about one issue in criminal theory can illuminate any number of others—even when commentators seldom connect them.

If the conclusion I defend here is correct, and persons who are culpably ignorant that Φ is wrong are almost always less blameworthy for Φ than those who know it to be wrong, why have so many moral and legal philosophers supposed otherwise? *One* of many possible explanations is that their intuitions are confounded because they confuse *culpable* action with *precipitate* action. According to Smith, in a precipitate action the agent's level of credence does not justify her performance of Φ at t2, the moment she engages in it.[77] Instead of performing Φ, she should defer until she gathers more information. As many instances of wrongful conduct involve both culpable action and precipitate action, it is easy to confuse the two possible sources of culpability for Φ: the agent's culpable ignorance, and the rashness of her action given that she lacks enough information to proceed. Suppose, for example, that a doctor

---

[76] Jurisdictions invoke a variety of rationales to reject this defense. Intoxication is governed by a special statute in *Model Penal Code* §2.08(2).

[77] Holly M. Smith: "Tracing Cases of Culpable Ignorance," in Rik Peels, ed.: *Moral and Social Perspectives on Ignorance* (London: Routledge Press, forthcoming, 2016).

culpably fails to Ω at t1—that is, to inquire about whether her patient has a condition that she knows would make taking a certain medication fatal. If she performs Φ at t2, that is, administers that very medication, the doctor's act is both culpably ignorant as well as precipitate. The doctor should have inquired at t1 whether the patient had the condition before administering the medicine. Even when she has not done so, however, she should have deferred from administering the medication at t2, when she is uncertain the patient does not have the condition. If the doctor is blameworthy for administering the medication, we cannot infer that culpable ignorance is what renders her responsible. Her blameworthiness may instead be due only to the precipitate nature of her action. Thus, in order to test whether culpable ignorance or the failure to discharge a duty to inquire makes a subsequent action blameworthy, we should focus on "pure" cases that do not involve precipitate action. In other words, at the time of wrongdoing, it must be true that the agent should no longer defer action to gain the information she should have obtained earlier, and that her performance of Φ is justified given her actual beliefs. Smith notes that these "pure" cases may be surprisingly rare.

In any event, the five conditions that would render C as culpable as A for their wrongful act Φ are rarely if ever satisfied—especially in the domain of morality rather than fact. I conclude that supposed duties of inquiry are of little help in resolving our basic question (Q). As a general matter, these duties do not exist. Even when they do exist, offenders may be unaware of them, so the original problem of attributing blame in the absence of knowledge of the duty that is breached remains untouched. When offenders are aware of a duty to inquire, its content will be very hard to specify, and discharging it will seldom rectify their ignorance. Even when these three problems are overcome, the claim that C is responsible for Φ because he breached his duty of inquiry Ω is vulnerable to counterexamples. Perhaps most important, the failure to discharge such a duty will rarely if ever render C, the ignorant defendant, as culpable as A, the defendant who knows his act is wrongful. Admittedly, tracing strategies or alleged duties of inquiry have played a central role in scholarly debates about the exculpatory significance of ignorance generally, and of ignorance of law in particular. Nonetheless, these strategies—and the theories of culpable moral ignorance that are constructed upon their foundation—are far less useful in resolving my basic question (Q) than a great many theorists have supposed.

Conclusion

This chapter is the most speculative—and the most difficult—in the entire book. Not coincidentally, it also contains the most philosophical content. Any debate about whether exculpation is deserved for wrongful conduct performed by persons who are morally ignorant depends on a general theory of responsibility. This topic is a quagmire of philosophical uncertainty. I describe a general theory of responsibility that will vindicate my claim that a defendant who commits conduct Φ in violation of law L typically deserves some degree of exculpation relative to someone who is aware his conduct is wrongful. My preferred theory grounds moral responsibility in the familiar idea of *reason-responsiveness.* I argue that this idea should be construed internally or subjectively for purposes of holding wrongdoers blameworthy. As it is hard to see how rational individuals can be expected to respond to reasons of which they are unaware, a theory of reason-responsiveness supports the conclusion that defendants typically deserve complete exculpation when they are ignorant of the wrongfulness of their behavior. Some of the most well-known competing theories—in particular, given versions of quality of will theories—also support a reduction in liability and punishment, although their support is more tenuous and may be less than total.

The conclusion I ultimately favor models the culpability of persons who make mistakes of law according to the same principles that govern those who make mistakes of fact. No deep disparity exists between the exculpatory significance of these two kinds of mistake. Accordingly, I distinguish different levels of blameworthiness for defendants who merit some amount of exculpation. The defendant who is reckless—who consciously disregards a substantial and unjustifiable risk his conduct is wrongful—deserves some degree of blame for his wrongdoing, but less than the defendant who fully understands his conduct is wrongful. This theory allows us to be fully blameworthy for what we do only when we act akratically—that is, contrary to the balance of reasons as we ourselves conceive them. Many theorists oppose my view by invoking a quality of will theory to show why defendants may be blameworthy despite their failure to realize their conduct is wrongful. I suggest that even quality of will theories should include information about what agents believe about the morality of their conduct when making inferences to the quality of their will. If I am correct, each kind of theory differentiates between the amount of blame deserved by A and B, both of whom commit Φ in violation of L, when A but not B recognizes Φ to be wrong. Only a very different kind of account of the foundations of blameworthiness would withhold any amount of exculpation from persons who are ignorant of law.

Many philosophers who generally sympathize with my claim that morally ignorant defendants are entitled to some degree of exculpation allow a reduction in blame only when their ignorance is *non-culpable*. Quite a few morally ignorant persons, however, *are* culpable for their ignorance, and thus merit no exculpation and should be treated comparably to those who are aware their conduct is wrongful. Ignorance is culpable, these philosophers continue, when it can be traced to or originates in a prior culpable act consisting in a duty to inquire. In Part C I provided a number of reasons to reject this use of tracing strategies in efforts to answer my basic question (Q). For five reasons, the supposition that mistaken defendants should be held responsible because they fail to discharge their duties to inquire about the law at an earlier time will seldom if ever show them to be fully culpable for the wrongful act they subsequently perform.

4

Refinements, Qualifications, Complexities

I have claimed that persons almost always deserve some degree of exculpation when they are unaware their conduct Φ is wrongful. Quality of will accounts cannot be rejected out of hand, but even these theories should reduce the blame directed to wrongdoers who act in moral ignorance. My preferred alternative, however, awards total exculpation to nearly all ignorant wrongdoers. As persons who are rational cannot be expected to respond to reasons of which they are unaware, a subjectivist reason-responsive theory of moral responsibility withholds all blame for wrongful acts committed in ignorance. Nor is blame likely to be deserved for Φ even when such persons are culpable *for* their ignorance. But my account requires a great deal of additional explication. In this chapter I propose a number of crucial refinements, qualifications, and complexities that provide further content to my ideal theory of ignorance of law. As often is the case, the devil is in the details. Many of the issues I address in this chapter have not even been discussed by criminal theorists. They are among the hardest in all of philosophy, and I fear that little will be resolved.

In Part A, I offer further detail about exactly *what* the offender who knows his act to be wrongful must believe in order to be fully responsible for it. First, I argue that a *latent* belief in the wrongfulness of conduct is probably all that is needed to render the wrongdoer responsible; an *occurrent* belief is not required. Second, I make a number of inquiries about the *content* of the belief required for culpability. Must defendants merely believe their conduct is presumptively wrongful, or must they also believe it is unjustified and unexcused? Must offenders who are reckless about the wrongfulness of their conduct believe that the risks they take are substantial and unjustifiable? Or is an externalist, objective account of these matters all that is needed? Finally, what is it *about* morality that offenders must believe in order to be responsible for their wrongful acts? Must they have some indication of *why* wrongful acts are wrongful in order to deserve blame? Obviously, competing answers to these questions have the potential to radically expand or contract the range of cases in which morally ignorant wrongdoers receive exculpation. As we will see, reflection about these issues will indicate that full responsibility for wrongdoing is likely to be unusual.

In Part B, I describe a number of *exceptions* to my position—circumstances in which even an ideal theory affords no exculpation whatever to those who are in ignorance of law. In these kinds of case, B should be punished every bit as severely as A. I am not altogether certain, however, exactly how many kinds of exceptions should be countenanced. I describe three possible such circumstances: cases in which B is *willfully ignorant* of law L, those in which B's conduct falls under what I call a *legal loophole,* and those in which B acts *in* but not *from* ignorance. In only the first circumstance am I confident that an exception to my general theory should be recognized. In the latter two instances, it is at least plausible to suppose that A and B should not be punished to the same extent.

Part C wrestles largely with the phenomenon of *malum prohibitum.* Many commentators are unwilling to exculpate ignorant wrongdoers who commit a *malum in se.* But their objections to exculpation wane elsewhere. If persons deserve punishment only when they violate the morality that underlies law, how can they ever deserve punishment when the crime they commit is not wrongful prior to and independent of law? I try to describe the various grounds on which persons act wrongfully, even when breaching a *malum prohibitum.* Contrary to the conventional wisdom expressed by many criminal theorists, I conclude that the contrast between these two categories of crime plays almost no role in a theory to resolve my basic question (Q).

Some persons make mistakes of law that are *negligent*; their mistakes would not have been made by a reasonable person in their situation. My account of responsibility in terms of reason-responsiveness precludes punishing defendants whose ignorance of wrongdoing is merely negligent. Rational persons cannot be blamed for failing to be guided by a reason they did not believe they had, even though a reasonable person in their situation would have realized that the reason applies to them. If liability for negligent mistakes of law should be imposed, the rationale for punishment must be unlike the rationale I have provided so far. I take seriously that a different defense of liability for negligent mistakes of law might be constructed. If persons ever are justifiably subject to liability when they make negligent mistakes of fact, the same should be true when they make negligent mistakes of law. In Part D I suggest that we should not be too hasty to rule out the possibility that some quantum of blame might be deserved by wrongdoers whose mistakes of law are unreasonable. Ultimately, I am agnostic about the matter, despite my inability to say much about how an argument in favor of liability for negligent conduct might be devised.

A. Knowledge of Wrongdoing

Some philosophers of criminal law may be tentatively prepared to accept my thesis that A, who engages in wrongful conduct Φ knowing it violates law L, deserves more blame and punishment than B, who commits the same crime while ignorant of law or the morality that underlies it. Yet these philosophers have good reason to withhold judgment until they are given more information about what they would be accepting. To this point, I have focused almost entirely on B: the defendant who is ignorant of law. But what about A? What exactly must A know to be fully responsible? And what exactly must someone know to be partly responsible? I have alleged that a person must know (to be fully culpable) or suspect (to be culpable to a lesser degree) that her conduct is wrongful, but this allegation is undeveloped in a number of important respects. Further specification of *what* A must know in order to be responsible for Φ is enormously controversial. In trying to resolve these controversies, we will see that the criteria for full responsibility are likely to be satisfied only rarely.

I begin by asking: In exactly *what* does A's knowledge of wrongfulness consist? As I propose to construe it, this question contains several distinct inquiries; I mention three of the most important here. First, what *kind* of belief must A possess in order to be fully responsible for Φ? Must his belief be occurrent, or might a non-occurrent belief suffice? Second, what must be the *content* of A's belief about Φ? To be fully culpable, must he believe not only that his conduct is pro tanto wrongful, but also that he lacks a justification and an excuse for performing it? And to have a lesser degree of culpability, what must he believe about the risk his conduct is illegal? Third, what must he believe *about* the moral reason(s) not to Φ in order to be blameworthy? Must he be able to identify this reason with tolerable accuracy? Even those legal philosophers who are quick to contest the doctrine of *ignorantia juris* seldom address these difficult philosophical issues. In this part I will do my best to clarify some of these matters by providing more detail about the role played by knowledge in a theory of ignorance of law. Unfortunately, few solutions will be forthcoming. I hasten to add, however, that the significance of many of these issues is independent of my particular theory of responsibility. Most must be answered *whatever* theory of responsibility one happens to hold. At the very least, I am confident I can show how different answers to these complex questions have the potential to make a thesis about the exculpatory significance of ignorance of law more or less radical—and thus more or less palatable to skeptics.

As we have seen, Michael Zimmerman famously contends that someone is responsible for Φ only when he either believes Φ is wrongful or is culpable for his ignorance that Φ is wrongful. In Chapter 3(C) I challenged the second disjunct: that a theory of culpable ignorance is likely to make the ignorant defendant as culpable for Φ as A (or indeed culpable for Φ at all). Zimmerman's first disjunct, however—that belief in the wrongfulness of Φ renders A fully culpable—seems unproblematic, and might be thought to express my own position. Important differences emerge, however, when one examines the *nature* of the belief Zimmerman thinks is needed for culpability. He contends (with a possible exception to be discussed below) that "it is . . . occurrent beliefs about wrongdoing that are . . . required for culpability."[1] I hope to show that this requirement is probably too demanding; A might be fully culpable for Φ even though his belief that Φ is wrong is not occurrent.

Before doing so, however, I emphasize what is at stake in the controversy about whether a person can be blameworthy for Φ even though his belief about its wrongfulness is not occurrent. As I reject tracing strategies and Zimmerman accepts them, it might appear that I withhold responsibility from wrongdoers far more frequently than he. But this appearance is deceptive, illustrating yet again what I call

---

[1] Michael Zimmerman: *Living with Uncertainty: The Moral Significance of Ignorance* (Cambridge: Cambridge University Press, 2008), p.191.

the "give-and-take" flavor of my theory. In many cases in which a tracing strategy might be invoked to explain how a person is culpable for Φ, I impose responsibility without tracing by allowing the belief that Φ is wrongful to be latent rather than occurrent. As a result, we might well agree that a particular defendant is responsible for acting wrongfully, even while disagreeing about why this is so. At the end of the day, it is hard to say which of us ultimately attributes or withholds responsibility from wrongdoers more often.

Before we can hope to decide whether Zimmerman is correct about the kind of belief required for culpability, we must clarify the nature of occurrent belief. Frankly, I doubt any such attempt at clarification will be successful; no consensus can be found among philosophers, many of whom resort to metaphorical terminology to describe occurrent beliefs. As a result, I confess to finding the concept of occurrent belief to be mysterious. Rik Peels, for example, uses several phrases interchangeably in the course of his explanatory efforts. He writes, if "S at some time t occurrently believes p, then at t S is considering p or thinking about p or reflecting on p, and believing that p."[2] Eric Schwitzgebel employs a different metaphor, alleging that beliefs are occurrent when they are at "the forefront of [the] mind."[3] At any rate, beliefs that are non-occurrent are generally described as *latent*.[4] Peels's explication of latent belief is wholly dependent on his account of occurrent belief. He continues: "If at t S latently believes p, then at t S is not considering p or thinking about p or reflecting on p, but still believes p." The most popular (but not the only) account of latent beliefs is *dispositional*. According to Jonathan Cohen, for instance, "belief that p is a disposition, when one is attending to issues raised, or items referred to, by the proposition that p, normally to feel it true that p and false that not-p."[5]

It is easy to think of clear cases in which Peels's criteria for occurrent belief are satisfied. Sometimes I have a pressing need to remember a proposition—involving, say, the name of an important person I am

---

[2] Rik Peels: "What Is Ignorance?" 38 *Philosophia* 57 (2010).

[3] Eric Schwitzgebel: "Belief," *Stanford Encyclopedia of Philosophy* (http://plato.stanford.edu/entries/belief/). (First published Aug 14, 2006; substantive revision Mar 24, 2015).

[4] On some accounts, non-occurrent beliefs are of two kinds: dormant and tacit. See Nikolaj Nottelmann and Rik Peels: "Some Metaphysical Implications of a Credible Ethics of Belief," in Nikilaj Nottelman, ed.: *New Essays on Belief: Constitution, Content, and Structure* (Palsgrave MacMillan, 2013), p.230.

[5] L. Jonathan Cohen: *An Essay on Belief and Acceptance* (Oxford: Clarendon Press, 1992), p.4.

about to greet—and I recite that person's name in my head over and over again. Silently, I think "the person I am about to meet is named Robert Barchi" repeatedly. In such a case, my belief that the person I will meet is named Robert Barchi is clearly occurrent. But if my belief is not occurrent at t unless I recite the proposition that expresses it to myself at that very time, almost none of my beliefs turn out to be occurrent. All but a small handful are latent. As I am writing this paragraph, I am not "considering," or "reflecting on," or "thinking" about the propositions "my name is Douglas Husak," or "the world is round," or "2+2=4"—although I *do* consider, reflect on, or think about these propositions as I type them.

Are *moral* propositions occurrent at the moment persons knowingly commit wrongful acts? If we take Peels's criteria literally—and I am unsure how else to construe them—virtually no instance of wrongdoing is accompanied by an occurrent belief in its wrongfulness at the instant it is undertaken. Credulity is strained by supposing that thieves such as Sabine have thoughts about the immorality of theft at the forefront of their consciousness when they abscond with stolen merchandise. If I can rely on my own introspective phenomenology, I almost never consider the proposition that my conduct is wrongful (or permissible, or superogatory, or has any normative property) at the moment I engage in it. And no thoughts about the wrongfulness of my act at a *different* time than when I perform it count toward making it occurrent. As Peels is careful to specify, judgments about whether a belief is occurrent are made at a given moment t. The fact that a belief was occurrent at an earlier time t-1, or at a later time t+1, is irrelevant to whether it is occurrent at t. If I am correct, virtually all of my moral beliefs about the actions I perform are latent. And they remain latent throughout whatever duration of time I need to perform the actions in question. I trust the same phenomenology is familiar to other wrongdoers as well.

Obviously, the conclusion that virtually no moral beliefs are occurrent at the time of wrongdoing can produce startling implications for how to understand and apply given theories about the exculpatory effect of moral ignorance. As Zimmerman recognizes, his position about the exculpatory effect of moral ignorance is already bound to strike many theorists as highly counterintuitive. But allowing responsibility only when A has an occurrent belief that his act is wrongful compounds this implausibility exponentially. If A must have an occurrent belief in the proposition "Φ is wrong" before he becomes blameworthy for it,

Zimmerman's view is a good deal more radical—far more so, in fact—than one might have suspected. I have repeatedly tried to downplay the extent to which my own theory of ignorance of law has devastating implications for our current practices of imposing blame and liability. Contrary to what Zimmerman himself concludes, for example, I do not think it requires us to abolish our retributive institutions of punishment.[6] But if an occurrent belief in the wrongfulness of Φ is needed before a person deserves to be blamed for it, and occurrent beliefs in moral propositions are exceedingly unusual at the moment actions are performed, almost no one will ever be responsible for anything. Although we have seen that Gideon Rosen resists holding persons blameworthy on epistemological grounds—third parties are almost never certain that wrongdoers actually have whatever beliefs render them blameworthy—Zimmerman's reluctance does not stem from third-party uncertainty. Instead, his demand that occurrent moral beliefs are required for blameworthiness would seem to all but guarantee that penal liability and punishment will be undeserved.

Fortunately, the ramifications of requiring an occurrent belief for responsibility may be less than meets the eye. As we have just seen, many philosophers (including Zimmerman) allow tracing strategies to show that a person can be blameworthy for Φ despite not knowing it to be wrongful at the time he performs it. According to these strategies, an agent's culpability for Φ can derive from (or originate in) her culpability for being ignorant that Φ is wrongful. When her culpability for Φ is imposed pursuant to a tracing strategy, she is blameworthy for her conduct at t even though she may have no belief of any kind—neither occurrent nor latent—about its wrongfulness. Frankly, I find it odd to allow blame to be imposed for conduct when someone lacks even a latent belief in its wrongfulness at the moment she engages in it. Moreover, I mentioned that Zimmerman allows a possible exception to his claim that blameworthiness requires an occurrent belief. "It may be true," he writes, "that routine or habitual actions are performed for reasons to which one does not advert."[7] In such cases, he takes seriously the possibility that a latent belief will suffice for responsibility. But why? And approximately what percentage of our actions are performed routinely or habitually? This unexplained qualification of Zimmerman's general thesis could turn out to be a whopping

[6] Michael J. Zimmerman: *The Immorality of Punishment* (Toronto: Broadview Press, 2011).
[7] Zimmerman: *Op.cit.* Note 1, p.191.

exception that all but swallows his rule. I reach two conclusions about Zimmerman's position, whatever his answers to these questions might be. First, he realizes that an occurrent belief in the wrongfulness of Φ is not needed for responsibility at t after all. Second, contrary to initial appearances, surprisingly many persons may actually turn out to be blameworthy for their wrongful conduct.

In any event, requiring a belief to be occurrent in order to impose blame seems far-fetched, and seldom is thought to be necessary in other contexts. Consider, for example, the familiar debate about the significance of intention versus knowledge to moral judgments about the extent to which wrongful conduct is blameworthy. Suppose a tactical bomber drops explosives on a factory he is aware is located in the middle of a densely populated city. Even though this pilot may lack the *intention* to kill civilians, all philosophers would agree he kills them *knowingly*. They would then proceed to judge his action and blame him accordingly—either just as much or less than the terror-bomber, who kills civilians intentionally. But would anyone be tempted to retract this judgment if they learned one of the pilots lacked an occurrent belief that civilians would die at the moment he dropped his bombs? Surely the pilot need not silently rehearse the proposition "these bombs will kill civilians" in order to kill them knowingly. Nor need he say to himself "it is wrongful to kill civilians" in order to knowingly commit the wrong and be eligible for blame.

Why does Zimmerman insist that blameworthiness presupposes an occurrent belief? His answer applies a reason-responsive theory of responsibility not unlike my own. He contends that a merely dispositional belief "plays no role in the reason for which one performs one's action; and, I am inclined to think, one incurs culpability for one's action only if one's belief concerning wrongdoing plays a role in the reason for which one performs the action."[8] I have no quarrel with the last premise in this argument, but I tend to dispute the first. Why should we think that a latent belief can play no role in the reason for which a person acts? Both first-person and third-person explanations of behavior cite pairs of belief and desire that need not be occurrent. To borrow a textbook illustration, I explain the behavior of drinking water by both myself and others by positing a desire to quench thirst and a belief that water will do the trick. I do not suppose the latter belief must be occurrent for the explanation to succeed. I would be surprised

---

[8] *Id.*

to learn that any philosopher has required a belief to be occurrent in the course of explaining conduct by reference to beliefs and desires. Practical reasoning proceeds perfectly well even though agents are not explicitly reflecting about their beliefs at the time they act.

I do not see why occurrent beliefs are needed to blame persons who commit wrongful acts knowingly. Is there any basis for supposing they are needed when persons commit such acts recklessly? Why might the nature of the belief involved in recklessness differ from that involved in knowledge? As far as I can see, statutory language is the only ground for a possible disparity. Definitions of recklessness typically require a defendant to be *consciously* aware of the substantial and unjustifiable risk the prohibited harm will occur. Knowledge, by contrast, is simply defined by the Code as "practical certainty" of such harm.[9] Presumably, a conscious belief is something more than a belief. Perhaps an occurrent belief is the elusive additional component in the former that is absent from the latter. Or perhaps it is not; maybe an occurrent belief need not be conscious. But if it need not be conscious, the mystery of what it means for an occurrent belief to be "before the mind," or for an agent to "advert" to it, is compounded. In any event, the presence of the term *conscious* in statutory definitions of recklessness, and its absence from statutory definitions of knowledge, is a poor basis for differentiating between the kind of belief required by the two culpable states. Reckless endangerment would seem to be a paradigm case of recklessness. Yet a builder who repeatedly throws bricks from the roof of a building need not silently rehearse the proposition "my behavior is risky" in order to qualify as reckless. For good reason, *no* worker should have the foregoing occurrent belief. A reckless builder who consciously adverts to the riskiness of his behavior would probably pose a greater danger to himself and others than one who focuses only on the details of what he is doing. If latent beliefs suffice to render a person blameworthy when she performs her wrongful act knowingly, they should suffice for the same purpose when she performs that act recklessly.

If a belief need not be occurrent in order for a person to be blameworthy for knowingly or recklessly committing a wrongful act, what kind of belief *is* required? Henceforth I will ignore non-dispositional analyses of latent beliefs to focus solely on dispositional analyses. These analyses offer the most promising account of latent belief, even though

---

[9] *Model Penal Code* §2.02(c) and (b).

they turn out to be problematic as well. According to dispositional analyses, S believes p latently when she has the disposition to behave in given ways, most notably when she has the disposition to assent to utterances of p in the right sorts of circumstances (for example, when she comprehends the language, has no stake in deception, and the like). Still, it is not easy to identify *which* dispositions are most relevant for purposes of deciding whether A latently believes Φ to be wrongful. Some answers might cite effects that are best explained as having been caused by given beliefs.[10] These effects may be purely physiological. Suppose Claire creates a substantial and unjustifiable risk by texting while driving. When should we hold her to be reckless—a culpable state requiring her to be *aware* of the risk? We have evidence that Claire knows she is creating a risk by texting while driving if her skin temperature rises slightly or if her heart beats a bit faster than when she texts in a safer environment. Other effects are wholly behavioral. We have evidence that Claire knows she is creating a risk by texting while driving if she makes more mistakes typing her message than when she does not multitask and is able to give the keyboard her undivided attention. Of course, such evidence is far from conclusive. The important point, however, is that Claire need not be adverting to her belief that texting is risky in order to be reckless.[11]

No single dispositional test to identify the content of Claire's belief is obviously correct. Perhaps the following test is the most apt—one I have previously applied to controversial cases in which persons cause harm by *forgetting* a material proposition or by being *distracted* from the task at hand.[12] According to my test, Claire should be prompted at the relevant time without being led to the correct answer. She should

---

[10] Clearly, lines will be hard to draw. A wealth of empirical research demonstrates that *unconscious* mental states—those of which we are unaware—exert tremendous influence on both our physiological states and our conduct. The behavioral effects best explained by beliefs (or unconscious mental states) are surprising and diverse. See Daniel M. Wegner: *The Illusion of Conscious Will* (Cambridge, MA: M.I.T. Press, 2002). Among the most spectacular examples is *blindsight*. See Lawrence Weiskrantz: *Blindsight: A Case Study and Implications* (Oxford: Oxford University Press, 1990).

[11] See Eric Luis Uhlmann, David A. Pizarro, and Paul Bloom: "Varieties of Social Cognition," 38 *Journal for the Theory of Social Behaviour* 293 (2008). Sometimes the term *metacognition* is used to describe the phenomenon by which unconscious beliefs explain our behavior.

[12] Douglas Husak: "Negligence, Belief, Blame and Criminal Liability: The Special Case of Forgetting," 5 *Criminal Law and Philosophy* 199 (2011); and Douglas Husak: "Distraction and Negligence," in Lucia Zedner and Julian V. Roberts, eds.: *Principles and Values in Criminal Law and Criminal Justice: Essays in Honour of Andrew Ashworth* (Oxford: Oxford University Press, 2012), p.81.

not be asked, for example: "Don't you know that you are creating a risk by texting while driving?" This question, I submit, is analogous to impermissibly leading a witness at trial or to contaminating a suspect during an interrogation. Instead, Claire should be asked a more neutral question such as: "Do you or do you not create an unjustifiable risk if you text while driving?"[13] This latter question is less likely to lead Claire in any particular direction. If she (sincerely) answers (or would answer) the more neutral question affirmatively, she satisfies a plausible dispositional test for belief. Thus she actually believes she creates a risk by texting at the time she drives, and we have good reason to conclude she is reckless.

The most glaring (but not the only) problem with the foregoing suggestion, however, is that a different but equally appropriate dispositional test yields the opposite result in the very cases in which I have suggested that attributions of blame are most compelling: those in which persons commit wrongful acts akratically. In instances of weakness of will, dispositional tests of belief invariably produce some evidence that the agent is unaware her act is wrongful. After all, persons who believe that theft is contrary to the balance of moral reasons seldom behave like Sabine, our weak-willed bicycle thief. Instead, they pay for whatever merchandise they take. The fact that Sabine behaves as she does is evidence that she does not *really* believe her act of theft is wrong after all. In this example, the dispositional tests I have mentioned threaten to pull us in contrary directions. The ultimate determination of whether a person believes she is acting wrongfully depends on *which* dispositional test of belief is privileged.

Thus dispositional analyses of latent belief turn out to be problematic. Despite the uncertainties that result from applications of these tests, I tentatively conclude that beliefs need not be occurrent to render wrongdoers culpable, regardless of whether they act knowingly or recklessly. In all probability, latent beliefs will suffice. As Zimmerman and I agree, however, the most important point is that a given belief must be able to play a role in the practical reasoning of a wrongdoer if it is to provide a basis for holding her culpable according to a subjectivist reason-responsive theory. Ultimately, it is less important whether we categorize the beliefs that are able to perform this function as occurrent or latent.

---

[13] Admittedly, complete neutrality is probably illusory. Any particular question is likely to have some tendency to prompt the answer respondents offer.

A host of additional questions about the nature of the belief required for blameworthiness must be confronted. I have said that a person is fully responsible when she knows her act is wrongful, and is responsible to a lesser degree when she knows she risks acting wrongfully. These accounts, however, are too imprecise. Exactly *what* must such persons know in order to be culpable? This question includes at least three dimensions. First, under what description must a defendant know his act is wrongful? Second, must the wrongdoer who is fully culpable believe only that Φ is pro tanto wrongful? Or must she also believe that Φ is wrongful all things considered; that is, must she also believe she lacks a defense for committing it? Third, what must the reckless defendant believe about the wrongfulness of her risky conduct in order to be blameworthy for performing it? In the context of matters of fact, statutory definitions of recklessness typically require a defendant to believe her conduct creates a *substantial* and *unjustifiable* risk.[14] How should we parse this definition? To satisfy it, must a defendant merely be aware of the risk that her conduct is wrongful, when this risk happens to be substantial and unjustifiable? Or must she also be aware that the risk of wrongdoing actually *is* substantial and unjustifiable? A comprehensive position on the responsibility of morally ignorant wrongdoers must answer these questions. Unfortunately, no solution to any of these problems is indisputably correct.

First, under what description must a defendant know his act is wrongful? He may understand perfectly well that some descriptions apply to his act, but may be unaware that other descriptions apply also. Suppose the former descriptions lead him to believe his conduct is permissible, but the latter make it wrongful, even according to his own lights. He may understand that he is distributing a chain letter, for example, and know that engaging in a pyramid scheme is wrongful, but fail to understand that chain letters amount to pyramid schemes. Does he possess enough knowledge to qualify for blame and liability? In statutory law, this question can arise in the context of illicit drug possession, an offense requiring the mens rea of knowledge. To be liable for possessing a controlled substance, a defendant must *either* (1) know the substance he possesses is controlled, even if he is unaware of exactly what controlled substance it is; *or* (2) know what substance he possesses, when what he possesses is controlled.[15]

---

[14] *Model Penal Code* §2.02(2)(c).
[15] *McFadden v. United States*, 576 U.S. ____ (2015).

My question involves the interpretation of clause (2). Under what description must the defendant "know" what substance he possesses? Suppose, for example, he knows he possesses a substance that he and his friends identify only by its popular street name, such as "Molly." He knows that Ecstasy is a controlled substance, but does not know that Molly is Ecstasy. Philosophers of language would refer to this problem as involving referential opacity. Is this defendant liable for knowing possession of a controlled substance?

This question is difficult, and my tentative answer is as follows. According to the view I have defended, what ultimately matters for purposes of responsibility is not the defendant's knowledge that his conduct is criminal, but rather his knowledge that his conduct is wrongful. Thus a provisional answer to questions involving referential opacity is that blameworthiness cannot be determined in the absence of additional information. If the defendant knows the properties of his conduct that render it wrongful, why need he know more to be blameworthy and eligible for punishment? A defendant who knows he is writing a chain letter, and knows that pyramid schemes are wrongful because of their exploitive feature, is liable as long as he knows that chain letters have this feature too. He need not also know that chain letters *are* pyramid schemes. The foregoing drug possessor would be blameworthy if (1) Molly is Ecstasy, (2) he knows he possesses Molly, (3) he knows possession of Ecstasy is wrongful, and (4) he knows Molly has whatever properties make the possession of Ecstasy wrongful. Unless each of these four conditions is satisfied, it is hard to see why his mental state would make him culpable for knowingly possessing Ecstasy.

Second, must the defendant who is fully culpable for her wrongful conduct know she lacks a defense for committing it? Must she know, that is, that she lacks both a justification and an excuse? After all, the absence of both a justification and an excuse is a prerequisite for liability and punishment. *One* part of this question is answered easily. Mistakes about the existence of an excuse are clearly irrelevant to the blameworthiness of the actor. Excusing conditions, we might say, are objective in the following sense: mistakes about whether they exist neither negate the wrongs that are committed nor the blameworthiness of the agent who commits them. As I have indicated, the presence of an excuse does not provide additional content to the formulation of the wrong proscribed. In other words, a complete description of the wrong against killing, for example, does not include an implicit *unless* clause, so that killings are wrong *unless* the killer happens to be insane or acts under duress. Excused killers are not permitted to kill, and the beliefs of the killer about the presence or absence of an excuse are immaterial to whether she has committed a wrongful act. Moreover, wrongdoers do not have an excuse of, say, insanity or duress, simply because they believe, however sincerely, that they are insane or act under duress when they perform their wrongful act. They lack blame when they *are* insane or act under an excuse of duress, not when they think they are. To be clear, the same is true about the exculpatory status of ignorance of morality or law. If ignorance of law should excuse, the rationale is not that a particular defendant believes ignorance of law should excuse. The rationale for exculpation resides in the correct theory of responsibility, regardless of whether the ignorant wrongdoer happens to accept or reject it.

Justifications however, present a much more difficult problem—a tangled set of issues that are among the most complex in the philosophy of criminal law. These difficulties have vexed criminal theorists for generations, illustrating once again the possible payoff of contrasting justification from excuse. Unlike excuses, justifications make conduct permissible, all things considered. Thus it is plausible to suppose that the existence of a justification *does* provide additional content to the formulation of the wrong proscribed. In other words, it is tempting to think that a complete description of the wrong against killing includes not only the explicit elements in the statutory definition of homicide, but also an implicit *unless* clause, so that killing is wrongful *unless* the killer possesses a justification such as self-defense. Moreover, it is important to note that the absence of a justification is among the explicit elements in statutory definitions of crimes involving recklessness (as well as those involving negligence). Thus a defendant who kills recklessly (or negligently) *cannot* commit a justified act; if his killing is justified, he can plead what I earlier characterized as a denial by alleging the offense did not occur at all.[16]

Nonetheless, we should not be too quick to concede that justifications (or, more precisely, their absence) are akin to elements inasmuch as they provide additional content to the formulation of the wrong proscribed. Several contested issues are discussed under

---

[16] See *Model Penal Code* §2.02(2)(c)&(d). It is not altogether clear, however, exactly *why* offenses of recklessness and negligence include the absence of justification in their statutory definitions.

the rubric of *unknowing justification*. Suppose a defendant performs a criminal act with mens rea: he knowingly kills another human being. Suppose further, however, that his particular act includes a justification. The defendant shoots a wrongful aggressor who was about to kill him, and the only way the defendant could have saved his own life was to kill the aggressor first. This pro tanto wrong is not wrong all things considered. Therefore, pursuant to the assumption I have made throughout this book, questions about the blameworthiness of this defendant simply do not arise. Yet this conclusion is controversial at best. Disagreement centers on situations in which the foregoing defendant is unaware of the existence of the justificatory circumstance that pertains to his conduct. To embellish my example, suppose he kills for malicious reasons, and is wholly unaware his victim happens to be a wrongful aggressor who is about to kill him. In such a case of unknowing justification, is it clear that the defendant cannot be blameworthy? After all, he knowingly killed another human being, thereby satisfying each of the statutory elements of the offense of murder. And he did so while having no idea of the existence of the circumstance that would justify him. Reams of scholarly ink have been spilled on this topic of unknowing justification, and I make no effort to survey the range of ingenious solutions that have been proposed.[17] On the level of intuition, which I admit to be untrustworthy, I am inclined to hold the unknowingly justified defendant blameworthy for the crime of murder. I tend to express this point by saying that the actor lacks a justification, even though his act is justified.[18] Perhaps we should say he is blameworthy because the act he performed—the knowing killing of another human being—is *presumptively* wrongful. The defendant understands he has a pro tanto moral reason not to do what he did, and he has no basis for thinking his reason is overridden or defeated. Is his knowledge of this pro tanto moral reason he does not believe to be overridden or defeated all that is needed to hold him responsible when he kills while unaware of the justificatory circumstance?[19]

[17] For an argument that the debate needs to be "relocated," see R.A. Duff: *Answering for Crime* (Oxford: Hart, 2007), p.281.

[18] See John Gardner: *Offences and Defences* (Oxford: Oxford University Press, 2007), chapter 11.

[19] Reasons to distinguish justifications from elements of offenses in a theory of responsibility are offered by George Fletcher: "The Right Deed for the Wrong Reason: A Reply to Mr. Robinson," 23 *U.C.L.A. Law Review* 293 (1975–1976).

For present purposes, the converse issue is even more central. That is, the more pressing question does not involve the defendant who is justified when he mistakenly believes he is not, but the defendant who is not justified when he mistakenly believes he is. This issue is familiar in the context of mistake of fact. Criminal theorists have long wrestled with the problem of whether *mistakenly justified* defendants are blameworthy and subject to penal liability, that is, whether defendants may be punished when they have false beliefs about facts that would comprise a justification if they were true. These defendants mistakenly believe, for example, that the innocent deliveryman they kill is an unlawful intruder who is about to kill them, and thus are incorrect about whether they actually possess a justification for killing him. They are justified on the facts as they believe them to be. But *are* they justified? Once again, theorists have defended different answers.[20] Common law adopts an "all-or-nothing" approach, holding reasonable mistakes about a justification to justify, but unreasonable mistakes about a justification not to justify. The Model Penal Code provides a more nuanced solution, matching the degree of culpability in the mistake the defendant makes with the degree of culpability required for liability under the statute breached.[21]

In the examples scholars have debated, the mistakenly justified defendant has false beliefs about the *facts* that would justify him. In the examples that concern *ignorantia juris,* however, the mistakenly justified defendant has false beliefs about the *morality* underlying the law he breaches. Thus we should imagine him to be aware he kills a victim who has insulted his mother, for example, but is unaware these facts do not justify his killing. He is mistaken, in other words, that he is justified to kill someone for insulting his mother. This defendant is ignorant of the all-things-considered wrongfulness of his act because he is ignorant about a supposed justification for committing it, that is, about a justification for breaching the statute proscribing murder. If a defendant must believe he is acting wrongly in order to be fully blameworthy, how can he possibly be blameworthy when he makes a mistake about the moral status of a supposed justification?

As far as I am aware, the foregoing question has not been discussed by legal philosophers who are highly critical of the doctrine of *ignorantia*

---

[20] For a recent novel proposal, see the discussion of the *warranted* in Duff: *Op.cit.* Note 17, pp.277–284.

[21] *Model Penal Code* §3.09.

juris. The wealth of commentary on mistakenly justified actors who are ignorant of the facts is matched by the poverty of commentary on mistakenly justified actors who are ignorant of the law or the morality underlying it. Perhaps commentators have thought about this issue, but balk at the prospects of explicitly allowing exculpation. Of course, the real worry does not involve defendants who erroneously believe they are justified to kill victims who insult their mothers. Despite its philosophical interest, the number of such cases is tiny as long as the scope of the inquiry is limited to sane adults. The larger problem involves ideologically driven zealots who erroneously believe they are justified to kill persons who oppose their political agenda. For dramatic effect, we might describe the most extreme such persons as *terrorists*—a group that includes fanatics who kill doctors who perform abortions. The proposal to acquit terrorists pursuant to a defense of ignorance of law because they mistakenly believe they have a moral justification for their heinous acts will strike many readers as the most devastating reductio of my theory thus far. As George Fletcher cautioned several years ago, "no theory of criminal law can tolerate the wholesale acquittal of revolutionary criminals."[22]

But how could my theory withhold exculpation from these "revolutionary criminals?" We respond to reasons by assigning approximate weights to the various considerations for and against the alternatives available to us. A terrorist who believes the value of purifying racial identity (or however he understands his twisted ideological agenda) outweighs the value of human life and therefore justifies mass killing is not behaving wrongfully by his own lights. Whatever else might be said about these villains, they do not behave akratically according to the conception I invoke here. How, then, can a subjectivist reason-responsive theory hold them responsible? To my mind, this problem constitutes the single most worrisome implication of a theory that affords some degree of exculpation to nearly all defendants who are ignorant of law. My normative thoughts about ignorance of law have painted me into a corner from which escape may be impossible.

I confess to enormous uncertainty about how to resolve this problem. As I will explain in Part C, I am not overly alarmed by the prospects of biting the bullet and exculpating garden-variety morally ignorant offenders, even when they commit a *malum in se*. Societies have long survived despite the numbers of parents who believe, for example,

---

[22] George Fletcher: *Rethinking Criminal Law* (Boston: Little, Brown and Co., 1978), p.749.

they are permitted to use corporal punishment when disciplining their disobedient children. Education rather than punishment is the more productive and humane response to those who perpetrate these relatively minor wrongs. Ideologically driven terrorists, however, threaten the very fabric of society and thus pose a more formidable problem. How does my theory allow us to protect ourselves from those who pose such a fundamental threat?[23] Three possible solutions at least mitigate the apparent absurdity of granting exculpation to all mistakenly justified actors—some of whom have committed the greatest atrocities in human history. I discuss each in turn and consider still other possibilities in part (C) .

First, we might try to borrow my proposed solution to the problem of the unknowingly justified defendant. I suggested such a defendant might be blameworthy because he realizes the act he performs is pro tanto wrongful; he lacks a justification even though his act is justified. In the converse situation, the acts of mistakenly justified actors are *not* justified, despite their belief to the contrary. Even the most zealous terrorist is likely to recognize his pro tanto moral reason not to kill, and his knowledge of this moral reason might be all that is needed to blame him. Inasmuch as the mistake of the terrorist is about a justification rather than about an element of the offense itself, the state might treat his ignorance differently from ignorance that he is perpetrating a pro tanto wrong. But I suspect I am guilty of wishful thinking in trying to use this strategy to reconcile blame with my general theory. After all, even *knowingly* justified defendants commit pro tanto wrongs, and no one proposes that *they* be blamed. But even if this proposed solution is indeed incompatible with my overall position, it might have to be implemented as a compromise between my theory and practical realities. At least this compromise would not be entirely unprincipled; as we have seen in the context of unknowingly justified actors, there is *some* basis for distinguishing between the blameworthiness of persons who make mistakes about the content of pro tanto wrongs and those who make mistakes about considerations that would justify the commission of such wrongs.

Second, I suspect that nearly all terrorists are at least reckless about whether their acts are morally justified. The substantial risk they might be mistaken about whether their political agenda provides a sufficient

---

[23] Some of the complexities involved in protecting ourselves from justified actors are explored in Heidi M. Hurd: *Moral Combat* (Cambridge: Cambridge University Press, 1999).

reason to kill has almost certainly occurred to most of them. How could it not? It is not hard to differentiate their culpability from that of persons who perform the same acts but understand perfectly well that their conduct is unjustified. Notwithstanding this differentiation, their recklessness would still make them responsible enough. After all, if their atrocities are sufficiently extreme—say, they kill scores of innocent victims while disregarding the risk their conduct might be wrongful—they would become eligible for an extraordinarily severe sentence. Punishment for multiple counts of (what I reclassify as) manslaughter is anything but lenient. Life imprisonment might still be deserved as a proportionate sentence under the theory of responsibility I have defended.

Finally, if all else fails, systems of preventive detention could be expanded to confine these misguided villains for purposes of public safety—as is already done with persons who are mentally ill and dangerous. Several theorists have suggested this mechanism should be employed for true psychopaths who do not recognize morality as reason-giving. A similar response might be given for persons who resemble but are not quite identical to psychopaths: those who recognize that morality gives reasons, but who systematically undervalue the *application* or *strength* of these reasons and believe they are easily overridden. If we opt for this last alternative for the class of wrongdoers who worry us most, the hard question is whether the goals of preventive detention are best pursued inside or outside the ambit of penal justice. I have contributed to the great deal of recent attention this issue has attracted.[24] Novel ideas to protect citizens from future harms through the criminal process are frequently defended,[25] although critics routinely denounce these proposals as a perversion of criminal justice.[26] The persons to be confined for preventive purposes might at least be *identified* through the criminal law, even if the sanctions ultimately imposed upon them

---

[24] For a defense of conceptualizing preventive detention *within* criminal justice, see Douglas Husak: "Lifting the Cloak: Preventive Detention as Punishment," 48 *San Diego Law Review* 1173 (2011); and "Preventive Detention as Punishment? Some Possible Reservations," in Andrew Ashworth, Lucia Zedner, and Patrick Tomlin, eds.: *Prevention and the Limits of the Criminal Law* (Oxford: Oxford University Press, 2013), p.178. See also Alec Walen: "A Punitive Precondition for Preventive Detention: Lost Status as a Foundation for Lost Immunity," 48 *San Diego Law Review* 1229 (2011).

[25] See Christopher Slobogin: "Plea Bargaining and the Substantive and Procedural Goals of Criminal Justice: From Retribution to and Adversarialism to Preventive Justice and Hybrid-Inquisitorialism," *William & Mary Law Review* (forthcoming, 2016).

[26] See Kimberly Kessler Ferzan: "Beyond Crime and Commitment: Justifying Liberty Deprivations of the Dangerous and Responsible," 96 *University of Minnesota Law Review* 141 (2011).

do not exactly qualify as *punishments*. But I need not try to resolve this controversy here. Although I tend to resist calls to bypass criminal justice in order to detain dangerous persons, candor that we are doing so may prove to be the least objectionable option if the state accepts my invitation to enlarge the exculpatory significance of ignorance of law and decides not to punish wrongdoers who believe they are morally innocent. In any event, we have a battery of options to ensure that ideologically driven terrorists are not released to prey upon innocent victims simply because we judge them to be neither mad nor fully blameworthy.

I do not pretend to have answered the complex questions involving mistaken justification. As I have indicated, I regard them as the single most troublesome aspect of my theory of ignorance of law. Compromises with my theory would be needed if the criminal justice system is disabled from coping with an overwhelming volume of totally misguided wrongdoers bent on serious mayhem. Nonetheless, I move to the second dimension of the issue I have raised. Consider a defendant who is reckless about whether she is acting wrongfully. What exactly must she believe about her conduct? Of course, she must suspect she is imposing a risk her behavior is wrongful. I have already discussed the question of whether she must be aware her conduct is unjustifiable. But what must she believe about the *extent* of the risk she knows she creates? Must this defendant not only believe she is imposing a risk that her conduct is wrong, but also believe that the risk she is imposing is substantial? Or is she blameworthy simply because she knows she is imposing a risk that is in fact substantial, even though she herself mistakenly regards it as trivial?

Pursuant to the presumptive symmetry I favor, this issue should be resolved in the same way for mistakes of law and for mistakes of fact. Even in the latter domain, however, the question has not been answered definitively. In either case, however, I propose that the defendant must actually believe the risk he creates is substantial. In the domain of fact, part of the rationale for requiring the reckless defendant to believe he has created a risk he knows to be substantial is that he might not take himself to be acting wrongfully if he thought the risk were minor. We all run small risks every day in any number of situations, simply by getting out of bed in the morning. Recycling again offers a perfect illustration. Am I really allowed to throw those plastic wrappers into the same can as my ordinary garbage? Even when I am a tourist in a city I know has progressive environmental policies? A mere inkling of a low probability of wrongdoing is insufficient for penal blameworthiness;

more is required than that the defendant cannot rule out the possibility altogether. I assume she must have some positive reason to think her conduct might actually be wrongful. Of course, the line between substantial and non-substantial risks is incredibly hard to identify. But such problems of "line-drawing" persist *whatever* formula is used and *however* statutory definitions of recklessness are formulated in the context of fact or law. If more perspicuous terminology can be devised to contrast permissible from impermissible levels of risk, legislators should be encouraged to employ it in both of these domains.

My third question about what A must believe about the wrongfulness of his conduct in order to be blameworthy for it raises an entirely different set of issues. Although I continue to describe my inquiry as involving ignorance of *law*, I have contended that defendants are not responsible unless they are knowledgeable of the *immorality* rather than the *illegality* of their wrongful conduct. As long as we remain interested in a moral justification of liability and punishment, exculpation is owed to defendants who are ignorant of the morality that underlies the law, rather than of the law itself. Two separate strains of argument lead to this conclusion. First, if the mere existence of a statute does not create an obligation of conformity in citizens where none existed previously, why is an obligation suddenly created when offenders happen to be aware of the law they violate? If the statute does not proscribe a moral wrong, knowledge of it does not create an obligation that was not present already, and ignorance of it cannot preclude an obligation that did not exist in the first place. Second, recall the line of cases in Chapter 2(D), discussed in the course of showing that ignorance of law sometimes exculpates as a denial of a mens rea element of the statute. In these cases, courts frequently interpret legislation to ensure that innocent defendants are not punished. The sense of *innocence* in question, however, is best construed as moral rather than legal. The commission of a legal wrong—a breach of the penal law—may provide a necessary condition for a legally justified punishment, but my normative focus as a philosopher is on a moral justification of penal sanctions.

Suppose, however, I am mistaken and persons *have* a prima facie obligation to obey the law—*all* law, or at least all law enacted in a reasonably just state that is not unconstitutional, illiberal, or violates a fundamental right, even if it is silly.[27] At first blush, a theory of ignorance

---

[27] See Dan Markel: "Retributive Justice and the Demands of Democratic Citizenship," 1 *Virginia Journal of Criminal Law* 1 (2012).

of law would seem to become much simpler. Persons would commit *a prima facie* moral wrong *whenever* they breach a statute; we would not need to undertake a separate inquiry into whether they had or lacked an obligation to conform to the particular law breached. Immoral conduct would still be required to explain why punishment is justified from a moral point of view, but the moral wrongfulness of conduct would be guaranteed whenever a law is broken. Nonetheless, on closer inspection, appearances on this matter are deceptive—as I have stressed. We still would need to assess the responsibility of persons who break the law but do not believe they have done so. The fact that they are acting wrongfully simply by acting illegally hardly establishes they are blameworthy for so doing. Our basic question remains: Why should rational persons respond to a moral reason they did not take themselves to have? If I am correct, the debate about the existence of a *prima facie* obligation to obey the law turns out to be something of a red herring that is orthogonal to my inquiry. This issue is important only if such an obligation exists *and* a defensible conception of responsibility supports the punishment of those who are so obligated. Both conditions need to be satisfied before an offender would act wrongfully according to her own lights and becomes blameworthy pursuant to my reason-responsive theory.

My requirement that defendants be cognizant of the morality underlying the law and not the law itself may avoid or even solve some problems, but raises other puzzles involving the significance of legality. Why does the law matter at all? I will return to this difficult topic in Chapter 5(A). At this point, I ask: What is it *about* morality that wrongdoers must believe in order to be responsible? Actions proscribed by law may be wrongful on a variety of different grounds. Some are *mala in se*; others are *mala prohibita*. It is incorrect to suppose that offenders cannot act wrongfully when they breach a *malum prohibitum;* after all, *mala prohibita* are still alleged to be *mala*. As I will explain further in Part C, the ground for supposing given *mala prohibita* are wrongful varies from case to case. Some statutes are wrong to breach because defendants have agreed to conform to them, others are wrong to breach because of duties of fair play, others may be wrong to breach for different reasons altogether, and still others may not be wrong to breach at all. For present purposes, the important point is that a defendant who is blameworthy for violating a given *malum prohibitum* need have no precise understanding of *why* her act is wrongful. Nor need she know exactly *which* wrong she is committing. If she jumps a

turnstile in a subway without paying the toll, she need have no conception that her free-riding violates a deontological constraint in order
to be aware her action is immoral. The only true belief she must have
in order to be responsible is that her act *is* wrongful.

Each of the above issues is difficult. Solving them is important to
apply my theory and to help us assess the extent to which it has radical
implications for the real world of criminal justice. Will a great many
defendants who are punished at present be exculpated if my theory is
implemented? I have continually emphasized that the repercussions
of my position would not be earth-shattering, although it is hard to
be sure. Much of the uncertainty derives from unanswered empirical
questions: How many defendants do *not* know or even suspect that
their criminal acts are wrongful? Terrorists aside, we need not be overly
alarmed when we focus on many of the offenses that worry us. It seems
hard to believe that bank robbers or burglars do not understand their
acts are wrongful—especially when we recall that my view applies
only to sane adults. In the case of offenses that probably alarm us
less, however, the potential for exculpation grows. Drug offenders, in
particular, may believe that what they are doing is permissible. I see no
reason to balk at the implication that such persons are not responsible
for their offenses. As I have argued at length elsewhere, I strongly doubt
that most drug offenses *are* wrongful.[28] At least, no one has *shown* them
to be wrongful, and the burden of proof should always be placed on
those who advocate criminalization and punishment. I would welcome
rather than resist the conclusion that my position provides yet another
ground on which to spare most drug offenders from penal liability.

I end this section with a final note of uncertainty about whether
my theory has profound ramifications for the real world of criminal
justice. My quandary about this matter derives both from empirical
conjectures and from further confusions about exactly what a defendant must believe about the wrongfulness of his conduct in order to
be eligible for blame. I stipulated that Sabine, my bicycle thief, acts
akratically. If we do not resort to stipulation, however, determinations
often become more unsettled—as Gideon Rosen frequently reminds
us. Persons demonstrate a remarkable ability to rationalize their
wrongful behavior in the circumstances in which they act; few of us
are willing to admit our acts are impermissible. Even when we engage
in conduct we realize to be bad, we cite extenuating circumstances

---

[28] Douglas Husak: *Drugs and Rights* (Cambridge: Cambridge University Press, 1992).

designed to show it is *less* bad than our accusers take it to be. Many of these techniques are learned at a very young age, and are common to white-collar offenders and juvenile delinquents alike. A brief summary of these mechanisms of rationalization is helpful in further muddying the waters about exactly what criminal defendants must believe about the wrongfulness of their conduct in order to be fully responsible for it.

Sociologists have long described several of the rationalizing mechanisms typical of offenders.[29] I mention five of the most familiar such devices, although further examples could be added to the list.[30] First, defendants frequently deny responsibility by alleging an inability to prevent the transgression. Wrongdoers protest they were impaired by drugs or alcohol, or their conduct was accidental, or they were caused to offend by forces outside of their control. They sometimes allege they "went crazy," were influenced by a "bad crowd," or "knew no better" because of their impoverished neighborhood and upbringing. Second, they often minimize the severity of the harm they inflict. They reason, for example, that the stolen car was actually insured, or that the person attacked was a seasoned fighter whose injuries are not so grave. Third, they may deny the status of the victim. They depict the injured party as a perpetrator or, at least, as a person of little moral worth. A common version of this rationalization is "they started it," so the ensuing conduct is transformed into an instance of self-defense. Fourth, they might condemn the condemners, implying that their accusers are themselves wrongdoers with no right to pass judgment. How do the robber barons of the capitalist class have standing to stigmatize blue-collar workers? Finally, defendants sometimes allege that their behavior is widespread and thus does not really violate norms. Elsewhere, I have questioned whether some of these pleas—such as the allegation that "everyone does that"—might actually enjoy more exculpatory significance than penal theorists are inclined to allow.[31] At this point, however, I mention these rationalizations simply because they cast additional doubt on my supposition that many wrongdoers are fully aware they are acting

---

[29] The classic source is G. Sykes and D. Matza: "Techniques of Neutralisation: A Theory of Delinquency," 22 *American Sociological Review* 664 (1957).

[30] See Darren Thiel: "Criminal Ignorance," in Matthias Gross and Linsey McGoey, eds.: *The International Handbook of Ignorance Studies* (Routledge, forthcoming).

[31] See Douglas Husak: "The 'But Everyone Does That!' Defense," in Douglas Husak, ed.: *The Philosophy of Criminal Law* (Oxford: Oxford University Press, 2010), p.338.

against the balance of moral reasons and thus deserve blame. At face value, the foregoing sociological considerations may show that persons are ambivalent about whether they are indeed committing wrongs.[32] What is unsettled, however, is the extent to which wrongdoers *really* believe their own rationalizations—some but not all of which are transparent ruses alleged in a desperate ploy to avoid or reduce blame. It is hard to be sure. Perhaps some of these persons should be deemed reckless and thus eligible for less than the full quantum of punishment the law authorizes for their offense.

These and other questions about exactly *what* A must believe in order to be fully responsible present some of the most difficult and unresolved challenges faced by my theory about the exculpatory significance of ignorance of law. In light of these many challenges, it may be helpful to summarize the several conditions under which wrongdoers are fully responsible and thus eligible for the maximum punishment the law allows. Recall that A is a sane adult with the capacity for moral responsibility—a capacity that may not be present in psychopaths. He does not possess any of the familiar defenses (either a justification such as self-defense or an excuse such as duress) for his criminal act Φ. He recognizes his act is wrongful, so whatever environmental factors tend to inhibit his awareness are not effective in his case. Although he is akratic in that he acts against what he takes to be the balance of moral reasons, he does not suffer from a compulsion sufficiently strong to mitigate his blame. He does not really believe any of the rationalizations that would make his behavior permissible. Perhaps additional conditions must be satisfied as well. But the sheer length of this list should persuade us that *full* responsibility as I have characterized it is relatively unusual. Penal offenses typically allow a wide range of sentences for which perpetrators become eligible. Most criminals, I am sure, deserve less than the maximum sentence the law authorizes for their crime. I hope this conclusion strikes most readers as an *advantage* of my theory. Our existing system of criminal justice punishes far too severely, and my account offers a principled basis to

---

[32] Some moral philosophers who agree that akratic actions are blameworthy sometimes take account of this sociological data by requiring the wrongdoer to act with *clear-eyed akrasia*. See Gideon Rosen: "Culpability and Ignorance," 103 *Proceedings of the Aristotelian Society* 61 (2003).

combat this phenomenon. The criteria of *full* responsibility, as I have construed it, are rarely satisfied.

B. Hard Cases and Possible Exceptions

I have argued that A should be punished more severely than B for the same act Φ that violates law L when A knows Φ is wrongful but B does not. As we will continue to see, efforts to incorporate this position into the real world of statutory law almost certainly require a number of compromises. In this part, however, I do not describe the inevitable retreats that must be made from what I take to be an ideal of retributive desert. Instead, I describe a number of *exceptions* to my position—circumstances in which even ideal theory affords no exculpatory force whatever to ignorance of law. In these kinds of case, B should be punished every bit as severely as A. I am not altogether certain, however, exactly how *many* kinds of exceptions should be countenanced. In what follows, I will examine three possible such circumstances: cases in which B is *willfully ignorant* of law L, cases in which B's conduct falls under what I call a *legal loophole,* and, finally, cases in which B acts *in* but not *from* ignorance. In each of these types of example, it is at least plausible to suppose that A and B should be punished the same amount, even if we accept that their blameworthiness *usually* differs. The difficulty, of course, is to find principled grounds for granting (or denying) an exception. In the first of the scenarios I will discuss, I am sure an exception to my general theory should be recognized: A and B *are* equally blameworthy. I am less confident and thus withhold judgment about the final two kinds of case; *perhaps* B is just as blame-worthy as A in these latter situations. At any rate, I am unaware of *other* plausible exceptions to the generalizations of my theory, even though I have no idea how to "prove a negative" that no further kinds of case exist. Moreover, compromises are hard to contrast from exceptions. As I have admitted, I cannot bring myself to exculpate terrorists who believe they have a justification for committing wrongful actions, and my unwillingness to do so may require a compromise rather than a principled exception. In any event, legal philosophers are welcome to offer additional candidates for exceptions and/or compromises.

I now move to real or possible exceptions heretofore barely mentioned. First, consider the phenomenon of *willful blindness* (or *willful ignorance*). I have contended that we need not be too concerned about how B *came* to be ignorant of law in order to conclude that she is entitled to some degree of exculpation relative to A. In particular, an unfulfilled duty to inquire about L rarely if ever provides a sound rationale for holding B as culpable for Φ as A. I now want to acknowledge an important exception to this contention about the irrelevance of history to a judgment of B's degree of blameworthiness. In cases of what I will call *willful blindness,* the story about how and why B came to be or remains ignorant of her wrongdoing has a special salience. We must clarify exactly what is meant by willful blindness to understand this salience. I do so by explaining the significance of willful blindness in the more familiar context of mistake of fact. This explanation is important because my subsequent approach takes a similar path when defendants are willfully blind about a proposition of law.

A number of penal statutes—such as those proscribing the possession of illicit drugs—require the mens rea of knowledge. A defendant is not liable for possessing cocaine, for example, unless he knows the substance he possesses is illicit. If he believes the substance he has just purchased is sugar, he is not guilty of the crime of illicit drug possession. But almost all courts and commentators agree that a mental state they describe as "willful blindness" satisfies the knowledge requirement. *United States v Jewell*[33] remains the leading case in which the concept of willful blindness was invoked to uphold a conviction. The defendant was arrested after driving an automobile in which 110 pounds of marijuana had been concealed in a secret compartment between the trunk and rear seat. He testified that he had been paid $100 by a stranger to drive the car into the country, and that he was not actually aware it contained contraband. Liability required that the defendant knowingly bring the drugs into the country. The court affirmed the defendant's conviction, upholding the following instruction: "The Government can complete their burden of proof by proving, beyond a reasonable doubt, that if the defendant was not actually aware that there was marijuana in the vehicle he was driving when he entered the United States his ignorance in that regard was solely and entirely a result of his having made a conscious purpose to disregard the nature of that which was in the vehicle, with a conscious purpose to avoid learning the truth."[34] The court added that "knowingly" should not

---

[33] 532 F.2d 697 (9th Cir. 1976).
[34] *Id.,* p.700.

be equated with "positive knowledge" because such an interpretation "would make deliberate ignorance a defense."[35]

What exactly *is* the mental state of willful blindness possessed by the defendant in *Jewell*? I take this term to be stipulative, with a technical meaning in law. To explicate it, we must attend to the purposes it is designed to serve. *My* purpose is relatively clear; the concept allows conviction in cases such as *Jewell*: those in which defendants may lack genuine (or "positive") knowledge of what they possess and who otherwise would have to be acquitted.[36] This purpose can be accomplished either by describing a mental state that *is* a kind of knowledge, or a mental state that is *not* a kind of knowledge but can plausibly be construed to be the moral equivalent of it. The draftsmen of the *Model Penal Code* sought to achieve this purpose in the following way. The Code generally defines "knowledge" of the "nature of [a defendant's] conduct" to require that "he is aware that his conduct is of that nature."[37] But a subsection of the Code provides that "knowledge of the existence of a particular fact" is established "if a person is aware of a high probability of its existence, unless he actually believes that it does not exist."[38] The commentaries explain that this subsection is designed to deal with the phenomenon of "willful blindness," in which the defendant "is aware of the probable existence of a material fact but does not determine whether it exists or does not exist."[39] The explanatory note alleges that this subsection "elaborates on the definition of 'knowledge.'"[40]

If intended as a definition of willful blindness that serves its normative purpose, the foregoing provision of the *Model Penal Code* is defective on a number of grounds.[41] First, not all cases in which a defendant would seem to be willfully blind involve "aware[ness] of a high probability" of the "existence of a particular fact." Consider the

---

[35] *Id.*, p.703.

[36] I do not deny that different conceptions of willful blindness are defensible in contexts other than those in which blameworthiness and/or punishment are at stake. Nor do I explore the similarities and differences between willful blindness as I characterize it and what has been called *motivated ignorance*. See Michelle Moody-Adams: "Culture, Responsibility, and Affected Ignorance," 104 *Ethics* 291 (1994).

[37] *Model Penal Code* §2.02(2)(b)(i).

[38] *Id.*, §2.02(7).

[39] *Id.*, Commentary, p.248.

[40] *Id.*, Explanatory Note, p.228.

[41] My account draws on Douglas Husak and Craig Callendar: "Willful Ignorance, Knowledge, and the 'Equal Culpability' Thesis: A Study of the Deeper Significance of the Principle of Legality," in Douglas Husak, ed.: *Philosophy, Op.cit.* Note 31, p.200.

following counterexample. Suppose that a foreigner approaches two American tourists who are about to return home. He offers to pay either of them $100 to deliver a suitcase to a contact in America. When the tourists inquire about the contents of the suitcase, the foreigner replies: "You have no need to know." Both tourists are tempted, but decline because they are apprehensive; they suspect but do not know the truth of the proposition "the suitcase contains illicit drugs." So the foreigner modifies his offer in order to persuade them. He proposes to pay each of them $100 to deliver *two* suitcases, and assures them that one (he will not identify which) of the suitcases is empty. Each tourist accepts this modified offer. Suppose that the tourists are stopped by customs officials, who open the suitcases and discover that one contains illegal drugs. Can the tourist whose suitcase contained the drugs be convicted under a statute that forbids knowingly possessing a controlled substance?[42] If either tourist had accepted the foreigner's original offer, his mental state would depict a paradigm case of willful ignorance. But what is to be said about the state of mind of the arrested tourist who accepts the modified proposal? This question must be answered by inquiring whether categorizing his mental state as willful blindness helps to achieve the purpose for which that concept was invented. By this standard, it seems clear that the question should be answered affirmatively. Anyone who agrees that the tourist in the original hypothetical should be convicted for violating a statute that requires that he act knowingly is unlikely to change his mind when the example is modified. It seems more plausible to conclude that the tourists are willfully blind in both the original and the modified hypotheticals, even though the tourist in the latter example does not believe it is highly probable that he is carrying contraband. Thus, the "highly probable" component of the *Model Penal Code* account of willful blindness must be rejected.

Moreover, it is not even clear that the foregoing account is correct in specifying that a defendant cannot be willfully blind of a material fact that "he actually believes . . . does not exist." As further modifications of the foregoing example indicate, some defendants who seem to be willfully blind would estimate the probability of a given proposition p (such as "my suitcase contains illegal drugs") as less than 50 percent.

---

[42] In my modified example, Peter Westen has pointed out that liability might be imposed under doctrines of conspiracy. But this concession does not settle the question of whether the defendant is also willfully blind.

Suppose my example is altered further to involve three tourists, two of whose suitcases are known to be empty. If so, each tourist would actually attach a higher degree of credence to the proposition that his suitcase does *not* contain illegal drugs. But this fact does not entail that none of these defendants could be willfully ignorant. Thus the agent's estimation of the probability of the truth of a proposition does not seem to be essential to judgments about whether he is willfully blind. Even a belief in the existence of the material fact is not an essential component of the phenomenon of willful blindness. Reconsider the foregoing hypotheticals. If a defendant need not actually believe p in order to be willfully blind about it—and might actually *dis*believe p— what mental state must he have? In the last example, all three defendants would appear to be willfully blind because they are *suspicious* that the suitcase contains drugs. This conclusion indicates that the complex relationship between belief and probability is somewhat tangential to the analysis of willful ignorance.

Willful blindness cannot be equated with suspicion alone, however. Although a precise characterization of this stipulative term is controversial, I hold that at least two non-mental conditions differentiate the willfully blind defendant from the suspicious defendant. The first might be called the *availability* condition. Typically, the willfully blind defendant will not have evaluated all of the evidence that an honest person in his circumstances would have considered. If he has the means to learn the truth (or to gather more evidence) about the significance of his actions, and is aware of these means, his inexcusable failure to act on these suspicions is a plain sign of willful blindness. He cannot simply fail to pursue unreliable, time-consuming, or extraordinary means to learn the truth. The facts must be readily available to anyone disposed to discover them. The second condition to differentiate the willfully blind defendant from the suspicious defendant might be called the *motivational* condition. The willfully blind defendant must have a given motive for remaining unaware of the truth: he must consciously desire to preserve a possible defense from blame or liability in the event he is apprehended. His failure to gain more information cannot be due to mere laziness, stupidity, or the absence of curiosity. Thus he is unlike the person who does not open a gift-wrapped package because he does not want to spoil the surprise until his birthday.

In summary, a defendant is willfully blind of an incriminating proposition of fact p when he is suspicious that p is true, fails to pursue reliable, quick, and ordinary measures that would enable him to learn the truth of p, and, finally, has a conscious desire to remain ignorant of p in order to avoid blame or liability in the event the truth emerges. In a paradigm case of willful blindness, the defendant suspects his trunk contains contraband, could easily open it to find out, but chooses to remain ignorant in order to retain a possible defense if he is apprehended. This characterization of willful blindness is defensible in light of the normative purpose for inventing the concept: to specify a culpable mental state that allows conviction in cases such as *Jewell*. Arguably, this mental state is the moral equivalent of knowledge. Thus it is plausible to hold this defendant liable for violating a statute that requires him to act knowingly.

The phenomenon I have described can be applied indifferently to both ignorance of law and ignorance of fact. The defendant who is willfully blind about his wrongdoing is indeed unaware that his act is immoral. As we have seen, however, some defendants have a culpable state that is not adequately captured either by complete ignorance or by full knowledge. In every case of what I call willful blindness of law, B is at least reckless with respect to the law she breaks. That is, she consciously disregards a substantial and unjustifiable risk that her conduct Φ breaches L. If she lacks any degree of suspicion that her conduct is illegal, the willfulness of her behavior would be inexplicable. The mystery would derive from the requirement that the willfully blind offender must satisfy the motivational condition and deliberately fail to take reasonable steps to discover the truth. She is motivated not to inquire about L because she prefers not to know the truth in order to preserve her ignorance in the event her inquiry would reveal her conduct to be illegal. We can easily imagine a defendant who thinks she may be acquiring a prescription drug but deliberately puts her hand over the label on the bottle to conceal the icon that indicates it contains a controlled substance. In such a case, I submit, this defendant B would be willfully blind about her wrongdoing and deserve no exculpation relative to A, who is aware his conduct is illegal.

Consider how the phenomenon of willful blindness applies to a case I have already discussed. In Chapter 3(C), I presented an example of a weightlifter who curses without realizing that profanity has been banned in his health club. He did not read a sign on the wall of the gym that explicitly prohibits his foul language. Suppose I embellish the example so that the weightlifter deliberately refrains from reading the sign whenever his gaze wanders to it. He purposely fails to read the sign precisely because he fears it might prohibit profanity, and he prefers to remain ignorant of the rule in order to remain blameless whenever he violates it. I deny that persons can orchestrate the conditions of their own lack of responsibility by this sort of connivance. When the example is embellished in this way, the willfully ignorant weightlifter is just as blameworthy as someone who violates the rule knowingly.

Cases of willful blindness are the clearest exceptions to my theory that otherwise grants some degree of exculpation to defendants who are ignorant of law. I am more ambivalent about what to say in two additional kinds of case I discuss. The first set of worries involves defendants I call (for lack of a better term) *legal loopholers*. In each of the type of case I have in mind, the defendant engages in conduct Φ knowing it to be morally wrongful and correctly believing the state has ample reason to criminalize it. In the easier of two variants, the loopholer believes Φ is *not* prohibited by law. But his belief is mistaken; a law L *does* prohibit Φ. I see no reason to allow this defendant to be acquitted, despite his mistake of law. His act is both legally proscribed as well as knowingly wrongful, so no exculpation should be available to him. In short, his mistake of *law* is beside the point. In the second and more difficult of the two variants, the loopholer again knows his conduct to be wrongful and correctly believes the state has ample reason to criminalize it. Now, however, he believes Φ *is* prohibited by law. But this latter belief is mistaken; no law actually prohibits Φ. If what matters to responsibility is immoral behavior knowingly performed, why should this defendant not be punished? Examples that conform to this variant need not be contrived; spousal rape may provide a perfect illustration. Suppose a defendant rapes his spouse in 1990, believing it to be morally wrongful as well as illegal. In the U.K., his (now mistaken) belief about the law would have been correct until 1992. The loopholer thinks an unjustifiable gap in the law permits him to perform an act he knows to be wrong. Existing doctrine, of course, would require his acquittal. The principle of legality precludes punishment because the loopholer is not actually violating a law, despite his belief to the contrary. Is this result defensible?

I again contend that no injustice would be done to the latter defendant if he incurs liability while trying to pass through a legal loophole. But should such persons really be punished? If not, why not? In my judgment, any rationale for a failure to punish must appeal to some factor other than desert. Paul Robinson usefully identifies a number of *non-exculpatory* public policy defenses—grounds on which punitive sanctions should not be inflicted even though they would do no injustice to the defendant.[43] As I have indicated, Michael Cahill believes these considerations apply in nearly every case in which a defense of ignorance of law should be granted. Arguably, he is correct about the type of case I examine here: those in which loopholers knowingly commit wrongs they mistakenly believe have been proscribed. In this peculiar circumstance, at least, policy grounds militate against punishment. In the absence of a preexisting statute, legal officials should probably lack confidence—beyond a reasonable doubt—that the type of case represented by the loopholer is before them. Just as we should withhold the power to conduct illegal searches or to punish persons twice for the same crime, we should withhold the power to enforce the rules of public morality without first codifying them in statutes. Historical examples from Nazi Germany and the Soviet Union in which states claimed the authority to punish wrongdoers who did not clearly violate the law—which involve the infamous *principle of analogy*—serve as chilling reminders that such powers are best withheld.[44] In short, too much authority would be granted to officials in a state that enforced morality rather than public wrongs codified in advance. Allowing loopholers to escape their just deserts is probably a small price to pay to keep state power within acceptable boundaries.

A clarification is needed. When I said that no injustice would be done to the loopholer who is punished if he knows he has committed a wrong that should have been proscribed but happens not to be, I am of course referring to *moral* injustice. Unless the concept is unintelligible, it is patently clear that this defendant would suffer a *legal* injustice. Legal theorists would be sure to protest vehemently if my loopholer were punished in contravention of legality. They should be pressed to identify the exact basis of their outrage. They might cite such cases as *Shaw v. Director of Public Prosecutions*—a staple in many criminal law textbooks.[45] Shaw was convicted for the common law crime of "conspiracy to corrupt public morals," which he allegedly committed by including the names of prostitutes in a magazine for publication and sale. I suspect the vast majority of criminal theorists concur that Shaw's conviction should have been reversed. But do they reach this conclusion because they regard his punishment as a moral

---

[43] Paul Robinson: *Criminal Law Defenses* (St. Paul, MN: West 1984), §26.
[44] Note: "The Use of Analogy in Criminal Law," 47 *Columbia Law Review* 613 (1947).
[45] [1962] A.C. 220.

injustice? Many of the several opinions in this case recite the policy grounds to which I have alluded. And whatever reservations we have about conviction from a moral rather than a legal point of view may derive from doubts about whether Shaw's conduct is wrongful in the first place. Moreover, even if his conduct *is* wrongful, it is far from clear that Shaw himself knew as much. Thus the moral lesson about the importance of legality derived from *Shaw*—or from any other case of which I am aware—is not altogether clear. I suggest that situations in which defendants (1) knowingly engage in wrongful conduct that (2) should be proscribed but (3) happens not to be prohibited are best treated as occasions in which my theory about the exculpatory force of ignorance of law should be qualified to further important social objectives independent of moral justice and desert.[46]

I turn next to the third and final possible exception to my theory. This class of cases raises the problem counterfactuals present for my analysis.[47] What judgment should we make about B, who is genuinely mistaken about the moral and legal status of her conduct Φ, if we stipulate that she *would* have committed Φ in any event, that is, even if she had known the truth? According to the scenario I have in mind, B acts *in* ignorance but not *from* ignorance; her mistake is materially irrelevant, making no difference to her behavior. This situation is probably fairly common. Suppose a waitress sincerely believes her tips are not taxable income and that she has no moral duty to declare them as such. In addition, however, she would continue to fail to declare them on her tax return even if she learned she is incorrect and tips are subject to taxation after all. What is the exculpatory status of her mistake under these circumstances? I am genuinely torn. According to my theory, her mistake would seem to have exculpatory significance; she cannot rationally respond to a reason she does not believe she has. Yet a harsher verdict might well be warranted, and a quality of will theory could offer a better perspective on why this is so: the waitress possesses an objectionable quality of will if correcting her mistake would not cause her behavior to change.

Indeed, some philosophers who hold quality of will theories are prepared to invoke counterfactuals to make a number of fine-grained

---

[46] For a different attempt to deal with the problems posed by legal loopholers, see Steven Garvey: "Authority, Ignorance, and the Guilty Mind," *Southern Methodist University Law Review* 545 (2014).

[47] See Alan C. Michaels: "Acceptance: The Missing Mental State," 71 *Southern California Law Review* 953 (1998).

judgments about the relative blameworthiness or praiseworthiness of agents. The responsibility of persons who care too little about moral reasons might increase or decrease depending on how *much* weight they take such reasons to have. Counterfactuals can be used to identify what changes in their circumstances would need to occur before their behavior would improve. Praise may be similar in this regard. Suppose Karen and Kathy both do the morally right thing in helping an elderly lady across the street with her groceries. We might suppose that the extent to which their actions are praiseworthy is a function (*ceteris paribus*) of the depth of their moral concern in performing them.[48] Depth of concern is plausibly measured by counterfactuals. Suppose Karen would have left the lady to struggle if someone had offered her one dollar to do so, but Kathy would need a bribe of fifty dollars before altering her conduct. Thus Kathy has a greater degree of moral concern than Karen. Does the truth of these counterfactuals affect the amount of praise each deserves when they perform the same good deed for the same good reason? Reasonable minds disagree.

Positive law has said little about the significance of counterfactuals to penal liability, and not simply because it is wedded to the draconian rule of *ignorantia juris*. The more obvious explanation of this failure is epistemological; we seldom are in a position to be confident how persons would have behaved had they known what they did not. Even the defendant *herself* may be unable to reliably predict her behavior under counterfactual conditions. Thus we can hardly expect the law to make the fine-grained distinctions in blameworthiness that many moral philosophers are prepared to recognize. As standards of proof for penal liability are high—defendants are protected by a presumption of innocence requiring proof beyond a reasonable doubt—particular defendants should probably be given the benefit of the doubt about the role ignorance plays in their behavior. Of course, this conclusion does not resolve the question on principled grounds. Does a given ignorant defendant deserve any degree of exculpation even if we *could* be sure she would persist in her wrongful behavior when she learns the truth?

Assistance in answering this question might come from applying my presumption that ignorance of fact and law should be treated symmetrically. Suppose a defendant makes a mistake of fact when

---

[48] Nomy Arpaly: *Unprincipled Virtue: An Inquiry into Moral Agency* (Oxford: Oxford University Press, 2003), p.84.

committing, say, a homicide. She intentionally shoots and kills a victim who happens to be her spouse, sincerely believing him to be an animal prowling in her garage. No system of criminal law of which I am aware would hold her to be liable for murder just because she *would* have shot and killed if she had known she was aiming at her spouse. This result obtains even if she had entered her garage to prepare to get into her car to find and murder the very victim she happens to shoot. In this situation, the actus reus and mens rea of the offense would not correspond. Of course, resort to arcane legal doctrines involving correspondence hardly settles the issue normatively. Arguably, defendants who kill *in* but not *from* ignorance should be liable, regardless of what the law happens to say about their factual or legal mistake. Given my ambivalence about this issue—which I take to be shared by many legal and moral philosophers—it is fortunate we can rarely be confident it arises in the real world.

I have defended a normative theory about ignorance of law and have described three kinds of case in which it may admit of exceptions. I have been definitive about only the first, admitting to uncertainty about the next two. Moreover, I do not pretend that additional hard cases may not arise—situations in which defendants are justifiably punished to the full extent despite being mistaken about whether morality or the law prohibits their conduct. The challenge is to rationalize potential counterexamples without allowing them to undermine the foundations of the theory I have constructed. I turn now to what may be the broadest class of hard cases for my claim that morally ignorant defendants deserve exculpation.

C. The Doubly Problematic Case of *Mala Prohibita*

Subject to the refinements and clarifications I have mentioned, my basic question (Q) asks whether the law should differentiate between the punishments deserved by A and B, each of whom commits the same act Φ that violates law L, when the latter but not the former is unaware Φ violates L, because of her mistake of law. Criminal theorists should have suspected from the start that no *general* answer can be found. Perhaps different types of laws are amenable to different analyses. After all, we have seen that the schema to which (Q) responds is literally incoherent when L allows for a denial of mens rea (or the mens rea of criminality). In this part I examine whether a different answer to (Q) must be provided depending on whether L is an instance of a *mala prohibita* or a *mala in se*. I argue that no different answer need be given. Contrary to conventional wisdom, this cryptic contrast plays no important role in a normative theory of ignorance of law. Even so, I will argue that the existence of *mala prohibita* offenses is *doubly problematic* for a theory of penal responsibility. These offenses raise distinct questions about how the wrongfulness *and* blameworthiness conditions of deserved punishment can be satisfied. These latter two conditions, of course, pertain to *all* offenses, *mala prohibita* and *mala in se* alike. Thus the problem, as we will see, is not that different standards apply, but rather how to determine whether and under what circumstances these common standards are satisfied in the case of offenses that are *mala prohibita*.

Philosophers are fond of distinctions, and philosophers of law are no exception. The distinction between *mala in se* and *mala prohibita* has played a pivotal role in the history of scholarly treatments of ignorance of law. Criminal theorists have been uniformly unwilling to allow such ignorance to provide any degree of exculpation when a statute proscribes a preexisting moral wrong. Yet many of these same commentators are far more open-minded about allowing exculpation in cases of *mala prohibita*. Superficially, this pair of positions seems easy to motivate. The very suggestion that a perpetrator of a serious *malum in se* might escape his just deserts is regarded by many legal philosophers as a reductio of the claim that ignorance of law has exculpatory force across the entire spectrum of penal offenses. My own theory, which locates responsibility in a defective response to reasons from an internalist or subjectivist perspective, threatens to exculpate some of the most notorious villains in human history. Yet there is nothing nearly as counterintuitive about conceding some amount of exculpation to those defendants who breach an obscure regulatory offense of which few citizens are aware. It is no coincidence that each of the examples in Chapter 2 in which statutes are construed to contain an explicit or implicit clause allowing defendants to gain exculpation by denying mens rea would seem to be an instance of a *malum prohibitum*. It is less likely—and perhaps unthinkable—that courts would offer a novel interpretation of a culpability term to allow a defendant who is ignorant of law to evade liability by denying mens rea when a *malum in se* is charged.[49]

Some of the most distinguished commentators in the history of criminal theory have embraced this pair of positions. I mention only one: Henry Hart. He maintains that the "essential rationale" of the "much misunderstood" maxim of *ignorantia juris* is that any person who engages in intrinsically wrongful, prohibited acts "without knowing that they are criminal is blameworthy, as much for his lack of knowledge as for his actual conduct."[50] He holds that "even if an offender somehow did not know that murder violates the criminal law, he would be blameworthy and deserving of criminal punishment nonetheless, as much because he did not know that murder was wrong as because he killed." Hart was quick to add, however, that his reasoning applies only to statutes that are *mala in se,* not to those that are *mala prohibita.*[51] One would have expected a commentator as astute as Hart to realize that the alleged culpable state of not knowing what one should know—which is the textbook definition of negligence—is not equivalent to the culpable state of actual knowledge. Does he really think that someone who kills not knowing killing is wrong is just as culpable as someone who actually has this moral knowledge? My present point, however, is only that Hart's reasoning parallels that of countless commentators who uncritically adopt a pair of positions about the normative status of *ignorantia juris*—a status that depends on the contrast between *mala in se* and *mala prohibita.* Despite its apparent intuitive appeal and support from a number of prominent criminal theorists, however, I will argue in this part that the contrast between *malum in se* and *malum prohibitum* has no deep normative significance in a theory of the conditions under which ignorance of law should have exculpatory force. We should not infer, however, that the existence of this type of offense is entirely unproblematic from the perspective of my theory.

---

[49] As I have indicated, the Mens Rea Reform Act of 2015 introduced by Orin Hatch would radically expand the defense of ignorance of law. Pursuant to §28(a)(1)(B)(iii), knowledge of criminality is not required, however, when an offense "involves conduct which a reasonable person would know inherently poses an imminent and substantial danger to life or limb." This exception disallows the defense for all *mala in se* offenses but allows it for most *mala prohibita* offenses; *available at* http://www.hatch.senate.gov/public/_cache/files/56edc2e6-c658-4a2a-bdb5-e259819c48a4/HEN15E40.pdf.

[50] Henry M. Hart, Jr.: "The Aims of the Criminal Law," 23 *Law and Contemporary Problems* 401, 413 (1958).

[51] *Id.,* p.419.

I begin with three preliminaries. First, I said this contrast lacks *deep* normative significance. I mean that any apparent importance this distinction may possess is due to other factors—factors that only contingently track the distinction itself. To be sure, persons are far more likely to be ignorant of a *malum prohibitum* than of a *malum in se.* This contingent empirical fact, however, is not a principled ground for regarding the contrast as normatively significant. I also said it is *superficially* easy to motivate the importance of the contrast between *malum prohibitum* and *malum in se* in a theory of when ignorance of law exculpates. On the level of intuition, I admit we are more likely to sympathize with defendants who unwittingly perpetrate an instance of the former than an instance of the latter kind of offense. But this intuition is not so easy to defend. Do we simply regard it as socially unacceptable for perpetrators of a *malum in se* to evade punishment? If prevention underlies our intuition, we have failed to ground it in terms of blameworthiness and desert. Hart indicates that a person who does not realize a *malum in se* is wrong would be blameworthy *for* his lack of knowledge. Is ignorance itself culpable? Or is Hart implicitly presupposing a quality of will theory, according to which persons are blameworthy when their will expresses whatever objectionable traits are manifested by committing the *malum in se* in question? No answer to any of these questions is obvious.

Next, my reservations about awarding a prominent place to this distinction in my theory have nothing to do with the notorious difficulty of drawing a precise boundary between *mala prohibita* and *mala in se.* This "line-drawing" problem is recited by nearly all theorists, leading some to conclude that the contrast is illusory and should be banished from legal discourse altogether. Entire treatises have been written in the philosophy of criminal law in which these terms fail to appear. In the event hard cases of categorization are needed, return to Jacob and his failure to recycle batteries. Is his offense *malum in se* or *malum prohibitum*? An argument can be devised for either answer. I admit that no criteria to draw this line are unproblematic; no single account can serve each of the many diverse purposes to which this distinction has been put. In any event, I make no concerted effort to overcome this definitional problem. For present purposes, I take offenses to be *mala in se* when they proscribe conduct that is morally wrongful prior to and independent of law, whereas offenses are *mala prohibita* when they proscribe conduct that is not morally wrongful prior to and independent of law.[52] Hopefully, greater precision is not needed. On *any* sensible way to draw the contrast, I will contend it to lack deep normative significance in a theory of when ignorance of law should be exculpatory.

Third, it is important to notice that the obstacles to punishing persons for *mala prohibita* offenses do not derive solely from my own peculiar account of the foundations of moral and legal responsibility. These problems resurface, albeit in a slightly different guise, even if one rejects my claim that the akrasia in defective deliberation provides the locus of full moral blameworthiness. Suppose instead that one of the many versions of a quality of will theory is correct, and persons become eligible for blame when their conduct betrays an objectionable configuration of beliefs and attitudes. It is manifestly unclear how these beliefs and attitudes are conveyed by the breach of a *malum prohibitum*. As I have said, no one can say with a straight face that Battersby, for example, showed disregard for the interests of others by failing to appreciate that weekends count toward the amount of time required to obtain a license to supervise children. Most of the problems I discuss below plague nearly *any* foundational theory of moral responsibility that would punish defendants for perpetrating a *malum prohibitum*.

With these three preliminaries out of the way, I begin with *mala in se*—the counterpart to *mala prohibita* that is thought to be easy for a theory of ignorance of law. Easy, that is, for everyone but me. The orthodox view is that ignorant defendants are *not* exculpated when they perpetrate an instance of this type of crime. Indeed, as we have seen, the specter that an offender might be spared from punishment because he is unaware of his serious moral wrong that exists prior to and independent of law has haunted scholarly commentary about this topic since its inception. Return to the case of Hernan, who enslaves captives of a conquered population but sincerely believes his acts are morally permissible. According to my theory, Hernan is not culpable at all if he does not even *suspect* involuntary servitude is wrongful. Do our intuitions recoil at this result? Is it fatal to my normative theory? My conclusion may only reinforce popular prejudice that we philosophers live in a fantasy realm far removed from reality. I have already had occasion to imagine the howls of protest from laypersons if some

---

[52] A *malum prohibitum* proscribes conduct that is not morally wrongful prior to and independent of *law,* but that law need not be *criminal.* See R.A. Duff: "Political Retributivism and Legal Moralism," 1 *Virginia Journal of Criminal Law* 179, especially p.198 (2012).

of the most diabolical villains in history were acquitted of the most serious crimes known to man.

Some even regard perpetrators of a serious *malum in se* as *more* culpable if they are unaware their conduct is wrongful. This possibility is embraced by Michelle Dempsey, who finds incredible Zimmerman's willingness to exempt Rudolph Hess (and his Nazi ilk) from blame for mass murder because he apparently believed his atrocities were justified. Dempsey counters that it is "more plausible" to suppose that "their ignorance *exacerbates* blame, such that these people are thereby shown to be an even more horrific moral monsters [sic] in virtue of their failure to recognize the wrongness of their conduct."[53] Although I understand her revulsion, I submit that Dempsey's comparative claim is mistaken. I trust she would not hold Hess to be *less* culpable if he continued to murder after coming to his senses and appreciating the enormity of his wrongs.

As I reject the orthodox view about the blameworthiness of persons who are mistaken about the wrongfulness of a *malum in se,* it is finally time to collect in one place a number of distinct replies to this allegedly insuperable objection. Although no one of the following eight responses may be conclusive by itself, I hope they remove the sting of the absurdity when evaluated together. First, as I have said, many of the most disturbing counterexamples are unrealistic, and we should be skeptical whenever unusual cases are invoked to reject a normative theory. I have stipulated that my position about ignorance of law applies only to sane adults (and may not apply to psychopaths or those who act compulsively), and it is hard to imagine (in this day and age) that many such persons hold some of the preposterous moral beliefs my opponents would describe. Recall Carlos, the character I introduced in Chapter 3(B): a sane adult who is a responsible agent and thus responsive to moral reasons, but who does not believe that the fact he will kill innocent persons is a moral reason not to act. One can only wonder what Carlos *does* take to be a moral reason to which he would respond. I do not pretend that no real person conforms to the description of Carlos. Terrorists, even when sane and not psychopathic, pose grave public threats. Fortunately, however, they remain unusual. Second, notice that similar alleged counterexamples could be marshaled against the treatment criminal codes afford to defendants

---

[53] Michelle Dempsey: "Book Review: Michael J. Zimmerman, *The Immorality of Punishment,*" 32 *Law and Philosophy* 333, 336 (2013).

who make elementary mistakes of *fact*. Imagine the public reaction to the acquittal of a defendant accused of murder for pouring gasoline on a victim and lighting a match if he believed only that gasoline is smelly but not flammable when ignited. Yet this is the result the law must reach; this defendant lacks mens rea because he did not know his act would cause death or grievous bodily harm. If I am correct, we should pause before citing these supposedly counterintuitive implications against only those theories about the responsibility of defendants who are ignorant of *law* or the morality that underlies it. Third, if we are genuinely concerned about the disastrous impact of an acquittal in the real world, it is reassuring to point out that a defendant would find it nearly impossible to persuade a judge or jury of her sincere ignorance of basic moral propositions. What story could she tell that might convince us? Unless her account of how she could believe something so outrageous is persuasive, juries would conclude she is lying. Wherever the burden of proof about such matters is placed, I strongly doubt that our penal justice system would allow the most heinous individuals to walk among us. Fourth, enlightened views about morality are available to most everyone, so it is virtually impossible to suppose these wrongdoers would not at least be reckless for harming their victims. Are we to further imagine that, say, perpetrators of hate crimes do not even *suspect* their actions might be wrong? If they are reckless, of course, conviction is appropriate, and the punishments for which these defendants would become eligible hardly resemble a slap on the wrist.

Fifth, it is not coincidental that the alleged counterexamples to my view typically involve the most terrible villains in history. The names of Hitler, Stalin, and Mao routinely appear in putative reductios of a subjectivist reason-responsive theory. When wrongdoing is massive, even those of us who are the most philosophically sophisticated tend to allow our judgments about first-order morality to seep into our judgments of blameworthiness. To prevent this sort of contamination, we are best advised to focus on cases in which wrongdoing is more mundane, as in the example of Sabine, our bicycle thief. Sixth, the supposed intuition that "moral monsters" might even be *more* culpable for their conduct can be explained away. This intuition seemingly confuses judgments of moral blameworthiness with something else— probably judgments about the character of the perpetrator. Although these two objects of evaluation can be difficult to disentangle, only culpability, and not character, clearly concerns the criminal law and provides the focus of my inquiry. Expressed somewhat differently, the fact that these villains may lack *moral* blame for what they do does not entail they are not thoroughly reprehensible along a number of other evaluative dimensions.[54] Seventh, I have grounded my position in a theory of moral responsibility. The whole point of a philosophical argument is to require those who object to its conclusion to indicate where the reasoning has gone awry. My adversaries owe me a counterargument, not an intuition—especially when I have provided reason to believe these intuitions are unreliable. Eighth and finally, if all else fails, I am willing to bite the bullet on the level of ideal theory. Even though I am aware that my judgment on this matter tends to diverge from that of most respondents, what I have called *full* responsibility—the maximum amount of blame one can merit—may well turn out to be quite rare. I believe B *really is* less blameworthy than A, who understands perfectly that his deed is immoral. Recall, however, my willingness to devise some way to preventively detain defendants who mistakenly believe they have a justification for their crimes. As I will further explain in Chapter 5(B), consequences too awful to contemplate provide a firm basis to retreat from ideal theory and find a position that does not bring the criminal law into disrepute. Hopefully this combination of eight replies helps to demonstrate why we should not regard the application of my theory to *mala in se* to be nearly as preposterous as many commentators seem to think. This supposedly absurd result would have virtually no impact on the real world of criminal justice.

I turn now to my central topic of *mala prohibita,* where ignorance of law and the morality that underlies it is ubiquitous. The phenomenon of overcriminalization is the main culprit in this narrative. Because these laws have become so plentiful and far-reaching, it is easy to see how a defendant may be mistaken about the content of a statute that prohibits conduct that is not wrongful prior to or independent of law. In fact, however, the difficulties for criminal theory created by the existence of these offenses extend well beyond the present inquiry. As I have indicated, *mala prohibita* turn out to be doubly problematic. Assessing the blameworthiness of persons who are ignorant of these laws is only the tip of the normative iceberg. The deeper problem is not

---

[54] One commentator alleges such persons possess *character-fault* rather than *blame-fault.* See Bruce Waller: *Against Moral Responsibility* (Cambridge, MA: MIT Press, 2011), chapter 9. Others distinguish *ordinary* blameworthiness from *objective* blameworthiness. See Elinor Mason: "Moral Ignorance and Blameworthiness," 172 *Philosophical Studies* 3037 (2015).

about blameworthiness, but rather about wrongfulness—two different
normative judgments that can be all too easy to blur, especially in
the context of *mala prohibita*. In my opinion, *no* respectable theory of
criminal responsibility—my own or any other—should allow persons
to be punished unless their conduct is wrongful. I have assumed that
questions about responsibility do not even arise unless conduct satisfies
this constraint. But what could possibly be wrongful about, say, the
failure to obtain a license to provide foster care for more than thirty
consecutive days that do not include weekends? As this question
suggests, the more basic difficulty is to explain why a person acts
impermissibly by perpetrating a *malum prohibitum, whether or not she is
aware of its content.* We will be unable to solve the problems involving
ignorance of law and *mala prohibita* unless we determine whether and
under what conditions we have moral reasons to obey these laws in
the first place. In what follows, I take an extended detour to discuss
some possible views about the wrongfulness of *mala prohibita* before
returning to the implications of my analysis for the blameworthiness
of defendants who are ignorant.

No general solution exists to the problem I tackle, so my subsequent
thoughts on whether and under what conditions we have moral reasons
to obey given *mala prohibita* statutes are best described as fragmentary.
On one point, however, I remain emphatic. I reject a possible solution
that would make the problem simple—an answer to which a number
of legal philosophers are attracted. I deny that persons have a prima
facie moral obligation to obey the law as such. That is, the mere fact
that a law has been duly enacted, even in a liberal democracy, does
not by itself give rise to a moral duty of compliance. But doesn't the
law have authority? Almost certainly. What is at issue, however, is
not *whether* the law has authority, but *what* authority *is*. In my view,
philosophers are mistaken to analyze authority in terms of preemptive,
content-independent reasons to conform to directives.[55] I will not,
however, embellish my position on these matters. The philosophical
literature on the authority of law and the supposed obligation to obey
it is vast, and any attempt to engage it here could only be superficial.[56]
Despite its relevance, this topic yet again lies beyond the scope of the
present inquiry. Nonetheless, it is clear that the narrower problem that
I address becomes more difficult once we reject a general duty to obey

---

[55] See Joseph Raz: *The Authority of Law* (Oxford: Clarendon Press, 1979).
[56] See the nuanced view defended by Markel: *Op.cit.* Note 27.

the law as such. Unless we countenance this duty, how can we possibly have a moral obligation to conform to a statute that proscribes conduct that is not wrongful prior to and independent of law? In what follows, I struggle mightily to determine whether and under what circumstances the breach of such laws might be wrongful.

Before proceeding, it is crucial to be reminded yet again that insuperable difficulties remain even if the commission of *each malum prohibitum* somehow qualifies as impermissible. Suppose my views about political philosophy are incorrect, and citizens have a moral obligation to obey every single law, regardless of its classification as a *malum in se* or a *malum prohibitum*. Even so, we must recall that (Q) asks not about first-order judgments of wrongfulness, but rather about whether persons are blameworthy for their wrongful actions. Why think that persons deserve blame for breaching their political obligations, even when they are unaware these obligations exist? No account of political obligation is directly responsive to *this* question. As I contended in Chapter 3(C) when critiquing the supposition that a failure to discharge a duty of inquiry establishes that legally ignorant offenders are blameworthy for their subsequent offenses, no progress is made in demonstrating why a mistaken defendant is responsible by multiplying the number of wrongs he is alleged to have committed.

But *is* it wrongful to commit a *malum prohibitum*? In the present context, this question first arose in the course of examining statutes that allow defendants to deny criminality by contesting a mens rea element of the offense charged. Recall my discussion in Chapter 2(D): courts frequently interpret the meaning or scope of culpability terms in penal statutes to protect persons deemed to be morally innocent. As far as I can see, however, the examples of innocence provided by courts do not require defendants to be ignorant of the law they break. Consider two of many possible illustrations. Return to the statute in *Skilling*.[57] Does the hypothetical employee who makes a few personal calls on the company phone during working hours lose her innocence if she has been informed that her behavior is legally proscribed? Or recall the statute in *Liparota*.[58] Does the conduct of the hypothetical recipient who throws away his food stamps become impermissible once he becomes aware a statute prohibits it? Surely our reluctance to punish in these cases is not due solely to ignorance of law on the part of

---

[57] *Skilling v. United States*, 130 S. Ct. 2896 (2010).
[58] *United States v. Liparota*, 471 U.S. 419 (1985).

defendants who act wrongfully. Instead, our reluctance to punish derives mostly from doubts the conduct is wrongful in the first place. The defendants in these cases are innocent not because they are ignorant of the wrong they have done, but because they have done no wrong. Permissible conduct is not transformed into wrongful conduct because the perpetrator is aware it has been prohibited. At the very least, it is unclear which of two variables in these cases explains our willingness to acquit: ignorance of law, or uncertainty the statutes in question proscribe wrongdoing. The basis of our judgment is overdetermined.

Still, the first hurdle is to explain how a given *malum prohibitum* could possibly create a moral obligation. By what moral magic are legislators able to create duties where none existed before? Are they alchemists? How can *mala prohibita* offenses be *mala*? No *general* answer to these questions is forthcoming. The beginning of wisdom in producing an account of how a person can act wrongfully by committing a *malum prohibitum* is to recognize the existence of several different *kinds* of such offenses.[59] What makes various statutes members of a given kind? If our purpose is to explain how a person can act wrongfully and thus become eligible for blame, the basis for grouping distinct laws into a single type is straightforward. Offenses should be sorted into a given kind because persons who commit them act wrongfully for the same reason. Once we have identified all of the several grounds on which a person can act wrongfully by violating a statute that is not a *malum in se*, we will have produced a complete inventory of the kinds of *mala prohibita* offenses needed for present purposes. In what follows, I discuss at least three such reasons. Each conceptualizes the wrongfulness of violating a *malum prohibitum* by relating that offense to a correspond-ing *malum in se*. A discussion of these reasons indicates how legislators appear able to "create" wrongs despite lacking magical powers. At the end of the day, breaches of quite a few *mala prohibita* will turn out to be wrongful. Thus persons have a prima facie moral obligation to obey a great many penal statutes that do not proscribe conduct that is wrongful prior to and independent of law. If I am correct, such persons become eligible for full responsibility when they break these laws knowingly, and the application of my theory of ignorance of law will not have radical implications for legal practice. Still, the violation of quite a few *mala prohibita* offenses is *not* wrongful, and criminal

---

[59] My account draws on Douglas Husak: "*Malum Prohibitum* and Retributivism," in *Op. cit.* Note 31, p.410.

liability and punishment would be morally indefensible. I will try to make some progress in identifying which *mala prohibita* do or do not impose obligations.

First and most important, many crimes are neither wholly *malum in se* nor wholly *malum prohibitum*. I call these *hybrid offenses* because they contain a bit of each category. According to Antony Duff, offenses of this kind "involve a more or less artificial, stipulative determination of a genuine *malum in se*."[60] His examples of hybrid offenses—statutory rape and drunk driving—nicely illustrate the entire class. Duff contends that the genuine *mala in se* that correspond to these two hybrids are (roughly) "having sexual intercourse with a young person who is not yet mature enough to be capable of making rational decisions about such matters" and "driving when one's capacities are impaired by alcohol or drugs." But these latter behaviors are not the elements of penal prohibitions, probably because legislators prefer to furnish more concrete guidance to citizens and legal officials about the exact conduct that is proscribed. Thus the state *specifies* these wrongs by giving them more concrete content. It does so by prohibiting "sexual intercourse with anyone under a specified age" and "driving with more than the specified amount of alcohol in one's blood." These latter offenses are hybrids—neither fully *mala in se* nor wholly *mala prohibita*. Hybrids are similar to but different from pure *mala prohibita* or *mala in se* in the following respect. Persons *can* and frequently *do* engage in these behaviors without doing anything wrongful prior to and independent of law. This is not the case with pure *malum in se* offenses. But some (and probably most) instances of these behaviors *are* wrongful prior to and independent of law. This is not the case with pure *mala prohibita* offenses.

I make two observations about Duff's remarks before I continue. First, I assume he characterizes the *mala in se* offenses that correspond to these respective hybrids as "rough" because the exact content of moral wrongs may be controversial. Among other difficulties, it is unclear at what level of generality these wrongs should be described. Is the *malum in se* that corresponds to the drunk driving statute the wrong of driving while impaired by alcohol, driving while impaired by anything, driving dangerously, or doing something dangerous, whether or not it involves driving? This controversy may be important for present

[60] Antony Duff: "Crime, Prohibition, and Punishment," 19 *Journal of Applied Philosophy* 97, 102 (2002).

purposes. Depending on how broadly or narrowly we depict the corresponding *malum in se,* it becomes more or less plausible to suppose a given defendant could be ignorant of it. Second, Duff characterizes the specification of the hybrid as "more or less artificial." By *artificial,* he does not mean *arbitrary.* Some candidates for specifying these offenses are preferable to others, although it is not obvious what makes a given alternative optimal. For example, why choose the status of having a given blood-alcohol content rather than the behavior of the driver as an element of a drunk-driving statute? If the defendant is driving safely, why should we care what percentage of alcohol is in his bloodstream? And even if blood-alcohol content is selected as an element in this offense, how should that limit be established?[61] No one would set the blood-alcohol amount for drunk driving at a barely detectable trace, just as no one would set it at a point where most persons lose consciousness. If legislators ultimately choose a non-optimal statutory specification, it becomes more difficult to regard each breach as wrongful. Scholarly discussions of hybrids frequently gloss over these quandaries.

In any event, no special difficulty arises in understanding how a defendant acts wrongfully when he breaches a hybrid offense by engaging in conduct that is both *malum in se* as well as *malum prohibitum.* That is, no difficulty occurs when the sexual partner of a given defendant is *both* under the age at which she is sufficiently mature to consent *and* under the age specified by the statute. Similarly, no difficulty occurs when the driver is *both* dangerously impaired *and* over the blood alcohol level stipulated by law. The problem becomes manifest, however, when the latter but not the former is true, that is, when the conduct of the defendant is *malum prohibutum* without simultaneously being *malum in se.* Some defendants, in other words, perpetrate a hybrid offense despite the fact that their conduct is not a *malum in se* of the appropriate kind. Because these offenses are hybrids, this possibility is all but inevitable. When the law proscribes sexual intercourse with anyone under a specified age, Duff admits "we know that there are some individuals under that age who are fully capable of rational consent (more so than some above that age)." Moreover, when the law proscribes driving with a given blood alcohol content,

---

[61] For a discussion of this problem in the context of drug impairment, see Andrea Roth: "The Uneasy Case for Marijuana as Chemical Impairment under a Science-Based Jurisprudence of Dangerousness," 103 *California Law Review* ___ (2015).

"we know that some people could still drive safely (more safely than many of those who are under the legal limit) when they are above the limit."[62] Suppose, for example, legislators decide to set the BAC (blood alcohol concentration) limit for drunk driving at the point at which more drivers than not become significantly impaired. Suppose further that a given driver is in the sizeable minority who is *not* impaired, even though his BAC is over the statutory limit. In such circumstances— when a defendant commits a hybrid offense by engaging in conduct that is *malum prohibitum* even though it is not simultaneously *malum in se*—how can he be said to commit a moral wrong that renders him a candidate for blame? An act is not wrongful simply because it tokens a type that is wrongful when performed by others, even if these others comprise a statistical majority.

Without relying on a supposed obligation to obey the law as such, it is hard to see why a man commits a moral wrong by having consensual sex with a woman sufficiently mature to be able to consent, even if her age happens to be below whatever line is specified in the statutory rape law of his jurisdiction. Similarly, it is hard to see why a driver commits a moral wrong by driving over the statutory BAC limit if his conduct does not create a substantial and unreasonable risk. Consider just one of many peculiar implications of the contrary position. As the age of consent or the blood-alcohol limit for drunk driving can and does vary from one jurisdiction to another, and can and does change over time within a single jurisdiction, do only those persons who breach the law in one time and place but not in another commit the moral wrong in question? How can the content of morality be so sensitive to these differing specifications of a *malum in se*—especially when we admit, as we must, that these specifications are "more or less artificial"? If wrongful conduct is a condition for justified punishment, as I believe it to be, why does a defendant who perpetrates a hybrid offense without simultaneously committing a *malum in se* deserve to be punished at all?

Admittedly, practical problems abound. The most obvious is epistemological. My examples stipulate that a given partner is sufficiently mature to consent to sex, or that a given driver is sufficiently unimpaired to drive safely, even though the defendants breach the hybrid statutes that specify the content of the corresponding *mala in se*. How can a defendant be so sure her conduct conforms to my stipulation? On

---

[62] *Op.cit.* Note 60, p.102.

the other hand, how can third parties be so sure the contrary is true? I see no general reason to prefer either answer. Of course, defendants may succumb to wishful thinking and err on the side that allows them to proceed. Nonetheless, individuals tend to be in a better position than legislators to appreciate the particular circumstances that bear on their conduct. Perhaps we should recommend that prudent agents defer to legislators in the face of moral uncertainty. But whether or not this recommendation is sensible, it opens a new inquiry that does not respond directly to my conundrum. I ask how persons act wrongfully (let alone are blameworthy) in cases in which it is true (by stipulation) that their conduct is not a *malum in se* despite breaching a hybrid statute.

Duff has not wavered in his assurance that such persons *do* act wrongfully, although his explanation of *why* this is so has evolved over time. His most recent thoughts are nuanced and qualified, providing different analyses for different kinds of cases. Generally, however, he no longer relies quite so much on the concept of *civic arrogance* that loomed so large in his earlier accounts.[63] In conjunction with Sandra Marshall, he now places more emphasis on the "associative duties that belong with citizenship in a republican polity."[64] We show solidarity with our fellow citizens when we share in legal burdens that are imposed for the common good. Although I am skeptical, I am not certain Duff is mistaken. We should always be willing to entertain novel arguments about why a person acts wrongfully despite committing a *malum prohibitum*. For present purposes, however, a crucial point remains: *if* those defendants who conform to my stipulation (by engaging in conduct that is not a *malum in se* despite breaching a hybrid statute) commit no moral wrong, they do not deserve to be punished *whether or not* they are fully cognizant of the content of the statutes they breach. Any doubts we may have that such persons act wrongfully and are eligible for blame when they are aware they are breaking the law apply with even greater force when they are unaware of their transgression.

Of course, at least *some* persons who commit an act that is both *malum in se* and *malum prohibitum are* unaware their conduct is morally

---

[63] *Op.cit.* Note 17, especially pp.166–172.

[64] R.A. Duff and S.E. Marshall: "'Remote Harms' and the Two Harm Principles," in A.P. Simester, Antje Du Bois-Pedain, and Ulfred Neumann, eds.: *Liberal Criminal Theory: Essays for Andreas von Hirsch* (Oxford: Hart, 2014), pp.205, 222–223.

wrongful. That is, they are unaware that it is wrongful to have consensual sex with a partner too immature to consent, even when their
partner is below the age specified in the offense of statutory rape.
Or they are unaware that it is wrongful to drive with faculties that
are seriously impaired, even when their blood alcohol level is above
that specified in the offense of drunk driving. What should we say
about the culpability of such persons? My answer has already been
given. Defendants who are unaware that these behaviors are morally
wrongful are not as culpable as defendants who are aware of these
moral truths, and may not be culpable at all. Fortunately, however, sane,
normal, and non-psychopathic adults who are not cognizant of these
moral truths are unusual at best, so I plead yet again that my theory has
few counterintuitive implications for the real world.

If I am correct, the category of *mala prohibita* I describe as hybrids
does not present a special problem for understanding how many
(but not all) offenders may be blameworthy. As many if not most
mala prohibita offenses are hybrids, this conclusion goes a long way
toward dispelling the worry that my theory has radical consequences
throughout the universe of *mala prohibita* crimes. Some examples help
to illustrate this point. First, consider the offense of driving on the left
side of the road in a country that mandates that persons drive on the
right. This offense is typically cited as a paradigm of a *malum prohibitum*.
Yet this offense is better conceptualized as a hybrid. Roughly (again),
the corresponding *malum in se* is the wrong of endangering persons
and property by driving on a side of the road different from that of
other persons. The law attaches a *malum prohibitum* component to this
offense by specifying the side of the road on which it is safe to drive.
Of course, it is possible to imagine a driver is unaware of what side
of the road is specified by the law as safe. But it is barely possible to
imagine a sane adult who does not understand it is morally wrong to
endanger others by proceeding on a side of the road different from that
of other drivers. Ignorance of the *malum in se* specified by this hybrid
will be rare indeed.

Unfortunately, not all *mala prohibita* offenses are amenable to this
analysis. That is, not all *mala prohibita* offenses are hybrids that specify
the content of a *malum in se*. A different account is needed to solve the
mystery of how (or whether) the enactment of a pure (that is, a non-
hybrid) *malum prohibitum* offense is able to create a moral obligation
where none existed before. To develop this account, I draw from (and
adapt to my own purposes) the account of *triggering* reasons recently

described by David Enoch.[65] I begin by borrowing his example of how a new nonmoral fact can appear to generate reasons for action. Suppose my neighborhood grocer raises the price of milk, thereby giving me a reason to decrease my milk consumption. But did she really create a new reason from whole cloth? More plausibly, my grocer merely manipulated non-normative circumstances in such a way as to trigger a dormant reason that existed all along, independently of her actions. Each of us has a preexisting reason to save money. By raising the price of milk, the grocer triggered this preexisting reason, making it the case that I have a reason to reduce my consumption. We already had a conditional reason to buy less of something if its price goes up—the existence of which does not depend on the grocer's actions. Simply by altering facts, the grocer's behavior transformed this conditional reason into an unconditional reason.

It is important to notice that the fact altered by the grocer need not itself *be* normative in order to play its triggering role. All that is required to play this triggering role is that the fact be *normatively significant*. A fact is normatively significant if some normative statement is sensitive to whether that fact obtains. My reason to save money and to buy less of something if its price goes up is prudential; I commit no moral wrong if I fail to change my consumption in response to the grocer's action. But other normative statements that are sensitive to whether a fact obtains *are* moral. When facts trigger these moral conditionals, new moral obligations are created where none existed before. Consider, for example, how the fact that I have made a promise generates an obligation. This phenomenon is not a mysterious instance of an "is" creating an "ought." Instead, the fact I have made a promise creates a moral reason to honor my commitment by triggering a conditional moral reason that existed all along, independently of anything I did. In this instance, the antecedent reason is that persons have a moral obligation to keep their promises. To cite a second and more complex example, consider how an obligation is generated by the fact that I voluntarily accept a benefit from someone who does not intend to make a gift in a cooperative enterprise. This fact creates a moral reason to reciprocate by triggering a preexisting conditional moral reason, namely, a reason pertaining to considerations of fair play.

---

[65] David Enoch: "Reason-Giving and the Law," in Leslie Green and Brian Leiter, eds.: *Oxford Studies in Philosophy of Law* (Oxford: Oxford University Press, Vol. I, 2011), p.1.

The latter two conditional moral reasons—those involving promises and fair play—are important in understanding how illegal actions can be wrongful. I act wrongfully if I breach a law I have promised to obey, or if I fail to reciprocate after I have benefitted from the conformity of others to a law under the appropriate circumstances. In at least these two kinds of situation, I trigger a preexisting conditional moral reason. My central claim is that no pure *malum prohibitum* statute can create a moral obligation unless it does so by triggering a preexisting moral conditional. This account helps to explain the sense in which morality can *underlie* law and thus how persons are able to act wrongfully by violating even those statutes that lack moral content. The fact altered by the enactment of the law need only be morally significant.

A moral obligation to obey a given law might originate in a promise. Several of the activities governed by the penal law—like those pertaining to hunting and fishing—require a license. When obtaining these licenses, persons often make an explicit promise to abide by the applicable rules and regulations. If they violate one of these rules or regulations, it is an oversimplification to say their moral wrong consists in the violation itself. The rule or regulation, after all, is probably *malum prohibitum*. Instead, their moral wrong consists in the breach of their promise to conform to the rule or regulation.[66] Next, briefly consider how an obligation to obey the law might originate in a duty of fair play. When I voluntarily benefit from a public space supported by entrance fees paid by others, I act impermissibly as a free-rider by enjoying the space without paying the fee. Disagreement about the exact conditions that must be satisfied to make a promise or to generate a duty of fair play has consumed many social and political philosophers. I have no interest in entering this fray. Suffice it to say that these conditional moral principles are capable of explaining *some* duties to conform to statutes that are instances of *mala prohibita*. Perhaps additional duties to obey the law might be derived from other considerations.[67] No single explanation applies to each of the laws to which we are obligated, and several laws fail to obligate us at all. Thus we can account for moral obligations to obey a great many laws with no need to posit a general obligation to obey the law as such.

---

[66] For further thoughts, see Susan Dimock: "Contractarian Criminal Law Theory and *Mala Prohibita* Offences," in R.A. Duff et al., eds.: *Criminalisation: The Political Morality of the Criminal Law* (Oxford: Oxford University Press, 2014), p.151.

[67] See Margaret Gilbert: *Joint Commitment: How We Make the Social World* (Oxford: Oxford University Press, 2014).

My main topic, of course, is about blameworthiness rather than wrongfulness. How should we assess the blameworthiness of defendants who breach a pure *malum prohibitum* the wrongfulness of which derives from a triggering reason such as promissory obligation or the duty of fair play? When a moral obligation arises via a promise, nearly all wrongdoers will turn out to be blameworthy (in the absence of an excuse such as duress). I doubt that a person *can* make a genuine promise to perform a given act without intending to do so, although legal philosophers have usually debated such matters in the domain of contract law rather than criminal law. Admittedly, several tough issues remain. For example, many a term in a boilerplate agreement is unknown to the parties. Perhaps this admission merely shows that a duty to conform to these terms, if it exists at all, does not originate in a genuine promise. In addition, persons may well have forgotten a promise they once made. In this event, their practical reasoning at the time they behave illegally may well be impeccable. Can they be blameworthy for failing to conform to a commitment they forgot they had made? Despite these many unresolved problems, promissory obligation is a clear basis for creating a duty to obey a law that renders wrongdoers blameworthy, even when the law is an instance of a *mala prohibita*.

Ignorance of a moral duty created through fair play may seem easier to imagine than the parallel situation involving a promise. Most philosophical descriptions of the conditions that generate duties of fair play require persons to accept benefits *voluntarily*. Whatever else voluntariness may mean in this context, it probably entails knowledge. A person may be a free-rider without realizing it, blissfully unaware of the existence of the cooperative enterprise maintained by the sacrifices of others. In this event, it is hard to see how she is blameworthy for her failure to reciprocate. If knowledge indeed is required, individuals who benefit from cooperative schemes of which they are unaware either have no duty of fair play, or, more important, almost certainly are not blameworthy when they fail to discharge whatever duties they may have.

I hope to diffuse misguided objections by repeating four disclaimers about the foregoing analysis. First, the exact formulation of given preexisting conditional moral reasons may be controversial. For example, political philosophers have created an industry in trying to identify the circumstances under which persons come to have duties of fair play. Without entering this debate, I say only that *some* such circumstances can be found; duties of fair play unquestionably exist. Second, political philosophers have extensively criticized both of the triggering moral reasons I have described. Their well-known objections, however, are typically directed against attempts to use these accounts to explain the normativity of law generally. My own analysis is much less ambitious. I do not allege that promises or duties of fair play account for the wrongfulness of breaching *all* or even *many* laws.[68] I purport to offer no unified analysis of the moral force of *mala prohibita* offenses; different analyses explain different laws, and quite a few lack moral content altogether. Third, I do not insist that promises or fair play exhaust the possible rationales for creating moral obligations to obey pure *mala prohibita* laws. I reserve judgment about whether additional triggering reasons account for the wrongfulness of committing any *mala prohibita* offenses. Finally, I make no effort to determine the parameters of any of these triggering reasons. In particular, I do not attempt to decide whether specific examples of supposed obligations can be explained as instances of promissory obligation or a duty of fair play. Others have been less reticent about this final point. David Estlund, for example, alleges that citizens have promised, or have a duty to promise, to stop at a stop sign in the middle of the night on a deserted highway where visibility is unimpeded.[69] I doubt I have made such a promise and am sure I have no duty to do so. But I need not resolve these controversies here; I do not want to risk misapplications of my own theory. I maintain only that *unless* we have made such a promise, have a duty of fair play, or some other antecedent triggering reason can be found, we do not commit a moral wrong when we fail to stop at the sign on the deserted highway envisaged by Estlund.

This final point is crucial if my conclusions are to be applied to the real world. If nearly all *mala prohibita* offenses trigger preexisting moral conditionals, virtually all of these statutes create obligations to obey. If few of these offenses do so, obligations to conform turn out to be rare. Almost in passing, I simply offer one consideration in favor of believing that some *mala prohibita* do not trigger preexisting moral conditionals. Let me illustrate this consideration with a realistic scenario. Consider the horse-trading in which politicians regularly engage to support

---

[68] See, for example, Christopher Heath Wellman: "Rights Forfeiture and *Mala Prohibita*," in R.A. Duff et al., eds.: *The Constitution of the Criminal Law* (Oxford: Oxford University Press, 2013), p.77. Wellman endorses this rationale with only minor qualifications.

[69] David Estlund: *Democratic Authority: A Philosophical Framework* (Princeton, NJ: Princeton University Press, 2008), p.152. Controversy about the example of a stop sign in a desert looms large in debates about political obligation.

246 IGNORANCE OF LAW

or oppose given bills, or the way statutes are enacted in the wake of tragedies that evoke public sympathy and enable politicians to pander to the citizenry. It is hard (but not impossible) to believe that laws passed for these reasons trigger preexisting moral conditionals. If criminal theorists attend to the actual political processes that create penal legislation in the real world, they are bound to be quicker to doubt these statutes generate obligations of compliance. But I digress. Regardless of how frequently or infrequently this requirement is satisfied, I hold that obligations to comply with a given pure *malum prohibitum* depend on whether it triggers a preexisting moral conditional.

I have made a lengthy detour in a project about responsibility, and it is helpful to be reminded why this foray into the wrongfulness of *mala prohibita* needs to be taken in the context of an inquiry about ignorance of law. The answer is that we cannot decide how to assess the culpability of a defendant who is ignorant of his alleged moral obligation to conform to a given law unless we have some idea whether this obligation exists in the first place. In the case of *mala in se,* the answer is simple: the law itself proscribes a preexisting, independent moral wrong. In the case of *mala prohibita,* however, the answer has proved to be far more elusive. In many cases, defendants commit *no* moral wrong in breaching a *malum prohibitum*. In the absence of wrongfulness, questions about blameworthiness—and thus about our basic question (Q)—do not arise. But even when it *is* wrong to commit such an offense, no single account explains why this is so. Some obligations arise through a promise, others by a duty of fair play, and still others because the defendant simultaneously perpetrates a *malum in se* specified in a hybrid statute. Each of these kinds generates its own distinctive puzzles about the responsibility of the ignorant wrongdoer.

I hope to have shown that the difficulties involving pure *mala prohibita* offenses are more complex than many commentators seem to have supposed. But where in the real world do these complexities leave us? It is hard to know what to say about particular examples. Return yet again to *Battersby*. The defendant was unaware she needed a license because she believed that Friday and Monday were not consecutive days. Did she behave wrongfully? Arguably, the statute she breached is a hybrid; legislatures sought to supply content to a *malum in se* by specifying a corresponding *malum prohibitum*. Is Batterby's conduct an instance of a *malum prohibitum* that is not simultaneously a *malum in se?* Although arguments should be heard on both sides, morality is almost certainly silent on the question of whether *consecutive days* include or exclude weekends. What follows from this supposition? If morality is silent on this question, and wrongfulness is required for criminalization, and awareness of wrongfulness is needed for responsibility and punishment, the probable outcome is that the offense in *Battersby* should not have been part of the *criminal* law. If that law were non-criminal in nature, persons who exceed the regulations, knowingly or otherwise, would not be subject to punishment. This implication is hardly radical. A state is not powerless to regulate the child-care industry, but most of the regulations it enacts should generally be enforced through civil rather than criminal sanctions. Anyone injured by a child-care worker who breaches the applicable regulations is free to sue for damages. If I am correct, it should be clear that my theory has the resources to identify the questions that need to be addressed if we are to assess the justifiability of liability and punishment. These questions will not always be easy to resolve. But it is no defect of my theory, I hope, that difficult questions prove difficult to answer.

I conclude that *mala prohibita* offenses are doubly problematic for a theory of responsibility. It can be hard to determine, first, whether persons who breach these offenses act wrongfully, *and,* second, whether such persons are blameworthy for their breach. Of course, the requirements that conduct must be wrongful and that persons must be blameworthy are necessary conditions for *any* punishment to be deserved. These conditions do not differ depending on whether the offense in question is a *malum prohibitum* or a *malum in se*; no special rules apply to one type of offense that do not apply to the other. The fundamental problem is not that the nature or application of these conditions differs depending on the kind of offense in question. Instead, the fundamental problem is that it is frequently more difficult to determine whether these conditions are satisfied in the case of *mala prohibita* than in the case of *mala in se*.

D. Negligent Mistakes of Law

Clearly, the foregoing theory of responsibility that exculpates most defendants who are ignorant of law is incompatible with holding persons criminally responsible when their mistakes of law are merely *negligent*. A mistake is negligent when a reasonable person in the actor's situation (sometimes represented by the acronym *RPAS*) would not have made it. In other words, pursuant to the objective standard of the reasonable person, the defendant himself *should* not have made that mistake. This characterization of negligence pertains both to mistakes about propositions of fact and to mistakes about propositions of law. In either event, liability for negligence is ruled out by the theory I have constructed. As persons who make negligent mistakes are not acting wrongfully according to their own lights, but only according to a standard extrinsic to them, the general theory of responsibility I have invoked would not hold them responsible. To be sure, objectivist accounts of rationality deem negligent conduct to be among the paradigms of irrationality; persons who behave contrary to how a reasonable person in their situation would have behaved fail to conform to all of the objective reasons that pertain to them. Nonetheless, I contend that no one can be blamed for failing to respond to a reason of which she is unaware, and this stubborn fact is not altered just because a reasonable person in her situation *would* have been aware of this reason and thus *should* have responded to it.

Quite a few criminal theorists greet punishment for negligent mistakes of *fact* with skepticism on several grounds, many of which apply with at least as much force to proposals to punish persons for negligent mistakes of law. In the first place, it is notoriously difficult to specify the content of the beliefs of the hypothetical reasonable person—the objective standard used to contrast negligence, which some commentators allow, from strict liability, which is almost universally denounced.[70] The beliefs of the reasonable person cannot be identical to those of the defendant himself, or both the defendant and the reasonable person would be equally ignorant. Nor can his beliefs be identical to those of an omniscient being; he then would never be mistaken about anything. Where between these two extremes should we locate the beliefs of the reasonable person? As far as I am aware, no commentator has tackled this problem when defendants make mistakes of law, but a promising solution has been proposed by Peter Westen when defendants make mistakes of fact.[71] He suggests that the reasonable person in the actor's situation shares *all* of the physical and psychological attributes of the particular defendant with one important exception: the reasonable person has an appropriate degree of concern and regard for others. Thus the RPAS

---

[70] For example, see Larry Alexander and Kimberly Kessler Ferzan with Stephen Morse: *Crime and Culpability* (Cambridge: Cambridge University Press, 2009), esp. pp. 70–85.

[71] See Peter Westen: "Individualizing the Reasonable Person in Criminal Law," 2 *Criminal Law and Philosophy* 137 (2008).

could be blind or even a drug addict, but he cannot be malicious or uncaring. Although Westen himself does not express the point in quite this way, I construe him to hold that the reasonable person in the actor's situation *just is* this particular defendant, altered only so that his quality of will is not defective. Might this promising solution be applied to mistake of law? Seemingly not. A person whose quality of will is not defective would make few if any mistakes about the morality underlying the statute he has breached. Thus Westen's approach entails that a non-negligent offender in the actor's situation would rarely if ever make an exculpatory mistake of law—unless, of course, the law in question *lacks* a moral foundation. I am afraid I cannot improve on Westen's solution. In any event, I will assume for present purposes that we somehow are able to decide whether an RPAS would have been aware of a given proposition of law (or the morality that underlies it) just as easily (or with just as much difficulty) as we are able to decide whether she would have been aware of a given proposition of fact. How frequently an RPAS would make mistakes about morality must remain an open question.

An unwillingness to punish wrongdoers whose mistakes of law are negligent would seem to represent yet another significant departure from the status quo. Even in the domain of mistake of fact, every criminal justice system known to man imposes liability for negligence at least occasionally. Those who reject responsibility for negligent mistakes of either law and/or fact owe us some explanation of why legal systems as well as ordinary judgments of morality go awry on this matter.[72] Can my theory really produce results so discrepant from those of positive law? Perhaps not. Here, as elsewhere, the application of my theory may not be quite as radical as appearances suggest. Recall that I allow penal liability when defendants have latent beliefs about the wrongfulness of their conduct. If a latent belief is all that is required when a person is reckless about the facts, it should suffice when a defendant is reckless about the moral status of his behavior. It would be incredible to exempt a defendant from punishment because he does not advert to the proposition "Φ is wrongful" at the moment he commits his criminal act. As a result, quite a few of the cases other legal philosophers would conceptualize to involve negligence I would categorize as involving recklessness. Pursuant to my device for drawing the

---

[72] Misgivings about the absence of an explanation are expressed by Larry Alexander: "Hart and Punishment for Negligence," in C.G. Pulman, ed.: *Hart on Responsibility* (New York: Palgrave Macmillan, 2014), pp. 195, 204.

boundary between these two (alleged) culpable states, more defendants will become eligible for blame than we might have anticipated. Thus a rejection of liability for mistakes of law that are truly negligent would be only mildly discomforting to theorists who favor my proposal to treat defendants who are ignorant of law in much the same way as those who are ignorant of fact.

But should we really be so quick to jettison responsibility for negligent mistakes of law when defendants lack even a dispositional belief that their conduct is wrongful? Again, maybe not. One thing is crystal clear: if criminal liability for negligence should ever be accepted in the domain of fact or law, its defense must rest on an entirely different theoretical foundation than liability that depends on the subjective mental states of recklessness, knowledge, or purpose. In each of these latter instances, wrongdoers deserve some amount of blame by their own lights. Obviously, the same cannot be said of persons who are negligent. As my reason-responsive theory cannot justify impositions of liability for negligence, might my theory be supplemented so that wrongdoers can be held responsible according to a rationale heretofore unexamined? The short answer to this question is that I am unsure. I *am* sure, however, that it would be rash to rule out liability for negligence just because it is incompatible with the theory of responsibility I have defended thus far. Akrasia may suffice for responsibility, but perhaps it is not necessary. After all, no single rationale explains all excuses from blame.[73] Why, then, should we uncritically suppose there exists a single theory of *inculpation*—of the grounds on which persons are responsible? Here, as elsewhere in moral and legal philosophy, we should remain open-minded about pluralist accounts of responsibility and the conditions that would defeat it.

Thus a new basis of responsibility would be needed if liability for negligence is to be imposed.[74] Perhaps the most promising efforts for expanding the scope of punishment for persons who make negligent mistakes of law would seek to supplement a reason-responsiveness account of responsibility with a quality of will theory that does not require awareness of wrongdoing—even though I have tended to be critical of the latter. According to *one* possible way to combine these

---

[73] See Jeremy Horder: *Excusing Crime* (Oxford: Oxford University Press, 2004).

[74] Novel theories of negligence continue to appear. See, for example, George Sher: *Who Knew?: Responsibility without Awareness* (Oxford: Oxford University Press, 2009); and Joseph Raz: *From Normativity to Responsibility* (Oxford: Oxford University Press, 2011), Part Three.

theories, wrongdoers would be most blameworthy when they are insufficiently responsive to reason (either by knowing they are acting wrongfully or by consciously disregarding a risk that they might be doing so), and would be less blameworthy when their quality of will is objectionable according to external criteria. Any proposal to combine these kinds of theories of responsibility in the above manner (or, indeed, in any manner) is highly speculative. But such a theory would be needed if we are to justify the punishment of persons who are distracted, forgetful, or in a hurry—the sorts of traits that explain why sane adults are prone to make unreasonable mistakes of fact or law.[75] I mention it only to indicate a possible theoretical basis on which liability for negligent mistakes of law might conceivably rest.

Obviously, I would prefer to reach a less equivocal conclusion. But the bulk of my theory can be implemented regardless of our ultimate verdict about negligence. Until we are more confident about how to deal with wrongdoers who are guilty of negligent mistakes of fact, it is not surprising we will remain in the dark about what to say about wrongdoers who are guilty of negligent mistakes of law. Hopefully, a resolution of the former problem can be applied to solve the latter. Unfortunately, the definitive defense of punishment for offenders who make unreasonable mistakes of fact has yet to be written. No less than when defendants are unreasonably ignorant of fact, any rationale for holding defendants responsible when they are unreasonably ignorant of law must remain tentative and uncertain.

Conclusion

In this chapter I discussed a number of refinements, qualifications, and complexities about the general theory of ignorance of law I introduced in Chapter 3(B). In Part A, I sought to identify what a defendant must know in order to be fully responsible for her offense. I contended that a defendant need only have a latent, dispositional belief her conduct is wrongful to be fully blameworthy for it; an occurrent belief is probably not required. Moreover, even though it might be counterintuitive to withhold liability from a defendant who erroneously believes

---

[75] See the various bases for punishing negligence distinguished in Michael S. Moore and Heidi M. Hurd: "Punishing the Awkward, the Stupid, the Weak, and the Selfish: The Culpability of Negligence," 5 *Criminal Law and Philosophy* 147 (2011).

she has a justification for her criminal conduct, more than awareness of a pro tanto reason not to commit Φ is almost certainly needed for responsibility. Finally, the fully blameworthy defendant need only know her conduct is wrongful; she need not be able to describe the moral foundation on which this belief rests.

Part B addressed possible exceptions to my general theory. When B is willfully ignorant her conduct violates L, she should be treated as culpable as A—who knows her act is criminal. I am more ambivalent about two additional possible exceptions: those in which B's conduct falls under what I call a legal loophole, and those in which she acts *in* but not *from* ignorance. In the absence of strong reasons to prefer a deviation, perhaps we should retreat to the default position of symmetry and allow our theory of ignorance of law to conform to our theory about ignorance of fact on these difficult topics.

Part C investigated the thorny problems surrounding *mala prohibita*, the class of statutes about which commentators have tended to be most critical of the application of *ignorantia juris*. The more difficult problem about these kinds of laws involves wrongfulness, in the absence of which questions of blameworthiness do not arise. In this context, wrongfulness and blameworthiness can be hard to disentangle. In any event, the breach of many *mala prohibita* offenses *is* wrongful— for several different reasons I attempted to describe. When the breach of a particular *malum prohibitum* is *not* wrongful, however, even those defendants who are certain they are breaking the law should not be eligible for penal liability.

Finally, in Part D, I turned to negligent mistakes of law: mistakes that would not be made by a reasonable person in the actor's situation. My reason-responsive account of responsibility precludes impositions of blame on defendants whose ignorance of wrongdoing is merely negligent. Rational persons cannot be faulted for failing to be guided by a reason they did not believe themselves to have, even though a reasonable person in their situation would have known of it. If liability for negligent mistakes of law should ever be imposed, its basis must be unlike the rationale I invoke elsewhere. I take this possibility seriously, but remain agnostic. Until we decide whether persons are ever responsible for negligent mistakes of fact, we should remain uncertain about whether persons are ever responsible for negligent mistakes of law.

5

The Real World

Thus far I have focused almost entirely on *ideal* criminal theory. I have undertaken this exercise in order to defend a preliminary answer to the basic question (Q): What should the law say about persons whose conduct is illegal but who are ignorant of the law they violate? After presenting several background assumptions in Chapter 1 and drawing from what can be learned from positive law and scholarly commentary in Chapter 2, I proceeded in Chapter 3 to show how the exculpatory significance of ignorance of law can be supported by one or more theories about the foundations of moral responsibility. Chapter 4 introduced a number of important complexities, qualifications, and exceptions to the theory to which I am partial. I have defended my conclusions from a moral perspective, that is, a perspective designed to ensure that impositions of the penal sanction conform to what I take to be our best moral conceptions of blameworthiness and desert. I turn now to practical questions that bear more directly on the real world. First, I inquire how my theory might be implemented into positive law. Second, I entertain conjectures about the consequences my theory would produce if it is implemented. Reflection on both of these matters suggests that compromises from ideal theory are needed. Pursuant to my methodological assumption that the penal law should conform to morality presumptively, I believe we should regret these retreats from our ideal and do our best to find ways to avoid them. Nonetheless, retreat is almost certainly needed.

I cannot begin to describe each of the possible ways my theory could be tweaked. Once we start down the road to compromise, we can wind up nearly anywhere. Some of the most negative reactions to my theory could be mollified by any number of revisions. According to the reason-responsive theory I prefer, morally ignorant defendants merit total exculpation. An obvious compromise with this ideal would be to reduce their punishments without precluding them altogether. B would receive a less severe sentence than A for Φ, but both would be liable and subject to some amount of punishment. Although this position cannot be reconciled with the particular theory of responsibility I favor, it cannot be said to lack a plausible rationale. After all, some versions of quality of will theories might support this very outcome. If my commitment to a reason-responsive theory of responsibility is misguided, the state could implement a sentencing scheme likely to be more acceptable both to the public and to many moral philosophers.

In any event, I do not canvass the many possible reasons we might hold B to be subject to less punishment than A for violating L. Instead, I begin by asking more general questions: How would our criminal justice system actually recognize exculpation for defendants who are ignorant of law? Does the answer follow directly from whatever *kind* of consideration we decide ignorance of law to be? How is the answer responsive to my claim that it is really ignorance of the morality that underlies law, rather than ignorance of law itself, that is exculpatory? These are the main topics of Part A. As I propose to treat ignorance of law and ignorance of fact symmetrically, we have ample precedent for how a criminal code might afford exculpation in any case of ignorance. I describe how the model that applies to mistakes of fact could be adapted for mistakes of law. Although I ultimately favor an option that treats each kind of mistake symmetrically, I cannot bring myself to decisively reject an alternative that deviates slightly from the conformity I presumptively favor. Pursuant to this latter possibility, defendants who plead ignorance of law would not be allowed to evade liability by denying mens rea—unlike defendants who plead ignorance of fact. Instead, they would be exculpated by an excuse with a statutory source extrinsic to the offense charged. In Part B I speculate about how the principled considerations I have defended throughout this book may have to be compromised for consequentialist reasons. I describe both the probable advantages and disadvantages my theory would produce in the real world. A proposal to recognize some degree of exculpation for defendants who are ignorant of law is bound to give rise to inadvertent misunderstandings and deliberate distortions, so my theory may not be worth its cost in the complexity and confusion it doubtless would engender. Just as important, no theory should be allowed to cause our criminal justice system to lose too much credibility in the eyes of a cynical public. However defensible it may be in principle, my theory should not be incorporated into positive law if the foreseeable consequences of doing so are sufficiently dire.

A. Implementation and Practical Realities

How could my theory of the exculpatory significance of ignorance of law actually be implemented in the real world of criminal justice? The answer requires a device to incorporate my position into statutory law. Skill in the art of legislation will not solve this problem until two enormous difficulties are overcome. The first seems cavernous. At face value, the theory I have defended is not a theory of ignorance of *law* at all. Instead, it is a theory of when ignorance of *morality* is exculpatory. More precisely, it is a theory of when ignorance of the morality (if any) that *underlies* law is exculpatory. Have I painted myself into another corner? How *can* a theory about the latter possibly be codified in a system of statutory law? The second difficulty, by comparison, appears to be more manageable. My theory that affords some degree of exculpation to B relative to A has been noncommittal about the *type* of exculpatory claim we should create. To this point, I have usually been evasive about this matter, referring generically to exculpation without further elaboration. I have contended that B should be acquitted altogether when she has no inkling whatever that her conduct is wrongful. How exactly should this result be achieved? And how should codes deal with defendants who are reckless about whether they are violating the law and thus deserve some quantum of punishment for their wrongful act Φ, albeit less than that of A? Answers to either or both of these questions may involve a *compromise*—an occasion in which my ideal theory should not be implemented in the real world without some adjustments. We should try, however, to find a principled ground for a solution.

It would not be surprising if quite a few compromises were needed. The criminal law, like any institution in the real world, already contains countless such compromises. Perhaps the most familiar set of these respond to the phenomenon that the several variables that render one defendant more deserving of punishment than another are usually *scalar,* even though the criminal law itself typically treats them as *binary*.[1] Countless illustrations could be given. Why, for example, should a defendant become eligible for significantly more punishment if she possesses twenty-nine grams of cocaine than if she possesses twenty-seven, when the difference between these amounts is identical to the difference between twenty-five and twenty-three—even though the latter difference lacks a comparable impact on sentencing? The answer, I am sure, reflects practicalities. For reasons only historians are likely to fathom, an ounce came to contain twenty-eight grams. Citizens and legal officials alike need categories that are relatively easy to understand and administer. A workable position on ignorance of law must be relatively easy to understand and administer as well.

The need for bright-line categories that conceal scalar distinctions is apparent if any theory of criminal responsibility is to be applied in the real world. I have said that wrongdoers deserve some quantum of punishment when they are reckless, that is, when they suspect that their conduct might be wrongful but their level of credence falls short of knowledge. Obviously, suspicion admits of degrees. Ideally, those with higher levels of credence that their conduct may be wrongful should be eligible for more severe sentences than those whose levels are lower (but still exceed the threshold that makes the risk substantial). Such determinations, however, would require fine-tuning that probably exceeds our human capacities. Implementing a retributive, desert-based model into a real-world system of criminal justice thus involves retreats from an ideal. Some commentators argue that these compromises are so pervasive that they doom a retributive, desert-based model at its inception.[2] As we all know, however, it is far easier to criticize a normative theory of punishment than to defend a detailed alternative. Before we surrender, we should do our best to preserve and improve a model of criminal law and punishment rooted in desert.

I begin with the first of the difficulties I have mentioned. Why does the *law* bear on the sentence a defendant deserves? In order to make this problem a bit less formidable, it is helpful to be reminded yet again why it is ignorance of morality rather than ignorance of law that does the exculpatory work. Legal philosophers seek a moral justification for punishing wrongdoers. I assume a defendant must have committed a

---

[1] This phenomenon has been noted by many legal philosophers. For example, see Leo Katz: *Why the Law Is So Perverse* (Chicago: University of Chicago Press, 2011), part II.

[2] Finding such difficulties with retributivism is a recurrent theme of quite a few theorists, including Adam J. Kolber: "The Subjective Experience of Punishment," 109 *Columbia Law Review* 182 (2009).

moral wrong if an adequate justification for punishment is to be given; ideal theory would not allow persons to be punished when their conduct is morally permissible. Fortunately, most penal laws in Anglo-American codes *do* proscribe moral wrongs. Unfortunately, quite a few do not—although any particular example is bound to generate controversy and depend on the story we tell about *mala prohibita*—a topic I addressed in Chapter 4(C). We should welcome rather than oppose a theory that confines morally justified punishments to persons guilty of moral wrongs. As the Supreme Court has repeatedly emphasized in the line of precedents I surveyed in Chapter 2(D), a primary goal of statutory interpretation is to protect innocence, where innocence is understood in moral rather than in legal terms. In any event, a theory that punishes only those offenders who commit moral wrongs would produce results that differ from the status quo in which *all* offenders become subject to punishment, even when the law breached does not proscribe a moral wrong. If the status quo is mistaken, how can it be corrected in the real world?

I hasten to point out that the corner in which I may seem to have painted myself is not simply an artifact of the peculiar theory I have constructed. Many well-known accounts of criminal law and punishment must surmount a similar hurdle. Various strains of legal moralism, for example, construe retributive justice to permit (or even to require) only the punishment of culpable wrongdoers. These theories earn the moniker of legal *moralism* because they construe culpable wrongdoing in moral terms. One can retain the *legal* component of these theories by stipulating that punishment should not be imposed unless the instance of culpable wrongdoing is antecedently proscribed by statute. But why adopt this stipulation? Unless it can be independently motivated, it seems suspiciously ad hoc. Legality plays no more obvious a role in legal moralism than in my theory of ignorance of law. It is unfair to press an objection too strongly against a particular theory when a great many others are vulnerable to it as well. At any rate, an independent motivation for the requirement of legality is needed, and it is not obvious where it can be found. I do not exaggerate in saying that an extended defense of the principle of legality in criminal theory has yet to be offered.[3]

[3] For the best such attempt, see Peter Westen: "Two Rules of Legality in Criminal Law," 26 *Law and Philosophy* 229 (2007). See also Michael Moore: Act and Crime (Oxford: Clarendon Press, 1993), pp.243ff.

Although I urge legal philosophers to be mindful that few theories of criminal law and punishment are immune from this worry, I do not thereby mean to minimize its significance. It seemingly creates a huge obstacle to implementing my theory—and thus to accepting it. The problem might be expressed as follows: If morality does all of the inculpatory and exculpatory work as regards blameworthiness, what role is left for law? Expressed more bluntly, why do we care about law at all?[4] It is one thing to *object* to punishment when criminal conduct is morally permissible. It would be quite another thing to *allow* punishment whether or not the law antecedently proscribed the impermissible conduct in question. This problem becomes acute when the defendant *knows* his conduct is wrong, but the state has failed to enact legislation to prohibit it. On the one hand, why should legality stand in the way of treating this wrongdoer as he deserves? On the other hand, to deny that legality *is* important to punishment—a claim that would contravene centuries of thought that is virtually unchallenged by criminal theorists—seems too big a bullet to bite. We should not be hasty to jettison the principle of *nulla poena sine lege*. My tentative solution of this problem will indicate that it has much less practical import than initial appearances might suggest.

I hazard the following response. In an ideal realm, where everyone agrees upon the content of morality, the principle of legality would *not* be needed. Punishment would be morally justified when imposed on persons who culpably commit moral wrongs; a legislature would have no need to proscribe these wrongs in advance. Perhaps divine justice satisfies this description. Do theologians insist that God must abstain from exacting retribution against sinners unless he has specifically proscribed their transgressions ex ante? Can clever sinners really escape their just deserts by finding loopholes in God's commands?[5] In any event, justice in the real world must differ. I have argued for only a *presumption* that the criminal law should conform to morality, and the normative case for legality is sufficiently compelling to warrant a deviation. On the planet we inhabit, we have ample reason to employ a *surrogate* for morality. This surrogate, of course, is statutory law. A separate treatise would be needed to recount the many advantages

---

[4] Recall my discussion in Chapter 2(D) that legality and notice play an important normative role *apart* from desert—as when punishments are imposed unfairly because persons are not given opportunities to avoid them.

[5] For a discussion of loopholers who try to avoid prohibitions on work on the Sabbath, see Katz: *op.cit.* Note 1.

of resorting to statutory law in criminal justice rather than making a direct appeal to morality,[6] so the explanation I will provide is cursory.

The main (but not the only) reason to employ legislation is that laypersons and legal officials alike remain uncertain and divided about the content of our moral duties, and an authoritative device is needed to allow the political process to function while these disputes are ongoing.[7] Good citizens as well as bad have caused havoc because of their misplaced confidence about what morality permits and prohibits. The state uses statutory law rather than morality to identify persons eligible for liability and punishment because direct recourse to the normatively relevant factor—morality itself—would be too divisive and uncertain. Even if there is a "right answer" to all moral disputes, we cannot expect people to concur about what that answer is. As we lack a mechanism to settle on a canonical formulation of moral wrongs, law is our next best option. Even when we generally agree about what is permissible or impermissible, the most experienced philosophers continue to debate about the details—where law is most needed. As every legal theorist can attest, of course, statutory law itself is far less certain than we would like. But one can only imagine the interminable chaos that would ensue if a system of criminal justice empowered officials to enforce the rules of morality without resort to statutory language.[8]

A number of philosophers appeal to similar considerations to conclude that citizens *do* commit at least a pro tanto moral wrong whenever they break the law—at least in a basically just democratic state.[9] As I understand these philosophers, they construe breaches of the best surrogate for morality to *be* immoral.[10] The position I take here is different, although its practical import is similar. Imagine a defendant who is punished for violating a law despite not having committed a moral wrong. I deny the state is morally justified in punishing her. On

[6] See Frederick Schauer: *The Force of Law* (Cambridge, MA: Harvard University Press, 2015).

[7] One might call this the *settlement function* of law. See Larry Alexander and Emily Sherman: *The Rule of Rules: Morality, Rules, and the Dilemmas of Law* (Durham, NC: Duke University Press, 2001).

[8] Many philosophers have written extensively about how democratic systems of law should respond to the inevitability of disagreement. See the discussion of the *burdens of judgment* in John Rawls: *Political Liberalism* (New York: Columbia University Press, 1993), esp. pp. 54–58.

[9] See Stephen P. Garvey: "Was Ellen Wronged?" 7 *Criminal Law and Philosophy* 185 (2013).

[10] See Philip Soper: *The Ethics of Deference: Learning from Law's Morals* (Cambridge: Cambridge University Press, 2002).

some occasions, however, the state has little alternative but to proceed *as if* she behaved wrongfully when she breaches a law that does not proscribe a moral wrong. If so, her punishment should be regarded as an unavoidable injustice. Nonetheless, an unavoidable injustice remains an injustice; she is wronged when punishment is inflicted. We should view her fate as an occasion for regret, as an invitation to try to do better. As such persons are innocent in the moral sense, our attitude toward their punishment should resemble our attitude toward the punishment of persons who are wrongfully convicted despite the best efforts of criminal justice officials to ensure the fairness and accuracy of our legal process. I assume that wrongful convictions cannot be eradicated entirely, even when they are not caused by abuses of power. Convicting these unfortunate individuals is the price we must pay for a system that brings about tremendous benefits relative to no system at all or to a system that dispenses with legality altogether. If we could identify those persons who have broken a law but not committed a moral wrong, we would have sound reasons to demand their acquittal or release. The overwhelming utilitarian advantages of using law rather than morality do not literally provide a moral justification for punishing them. A surrogate adopted for consequentialist reasons should not be confused with the real thing.

The practical import of my position may be indistinguishable from one in which ignorance of law rather than ignorance of morality is what does the real exculpatory work. The person who is punished is unlikely to be assuaged when told the state is permitted to treat him *as if* his punishment were justified, even though it is *un*justified from the perspective of ideal theory. Similar complaints might be heard in other contexts, as when doctrines of imputed consent are applied. Consider Victor, an unconscious victim of an automobile accident who is given medical assistance by doctors who happen to find him. When he subsequently receives a reasonable bill for their care, he might object (if he is sufficiently ungrateful) that he never consented to pay it and would not have consented had he been asked. Victor is literally correct. Still, he should be made to pay anyway; doctors are permitted to treat him *as if* he had consented, despite the fact that he did not. The position I adopt here is similar. A defendant may object when he is punished despite having done nothing wrong to deserve it. Yet I hold that the state has little recourse but to treat him as if he deserves to be punished, even though he does not. Perhaps a few defendants will find solace in my position. On the level of the expressive message that is conveyed, a defendant should prefer to be told the state has no alternative but to treat her as though she deserves punishment than to be told that she actually deserves it.

Return to the converse situation—one involving persons I described as *legal loopholers* in Chapter 4(A). Why should legality create a decisive barrier *against* punishing persons who *do* knowingly commit a moral wrong that happens *not* to be proscribed by law? We might insist the state should be *estopped* from prosecution, but this answer, without further embellishment, is a conclusion in search of an argument. Unlike in the foregoing situation, I said that no injustice would be done to a defendant who is punished under these circumstances. If the state should abstain from punishment, the rationale must involve considerations other than desert. To my mind, the best rationale again refers to practical realities—to the lack of confidence that such persons can be correctly identified. Any procedure to detect them would be bound to generate social turmoil. Again, acquitting those individuals who deserve blame is the price we must pay for a system that brings about tremendous benefits relative to no system at all, or to a system that dispenses with legality altogether. Instances in which defendants knowingly engage in wrongful conduct not proscribed by law should be treated as occasions in which my theory about the exculpatory force of ignorance of law requires a compromise in order to attain important social objectives independent of justice and desert.

Legality is also important because of a controversial point I mentioned in Chapter 1(B): the presumption that the law should enforce morality does not apply (or is always rebutted) when persons commit *private* rather than *public* wrongs. As I construe them, public wrongs concern the community as well as the particular individuals who have been victimized. Recall my reticence to provide an account of which wrongs *are* private. If legal philosophers cannot be confident that particular wrongs are private rather than public, the comparable difficulty for citizens and officials is exponentially more acute. To resolve this uncertainty, we need a political process by which the interests of the public are authoritatively identified. This mechanism, of course, is statutory law, enacted by legislators on behalf of the citizenry in a democratic regime. In the absence of a statute that has been breached, it is harder to be sure the conduct in question amounts to a public wrong, even if we could be certain of its wrongfulness. For all *practical* purposes, therefore, law does all of the exculpatory and inculpatory work. Thus in what follows I will describe the exculpatory consideration I examine as ignorance of *law* rather than ignorance of the *morality* that underlies it. Our existing practices of arresting, prosecuting, convicting, and punishing have little recourse but to invoke law rather than morality. Again, however, we should not equate the conclusions we adopt for practical reasons with those that reflect the underlying moral grounds for deciding who does and does not deserve to be blamed and punished. The true normative basis of exculpation is ignorance of the morality underlying law, and not ignorance of law itself.

A second problem must be confronted before my theory can be implemented in the real world: we must decide what *kind* of exculpatory consideration is ignorance of law, and how it should be codified. Although this problem may seem less formidable than the first, I regard it as surprisingly difficult. Outside of the *Model Penal Code,* positive law offers little help in resolving it. As I explained at length in Chapter 2(D), the U.S. Code in particular currently implements no single solution, including a sizeable minority of statutes that require defendants to know they are committing an offense before liability can be imposed. Why some but not all? I can divine no rhyme or reason to explain why some statutes but not others allow legally ignorant defendants to evade liability. Factors such as statutory complexity account for why mistakes about some offenses are more prevalent than mistakes about others, but fail to provide a deep explanation of why a given defendant is regarded as blameworthy and eligible for punishment just because he makes a mistake few others would have made. Whatever the explanation, legally ignorant defendants who are accused of breaching a statute that *does* exculpate them plead either a denial of mens rea or a true defense— a distinction that can be difficult to draw. Courts have enlarged the number of these offenses in endeavors to protect persons alleged to be morally innocent, although it is hard to be sure whether they are thought to be innocent because they have done nothing wrong or because they lack responsibility for the wrongs they have done. In any event, as my examples illustrate, the U.S. Code contains a patchwork or hodgepodge of these offenses. Obviously, I prefer a generic approach that would permit legally ignorant defendants to evade liability for *all* crimes. Should we do so by creating a true defense, or by allowing them to deny mens rea?

The ideal solution would codify the exculpatory significance of mistake of law in exactly the same way as mistake of fact. As we have seen, the *Model Penal Code* consistently treats ignorance of fact as a denial of mens rea. Any legal philosopher worth her salt should be loath to recommend otherwise—and take a step more radical than any I have proposed to this point. The inclusion of mens rea in penal statutes has a long and celebrated history, and no living commentator, to my knowledge, argues that it should be removed as an element of core offenses. Hence if we are to maintain the symmetry I presumptively favor between the treatment of mistake of fact and mistake of law, the latter must be conceptualized as a denial of mens rea too, and not as a true defense. As a first pass, each and every offense could be redrafted to contain a mens rea term requiring awareness of wrongdoing. Murder, for example would no longer be defined as (roughly) "knowingly killing another human being," but would be redefined as "knowingly killing another human being while knowing it is wrong to kill another human being." Similarly, statutes could be redrafted to ensure a lesser sentence when the defendant is reckless, that is, when she consciously disregards a substantial and unjustifiable risk that her conduct is wrongful. Manslaughter, in turn, would no longer be defined as (roughly) "recklessly killing another human being," but would be redefined as "recklessly killing another human being while aware of the substantial and unjustifiable risk that it is wrong to kill another human being." If this strategy were followed, all penal statutes would allow defendants who are ignorant or reckless about the law to evade or reduce their responsibility for the relevant offense by denying mens rea. Ignorance of fact and law would be treated symmetrically.

Clearly, this ideal as characterized above produces offenses that are unwieldy and barely pass the laugh test. This worry, however, can be overcome easily. Legislators could simply borrow the *Model Penal Code's* device for solving this problem in the domain of mistake of fact. Section 2.02(1) specifies that culpability is needed with respect to *each* material element of (nearly all) penal statutes, even when a given statute does not indicate this need. The operation of this provision avoids cumbersome language and saves a lot of legislative ink. States could amend the current definitions of mens rea terms so that knowledge of wrongdoing would be required for all penal offenses, even when they do not say so explicitly. An additional statute would modify the first by specifying that recklessness of wrongdoing reduces the grade of the offense—perhaps to one-half, as I tentatively proposed in Chapter 3(C). Thus the literal wording of existing statutes such as murder and manslaughter could remain intact, but would implicitly require some awareness of wrongdoing as a precondition of liability.

Defendants without the needed level of awareness would evade punishment by denying mens rea.

Apart from the other advantages of symmetry, allowing ignorance of law to function as a denial of mens rea would reap an enormous benefit: we would be spared once and for all from wrestling with the elusive distinction between the two kinds of mistake. No longer would we need to categorize given mistakes as one type or the other—as factual or legal. All we would have to determine is whether the defendant made a material mistake, that is, a mistake that negates his culpability. Thus positive law would implement the same theory to exculpate persons who made either kind of mistake. This advantage should not be taken lightly, even though I have contended in Chapter 2(C) that the difficulties in contrasting the two kinds of mistake are often exaggerated.

Still, my theory might be codified in a different way. A second alternative would not conceptualize ignorance of law as a denial of mens rea but would require the enactment of one or more new statutes that create two tiers of culpability (or possibly three or four, if purpose and/ or negligence are included among the culpable states). The scheme would be modeled after 18 USC Section 1902. As I indicated in Chapter 2(D), this statute specifies: "No person shall be deemed guilty of a violation of any such rules, unless prior to such alleged violation he shall have had actual knowledge thereof." *All* penal offenses would be governed by this sort of provision. More precisely, the statute should specify: "No person shall be guilty of a violation of any penal statute unless he is aware his conduct is wrongful." A second statute should be enacted to qualify the first and impose liability but reduce the severity of the sentence by a specified amount when a defendant is aware of a substantial and unjustifiable risk his conduct is wrongful.

This second alternative departs from symmetry in not treating mistakes of law as a denial of mens rea. It also deviates from symmetry in an additional respect I regard as advantageous rather than troubling. Apart from a handful of cases such as homicide, few existing statutory schemes expressly provide that persons who commit a crime recklessly are eligible for a lesser sentence than those who commit that same crime knowingly. Instead, offenses generally specify a single culpable state, often recklessness, as sufficient to convict. Defendants who commit that offense with a higher degree of culpability do not automatically qualify for a more severe punishment than those whose culpability is at the minimum statutory threshold. This feature of existing law is puzzling, and has received too little criticism from philosophers of criminal law. Statutes should explicitly provide that, *ceteris paribus,* more culpable defendants should be punished more severely than less culpable defendants. My theory would ensure that wrongdoers whose mistake of law is reckless are sentenced less severely than wrongdoers who violate the law knowingly. This feature should be implemented into positive law, regardless of whether the defendant makes a mistake of fact or a mistake of law.

Despite its slight departure from perfect symmetry, the second of these solutions has much to recommend it. Defendants who are ignorant of law would evade liability not by denying mens rea, but by invoking an altogether new defense. The main (but not the only) advantage of not making awareness of wrongdoing an explicit or implicit mens rea element of penal offenses involves the implications for burdens of proof. We might at least allow the possibility that the burden of persuasion should be allocated to the defendant regarding her ignorance of law; the prosecution should not necessarily be required to prove she is aware of the law she violates. The presumption of innocence traditionally applies to every crime, and crimes, as I have said, are comprised of their several elements. Unless the presumption of innocence should extend to the plea of ignorance of law, it might be preferable not to allow mistaken defendants to evade liability by denying the mens rea included in the offense. Instead, defendants who are ignorant of law would plead a genuine defense separate from the offense. Frankly, I am ambivalent about how the burden of proof should be allocated with respect to ignorance of law. Assigning this burden to defendants rather than to the state might be advisable for practical reasons, helping to diffuse the political backlash that is bound to occur if my views are perceived as too radical. Perhaps jurisdictions should be encouraged to experiment with different assignments of the burden of proof so that legislators and commentators are able to gather real-life data about which option is more manageable and just.

A second possible rationale for preferring the second of the above alternatives—despite its slight deviation from symmetry—returns to my worries about how the state might secure protection from zealous terrorists who are unaware of wrongdoing. I proposed that systems of preventive detention outside the ambit of penal justice might have to be enlarged to confine misguided villains for purposes of public safety. If these persons were acquitted on the ground that they had not violated the statute at all, sensible measures of social protection might be harder to devise. At the present time, many such measures are secured through collateral consequences of conviction.[11] For example, the passage of the federal sex offender registration law in 2006 and the proliferation of similar state laws have led to the registration of approximately three-quarters of a million persons nationwide.[12] These collateral consequences, however, are usually predicated on having committed an offense, that is, on having breached a statute.[13] If defendants are found not to be liable because they possess a defense extrinsic to the statute breached, it could be easier to require them to suffer whatever collateral consequences are deemed to be desirable. Just as states may commit dangerous persons found not guilty by reason of insanity, states might impose whatever collateral consequences are needed to protect the public from persons who are found not guilty because of their ignorance of law. Obviously, the justifiability of collateral consequences is a highly controversial topic, and I do not want to give any of them my unqualified endorsement.[14] Each must be assessed on its own merits. But the imposition of some of these consequences should remain a viable option I suspect could be exercised more easily if ignorant defendants were unable to evade liability by denying the mens rea elements of the statutes they breach.

My final reservation about implementing a perfectly symmetrical position is even more speculative, and depends on the rationale for why the Code presently attaches a culpability requirement to each individual element of an offense rather than to offenses as a whole. The Code allows different culpability requirements to apply to different elements of a single statute because a defendant who makes a factual mistake about one element may or not be as blameworthy as a defendant who makes a factual mistake about another. Consider, for example, the crime of "Endangering Welfare of Children."[15] A guardian who "supervises the welfare of a child under 18" does not commit this

---

[11] See Margaret Colgate Love, Jenny Roberts and Cecelia Klingele: *Collateral Consequences of Criminal Convictions: Law, Policy and Practice* (Eagan, Minnesota: Thomson Reuters, 2013).

[12] *See Registered Sex Offenders in the United States*, National Center for Missing and Exploited Children, *available at* www.missingkids.com/SOTT (data as of 2014).

[13] Admittedly, states occasionally impose these consequences on defendants who successfully avoid liability by a denial of mens rea. See, for example, *Kansas v. Hendricks*, 521 U.S. 346 (1997). But this practice seems more problematic and has been roundly criticized by commentators. Collateral consequences are more easily imposed after *conviction*.

[14] For a balanced view, see Sandra G. Mayson: "Collateral Consequences and the Preventive State," 91 *Notre Dame Law Review* (forthcoming, 2016).

[15] *Model Penal Code* §230.4.

offense unless he "knowingly endangers the child's welfare by violating a duty of care." Suppose the defendant mistakenly believes the person whose welfare he knowingly endangers is an adult rather than a child. Through the operation of Section 2.02(3), this defendant is not liable for this crime unless he is at least *reckless* in his mistaken belief about the age of the child he endangers. Still, he must *know* his conduct actually endangers his victim's welfare. Thus no single culpability term applies to each of the different elements of this offense. It is not exactly clear *why* a defendant who makes a factual mistake about the age of the person he knowingly endangers is thought to differ in blameworthiness from a defendant who makes a factual mistake about whether his conduct really involves endangerment. As far as I can see, only intuitions govern the decision about how the content of this wrong should be formulated.

In any event, these same considerations might apply to mistakes of law. I asked in Chapter 1(A) whether we should equate the defendant who is wholly unaware the law proscribes sex with very young women with another who is mistaken of the exact age at which very young women are able to convey effective consent. It is hardly obvious that each of these defendants deserves comparable amounts of blame when they commit the actus reus of the offense. Should we then replicate the above feature of the Code in the context of mistake of law? Return to the crime of Endangering Welfare of Children. We might be tempted, for example, to differentiate between the culpability of a guardian who does not believe he owes a given child any duty of care whatever from the culpability of a guardian who does not believe he has a duty, for example, to secure an education or medical care for his child. But if we do not want to differentiate between the blameworthiness of these two individuals, we would simply ask how severely a defendant who commits this offense because of either mistake should be punished relative to a defendant who commits neither. We would have no need to subdivide the statute into its several elements with different mens rea requirements. The finer gradations of culpability required in the context of ignorance of fact would have no counterpart in a normative theory of ignorance of law.

Is the blameworthiness of a defendant who makes a mistake of law about one element greater than that of a defendant who makes a mistake of law about another? *Should* we differentiate between the culpability of the guardian who does not believe he owes a given child any duty of care whatever from the culpability of the guardian who does not believe he has a duty to educate or obtain medical care for his child? I admit to feeling a slight tug of the intuition that these individuals differ in their desert. For reasons I belabored in Chapter 1(C), however, I attach little credence to these intuitions. The general theory of responsibility on which I rely does not explain why the blameworthiness of these two defendants should be differentiated. Neither person should be expected to conform to reasons of which he is unaware, even when the content of these reasons differs. Moreover, allowing their culpability to be differentiated would add complexity to the criminal law, a complexity offset by little if any gain. I tentatively conclude that we have no clear basis to attach different culpability terms to different elements of the law L about which a defendant is ignorant.[16] The culpable states that are most clearly relevant to assessing the blameworthiness of defendants who are ignorant of law—knowledge and recklessness—can apply to entire statutes rather than to particular elements within statutes. If so, the exculpatory significance of ignorance of law can just as easily be derived from a statute extrinsic to the offense charged rather than from a denial of the mens rea in the offense itself.

None of the above reasons for deviating from the symmetry I generally favor between fact and law is decisive. Thus I propose that defendants who are ignorant of fact or ignorant of law should evade punishment by denying mens rea. This solution, however, leaves us with a theoretical puzzle. This puzzle can be introduced simply, even if its resolution involves a bit of conceptual uncertainty. We have seen that ignorance of fact amounts to a denial of mens rea, and I have proposed that ignorance of law should do so as well. If so, can this symmetrical position allow us to regard ignorance of law as an *excuse*? Ignorance of *fact* is not regarded as an excuse. But recall Fletcher's response to Hall's argument on behalf of the doctrine of *ignorantia juris*. His response presupposed that ignorance of law *is* an excuse, and I see no basis for contending Fletcher is mistaken. If these two kinds of mistake are to be treated symmetrically, how can one be an excuse and the other not?

I tentatively respond to this puzzle as follows. Even though penal codes afford exculpatory significance to mistake of fact as a denial of mens rea, it should not be thought to follow that mistake of fact is not an excuse. Contrary to what many criminal theorists tend to

---

[16] Thus I depart from some of the tentative positions I defended in Douglas Husak: "Mistake of Law and Culpability," 4 *Criminal Law and Philosophy* 135 (2010).

THE REAL WORLD   269

suppose, ignorance of fact *is* an excuse. So too is ignorance of law. Thus I ultimately preserve the symmetry between mistake of fact and mistake of law by conceptualizing mistake of fact as an excuse, not by conceptualizing mistake of law as some other species of exculpatory plea. As both pleas are excuses, they presuppose the defendant has committed a wrong. The wrong, in both instances, is the act committed without culpability or mens rea. Of course, existing law *affords* the excuse of mistake of fact exculpatory significance as a denial of a mens rea term included within the text of the statute breached. But the fact that codes afford exculpatory significance to a given plea by allowing it to deny mens rea should not mislead us into drawing false inferences about its true normative character. As every moral philosopher could have told us, ignorance of fact *is* an excuse, notwithstanding its codification as a denial of mens rea. Such ignorance is an excuse the absence of which must be proved by the prosecution pursuant to a straightforward application of the presumption of innocence.

My solution, however, may simply push the puzzle elsewhere. If ignorance of fact *is* an excuse, why does the structure of penal codes suggest otherwise? Nearly all excuses are afforded exculpatory significance through a statute extrinsic to the offense charged. I have not entirely ruled out the possibility that the exculpatory significance of ignorance of law should be codified this way as well. Why should the excuse of ignorance of fact possibly stand alone in being codified differently, allowing defendants to evade liability by denying a mens rea element of the statute? These questions invite us to ponder the explanation for including mens rea as an element of all core penal offenses. If a wrong can be perpetrated without mens rea, as I believe to be the case, why incorporate mens rea into the content of an offense? Although the inclusion of mens rea in penal offenses is widely celebrated and seldom challenged, it is rarely explained.

Perhaps the best rationale for including mens rea in criminal statutes is political: requiring persons to defend themselves when they have committed a moral wrong without mens rea would bring too many persons within the ambit of state power.[17] After all, it is burdensome to ask citizens to *respond* or to *answer* to a charge of criminal conduct—the criterion by which Antony Duff proposes we contrast the exculpatory considerations that should be treated as defenses from

---

[17] See R.A. Duff: *Answering for Crime* (Oxford: Hart, 2007).

those that should be treated as denials of an element of the offense.[18] According to this rationale, the authority of the state should not extend to those who lack blameworthiness because of their excuse of mistake of fact, even though they may have committed a public wrong. The unresolved question is whether this very same rationale applies with equal force to persons who make mistakes of law. Is state power abused just as badly when defendants who are ignorant of law are required to plead an excuse with a statutory source extrinsic to the offense charged? Probably. But I confess to some uncertainty about these matters, and my ambivalence is reflected by my willingness to entertain the possibility that the burden of proof should be allocated to defendants who plead ignorance of law. Although reasonable minds may differ about these complex matters, I tentatively conclude that we should preserve symmetry by allowing defendants who plead ignorance of law to avoid liability by invoking the same kind of defense as those who plead ignorance of fact: an excuse that denies mens rea.

B. Consequences and Compromises

I have argued in favor of an ideal to which our criminal justice system should aspire if the penal law is to conform to morality. To oversimplify a bit, I have concluded that the penal law should answer the basic question (Q) by imposing different quanta of blame and punishment on A and B. An adequate theory of ignorance of law should countenance at least two (and possibly as many as four) different culpable states. Defendants should be held fully responsible and subject to the maximum sentence a statute authorizes only when they act akratically, fully aware their conduct does not conform to the balance of moral reasons. This will be fairly unusual. Contra Rosen or Zimmerman, however, I claim we are sometimes responsible and blameworthy even though we do not commit a wrongful act akratically. Wrongdoers should also be held responsible when they are aware they create a substantial and unjustifiable risk that their conduct may be wrongful. Still, the latter offenders should be subject to a less severe punishment than

---

[18] See Duff: *id.,* especially chapter 9. It is worth noting that Duff would not endorse the above solution. He believes that persons should be made to answer when they are *responsible,* and responsibility consists in committing an offense—which includes mens rea.

the former. Unlike many other commentators who are critical of the existing rule of *ignorantia juris,* I extend exculpation even to defendants who commit a *malum in se* offense—although the special difficulties involving *mala prohibita* are sufficiently important to have merited a separate section. I am sure a great many legal philosophers will report initial intuitions that are at odds with some or all of my positions. Even those philosophers who agree that moral ignorance should excuse in nearly every case admit their views encounter emphatic resistance when they are first presented. Although I believe reflection ultimately favors my conclusions, a theory of ignorance of law should not depend solely on intuitions. Thus I have tried to ground my position in a conception of responsibility, fully aware that the particular conception I invoke is the Achilles heel in my project. I take solace in believing it is the weak link in *any* project that explicitly identifies the theory of responsibility on which it rests.

Ideas have consequences, and criminal theorists who wish to be taken seriously must attend to them. I complained in my Introduction that many philosophers who advocate the abolition of punishment fail to offer details about the mode of social control that should take its place. What would a world without punishment really be like? What kinds of responses to wrongdoers would substitute for penal institutions, and why should we believe they would improve upon them? In this part I speculate briefly about similar questions involving ignorance of law. If my theory (or a close approximation of it) were implemented in our criminal codes, what would be its probable effects? Even the best ideas defensible on principled grounds and accepted by the community of legal philosophers have indirect consequences that must be carefully evaluated. In all likelihood, these effects would be both positive and negative. Would the good outweigh the bad? We philosophers should be cautious about making empirical predictions. Nonetheless, I hazard the following informed guess: in a world of moderately rational agents generally persuaded by sound normative arguments, the pluses would outweigh the minuses. Unfortunately, in the world we actually inhabit, the opposite prediction is just as probable. Compromise or even outright repudiation of some of my ideals may be necessary.

I begin with what I take to be the single greatest advantage of the theory I have defended: it could help to lessen the number of persons we punish and the severity of the draconian sentences we presently impose. Most important, it would do so on principled rather than on pragmatic grounds: punishing the morally ignorant is *unjust* rather than merely *inexpedient*.[19] Few proposed reforms (or compromises) meet this standard. Almost certainly, states could save money without jeopardizing public safety by adopting a number of changes in how offenders are sentenced. For example, elderly inmates, whose criminal careers are a distant memory, could be released from prison. But even such economically sensible ideas are bound to encounter resistance unless they can be supported on grounds of desert. Apart from implementing a better theory of criminalization—and repealing unjustifiable offenses such as drug proscriptions—I am unaware of a single reform defensible on grounds of justice that could be more effective in reducing the amount of punishment than the theory I have described here. I have no doubt this achievement would have positive repercussions throughout all of society. Nonetheless, theorists who seek to depict this advantage solely in terms of costs and benefits miss the point of a deontological moral philosophy. The main beneficiaries of my theory would be those offenders who would otherwise be punished in excess of their desert. In this era of mass incarceration, any reasonable person should support an idea that decreases the sentences of offenders by conforming more closely to the demands of proportionality.

The foregoing advantage can be secured even if we are uncertain my theory is correct. As I frequently admit, no decisive argument favors *any* underlying theory of responsibility—including a theory that affords exculpatory significance to ignorance of law. How should our criminal justice system respond to this uncertainty? Unlike mere judgments that persons are blameworthy from a moral point of view, the real-world ramifications for personal autonomy and well-being can be catastrophic when criminal liability and punishment are inflicted. For this reason, in cases of reasonable doubt, we have special grounds to cast the net of penal responsibility narrowly.

Who else besides blameless and less-than-fully-responsible defendants would benefit from the implementation of my theory? In the long run, I anticipate the behavior of legal officials would be improved in several ways if the law became more charitable to offenders who are unaware their conduct is wrongful. I draw inspiration from reflection about the impact of exclusionary rules in constitutional law. Just as rules that bar the admissibility of given kinds of evidence shape the practices of law enforcement, a robust defense of ignorance of law would alter the incentives of criminal justice officials. The first such change would

---

[19] As some politicians have begun to appreciate. See *infra* Note 22.

take place in the legislature; the second would occur throughout our political system more generally. I briefly describe each in turn.

First, abolishing the doctrine of *ignorantia juris* might finally lead legislatures to take steps to combat the problem of overcriminalization—a phenomenon I have previously discussed at length.[20] Commentators from all points along the political spectrum have begun to agree that the size of the criminal law and the amount of punishment we inflict are out of control and need to be curtailed.[21] Legislators should respond to an expansion of the exculpatory significance of ignorance of law by asking *why* citizens make so many such mistakes in the first place. More specifically, they should ask *what it is* about our criminal law that contributes to the unacceptable number of these errors. Of course, no single cause explains all instances of ignorance, and no single change would eliminate them entirely. Still, legislators could play a huge role in reducing their prevalence. As politicians have come to realize, a major factor producing ignorance of law is the unbelievable complexity and obscurity of our criminal codes.[22] Legislators who hope to reduce the impact of a defense of ignorance of law on the operation of penal justice would be well advised to address this root cause by simplifying the number and content of penal statutes. Our tendency to enact laws that do not proscribe conduct citizens believe to be wrongful cannot be a good idea. Conscientious defendants should not be forced to guess whether broad offenses apply to their conduct. Thus the first general benefit I would expect my proposals to produce is a more sensible criminal code with less complexity and obscurity.

Let me elaborate. Nonspecialists would not be surprised to learn that commentators who have spent the better parts of their lives studying criminal justice agree that some of our penal laws are unintelligible. But laypersons might be appalled by the true extent of this problem. *No*

---

[20] Douglas Husak: *Overcriminalization* (Oxford: Oxford University Press, 2008).

[21] See Inimai M. Chettiar et al. eds.: *Solutions: American Leaders Speak Out on Criminal Justice* (New York: Brennan Center for Justice, 2015).

[22] Some even agree with me by construing this excuse as a denial of mens rea. According to Orrin Hatch, member and former Chairman of the Senate Judiciary Committee, "without adequate *mens rea* protections—that is, without the requirement that a person know his conduct was wrong, or unlawful—everyday citizens can be held criminally liable for conduct that no reasonable person would know was wrong. This is not only unfair; it is immoral." The main culprit, Hatch continues, is that "for too long, Congress has criminalized too much conduct and enacted overbroad statutes that sweep far beyond the evils they're designed to avoid." Press Release (September 15, 2015), http://www.hatch.senate.gov/public/index. cfm?p=releases&id=090FFA70-5ABF-4160-8ED5-D512EBEBEB6F.

one—practitioners, legislators, or law professors—is familiar with more than a tiny handful of the criminal statutes to which we are subject. To illustrate this point, we should not focus simply on the amusing stories of antiquated statutes that continue to survive on our books.[23] To be sure, Alabama makes it a felony to maim oneself to excite sympathy, England forbids MPs from wearing armor in Parliament, and Indiana bans the coloring of birds and rabbits. But these laws are seldom if ever enforced, so defendants have little or no occasion to plead ignorance when charged with their violation. As I have indicated, however, other examples present problems that arise all too frequently in the real world.

Sheer numbers are a large part of the problem. Amazingly, no respectable commentator is prepared to estimate how many state and federal laws subject persons to punishment in the United States. Everyone agrees the figure is high, whatever the final tally may be. But counting the number of statutes tends to understate the explosive growth in the size of the criminal law. Because much of the recent expansion consists in amendments to existing statutes, some of which are located outside of criminal codes altogether, we cannot meaningfully say that the number of offenses has doubled, tripled, or multiplied tenfold. Despite the formidable difficulties in measuring the extent of criminalization, we can count the words or pages in penal codes to illustrate the trend. Paul Robinson and Michael Cahill employ this method to demonstrate the expansion in the criminal code of Illinois—even though commentators (including Robinson himself) tend to rank the overall quality of this state code as well above average. When enacted in 1961, the Illinois Code contained fewer than 24,000 words. Within forty years, that number had swelled to more than 136,000—a sixfold increase.[24]

But numbers tell only part of the story. A more accurate picture of the problem is presented by examining the different kinds of laws that have led to this expansion. *Mala prohibita* are the main culprit, but I propose to be more concrete. I briefly mention only one of several categories of *mala prohibita* offenses that should be ripe for reconsideration.[25] Norman Abrams calls these offenses *ancillary*.[26]

---

[23] See Eric Luna: "The Overcriminalization Phenomenon," 54 *American University Law Review* 703 (2005).

[24] Paul H. Robinson and Michael T. Cahill: "Can a Model Penal Code Second Save the States from Themselves?" 1 *Ohio State Journal of Criminal Law* 169, 170 (2003).

[25] Offenses of *risk-prevention* comprise an additional category. See Husak: *Op.cit.* Note 20.

[26] Norman Abrams: "The New Ancillary Offenses," 1 *Criminal Law Forum* 1 (1989).

Roughly, ancillary offenses function as proxies or surrogates for the prosecution of primary or core crimes. They are created mostly for situations in which a defendant is believed to have committed a *malum in se*, but prosecution is unlikely to be successful. On some occasions, the state cannot prove the commission of the core offense, or its evidence of this offense is inadmissible because it has been obtained illegally. These occasions have led to the enactment of growing numbers of ancillary offenses that surround core crimes. Several of these laws venture into the "gray zone of socially acceptable and economically justifiable business conduct."[27] Because most of these statutes have neither common-law analogs nor well-established public meanings, legislators have broad latitude to define them expansively. The features of many of these offenses—the absence of culpability requirements, the shifting of burdens of proof, the imposition of liability for omissions, and the implicit trust in prosecutorial discretion to prevent abuse—undermine fundamental principles long held sacrosanct by philosophers of criminal law, and surely contribute to the incidence of ignorance of law among offenders. Theorists have raised doubts about the justifiability of these ancillary offenses. Abrams himself frequently indicates his misgivings, yet admits "it is difficult to grab hold of the specific objection that underlies such an intuition."[28] Ronald Gainer is less reticent, expressing his dissatisfaction with this category of crime as follows: "Sometimes the operating philosophy seems to be that, if government cannot prosecute what it wishes to penalize, it will penalize what it wishes to prosecute. . . . Moving beyond penalization of collateral misconduct to the penalization of collateral, seemingly innocent conduct, that causes no real independent harm but that may be associated with either lawful or unlawful actions, raises jurisprudential questions that lawmakers have not frequently chosen to face."[29] I agree these problems are acute, and have discussed them in the context of such crimes as money laundering.[30] I trust lawmakers would be more willing to confront these problems if defendants were afforded some degree of exculpation when they are ignorant of law. In

---

[27] *United States v. United States Gypsum Co.*, 438 U.S. 422, 441 (1978).

[28] Abrams: *Op.cit.* Note 26, p.29.

[29] Ronald Gainer: "Federal Criminal Code Reform: Past and Future," 2 *Buffalo Criminal Law Review* 45, 63 n.38 (1993).

[30] See Husak: *Op.cit.* Note 20. For a critical discussion, see Robert Young: "Douglas Husak on Dispensing with the *Malum Prohibitum* Offense of Money Laundering," 28 *Criminal Justice Ethics* 108 (2009).

sum, it would be appropriate for legislators to respond to the adoption of my theory by cleaning up criminal codes to ensure that penal laws proscribe behavior nearly all persons recognize to be morally wrong. Ancillary laws would be a sensible place to begin.

I turn now to a second beneficial consequence that the implementation of my theory might be expected to produce in the real world—a benefit that extends beyond the impact on blameless defendants. If ignorance of law were accepted either as a complete defense or as a consideration that reduces the grade of an offense, states would have reason to respond by undertaking greater efforts to inform citizens of the laws to which they are subject. It is not enough to ensure that statutes are somehow available to citizens who are sufficiently heroic to discover them; the political process itself must take positive steps to prevent us from remaining ignorant. Concerted efforts in this direction would be welcome. Andrew Ashworth, a longtime critic of the doctrine of *ignorantia juris,* laments that almost none of the scholarly discussion involving criminal responsibility focuses on the duties of states to inform citizens about the law, emphasizing instead the duties of citizens to inquire and conform to it. Obviously, states have obligations to enact statutes to protect the public and to prosecute those who breach them. "But," Ashworth continues, "the highest priority should be given to the use of education and information in order to reduce the number of offences being committed. Waiting until a case arises, imposing strict liability as to knowledge of the law so as to convict the person concerned, and then following it with a disproportionate sentence so as to use this offender as a means (adequate or not) of warning others is monumentally unjust."[31] Who can contest Ashworth's claim? Surely "it is better that crimes do not occur in the first place than that we convict people after they have committed them."[32] If the criminal justice system took greater measures to prevent wrongful conduct ex ante than to punish it ex post, it might seem less heretical to confine penal sanctions to those who know or at least suspect their conduct is wrongful.[33] Needless to say, Anglo-American states have done a poor job meeting their obligations under what Ashworth describes as their "highest priority."

---

[31] Andrew Ashworth: "Ignorance of the Criminal Law, and Duties to Avoid It," in Andrew Ashworth, ed.: *Positive Obligations in Criminal Law* (Oxford: Hart, 2013), pp.81, 92.

[32] *Id.,* p.101.

[33] See also Samuel Buell and Lisa Kern Griffin: "On the Mental State of Consciousness of Wrongdoing," 75 *Law and Contemporary Problems* 213 (2012).

I add a single refinement to Ashworth's sensible recommendations. On my view, it is desirable not only that the state does a better job informing citizens of the content of the law, but also that it does a better job educating citizens about the moral reasons that led it to enact the law in the first place. After all, it is these reasons, and not the law per se, that generate duties of compliance. What, for example, is the moral rationale of penal laws proscribing the use of illicit drugs? As legislators have made no serious effort to tell us, we citizens are forced to guess. An ongoing dialogue about the supposed moral basis for given laws could only be beneficial in a democratic society that aspires to limit its intrusions on liberty.

I do not pretend to offer much concrete advice about what steps should be taken by our political process to reduce the extent of moral and legal ignorance among our citizens. Obviously, efforts should be targeted on individuals most likely to engage in the type of conduct proscribed. With respect to laws of more general application, however, Ashworth advances four specific proposals: the creation of a free electronic database of penal laws, the simplification of statutory language to better guide persons in how to avoid the conduct proscribed, a requirement that those who sponsor new legislation be made to describe how information of its content is to be disseminated, and, most important, a strategy for more effective education in public schools. Of course, efforts to disseminate information need not be limited to educational institutions. Return yet again to Jacob, our camper who disposes of batteries in ignorance of recycling laws. Why shouldn't the labels on batteries contain information about proper recycling? If jurisdictions differ too much to make this goal possible, states have incentives to seek more uniformity so environments are not contaminated. Still, schools would be a reasonable place to start. As all citizens should cooperate with recycling efforts, it would be sensible for educational institutions to include information about these laws as part of its curriculum. Some already do so. In most municipalities, unfortunately, schoolchildren are most likely to come into contact with legal officials when they are subjected to DARE programs that warn them of the punishments they face if caught using an illicit drug. I am sure we can do better.

So much for the several advantages. I now mention what I fear would be a huge *disadvantage* of my proposal—a disadvantage so great it might necessitate a wholesale repudiation of the ideal I have defended. How would our political process and citizenry *really* react to an expansion in the exculpatory significance of ignorance of law? At the present time, I am skeptical we are willing and able to overcome our proclivity to politicize a law-and-order issue to further an ideological agenda. For whatever reason, even the best (not to mention the worst) media have done a poor job educating citizens about criminal justice and the principles that underlie it. To cite one of several examples, much of the electorate continues to believe crime rates are increasing, even though they have been decreasing, often precipitously, throughout nearly all of the United States for the past few decades. Many citizens are certain police brutality is rising, when the better hypothesis is that bad behavior is more difficult to conceal in an era in which most of us are readily equipped with video cameras. In the wake of such disinformation, a caricature of my theory is destined to add to the low esteem in which our system of criminal justice is currently held. I can only wince at the spin my proposal is likely to receive in the popular press, already far too cynical about the alleged leniency shown to wrongdoers. My frequent efforts to downplay the radical implications of my theory are bound to be discounted or ignored. Commentators who sign on to my conclusions run the risk of being further discredited by a public persuaded that academics generally, and philosophers in particular, live on a distant planet unconnected to the real world. If the prospects that brutal villains might qualify for some degree of exculpation is regarded as a possible reductio by thoughtful philosophers, it is guaranteed to be ridiculed by politicians and laypersons. As a precedent for the reception my proposal is certain to receive, one need only examine the misunderstandings and exaggerations that surround the insanity defense and the various ideas to reform it.[34] I do not fully understand the sociological factors that make so many of us prepared to believe the worst about our legal officials and political process. Expertise about these matters involves proficiency in empirical issues that philosophers rarely possess. Still, I fear these forces would operate to counterbalance many of the advantages of my theory, and quite possibly would outweigh them altogether.

In some respects, my pessimism derives from a corollary of a thesis long defended by Paul Robinson. As I mentioned in Chapter 1(C), Robinson has argued that respect for the penal law is fostered

---

[34] See T. Daftary-Kapur, J. L. Groscup, M. O'Connor, F. Coffaro, and M. Galietta: "Measuring Knowledge of the Insanity Defense: Scale Construction and Validation," 29 *Behavioral Sciences & The Law* 40 (2011).

when its rules and doctrines conform to judgments of desert made by laypersons.[35] Voluntary compliance is maximized when the law expresses what citizens intuitively believe to be correct. Although I have strived to ground my position in a theory of moral responsibility, I have conceded all along that my views are highly controversial and conflict with the intuitions most respondents are likely to bring to the table. As laypersons will unreflectively reject my theory, its implementation might erode rather than promote respect for law. Unfortunately, treating wrongdoers in the manner that *philosophers* believe they deserve rather than as the *public* believe they deserve may undermine rather than bolster the credibility of our penal institutions. Should we then preserve the status quo of *ignorantia juris* because it corresponds to the judgments of the citizenry, even if we have good reason to doubt these judgments are able to withstand critical scrutiny? More generally, would this negative consequence swamp the several positives my theory would bring about—advantages I have described at greater length? I am unsure. Even Gideon Rosen, famous for championing an expanded exculpatory consideration of ignorance in the moral domain, is ambivalent about its implications for the criminal law.[36] Notice, however, that Rosen tries to soften the counterintuitive flavor of his view in the moral sphere by reminding us just how *awful* moral blame can be.[37] Surely we all should agree that penal punishment, when piled on top of moral blame, is more awful still.

I would like to conclude on a more optimistic note. Change can come quickly in ways few of us are able to anticipate. Some reformer must be willing to take the first step to articulate and defend a novel idea before it has any chance of gaining acceptance through our democratic process. Some proposals seem fantastic until they permeate popular consciousness. In 1930, Senator Morris Sheppard, author of the Eighteenth Amendment that brought about the prohibition of alcohol, wrote "there is as much chance of repealing the Eighteenth Amendment as there is for a hummingbird to fly to the planet Mars with the Washington Monument tied to its tail."[38] Three years later,

[35] Paul H. Robinson: *Distributive Principles of Criminal Law: Who Should Be Punished How Much?* (Oxford: Oxford University Press, 2008).

[36] Gideon Rosen: "Culpability and Ignorance," 103 *Proceedings of the Aristotelian Society* 61, 86 (2003).

[37] *Id.*, p.81.

[38] Quoted in Daniel Okrent: *Last Call: The Rise and Fall of Prohibition* (New York: Scribner, 2010), p.330.

Prohibition had been repealed. Pleas to decriminalize marijuana or to legalize gay marriage seemed unthinkable a short time ago. Soon it will be hard to remember what all of the fuss was about.

What, then, is the ultimate verdict on my theory of how a system of criminal justice should treat defendants who act in ignorance of law? To what extent should my ideal be implemented? We philosophers have no special competence in making predictions about the real world, even if we are reasonably good at achieving what I take to be the central objective of criminal theory: describing what the law ought to be. But I am certain that no idea is so compelling that it cannot be subverted by people of ill will or by those who are unprepared to reexamine their prejudices. Although compromises may be inevitable, we should continue to aspire to the ideal from which retreats must regrettably be made.

Conclusion

Implementing my theory in the real world would almost certainly necessitate a number of compromises and retreats from the ideals I have defended—although I cannot begin to describe all of the possible revisions my theory might be forced to undergo in order to win acceptance. Legality itself, as a surrogate for morality, involves such a compromise. Even though laypersons may be unable to appreciate the difference, the need to treat some persons *as if* they are blameworthy and deserving of punishment is not equivalent to the judgment that they *are* blameworthy and deserving of punishment. A just state should aspire to the latter rather than to the former; we should not accede to a compromise without a fight.

Ideally, the kind of exculpatory consideration employed when wrongdoers make mistakes of fact should be replicated when wrongdoers make mistakes of law. Both kinds of mistake should be conceptualized as excuses that deny mens rea—although penal theorists rarely regard mistake of fact as an excuse. Even so, I have no decisive objection against allowing codes to recognize ignorance of law by creating a stand-alone excuse rather than by denying a mens rea element explicitly or implicitly included in the statute breached. In particular, this latter device would allow the burden of proof about ignorance of law to be allocated to defendants—if indeed this allocation is deemed advisable. Despite some ambivalence about this matter, I ultimately favor a symmetrical solution that conceptualizes both the plea of ignorance of fact and the plea of ignorance of law as a denial of mens rea.

I concluded by briefly speculating about the probable advantages and disadvantages my theory might bring to legislation as well as to our democratic political process more generally. The main benefit, of course, is the increase in justice afforded to defendants themselves. Moreover, better criminal laws and greater efforts to educate citizens of its underlying moral rationale are long overdue. Unfortunately, inadvertent misunderstanding and deliberate distortion might offset these advantages. Experimentation is probably needed before jurisdictions are in a good position to decide how much of my theory should be implemented in the real world of criminal justice. My central objective throughout this book, however, has been to describe the ideal to which I believe our systems of criminal justice should aspire.

References

11 *Criminal Law and Philosophy* (forthcoming, 2016).

§17 StGB.

18 *P.A. Cons. Stat.* § 3503(a).

8 *Criminal Law and Philosophy* 283–525 (2014).

Abrams, Norman: "The New Ancillary Offenses," 1 *Criminal Law Forum* 1 (1989).

Alexander, Larry: "Hart and Punishment for Negligence," in C.G. Pulman, ed.: *Hart on Responsibility* (New York: Palgrave Macmillan, 2014).

_____. "Inculpatory and Exculpatory Mistakes and the Fact/Law Distinction: An Essay in Memory of Mike Bayles," 12 *Law and Philosophy* 33 (1993).

Alexander, Larry and Kimberly Kessler Ferzan with Stephen Morse: *Crime and Culpability* (Cambridge: Cambridge University Press, 2009).

Alexander, Larry and Emily Sherman: *The Rule of Rules: Morality, Rules, and the Dilemmas of Law* (Durham, NC: Duke University Press, 2001).

Alter, Adam L., Julia Kernochan, and John M. Darley: "Morality Influences How People Apply the Ignorance of Law Defense," 41 *Law & Society Review* 819 (2007).

Apuzzo, Matt and Eric Lipton: "Rare White House Accord with Koch Brothers on Sentencing Frays," *New York Times* (Nov. 24, 2015), p.A1, http://www.nytimes.com/2015/11/25/us/politics/rare-alliance-of-libertarians-and-white-house-on-sentencing-begins-to-fray.html?r=0.

Arpaly, Nomy: *Unprincipled Virtue: An Inquiry into Moral Agency* (Oxford: Oxford University Press, 2003).

Ashworth, Andrew: "Excusable Mistake of Law," *Criminal Law Review* 652 (1974).

_____. "Ignorance of the Criminal Law, and Duties to Avoid It," in Andrew Ashworth, ed.: *Positive Obligations in Criminal Law* (Oxford: Hart, 2013).

_____. *Principles of Criminal Law* (Oxford: Oxford University Press, 5th ed., 2006).

Austin, John: in Robert Campell, ed: *Lectures on Jurisprudence* (London: Gale, 5th ed., Vol. 1, 1885).

Baude, William: "State Regulation and the Necessary and Proper Clause," 65 *Case Western Reserve Law Review* 513 (2015).

Bedau, Hugo: "Retribution and the Theory of Punishment," 75 *Journal of Philosophy* 601, 608 (1978).

Blackburn, Simon: "AntiRealist Expressivism and Quasi-Realism," in David Copp, ed.: *The Oxford Handbook of Ethical Theory* (Oxford: Oxford University Press, 2006).

Bowers, Josh: "Legal Guilt, Normative Innocence, and the Equitable Decision Not to Prosecute," 110 *Columbia Law Review* 1655 (2010).

Bryant v. United States, 524 U.S. 184 (1998).

Buell, Samuel W.: "Culpability and Modern Crime," 103 *Georgetown Law Journal* 547, 602–603 (2015).

Buell, Samuel and Lisa Kern Griffin: "On the Mental State of Consciousness of Wrongdoing," 75 *Law and Contemporary Problems* 213 (2012).

Cahill, Michael: "Mistake of Law as Nonexculpatory Defense" (forthcoming).

Celano, Bruno: "Publicity and the Rule of Law," in Leslie Green and Brian Leiter, eds.: *Oxford Studies in Philosophy of Law* (New York: Oxford University Press, Vol. 2, 2013).

Cheek v. United States, 498 U.S. 192 (1991).

Chettiar, Inimai M. et al. eds.: *Solutions: American Leaders Speak Out on Criminal Justice* (New York: Brennan Center for Justice, 2015).

Chin, Gabriel S., Reid Griffith Fontaine, Nicholas Klingerman, and Melody Gilkey: "The Mistake of Law Defense and an Unconstitutional Provision of the Model Penal Code," 93 *North Carolina Law Review* 139 (2014).

City of Chicago v. Morales, 527 U.S. 41 (1999).

Clarke, Randolph: "Negligent Action and Unwitting Omission," in Alfred Mele, ed.: *Surrounding Free Will* (Oxford: Oxford University Press, 2015), pp.298, 299.

_____. *Omissions: Agency, Metaphysics, and Responsibility* (Oxford: Oxford University Press, 2014).

Coates, D. Justin and Neal A. Tognazzini: "The Contours of Blame," in D. Justin Coates and Neal A. Tognazzini, eds.: *Blame: Its Nature and Norms* (Oxford: Oxford University Press, 2013).

Cohen, L. Jonathan: *An Essay on Belief and Acceptance* (Oxford: Clarendon Press, 1992).

Comments to *Model Penal Code* §2.04(3).

Connally v. General Construction Co., 269 U.S. 385, 391 (1926).

Cox v. Louisiana, 379 U.S. 559 (1965).

"Criminal Code Improvement Act of 2015" Subchapter C, §11.

Davies, Sharon: "The Jurisprudence of Willfulness: An Evolving Theory of Excusable Ignorance," 48 *Duke Law Journal* 341 (1998).

Daftary-Kapur, T, Groscup, J.L., O'Connor, M, Coffaro, F. and Galietta, M: "Measuring Knowledge of the Insanity Defense: Scale Construction and Validation," 29 *Behavioral Sciences & The Law* 40 (2011).

Dempsey, Michelle: "Book Review: Michael J. Zimmerman, *The Immorality of Punishment*," 32 *Law and Philosophy* 333 (2013).

Dimock, Susan: "Contractarian Criminal Law Theory and *Mala Prohibita* Offences," in R.A. Duff et al., eds.: *Criminalisation: The Political Morality of the Criminal Law* (Oxford: Oxford University Press, 2014).

Conley v. United States, No. 11-CF-589 (D.C. 2013).

"*Don't Change the Legal Rule on Intent*," The New York Times (December 6, 2015).

Doris, John: *Talking to Our Selves: Reflection, Ignorance, and Agency* (Oxford: Oxford University Press, 2015).

Driver, Julia: "Appraisability, Attributability, and Moral Agency," in Randolph Clarke, Michael McKenna, and Angela M. Smith, eds.: *The Nature of Moral Responsibility: New Essays* (New York: Oxford University Press, 2015).

Duff, Antony: "Crime, Prohibition, and Punishment," 19 *Journal of Applied Philosophy* 97, 102 (2002).

Duff, R.A.: *Answering for Crime* (Oxford: Hart, 2007).

_____. *Criminal Attempts* (Oxford: Clarendon Press, 1996).

_____. "Legal Moralism and Private Wrongs," in Kimberly K. Ferzan and Stephen Morse, eds.: *Legal, Moral, and Metaphysical Truths: The Philosophy of Michael S. Moore* (Oxford: Oxford University Press, 2016).

_____. Political Retributivism and Legal Moralism," 1 *Virginia Journal of Criminal Law* 179 (2012).

Duff, R.A. and S.E. Marshall: "'Remote Harms' and the Two Harm Principles," in A.P. Simester, Antje Du Bois-Pedain, and Ulfred Neumann, eds.: *Liberal Criminal Theory: Essays for Andreas von Hirsch* (Oxford: Hart, 2014), pp.205, 222–223.

Edwards, James: "Reasons to Criminalise," *Legal Theory* (forthcoming).

Elonis v United States, 572 U.S. ___ (2015).

Elster, Jakob: "How Outlandish Can Imaginary Cases Be?" 28 *Journal of Applied Philosophy* 241 (2011).

Endicott, Timothy: "The Value of Vagueness," in Andrei Marmor and Scott Soames, eds.: *Philosophical Foundations of Language in the Law* (Oxford: Oxford University Press, 2011).

Enker, Arnold: "Error Juris in Jewish Criminal Law," 11 *The Journal of Law and Religion* 23 (1994–1995).

Enoch, David: "Reason-Giving and the Law," in Leslie Green and Brian Leiter, eds.: *Oxford Studies in Philosophy of Law* (Oxford: Oxford University Press, Vol. 1, 2011), p.1.

Estlund, David: *Democratic Authority: A Philosophical Framework* (Princeton, NJ: Princeton University Press, 2008).

Ferzan, Kimberly Kessler: "Beyond Crime and Commitment: Justifying Liberty Deprivations of the Dangerous and Responsible," 96 *University of Minnesota Law Review* 141 (2011).

Fischer, John Martin: *Deep Control: Essays on Free Will and Value* (Oxford: Oxford University Press, 2012).

Fischer, John Martin, et al.: *Four Views on Free Will* (Malden, MA: Blackwell, 2007).

Fischer, John Martin and Mark Ravizza: *Responsibility and Control: A Theory of Moral Responsibility* (Cambridge: Cambridge University Press, 1998).

Fischer, John Martin and Neil A. Tognazzini: "The Triumph of Tracing," 43 *Nous* 531 (2009).

Fiske, Alan Page and Tage Shakti Rai: *Virtuous Violence: Hurting and Killing to Create, End, and Honor Social Relationships* (Cambridge: Cambridge University Press, 2014).

Fitzpatrick, William J.: "Moral Responsibility and Normative Ignorance: Answering a New Skeptical Challenge," 118 *Ethics* 589, 610 (2008).

Fletcher, George: *Rethinking Criminal Law* (Boston: Little, Brown and Co., 1978).

_____. "The Right Deed for the Wrong Reason: A Reply to Mr. Robinson," 23 *U.C.L.A. Law Review* 293 (1975–1976).

Frankfurt, Harry: "Freedom of the Will and the Concept of a Person," 68 *Journal of Philosophy* 5 (1971).

Frankfurt, Harry G.: "Alternate Possibilities and Moral Responsibility," 66 *Journal of Philosophy* 829 (1969).

Fuller, Lon L.: *The Morality of Law* (New Haven, CT: Yale University Press, 1964).

Gainer, Ronald: "Federal Criminal Code Reform: Past and Future," 2 *Buffalo Criminal Law Review* 45, 63 n.38 (1993).

Gardner, John: *Offences and Defences* (Oxford: Oxford University Press, 2007)

Garvey, Steven P.: "Authority, Ignorance, and the Guilty Mind," 67 *Southern Methodist University Law Review* 545 (2014).

_____. "Dealing with Wayward Desire," 3 *Criminal Law and Philosophy* 1 (2009).

_____. "Was Ellen Wronged?" 7 *Criminal Law and Philosophy* 185 (2013).

Gilbert, Margaret: *Joint Commitment: How We Make the Social World* (Oxford: Oxford University Press, 2014).

Grant v. Borg (1982) 1 WLR 638, 646B.

Greenberg, Mark: "How Mistakes Excuse: Genuine Desert, Moral Desert, and Legal Desert," 11 *APA Newsletter on Philosophy and Law* 8 (2011).

Guerrero, Alexander A.: "Deliberation, Responsibility, and Excusing Mistakes of Law," 11 *APA Newsletter on Philosophy and Law* 2 (2011).

_____. "Don't Know, Don't Kill: Moral Ignorance, Culpability, and Caution," 136 *Philosophical Studies* 59 (2007).

Gur-Arye, Miriam: "Reliance on a Lawyer's Mistaken Advice—Should It Be an Excuse from Criminal Liability?" 29 *American Journal of Criminal Law* 455 (2002).

Hall, Jerome: *General Principles of Criminal Law* (Indianapolis: Bobbs-Merrill, 1947), chapter XI.

Harman, Elizabeth: "Does Moral Ignorance Exculpate?" 24 *Ratio* 443 (2011).

_____. "Ethics Is Hard! What Follows?" (forthcoming).

Hart, H.L.A.: *Punishment and Responsibility* (Oxford: Oxford University Press, 2d ed., 2008).

Hart, Harry M., Jr.: "The Aims of the Criminal Law," 23 *Law and Contemporary Problems* 401, 413 (1958).

Hatch, Orin: Press Release, September 15, 2015, http://www.hatch.senate.gov/public/index.cfm?p=releases&id=090FFA70-5ABF-4160-8ED5-D512EBEBEB6F.

Heien v. North Carolina, 135 S. Ct. 530 (2014).

Heyman, Gene H.: *Addiction: A Disorder of Choice* (Cambridge, MA: Harvard University Press, 2009).

Hieronymi, Pamela: "Reflection and Responsibility," 42 *Philosophy and Public Affairs* 3 (2014).

Holmes, Oliver Wendell, Jr., in Mark DeWolfe Howe, ed.: *The Common Law* (Boston: Little, Brown and Co., 1963).

Horder, Jeremy: *Excusing Crime* (Oxford: Oxford University Press, 2004).

Huemer, Michael: *Ethical Intuitionism* (New York: Palgrave MacMillan, 2005).

Hughes, Brennan T.: "A Statutory Element in Exile: The Crucial 'Corrupt Intent' Element in Federal Bribery Laws," (forthcoming).

Hurd, Heidi M.: *Moral Combat* (Cambridge: Cambridge University Press, 1999).

_____. "Paternalism on Pain of Punishment," 28 *Criminal Justice Ethics* 49 (2009).

Husak, Douglas: "'Broad Culpability' and the Retributivist Dream," 9 *Ohio State Journal of Criminal Law* 449 (2012).

_____. The 'But Everyone Does That!' Defense," in Douglas Husak, ed.: *The Philosophy of Criminal Law* (Oxford: Oxford University Press, 2010).

_____. "The Criminal Law as Last Resort," 24 *Oxford Journal of Legal Studies* 207 (2004).

_____. "Distraction and Negligence," in Lucia Zedner and Julian V. Roberts, eds.: *Principles and Values in Criminal Law and Criminal Justice: Essays in Honour of Andrew Ashworth* (Oxford: Oxford University Press, 2012).

_____. *Drugs and Rights* (Cambridge: Cambridge University Press, 1992).

_____. "Ignorance of Law and Duties of Citizenship," 14 *Legal Studies* 105 (1994).

_____. "Lifting the Cloak: Preventive Detention as Punishment," 48 *San Diego Law Review* 1173 (2011).

_____. "*Malum Prohibitum* and Retributivism," in Douglas Husak, ed.: *The Philosophy of Criminal Law* (Oxford: Oxford University Press, 2010).

_____. "Negligence, Belief, Blame and Criminal Liability: The Special Case of Forgetting," 5 *Criminal Law and Philosophy* 199 (2011)

_____. "On the Supposed Priority of Justification to Excuse," in Douglas Husak, ed.: *The Philosophy of Criminal Law* (Oxford: Oxford University Press, 2010).

_____. *Overcriminalization* (Oxford: Oxford University Press, 2008).

_____. "Partial Defenses," in Douglas Husak, ed.: *The Philosophy of Criminal Law* (Oxford: Oxford University Press, 2010).

_____. "Preventive Detention as Punishment? Some Possible Reservations," in Andrew Ashworth, Lucia Zedner, and Patrick Tomlin, eds.: *Prevention and the Limits of the Criminal Law* (Oxford: Oxford University Press, 2013).

_____. Reply: The Importance of Asking the Right Question: What Is Punishment Imposed For?" in Russell L. Christopher, ed.: *Fletcher's Essays on Criminal Law* (Oxford: Oxford University Press, 2013).

_____. "The Sequential Principle of Relative Culpability" in Douglas Husak, ed.: *The Philosophy of Criminal Law* (Oxford: Oxford University Press, 2010).

_____. "Strict Liability, Justice, and Proportionality," in Douglas Husak, ed.: *The Philosophy of Criminal Law* (Oxford: Oxford University Press, 2010).

_____. "Varieties of Strict Liability," VIII *Canadian Journal of Law and Jurisprudence* 189 (1995).

_____. "What Do Criminals Deserve?" in Kimberly K. Ferzan and Stephen Morse, eds.: *Legal, Moral, and Metaphysical Truths: The Philosophy of Michael S. Moore* (Oxford: Oxford University Press, 2016).

_____. "Why Punish the Deserving?" in Douglas Husak, ed.: *The Philosophy of Criminal Law* (Oxford: Oxford University Press, 2010).

Husak, Douglas and Craig Callendar: "Willful Ignorance, Knowledge, and the 'Equal Culpability' Thesis: A Study of the Deeper Significance of the Principle of Legality," in Douglas Husak, ed.: *Philosophy, Op.cit.* Note 31, p.200.

Husak, Douglas and George C. Thomas III: "Rapes without Rapists: Consent and Reasonable Mistake," 11 *Philosophical Issues* 86 (2001).

Husak, Douglas and Andrew von Hirsch: "Culpability and Mistake of Law," ," in Stephen Shute, John Gardner and Jeremy Horder, eds: *Action and Value in Criminal Law* (Oxford: Clarendon Press, 1993).

Jacobellis v. Ohio, 378 U.S. 184, 197 (1964).

Kadish, Sanford H.: "Excusing Crime," 78 *California Law Review* 257, 268 (1987).

Kagan, Shelly: *The Geometry of Desert* (New York: Oxford University Press, 2012).

Kahan, Dan M.: "Ignorance of Law Is a Defense: But Only for the Virtuous," 96 *Michigan Law Review* 127 (1997).

Kansas v. Hendricks, 521 U.S. 346 (1997).

Katz, Leo: "Villainy and Felony," 6 *Buffalo Criminal Law Review* 100 (2002).

_____. *Why the Law Is So Perverse* (Chicago: University of Chicago Press, 2011).

Keedy, Edwin R.: "Ignorance and Mistake in the Criminal Law," 22 *Harvard Law Review* 75, 77 (1908).

Kerr, Orin: "A Confusing Proposal to Reform the 'Mens Rea' of Federal Criminal Law," *The Volokh Conspiracy* (November 25, 2015), https://www.washingtonpost.com/news/volokh-conspiracy/wp/2015/11/25/a-confusing-proposal-to-reform-the-mens-rea-of-federal-criminal-law/.

_____. *The Volokh Conspiracy* (June 18, 2015), http://lawprofessors.typepad.com/crimprof_blog/2015/06/ignorance-of-the-law-is-no-excuse-or-is-it.html.

Kinports, Kit: "Heien's Mistake of Law," *Alabama Law Review* (forthcoming, 2016).

Kolber, Adam J.: "Free Will as a Matter of Law," in Michael Pardo and Dennis Patterson, eds.: *Philosophical Foundations of Law and Neuroscience* (Oxford: Oxford University Press, forthcoming, 2016).

_____. "The Subjective Experience of Punishment," 109 *Columbia Law Review* 182 (2009).

Kreit, Alex: "What Will Federal Marijuana Reform Look Like?" 65 *Case Western University Law Review* 689 (2015).

Lambert v. California, 355 U.S. 225 (1957).

Larkin, Paul J., Jr.: "Taking Mistakes Seriously," 28 *B.Y.U. Journal of Public Law* 104–105 (2015).

Lee, Ambrose: "Public Wrongs and the Criminal Law," 9 *Criminal Law and Philosophy* 155 (2015).

Levy, Neil: "Culpable Ignorance and Moral Responsibility: A Reply to Fitzpatrick," 119 *Ethics* 729 (2009).

_____. "The Good, the Bad and the Blameworthy," 1 *Journal of Ethics and Social Philosophy* 1 (2005).

_____. *Hard Luck* (Oxford: Oxford University Press, 2011).

Levy, Neil, ed.: *Addiction and Self-Control* (Oxford: Oxford University Press, 2013).

Lewinsohn, Jed: "Philosophy in Halakhah: The Case of Intentional Action," 7 *Torah-U-Madda Journal* 97 (2006–2007).

Love, Margaret Colgate, Jenny Roberts and Cecelia Klingele: *Collateral Consequences of Criminal Convictions: Law, Policy and Practice* (Eagan, Minnesota: Thomson Reuters, 2013).

Low, Peter W. and Joel S. Johnson: "Changing the Vocabulary of the Vagueness Doctrine," (forthcoming).

Low, Peter W. and Benjamin Charles Wood: "*Lambert* Revisited," 100 *Virginia Law Review* 1603 (2014).

Luna, Eric: "The Overcriminalization Phenomenon," 54 *American University Law Review* 703 (2005).

Macnamara, Coleen: "Blame, Communication, and Morally Responsible Agency," in Randolph Clarke, Michael McKenna, and Angela M. Smith, eds.: *The Nature of Moral Responsibility: New Essays* (New York: Oxford University Press, 2015).

Malatesi, Luca and John Mcmillan, eds.: *Psychopathy and Responsibility* (Oxford: Oxford University Press, 2010).

Markel, Dan: "Retributive Justice and the Demands of Democratic Citizenship," 1 *Virginia Journal of Criminal Law* 1 (2012).

Marshall, S.E. and R.A. Duff: "Criminalization and Sharing Wrongs," 11 *Canadian Journal of Law and Jurisprudence* 7 (1998).

Mason, Elinor: "Moral Ignorance and Blameworthiness," 172 *Philosophical Studies* 3037 (2015).

Mayson, Sandra G.: "Collateral Consequences and the Preventive State," 91 *Notre Dame Law Review* (forthcoming, 2016).

McFadden v. United States, 576 U.S. ____ (2015).

McKenna, Michael: *Conversation and Responsibility* (Oxford: Oxford University Press, 2012).

_____. "Directed Blame and Conversation," in D. Justin Coates and Neal A. Tognazzini, eds.: *Blame: Its Nature and Norms* (Oxford: Oxford University Press, 2013).

McKenna, Michael and Paul Russell, eds.: *Free Will and Reactive Attitudes: Perspectives on P.F. Strawson's Freedom and Resentment* (Burlington, VT: Ashgate, 2007).

Meese, Edwin, III and Paul J. Larkin, Jr.: "Reconsidering the Mistake of Law Defense," 102 *Journal of Criminal Law & Criminology* 725 (2012).

Mele, Alfred R.: *Backsliding: Understanding Weakness of Will* (Oxford: Oxford University Press, 2013).

_____. *Free Will and Luck* (Oxford: Oxford University Press, 2006).

"Mens Rea Reform Act of 2015," §(A)(4), §28(a)(1)(B)(iii), *available at* (https://www.govtrack.us/congress/bills/114/s2298/text).

Michaels, Alan C.: "Acceptance: The Missing Mental State," 71 *Southern California Law Review* 953 (1998).

Model Penal Code §2.02(2), §2.02(2)(b) and 2.02(2)(b)(i), . §2.02(2)(c), and (d); §2.02(7), §2.02(9), §2.04(3)(a) and (b), §2.08(2), §211.2, §230.4, §3.09.

Moody-Adams, Michelle: "Culture, Responsibility, and Affected Ignorance," 104 *Ethics* 291 (1994).

Moore, Michael: *Act and Crime* (Oxford: Clarendon Press, 1993), pp.243ff.

Moore, Michael: "Stephen Morse on the Fundamental Psycho-Legal Error," 10 *Criminal Law and Philosophy* (forthcoming 2016).

Moore, Michael S.: "The Quest for a Responsible Responsibility Test—Norwegian Insanity Law after Brevik," 10 *Criminal Law and Philosophy* (forthcoming, 2016).

_____. "A Tale of Two Theories," 28 *Criminal Justice Ethics* 27 (2009).

Moore, Michael S. and Heidi M. Hurd: "Punishing the Awkward, the Stupid, the Weak, and the Selfish: The Culpability of Negligence," 5 *Criminal Law and Philosophy* 147 (2011).

Morse, Stephen J.: "Diminished Rationality, Diminished Responsibility," 1 *Ohio State Journal of Criminal Law* 298 (2003).

_____. "Lost in Translation?: An Essay on Law and Neuroscience," *Law and Neuroscience*, 13 Current Legal Issues 529 (ed. Michael Freeman, 2010).

_____. "Psychopaths and Criminal Responsibility," 1 *Neuroethics* 205 (2008).

Nichols, Shaun: *Bound: Essays on Free Will and Responsibility* (Oxford: Oxford University Press, 2015).

Nix v. Hedden, 149 U.S. 304 (1893).

N.J. Stat. Ann. §§2C:2-4(c)(3) (West 2005), 2C:14-9(a), 2C:18-2(a)(2).

Note: "The Use of Analogy in Criminal Law," 47 *Columbia Law Review* 613 (1947).

Nottelmann, Nikolaj and Rik Peels: "Some Metaphysical Implications of a Credible Ethics of Belief," in Nikilaj Nottelman, ed.: *New Essays on Belief: Constitution, Content, and Structure* (New York: Palsgrave MacMillan, 2013).

Okrent, Daniel: *Last Call: The Rise and Fall of Prohibition* (New York: Scribner, 2010).

Palmer, David, ed.: *Libertarian Free Will: Contemporary Debates* (New York: Oxford University Press, 2014).

Parfit, Derek: *On What Matters* (Oxford: Oxford University Press, 2011).

Peels, Rik: "What Is Ignorance?" 38 *Philosophia* 57 (2010).

People v. Marrero, 507 N.E.2d 1068 (1987).

Pereboom, Derk: *Living without Free Will* (Cambridge: Cambridge University Press, 2001).

Perry, Stephen: "Political Authority and Political Obligation," in Leslie Green and Brian Leiter, eds.: *Oxford Studies in Philosophy of Law* (New York: Oxford University Press, Vol. 2, 2013).

Pillsbury, Samuel H.: "Why Psychopaths are Responsible," in Kent Kiehl and Walter Sinnott-Armstrong, eds.: *Handbook on Psychopathy and Law* (New York: Oxford University Press, 2013).

Posner, Richard: *Economic Analysis of Law* (Aspen: Kluwer, 7th ed., 2007), pp.233–234.

Press Release, September 15, 2015, http://www.hatch.senate.gov/public/index. cfm?p=releases&id=090FFA70-5ABF-4160-8ED5-D512EBEBEB6F.

R v. Smith (David Raymond) [1974] 1 All E.R. 632.

Raley v. Ohio, 360 U.S. 423 (1959).

Ratzlaf v. United States, 510 U.S. 135 (1994).

Rawls, John: *Political Liberalism* (New York: Columbia University Press, 1993).

Raz, Joseph: *The Authority of Law* (Oxford: Clarendon Press, 1979).

_____. *From Normativity to Responsibility* (Oxford: Oxford University Press, 2011), Part Three.

Registered Sex Offenders in the United States, National Center for Missing and Exploited Children, *available at* www.missingkids.com/SOTT (2014).

Renteln, Allison Dundes: *The Cultural Defense* (Oxford: Oxford University Press, 2004).

Robinson, Paul H.: *Criminal Law Defenses* (St. Paul, MN: West 1984).

_____. *Distributive Principles of Criminal Law: Who Should Be Punished How Much?* (Oxford: Oxford University Press, 2008).

_____. "Imputed Criminal Liability," 93 *Yale Law Journal* 609 (1984).

Robinson, Paul H. and Michael T. Cahill: "Can a Model Penal Code Second Save the States from Themselves?" 1 *Ohio State Journal of Criminal Law* 169, 170 (2003).

Robinson, Paul H. and Jane A. Grall: "Element Analysis in Defining Criminal Liability: The *Model Penal Code* and Beyond," 35 *Stanford Law Review* 681 (1983).

Rosen, Gideon: "The Alethic Conception of Moral Responsibility," in Randolph Clarke, Michael McKenna, and Angela M. Smith, eds.: *The Nature of Moral Responsibility: New Essays* (New York: Oxford University Press, 2015).

_____. "Culpability and Ignorance," 103 *Proceedings of the Aristotelian Society* 61, 83 (2003).

_____. "Skepticism about Moral Responsibility," 18 *Philosophical Perspectives* 295 (2004).

Roth, Andrea: "The Uneasy Case for Marijuana as Chemical Impairment under a Science-Based Jurisprudence of Dangerousness," 103 *California Law Review* ___ (2015).

Roxin, C.: *Strafrecht Allgemeiner teil, Band I, Grundlagen, der Aufbau der Verbrechenslehre* (Munich: C.H. Beck, 4th ed., 2006).

Scanlon, T.M.: *Being Realistic about Reasons* (Oxford: Oxford University Press, 2014).

_____. "The Significance of Choice," Lecture I in *The Tanner Lectures on Human Values* (Salt Lake City: University of Utah Press, 1988).

_____. *What We Owe to Each Other* (Cambridge, MA: Harvard University Press, 1998).

Schauer, Frederick: *The Force of Law* (Cambridge, MA: Harvard University Press, 2015).

Schramme, Thomas, ed.: *Being Amoral: Psychopathy and Moral Incapacity* (Cambridge, MA: MIT Press, 2014).

Schwitzgebel, Eric: "Belief," *Stanford Encyclopedia of Philosophy* (http://plato.stanford.edu/entries/belief/). (First published Aug 14, 2006; substantive revision Mar 24, 2015).

Segev, Re'em: "Justification, Rationality and Mistake: Mistake of Law Is No Excuse? It Might Be a Justification!" 25 *Law and Philosophy* 31 (2006).

_____. "Moral Rightness and the Significance of Law: Why, How, and When Mistake of Law Matters," 64 *University of Toronto Law Journal* 33 (2014).

Sepielli, Andrew: "What to Do When You Don't Know What to Do When You Don't Know What to Do . . .," 48 *Nous* 521 (2013).

Sher, George: *Who Knew?: Responsibility without Awareness* (Oxford: Oxford University Press, 2009).

Shaw v. Director of Public Prosecutions, [1962] A.C. 220.

Shoemaker, David: "On Criminal and Moral Responsibility," in Mark Timmons, ed.: *Oxford Studies in Normative Ethics* (Oxford: Oxford University Press, Vol. 3, 2013).

_____. "Qualities of Will," 30 *Social Philosophy and Policy* 95 (2013).

Shute, Stephen, John Gardner and Jeremy Horder, eds: *Action and Value in Criminal Law* (Oxford: Clarendon Press, 1993).

Simons, Kenneth W.: "Ignorance and Mistake of Criminal Law, Noncriminal Law, and Fact," 9 *Ohio State Journal of Criminal Law* 487 (2012).

Singer, Richard and Douglas Husak: "Of Innocence and Innocents: The Supreme Court and Mens Rea since Herbert Packer," 2 *Buffalo Criminal Law Review* 859 (1999).

Sinnott-Armstrong, Walter: "Framing Moral Intuitions," in Walter Sinnott-Armstrong, ed.: *Moral Psychology: The Cognitive Science of Morality: Intuition and Diversity* (Vol. 2, Cambridge, MA: MIT Press, 2008).

Skilling v. United States, 561 U.S. 40, 130 S. Ct. 2896 (2010).

Slobogin, Christopher: "Plea Bargaining and the Substantive and Procedural Goals of Criminal Justice: From Retribution to and Adversarialism to Preventive Justice and Hybrid-Inquisitorialism," *William & Mary Law Review* (forthcoming, 2016).

Slote, Michael: "Is Virtue Possible?" 42 *Analysis* 70 (1982).

Smith, Angela: "Control, Responsibility, and Moral Assessment," 138 *Philosophical Studies* 367 (2008).

Smith, Angela M.: "Attitudes, Tracing, and Control," 32 *Journal of Applied Philosophy* 115 (2015).

Smith, A.T.H.: "Error and Mistake of Law in Anglo-American Criminal Law," 14 *Anglo-American Law Review* 3 (1985).

Smith, Holly M.: "Culpable Ignorance," 92 *Philosophical Review* 543 (1983).

_____. "Dual-Process Theory and Moral Responsibility," in Randolph Clarke, Michael McKenna, and Angela M. Smith, eds.: *The Nature of Moral Responsibility: New Essays* (New York: Oxford University Press, 2015).

_____. "The Subjective Moral Duty to Inform Oneself before Acting," 125 *Ethics* 1 (2014).

_____. "Tracing Cases of Culpable Ignorance," in Rik Peels, ed.: *Moral and Social Perspectives on Ignorance* (London: Routledge Press, forthcoming, 2016).

Soper, Philip: *The Ethics of Deference: Learning from Law's Morals* (Cambridge: Cambridge University Press, 2002).

State v. Fox, 866 P.2d 181 (1993).

State v. Striggles, 202 Iowa 1318 (1927).

Stephen, James Fitzjames: *A History of the Criminal Law of England* (Cambridge: Cambridge Library Collection, Vol. 2, 1883).

Strawson, Peter F.: "Freedom and Resentment," 48 *Proceedings of the British Academy* 1 (1962).

Sykes, G. and D. Matza: "Techniques of Neutralisation: A Theory of Delinquency," 22 *American Sociological Review* 664 (1957).

Symposium on "Actio Libera in Causa," 7 *Criminal Law and Philosophy* 549–636 (2013).

Tadros, Victor: *Criminal Responsibility* (Oxford: Oxford University Press, 2005).

_____. *The Ends of Harm* (Oxford: Oxford University Press, 2011).

The Joseph, 12 U.S. (8 Cranch) 451 (1814).

Thiel, Darren: "Criminal Ignorance," in Matthias Gross and Linsey McGoey, eds.: *The International Handbook of Ignorance Studies* (Routledge, forthcoming).

Toh, Kevin: "Legal Judgments as Plural Acceptances of Norms," in Leslie Green and Brian Leiter, eds.: *Oxford Studies in the Philosophy of Law* (Oxford: Oxford University Press, Vol. 1, 2011).

Tomlin, Patrick J.: "Extending the Golden Thread? Criminalisation and the Presumption of Innocence," 21 *Journal of Political Philosophy* 44 (2013).

Uhlmann, Eric Luis, David A. Pizarro, and Paul Bloom: "Varieties of Social Cognition," 38 *Journal for the Theory of Social Behaviour* 293 (2008).

United States v. Curran, 20 F.3d 560 (3d Cir. 1994).

United States v. Gurary, 860 F.2d 521 (2d Cir. 1988).

United States v. Jewell, 532 F.2d 697 (9th Cir. 1976).

United States v. Liparota, 471 U.S. 419 (1985).

United States v. McNab, 324 F.3d 1266 (2003).

United States v. Pennsylvania Industrial Chemical Corp., 411 U.S. 655 (1973).

United States v. Rogers, 18 F.3d 265 (4th Cir. 1994).

United States v. United States Gypsum Co., 438 U.S. 422, 441 (1978).

United States v. Wilson, 159 F.3d 280, 295 (1998) (Posner, J., dissenting).

van Verseveld, A.: *Mistake of Law* (The Hague: T.M.C. Asser Press, 2012).

Vargas, Manuel: *Building Better Beings: A Theory of Moral Responsibility* (Oxford: Oxford University Press, 2013).

_____. "The Trouble with Tracing," 29 *Midwest Studies in Philosophy* 269 (2005).

von Hirsch, Andrew: *Censure and Sanction* (New Brunswick, NJ: Rutgers University Press, 1987).

Walen, Alec: "A Punitive Precondition for Preventive Detention: Lost Status as a Foundation for Lost Immunity," 48 *San Diego Law Review* 1229 (2011).

_____. "Transcending the Means Principle," 33 *Law and Philosophy* 427 (2014).

Waller, Bruce: *Against Moral Responsibility* (Cambridge, MA: MIT Press, 2011).

Watson, Gary: "Two Faces of Responsibility," 24 *Philosophical Topics* 227 (1996).

Wegner, Daniel M.: *The Illusion of Conscious Will* (Cambridge, MA: M.I.T. Press, 2002).

Weiskrantz, Lawrence: *Blindsight: A Case Study and Implications* (Oxford: Oxford University Press, 1990).

Wellman, Christopher Heath: "Rights Forfeiture and *Mala Prohibita*," in R.A.Duff et al., eds.: *The Constitution of the Criminal Law* (Oxford: Oxford University Press, 2013).

Westen, Peter: "An Attitudinal Theory of Excuse," 25 *Law and Philosophy* 289 (2006).

_____. "Impossible Attempts: A Speculative Thesis," 5 *Ohio State Journal of Criminal Law* 523, 535 (2008).

_____. "Individualizing the Reasonable Person in Criminal Law," 2 *Criminal Law and Philosophy* 137 (2008).

Westen, Peter K.: "Two Rules of Legality in Criminal Law," 26 *Law and Philosophy* 229 (2007).

Wieland, Jan Willem: "What's Special about Moral Ignorance?," 28 *Ratio* ___ (2016).

Wiley, John Shepard, Jr.: "Not Guilty by Reason of Blamelessness: Culpability in Federal Criminal Interpretation," 85 *Virginia Law Review* 1021, 1046 (1999).

Wootton, Barbara: *Crime and the Criminal Law* (London: Stevens & Sons, 1963).

Yaffe, Gideon: *Attempts* (Oxford: Oxford University Press, 2010).

_____. "Excusing Mistakes of Law," 9:2 *Philosophers' Imprint* 1 (2009).

Yates v. United States, 574 U. S. ___ (2015).

Young, Robert: "Douglas Husak on Dispensing with the *Malum Prohibitum* Offense of Money Laundering," 28 *Criminal Justice Ethics* 108 (2009).

Zaibert, Leo: *Punishment and Retribution* (Burlington, VT: Ashgate, 2006).

Zimmerman, Michael: *Ignorance and Moral Obligation* (Oxford: Oxford University Press, 2014).

_____. "Ignorance as a Moral Excuse" (forthcoming).

_____. *Living with Uncertainty: The Moral Significance of Ignorance* (Cambridge: Cambridge University Press, 2008).

Zimmerman, Michael J.: *The Immorality of Punishment* (Toronto: Broadview Press, 2011).

_____. "Varieties of Moral Responsibility," in Randolph Clarke, Michael McKenna, and Angela M. Smith, eds.: *The Nature of Moral Responsibility: New Essays* (New York: Oxford University Press, 2015).

Index of Authorities

Index